James Abram
Jon Wright

unter Mitarbeit von
Philipp Fehrenbach
Petra Lehmann
Petra Veit
Marco Zimmermann
und der Verlagsredaktion

5th edition

crossover

2

Ausgabe Baden-Württemberg

Ein Lehrwerk für berufliche Gymnasien

KLASSE 12/13

Cornelsen

Verfasser	James Abram
	Jon Wright
Berater/Beraterinnen:	Philipp Fehrenbach, Nürtingen
	Petra Lehmann, Neuried
	Petra Veit, Stuttgart
	Marco Zimmermann, Geislingen
Redaktion:	Neil Porter
Wörterverzeichnisse:	Oliver Busch
Redaktionelle Mitarbeit:	Oliver Busch, Megan Hadgraft, Adam Hill, Valentin Olbrich
Projektleitung:	Shaunessy Ashdown
Bildredaktion:	Gertha Maly
Gesamtgestaltung und Coverbild:	Klein & Halm Grafikdesign, Berlin
Illustrationen:	Oxford Designers & Illustrators

Zu Band 2 von Ausgabe Baden-Württemberg sind ebenfalls erhältlich:

Workbook	ISBN 978-3-06-451132-3
Interaktives Workbook für mobile Endgeräte	ISBN 978-3-06-451471-3 (erhältlich auf cornelsen.de zur Nutzung in der Scook-App)
Handreichungen für den Unterricht mit Unterrichtsmanager (UM) und drei Audio-CDs	ISBN 978-3-06-451137-8
Unterrichtsmanager (UM) als Download	ISBN 978-3-06-451141-5
Kopiervorlagen zur Textproduktion	ISBN 978-3-06-451183-5
Communication Cards	ISBN 978-3-06-450968-9
Vokabeltrainer-App für Android, Apple und Windows	In dem jeweiligen App-Store

Soweit in diesem Lehrwerk Personen fotografisch abgebildet sind und ihnen von der Redaktion fiktive Namen, Berufe, Dialoge und Ähnliches zugeordnet oder diese Personen in bestimmte Kontexte gesetzt werden, dienen diese Zuordnungen und Darstellungen ausschließlich der Veranschaulichung und dem besseren Verständnis des Inhalts.

www.cornelsen.de

Die Webseiten Dritter, deren Internetadressen in diesem Lehrwerk angegeben sind, wurden vor Drucklegung sorgfältig geprüft. Der Verlag übernimmt keine Gewähr für die Aktualität und den Inhalt dieser Seiten oder solcher, die mit ihnen verlinkt sind.

1. Auflage, 2. Druck 2017

Alle Drucke dieser Auflage sind inhaltlich unverändert und können im Unterricht nebeneinander verwendet werden.

© 2016 Cornelsen Schulverlage GmbH, Berlin
© 2016 Cornelsen Verlag GmbH, Berlin

Druck und Bindung: Livonia Print, Riga

ISBN 978-3-06-451130-9
ISBN 978-3-06-451182-8 (E-Book)

PEFC zertifiziert
Dieses Produkt stammt aus nachhaltig bewirtschafteten Wäldern und kontrollierten Quellen.
PEFC/12-31-006
www.pefc.de

Vorwort

Crossover 2 – 5th edition, Ausgabe Baden-Württemberg ist ein Lehrwerk für die Klassen 12 und 13 an beruflichen Gymnasien. Es bereitet auf alle Teile der mündlichen und schriftlichen Abiturprüfung vor und deckt die Themenbereiche des aktuellen Lehrplans ab. Das Buch führt zu Stufe B2 des Europäischen Referenzrahmens, vertieft die Anforderungen dieser Stufe und erweitert sie teilweise auf Stufe C1.

Crossover 2 entfaltet in sechs Themengruppen eine Bandbreite aktueller, relevanter und beruflicher Materialien, die es der Lehrkraft leicht machen, die Abiturvorbereitung interessant und motivierend zu gestalten, die Sprachfertigkeiten systematisch zu verbessern sowie den besonderen Auftrag des beruflichen Gymnasiums zu erfüllen.

Während die Textauswahl nach lehrplanbezogenen Kriterien erfolgte, wurde bei den Fragen der Schwerpunktsetzung und Textsortenvielfalt die Gelegenheit genutzt, auch ungewöhnliche Aspekte und überraschende Perspektiven auf die jeweiligen Themenbereiche einzubringen. So finden sich im Buch auch literarische Texte – Gedichte, Lieder und ein Ausschnitt aus einem Drama.

Ein wichtiges Element in **Crossover 2** ist die Vorbereitung auf alle Teile der neuen Abiturprüfung am beruflichen Gymnasium in Baden-Württemberg. Zu erkennen sind die prüfungsrelevanten Aufgaben an dem Kästchen **EXAM PREPARATION** in der Randspalte. Hier finden sich Aufgaben zur systematischen Vorbereitung auf alle Prüfungsteile.

Neu in der 5th edition ist die Hervorhebung von Kompetenzen in der Rubrik **COMPETENCE TRAINING**, in der sowohl prüfungsrelevante Fertigkeiten als auch Lerntechniken ausführlich beschrieben und intensiv trainiert werden.

Der Bereich Textproduktion wird gründlich und Schritt für Schritt erarbeitet – wie man Texte strukturiert, wie eine gute Einleitung aussieht, wie man einen Absatz schreibt. Häufig werden sprachliche oder strukturelle Hilfen angeboten (*scaffolding*).

Die Simulation authentische Prüfungssituationen wird ermöglicht durch zwei Hörprüfungen (zentrale Klassenarbeiten), sechs schriftliche **Musterprüfungen** und sechs Kommunikationsprüfungen, die den jeweiligen *Topics* zugeordnet sind.

Wichtig für die erfolgreiche Bearbeitung der Aufgaben ist der Anhang, auf den in der Randspalte verwiesen wird:
· Der Buchstabe **S** verweist auf den Teil **Study Skills**, der einen handlichen Leitfaden mit Lernhilfen und wichtigen Formulierungen enthält.
· Der Buchstabe **G** verweist auf die **Grammar Summary**, in der die wesentlichen Bereiche der Grammatik übersichtlich zusammengefasst sind.
· Die Kästchen **EXAM PREPARATION** kennzeichnen Aufgaben, die auf die Anforderungen der neuen Abiturprüfung vorbereiten, und verweisen auf die Übersicht zur Abiturprüfung im Anhang.

Ebenso in der Randspalte finden sich Übersetzungen anspruchsvoller **Vokabeln**. Es empfiehlt sich, die fett gedruckten Wörter in den aktiven Wortschatz aufzunehmen. Die nicht fett gedruckten Wörter dienen lediglich zum Verständnis des jeweiligen Textes.
Zum Nachschlagen stehen umfangreiche Wörterverzeichnisse zur Verfügung. Die **Unit word list** enthält ausschließlich Wörter für den aktiven Wortschatz und bietet den Lernenden die Wahl zwischen Definitionen und Übersetzungen, um sich diese Vokabeln möglichst effektiv einzuprägen.

Nicht zu vergessen: die hintere Umschlagklappe. Im Unterricht lässt sie sich für den mündlichen Gebrauch ausklappen, die eingeklappte Seite hilft bei den Hausaufgaben.

Das Crossover-Team wünscht Ihnen mit diesem Lehrwerk viel Freude und Erfolg!

INHALT

TOPIC 3 Technology – risks and opportunities

TOPIC 4   Striving for equality

TOPIC 5   Britain – tradition and change

TOPIC 6   The USA – a fading superpower?

ANHANG

TOPIC 1

The world of work and consumerism

VA 1   1.02

consumer society *Konsumgesellschaft*
Industrial Revolution *industrielle Revolution*
mass production *Massenproduktion*
fundamental *grundlegend*
pattern of consumption *Konsumverhalten*
leisure activity *Freizeitaktivitäten*
wealthy elite *wohlhabende Elite*
possession *Besitztum*
wages *Löhne*
essentials *notwendige Güter*
basic needs *Grundbedürfnisse*

trade union *Gewerkschaft*
working conditions *Arbeitsbedingungen*
urban poverty *Stadtarmut*
child labour *Kinderarbeit*
healthcare *Gesundheitsfürsorge*
day of rest *Ruhetag*
computer-related skills *Computerkenntnisse*
job for life *lebenslange Beschäftigung*

growing demand *wachsende Nachfrage*
transportation *Transportwesen*
on offer *im Angebot*
buying habits *Konsumgewohnheiten*
non-essentials *Unwesentliches*
luxury item *Luxusgut*
standard of living *Lebensstandard*
conspicuous consumption *beträchtlicher Konsum*
identity statement *Produktidentität (seinen Sozialstatus durch teuren Konsum definieren)*
shopaholic *Kaufsüchtige/r*
easy access *leichter Zugang*
spending habits *Konsumgewohnheiten*
personal debt *Privatverschuldung*

The beginning of the consumer society

The Industrial Revolution changed the world of work by introducing factories to create mass production, which led to fundamental changes in patterns of consumption. Before industrialization, shopping as a leisure activity was the privilege of the wealthy elite. The rest of society had few possessions. 5 Clothes were usually made by members of the household, and were repaired and re-used or even passed from generation to generation rather than replaced. Fashion was a luxury beyond the reach of most. Following the Industrial Revolution, people moved away from the country to the cities to find regular work. In the factories they earned wages, which they spent on 10 essentials for their basic needs.

The rise of trade unions

As the number of workers increased and cities became overcrowded, more attention was paid to problems such as unsafe working conditions, urban poverty and child labour. The activities of trade unions and political 15 reformers gradually resulted in improvements that included education for children, healthcare, safer working environments and official days of rest. However, as permanent jobs in manufacturing were replaced with casual service jobs, so too did unions begin to lose their significance. Technological progress continues to cause changes to the way we work. The majority of 20 non-manual jobs now require computer-related skills, while the concept of a "job for life" has disappeared.

Changes in patterns of consumption

As people earned more money by working, they found new ways of spending their earnings, and so patterns of consumption changed. People began to 25 buy what they wanted rather than just what they needed. Growing demand and improvements to transportation led to an enormous increase in the range of goods on offer. As choice increased, so advertising developed to try to influence consumers' buying habits. One characteristic of modern life is that as salaries increase, more money is available for non-essentials such as 30 entertainment, holidays and fashion. Indeed, the ability to enjoy luxury items is a key element of how people evaluate their standard of living. We are living in an age of conspicuous consumption. Spending vast sums on goods or holidays is often an identity statement. The negative consequence of this is the large number of shopaholics. With easy access to credit cards, many people have spending habits that they cannot afford and live with 35 high levels of personal debt.

Advertising

We are surrounded by advertising. It saturates print news and magazines, funds our favourite websites, and decorates every city street. It has been estimated that the average Western adolescent is exposed to over 40,000
40 adverts a year. Advertising is designed to create a need. The basic message is: in order to be happy you need this. There are strict controls over cigarette and alcohol advertising, but companies find other ways of keeping their brands in the public eye, such as sponsorship of sporting events and product placement in popular films.

45 ## Consumers of the future

Typically, as a nation develops, a middle class starts to emerge. To show their status, the middle class aspires to the lifestyle of the people they looked up to before. This includes investing in education, housing and technology. The main development in patterns of consumption this century will be the rise of
50 the Asian consumer, in particular in India and China. Currently, Americans only constitute 5 % of the global population, but they consume around 25 % of the world's energy. It has been calculated that one American consumes as much as 13 Chinese or 31 Indians. Asia accounts for more than half the world's population, but only 28 % of the world's middle class. By 2020 that
55 percentage is expected to double, and by 2030 it is believed that two thirds of the world's middle class will live in Asia. The ecological consequences of the growth of consumption are hard to ignore: more exploitation of natural resources, more factories being built and increased levels of transportation for more goods that are being replaced more quickly.

60 ## Globalization: for and against

The process of integration and interaction among people, companies and governments of different nations has developed to such an extent that the economies of all the major countries are now interdependent. Economic problems in one country spread quickly and have negative effects on many
65 others, as the problems in the Eurozone have demonstrated. Proponents of globalization such as business leaders and governments argue that it allows poorer countries to raise the standard of living of their citizens. Critics say that multinational companies have benefited at the expense of local enterprises and local culture, and that exporting jobs and work to cheaper
70 countries creates unemployment at home.

(773 words)

saturate sth *etw durchdringen*
strict controls *strenge Kontrollen*
brand *Markenlogo*
in the public eye *im Bewusstsein der Öffentlichkeit*
sponsorship *Unterstützung, Förderung, Sponsoring*
product placement *Schleichwerbung*

middle class *Mittelschicht*
status *Status, Stand, Stellung*
aspire to sth *nach etw streben*
lifestyle *Lebensstil, -führung, -art*
look up to sb *zu jdm aufsehen*
constitute sth *etw zahlenmäßig ausmachen*
double *sich verdoppeln*
hard to ignore sth *schwer etw zu ignorieren*

interdependent *voneinander abhängig, verflochten*
proponent *Befürworter/in, Anhänger/in*
business leader *Betriebsleiter/in, Führungskraft*
multinational company *(multinationaler) Konzern*
local enterprise *lokales Unternehmen*

1 Match words from box A and box B to make collocations. They are all highlighted words from the text.

A	B
consumer	needs
mass	labour
basic	leaders
working	class
child	conditions
spending	production
middle	society
business	habits

2 Fill the gaps with the prepositions missing from these expressions.

1 People work hard to improve their standard … living.
2 I like looking around the shops to see what's … offer.
3 The social problems we are facing are hard … ignore.
4 There are … excess of a million young people without jobs.
5 The purpose of advertising is to keep products … the public eye.
6 Society encourages us to look … to people who work hard to achieve their goals.

3 Explain what the following are, and say what you know about them.

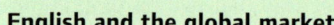

urban poverty – fairtrade organizations – trade unions – conspicuous consumption

4 Choose one of the section headings below. Do some research to answer the questions, then use your answers to prepare a 3-minute presentation to the class.

English and the global market	**Sport and globalization**
• Why is English a world language? • When did English become a world language? • Which professions use English? • How many non-native speakers speak English regularly? • Why do people talk about "world Englishes"?	• How much international sport is televized, and by which companies? • How much can sportsmen and women earn as professionals? • How can clubs afford these salaries? • What is the role of advertising in sport? • How international are clubs nowadays?
Tourism and globalization	**Globalization and work**
• When did air travel become affordable? • What is the connection between tourism and the environment? • When did holiday resorts develop as a business? • Which countries rely on tourism most? • How does tourism affect local culture and employment?	• What is the connection between globalization and (un)employment? • What are the advantages and disadvantages when companies use workers in other countries? • What sort of jobs cannot be easily done by people in other countries? • Which foreign languages are most useful in the world of business? Why? • What examples of multinational companies do you know? What do they do?

Advertising and the effects of consumerism

....

1 Look at the photos and do the following tasks.

1 Describe the photos. Say what is happening, and when and where the photos could have been taken.
2 Discuss the positive and negative things the photos say about our shopping habits.

2 Add the missing prepositions to these sentences. Then decide which photos they relate to.

a "We queued … the pavement … hours to get in, but it was worth it … the end."
b "It's so convenient. I get everything … the push … a button … the comfort … my own home."
c "We're so happy! So many bargains. Everything was reduced … 40 % … least!"
d "They are all … you, everywhere you look. Every surface is covered … them."

The effects of consumerism

Richard Docwra

Exposure to one advertisement can be powerful enough to influence someone. […] But when we are exposed to thousands of advertisements a day, and consumerism is promoted in most of the mental inputs we receive, this can trap us within a consumerist bubble and can mould our entire worldviews – our
5   aspirations, views, lifestyles and many other things. […]

Some of the effects of consumerism on us are what one might expect from a culture that promotes consumption. We slip into a cycle of wanting more things – whether it is the new iPod, another holiday abroad or simply a particular type of food – and the pursuit of these things takes up our time, energy, stress and
10 money. […] We also constantly compare ourselves with other people (both real and fictitious), wanting to be like them or in their position. This leads us into a

[1] **exposure** *Ausgesetztsein, Kontakt*
[3] mental input things in the outside world that make us think
[3] **trap sb** *jdn fangen*
[4] bubble Blase
[4] **mould sb/sth** form, influence sb/sth
[4] **worldview** the way we think of the world
[5] **aspiration** hope and ambition
[7] **slip into sth** easily fall into sth
[9] pursuit [pəˈsjuːt] *Streben*
[11] fictitious not real

12 dissatisfaction unhappiness

13 on edge nervous

19 dominate sth *etw dominieren*

19 potentially possibly

22 product placement
Produktplatzierung

22 imposition *Zumutung*

27 manipulate sb/sth control sb/
sth in a negative way

50 broaden your horizons
experience more of the world

51 prompt sb force sb

53 import-reliant dependent on
importing

57 finite limited

state of constant dissatisfaction – we are never happy with what we have and are always on edge. So, consumerism not only affects our behaviour (we spend more time on consumerist activities) but also our thinking (our aspirations, attitudes and worldviews). [...]

15

What is wrong with consumerism?

There is not necessarily anything morally wrong in buying and selling things, nor even in promoting them. But the extreme form of consumerism that now dominates the Western world has a number of unpleasant and even potentially dangerous characteristics.

20

1   – ? –

Advertising, selling and product placement is simply an annoying imposition on one's peace and personal space. Advertising is everywhere, and spoils many experiences and pleasant views. It is like having a stranger following you and shouting at you for several hours a day.

25

2   – ? –

Both advertising and consumerism itself try to manipulate us into adopting a particular view of how we should live rather than letting us decide for ourselves. [...] Modern advertising is not just about telling people about a product. It is now about creating wants and needs that we might not have had before seeing the advertisement. In other words, it creates false desires and needs in us by manipulating us. [...]

30

3   – ? –

Some people may believe that consumerism meets all their desires in life. But for an increasing number of people it does not. It creates impossible aspirations – quite simply, the principles it is based on make it a logical impossibility that it will make us happy. If the idea of consumerism is to continually create new needs in people and make them consume more, this will result in us constantly chasing after a carrot on a stick. [...]

35

4   – ? –

40

In its broadest sense, consumerism can be seen as a particular view of the 'good life' – a view that says life is better when you have more 'market goods' (products, services and activities). [...] There are, however, many other ways we could live (e.g. simple living or a focus on time and people rather than possessions), some of which people may feel are more appropriate for them. [...]

45

5   – ? –

Consumerism does not just restrict our choices. It is also a significant influence on our perspectives on the world. For example, if we are spending much of our time and energy seeking the next product or activity to consume, then we have less time and enthusiasm to learn about the world or broaden our horizons. Also, consumerism is unlikely to prompt us to question important things such as the availability of the resources that maintain our lifestyles, the capacity of the planet to hold the waste we generate or the vulnerability of the centralized, import-reliant food supply systems we currently use. [...]

50

6   – ? –

55

We live on a planet with a rapidly growing population (6.7 billion people and counting) and a finite set of natural resources for this population to consume. [...] We are already living way beyond the planet's limits.

60 Given this worrying situation, it seems obvious that we can't continue with the ever-increasing levels of consumption demanded by consumerism without major consequences. In fact, what we urgently need is precisely the opposite of consumerism – namely, a philosophy that urges us to reduce our levels of consumption. (706 words)

From: The website of lifesquared, 2009

59 given because of this situation

WORKING WITH THE TEXT

3 Match these missing section headings to spaces 1–6.

a It restricts our choices and lives
b It is unsustainable
c It is manipulative
d It is intrusive
e It affects our worldviews and characters
f It does not meet our needs

4 Entscheiden Sie, ob die Aussagen zum Text richtig oder falsch sind. Begründen Sie Ihre Entscheidung auf Deutsch in vollständigen Sätzen.

1 Advertising can affect the way we see the world.
2 Consumerism makes us try to model ourselves on other people.
3 The goal of consumerism is to promote happiness.
4 Consumerism can change how we behave, but not how we think.
5 There are alternatives to the consumerist lifestyle.
6 We are using up the world's resources faster than previously.

→) **EXAM PREPARATION**
Leseverstehen (p. 222)

S ▶ Doing comprehension tasks, p. 258

WORKING WITH WORDS

5 Discuss with a partner what the underlined words in these expressions mean.

1 (We are trapped) within a <u>consumerist bubble</u>. (l. 4)
2 We slip into <u>a cycle</u> of wanting more things. (l. 7)
3 (Advertising) creates <u>false desires and needs</u>. (l. 31)
4 … <u>broaden our horizons</u>. (l. 50)

6 a Match a verb from box A to a preposition in box B to form verb and preposition combinations from the text.

A verbs	B prepositions
(be) exposed …	for
compare (sb/sth) … (sb/sth)	in
spend …	on
decide … (yourself)	to
(be) based …	with
result …	
continue …	

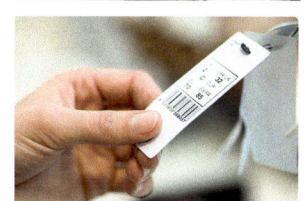

b Complete the following text with verb and preposition combinations from 6a in the correct form.

Advertising is at the heart of consumerism. Companies view the money they …[1] advertising as a necessary investment that can …[2] increased sales of their products. That's why we are …[3] huge quantities of advertisements every day. Adverts don't simply tell us about new products. The success of adverts is …[4] creating and fulfilling a need we might not even know we have. Many adverts work by making us …[5] ourselves … happy families or celebrities and their ideal lifestyles. Critics of consumerism say that it attempts to influence the way we think and to reduce our ability to …[6] ourselves. As we are using up the earth's resources more quickly than ever before, we simply cannot afford to …[7] current levels of consumption.

c Find other examples of verb + preposition combinations in the text.

LOOKING AT LANGUAGE

G ▸ The gerund and infinitive, p. 276

7 Rewrite the sentences starting with an *-ing* form and making any other changes necessary.

1 The primary goal of advertising is to influence people to buy.
   Influencing people to buy is the primary goal of advertising.
2 One of the key techniques of advertising is that they show us an ideal lifestyle.
3 It's difficult to persuade people to buy your products or services.
4 Consumerism does not want to let people decide for themselves.
5 Successful adverts aim to create and fulfil a need at the same time.
6 The only way we can preserve the resources of the planet is to reduce the amount we consume.

SPEAKING

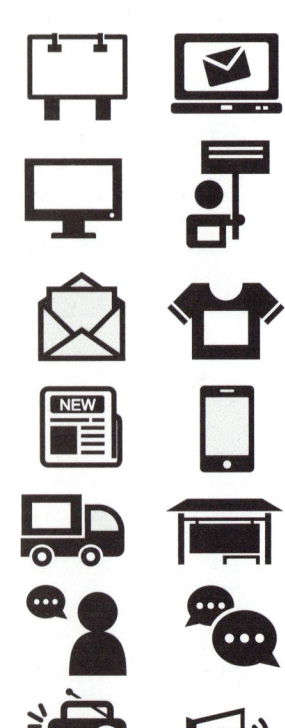

8 a Work in pairs. Look at the graphics in the margin. Name the different places you can find advertisements, and add to the list.

b Partner A: Explain which sorts of advertising you pay most attention to and why. Partner B: Say what you have bought as a result of advertising.

c Get together with three other pairs. Each person chooses one of the following products or services and prepares a two-minute presentation to the group on what advertisers do to make them attractive to consumers.

cars | chocolates and snacks | cosmetics | holidays | internet games and services | other food products | toothpaste | work and careers

DOING A CLASS SURVEY

9 Do a class survey on spending habits to find out the following:

· the percentage of essentials compared to non-essentials bought in the last week.
· the average number of shops visited.
· how many items, and what sort, were bought.
· the percentage of time spent shopping online as compared to in shops.

COMPETENCE TRAINING: ANALYSING A CARTOON ....

10 Cartoons are often found in news publications and websites. They usually employ humour to illustrate a sometimes serious point of view on current social and/or political topics. Cartoons often include speech balloons and/or captions. In order to understand a cartoon and its effect, you need to follow certain steps.

Look at the cartoon.

I'M NOT SURE WHAT IT IS BUT IT WAS IN THE SALE SO WE THOUGHT WE'D BETTER GET ONE BEFORE THEY SOLD OUT

FRAN

S ▶ Interpreting pictures and cartoons, p. 262

Step 1: Describe the cartoon.

Answer the following questions in order to describe the cartoon:
1 Who is in the cartoon?
2 Where are they?
3 What else is in the cartoon?
4 Is there a speech bubble cartoon? If so, what does it say?

Now write a paragraph describing the cartoon (cf. Language box 1).

> **→ TIP BOX**
> Always use the present progressive when describing what people are doing, wearing, saying and how they are feeling in cartoons or photos.

Step 2: Analyse the cartoon.

The following questions may help you when analysing a cartoon:
1 What sort of people are depicted: Are they well-known people, stereotypes, caricatures, etc.? Who are they and what is their role in connection with the topic of the cartoon? Are the people or issues presented in a positive or negative light? How is this impression achieved?
2 What point is the cartoonist trying to make? What means are used to get the message across?
3 Which of the headlines below do you think best sums up the cartoon?
   a Getting bargains makes people happy.
   b Everyone needs everything.
   c You will always find a use for everything.
   d People buy stuff they do not need.
   e Women are shopaholics
   f Good advertising can sell any rubbish.

Now write a paragraph analysing the cartoon (cf. Language box 2).

> **→ LANGUAGE BOX 1**
> On the left/right hand side of the cartoon …
> There are two women sitting …
> To the right of them …
> There is a speech bubble, in which one of the women is saying …

> **→ LANGUAGE BOX 2**
> The cartoonist has chosen two slightly old-fashioned women because …
> The women seem typically English as …
> This contrasts with the strange contraption …
> The contraption is a symbol of …
> By contrasting the women and the contraption, the cartoonist intends to …

Step 3: Evaluate the cartoon.

The following questions may help you when evaluating a cartoon:
1 Is the cartoon effective or not? Give reasons, using your background knowledge about the topic. (You may find the cartoon effective, while someone else might not.)
2 Does the cartoon reflect your own behaviour? Have you done something similar?

Now write a paragraph evaluating the cartoon (cf. Language box 3).

> **→ LANGUAGE BOX 3**
> The cartoon is humorous because …
> It gets its message across through/by …
> What I particularly like is …

TEXT 2   Our throwaway society

WARM-UP

1 Look at the pictures and do the following tasks.

1 Arrange the items in sequence according to how long each one normally lasts. Which are the most and least disposable?
2 Make a list of the different reasons for wanting to replace the items.
3 Choose two items and discuss ways you could make them last longer.

2 Before you read the text, look at the title of the article and discuss your predictions.

1 Do you think the article has a positive or negative view of the way we live? Explain your answer.
2 Which of the following do you think will be mentioned, and why?

advertising | drugs | repairing and recycling | shopping habits | the earth's resources | unemployment

The high cost of our throwaway society

Gaia Vince

Our global extractions are environmentally damaging and depleting some resources to the extent that they are in danger of running out. Many of those resources find their way into the goods, gadgets and machines that we find indispensable in our everyday lives. But do we really need so much stuff, or are we simply addicted to the new? There's no doubt that our consumption of resources from food to gadgets has risen dramatically over the past 60 years, and much of the world seems to be in the grip of a shopping epidemic.

There have been many times during my travels when I've needed something repaired, from rips in my backpack to holes in my clothes, zippers that have broken or memory cards that have lost data. From India to Ethiopia, I have had no trouble in finding someone who can sort the problem out, repair what is broken or find an ingenious solution to the issue. In rich countries, such items often would be thrown away and replaced with new ones without a second thought.

But then there are those items that seemingly can't be repaired. My camera shutter, battered by the dust and grime of travel, no longer works. I'm told I should throw away my camera, even though it works fine, apart from the shutter mechanism. Like the majority of consumer electronics, my camera has not been designed to be easily reparable.

5

10

15

---

[1] **deplete sth** use sth up
[2] **run out** be used up, be finished
[9] **rip** *Riss*
[9] **zipper** *Reißverschluss*
[10] **memory card** *Speicherkarte*
[12] **issue** *Problem*
[14] **camera shutter** *Kameraverschluss*
[15] **battered** in a bad condition through use
[15] **dust** *Staub*

Since the mobile phone handset market reached saturation in Europe and the
United States, we have chosen not to wait for our devices to fail. Almost all new
phones purchased are "upgrades", replacing functioning phones simply for reasons
of fashion or for technological additions that many of us rarely use, and which
could otherwise easily be achieved through software upgrades to existing handsets.

Made to fail

The idea that something that works fine should be replaced is now so ingrained in
our culture that few people question it. But it is a fairly recent concept, brought
about by a revolution in the advertising and manufacturing industries, which
thrived on various 20th century changes, including the mass movement of large
populations to cities, the development of mass production, globalization, improved
transport, international trade and public broadcast media.

The earliest example of manufacturers convincing people to frequently replace a
product may be the so-called "light bulb conspiracy", in which a group of companies
formed a cartel to prevent anyone from selling light bulbs with a longer than
1,000-hour lifespan, even though bulbs lasting more than 100,000 hours existed.

This way of selling more products by designing things that deliberately fail, cannot
be repaired, or have a set lifespan imposed is known as planned obsolescence. The
idea was born in the US during the 1930s depression as a way to get the economy
moving again by compelling people to buy more stuff. There were plenty of
factories and masses of unemployed, the trouble was the people who could afford
to buy things already had them. What was needed was a reason for shoppers to
buy things they already had, or didn't know they "needed".

By the 1950s, planned obsolescence had become the dominant paradigm in mass
production with things no longer built to last. A sophisticated advertising industry
persuaded people to shop. Mechanisms flourished to make this easier, from
department stores to credit. Consumerism was born. Some industries, such as
fashion, are predicated on planned obsolescence, with items being made to last a
single season or less.

Market forces

At the moment, there is little onus on manufacturers to improve. As Apple's
beautiful-looking and increasingly thin gadgets take an ever-larger share of the
market, other manufacturers are following suit. Motorola and Nokia, both of
which were known for their durable phones with easily replaced long-lasting
batteries, have now both released thin phones with glued-in batteries. But some
companies have been bucking the trend. HP and Dell release service manuals and
make computers that are easily upgradable and repairable.

Other companies are joining the move towards a circular economy, in which
economic growth is uncoupled from finite-resource use. Instead of the linear
manufacturing route: mining materials, fabricating, selling, throwing them away; a
circular economy is based around making products that are more easily
disassembled, so that the resources can be recovered and used to make new
products, keeping them in circulation.

The high-end outdoors clothing company Patagonia, for example, issues a
guarantee that it will repair any of its products for free over their lifetime. In
2011, it actually ran an advertising campaign asking consumers to buy less of the
stuff they don't need, to curb waste and environmental damage.   (768 words)

From: the website of the BBC, 29 November 2012

19 reach saturation *Sättigung erreichen*

23 handset *Handy, Mobilgeräte*

25 ingrained deeply rooted and difficult to change

26 bring about sth make sth happen

28 thrive do well

30 public broadcast media *öffentliche Rundfunkmedien*

33 cartel *Kartell*

36 planned obsolescence deliberately making sth so it does not last long

44 flourish do well

46 predicate on sth base on sth

52 durable lasting a long time

53 release sth sell sth; make sth public

53 glued-in fixed so it can't be removed

54 buck the trend do sth that goes against what everyone else is doing

54 service manual *Serviceanleitung, Wartungshandbuch*

57 uncouple sth separate sth

57 finite-resource use using up any of the limited resources

57 linear coming one after another in a line

60 disassemble sth take sth apart

61 in circulation available

62 issue sth provide sth

WORKING WITH THE TEXT

→ **EXAM PREPARATION**

Leseverstehen (p. 222)

S ▶ Doing comprehension tasks, p. 258

3 Entscheiden Sie, ob die Aussagen zum Text richtig oder falsch sind. Begründen Sie Ihre Entscheidung auf Deutsch in vollständigen Sätzen.

1 The author found it difficult to get her items repaired on her travels in developing countries.
2 In the West it was easier for her to get spare parts for her items.
3 Many people get new phones despite the fact that their old ones work well.
4 A group of companies decided to limit how long lightbulbs would work in order to increase profits.
5 The fashion industry designs clothes that are supposed to be worn for many seasons.
6 Some companies have started to make products that are more easily taken apart, so that the resources can be recovered and used to make new products.

4 Make a list of the examples in the text of different ways companies encourage consumers to make better use of resources.

WORKING WITH WORDS

5 Decide which is the closest in meaning to these words from the text.

1 indispensable (l. 4)	**a)** very popular	**b)** we can't manage without it
2 ingenious (l. 12)	**a)** cheap and easy	**b)** brilliantly clever
3 lifespan (l. 34)	**a)** a person's lifetime	**b)** the length of time a thing is likely to function
4 deliberately (l. 35)	**a)** by accident	**b)** not by chance
5 compel (l. 38)	**a)** help	**b)** force
6 follow suit (l. 51)	**a)** do something differently	**b)** do something in a similar way

6 Rewrite the sentences replacing the underlined words with a synonym from the box and making any necessary changes.

disposable | for now | lifestyle | repair | run out | second-hand | temporary | throw away

1 It's just a <u>short-term</u> solution but we'll think of something more permanent soon.
2 My mobile wasn't working properly so I <u>got rid of it</u>.
3 Our car is being repaired so we'll have to use our parents' car <u>for the time being</u>.
4 Brand new devices are often expensive, so I sometimes buy <u>pre-owned</u> models.
5 If our society carries on like this, the earth's resources will soon <u>be exhausted</u>.
6 Going shopping and buying things has become a big part of <u>the way we live</u>.
7 Many everyday items like coffee cups <u>are designed to be discarded after use</u>.
8 My laptop is broken and the technician says it can't be <u>made to work again</u>.

LOOKING AT LANGUAGE

7 Decide which verb form best completes these sentences.

G ▸ The simple present, p. 267
G ▸ The present perfect, p. 269

1 Consumption of the planet's resources <u>rises</u>/<u>has risen</u> dramatically in the last 50 years.
2 It <u>becomes</u>/<u>has become</u> normal to replace things even though they <u>work</u>/<u>have worked</u> well.
3 Some companies <u>start</u>/<u>have started</u> to publicize the fact that their products <u>are</u>/<u>have been</u> long-lasting.
4 I <u>have</u>/<u>have had</u> my mobile phone for several years. It <u>has</u>/<u>has had</u> all the basic functions I need.
5 Advertising <u>works</u>/<u>has worked</u> by showing us an idealized view of the life we could have.
6 We <u>get</u>/<u>have got</u> to a point now where many technology companies <u>produce</u>/<u>have produced</u> a new model every year.
7 I <u>buy</u>/<u>have bought</u> a number of things recently as a direct result of the advertising I <u>see</u>/<u>have seen</u>.
8 Advertising is everywhere you <u>look</u>/<u>have looked</u>. Since about 1960 it <u>invades</u>/<u>has invaded</u> every aspect of our lives.

COMPETENCE TRAINING: LISTENING

▸ Practising listening skills, p. 256

8 When you listen to a text in class, you are normally asked to find certain information in the text. Read the tasks well and make sure you know what you are looking for. In the exam there are three types of tasks: 1) answering questions in German; 2) completing sentences in German; 3) filling in grids.
In this section we will concentrate on filling in grids.

1.03

➔ EXAM PREPARATION
Zentrale Klassenarbeit Hörverstehen (p. 224)

Sie hören einen Bericht aus der Radiosendung „Green Living" über den Lebenszyklus eines T-Shirts. Nennen Sie die verschiedenen Phasen des Lebenszyklus und beschreiben Sie, was in jeder Phase stattfindet. Vervollständigen Sie die Tabelle auf Deutsch mit Informationen aus der Radiosendung.

Phasen	Beschreibung

Pre-listening

a Decide which English key words you need to listen out for to know when each *"Phase"* is being discussed. Which of the following might be used (three might occur; three are irrelevant)?

method | phase | production | row | stage | step

b You also need to listen out for signpost words, i.e. words that indicate that a new *"Phase"* is being discussed. Which of the following words may help you? (Can you think of any others?)

after … | finally, … | first of all, … | for example, … | obviously, … | once …, | secondly, … | then …

After the first listening

a Finding the first phase. You probably heard "First of all, there is the cultivation phase". If you are unsure what "cultivation" means, you can draw on your general knowledge. So write down which of the following might be the first stage of making a T-shirt.

getting the material to make it | packing it in a factory | selling it in a shop | planning a marketing conference

Moreover, you heard the following words which were used to describe this phase.

farming | irrigating | fields | water | plants | fertilising | ground | harvesting | heavy machinery | cotton | natural fibre | pesticides | crops

Now write down in one sentence what the first phase is about.

b Copy the table in the task and under *"Phasen"* write down the German words or phrases from the box below that you think is the best one to describe the first phase.

Anbau | Anbau des Stoffs | Produktion | Landwirtschaft

c In the first row under *"Beschreibung"* write in German a description of what this stage involves. (The words in the second box in **a** will help you.)

d Continue with the rest of the table in the same way. Then do task 9.

1.03

LISTENING

EXAM PREPARATION
Zentrale Klassenarbeit Hörverstehen (p. 224)

TIP BOX
Use techniques you learned in task 7.

9 Jetzt hören Sie den Bericht nochmals. Nennen Sie die Auswirkung jeder Phase des Lebenszyklus des T-Shirts auf die Umwelt. Kopieren und vervollständigen Sie die Tabelle auf Deutsch mit Informationen aus der Radiosendung.

Phasen	Auswirkung auf die Umwelt

SPEAKING ....

10 Produce an uninterrupted five-minute discourse based on the diagram below.

→ EXAM PREPARATION
Kommunikationsprüfung (p. 224)

→ TIP BOX
Use your notes from tasks 8 and 9 and describe the different stages of the lifecycle of a T-shirt, the impact on the environment and what can be done to minimize environmental damage.

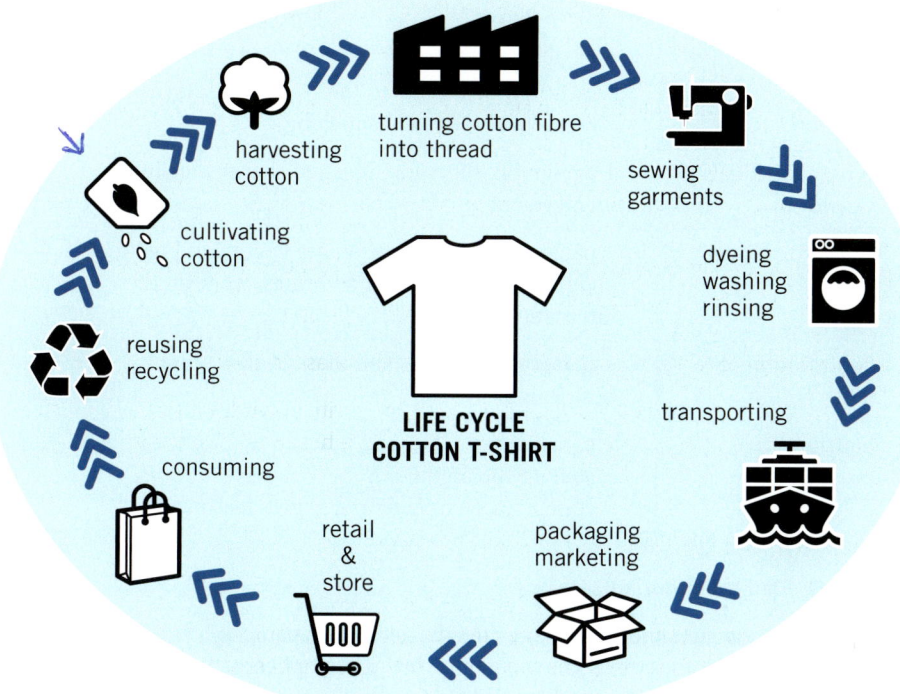

COMPETENCE TRAINING: STRUCTURING AN ESSAY .... **S ►** Writing an essay, p. 259

11 When writing a composition, you need to structure your essay logically so that the reader can follow your arguments.

This is the essay you have been given:

Who should be responsible for preserving the planet's resources: individuals or the government?

Step 1: Gather ideas.

a   Look at these ideas for the essay. Decide if they relate more to what individuals or the government can do.

heavy fines for pollution	set a good example
recycle more	reduce waste
pay attention to buying habits	reduce taxes for certain companies
grow own food	control advertising
use public transport	reduce road building
encourage renewable energy sources	avoid buying plastic

b   Think what families and schools could also do.
c   Decide which points are most important and which could be left out.

Step 2: Find a structure

An essay should follow a logical structure, with an introduction to the topic of the essay, the main part (or "body") of the text, and a conclusion, usually giving your own opinion.

Introduction:	• 1 paragraph:
	  – overview of threats to the planet's resources
	  – reasons why this is happening

What individuals can do	• 1 paragraph: recycling, lifestyle changes, political involvement
What government can do	• 1 paragraph: promote alternate energy and reduce pollution, pass new laws and fines, work on the international stage
Contribution of other groups	• 1 paragraph: families and local groups, schools, businesses

Conclusion:	• 1 paragraph:
	  – sum up the arguments
	  – state your own opinion and give reasons for it

Step 3: Plan the different sections.

a The introduction and conclusion should each be one paragraph.

b For the body of the text you will need a few paragraphs: each new issue should be presented in a separate paragraph.

c Give examples to support your main points.

d Make sure you cover the most important point or argument in sufficient detail. Generally, it helps to leave the key point until last so it makes the most impact.

e Use signposting: in the introduction, outline what you are going to say. Remember to use linking devices to connect your ideas, too.

WRITING

→ **EXAM PREPARATION**

Textproduktion (p. 223)

S ▶ Writing an essay, p. 259

12 **Using all the information you have from this unit and using the methods learned in task 11, write the essay.**

Discuss who should be responsible for preserving the planet's resources – individuals or the government.

TEXT 3   The global division of labour

1 With a partner decide which of the following categories the statements belong to.

China	India	both	neither
9, 3	1, 5, 8	2, 4, 7, 10	6

1 The country is developing rapidly, creating many new roads, airports and cities.
2 Millions of people are still living in poverty.
3 There is a single political party.
4 Rice growing and tea production are important to the national economy.
5 Religion is a key aspect of daily life for most inhabitants.
6 Although vast, the country is in a single time zone.
7 Although education is highly valued, millions of people are still illiterate.
8 It has a significant film industry.
9 It has invested in an ambitious space programme.
10 It has few natural resources so is dependent on imports for many everyday basics.

China and India – two different economic stories

1.04

If the last century is the story of how the United States transformed itself into a global economic powerhouse, this century will in all likelihood be the story of the rise of Asian countries. Numerous predictions suggest that China and India will be the largest economies in the world by 2050, but with significant differences.

5   Analysis of how the labour force is divided between the different sectors of economic activity reveals a great deal about a country, its wealth and its future prospects. The first – the primary sector – is the extraction of raw materials, which includes agriculture, fishing, forestry and mining. In the poorest countries, there tend to be more people working in this sector, as is the case with many African
10 nations today. The secondary sector is manufacturing, which involves the transformation of materials into goods, so here steel is made into cars, and textiles are made into clothes and bricks become houses. The tertiary sector involves the supply to consumers and businesses of services and intangible goods such as banking, entertainment, tourism, general retail and restaurant services.

15 These sectors also reflect stages in the development of society. In traditional civilizations, as much as 70 % of employment is in the primary sector, particularly agriculture. This is reduced to 50 % of employment in the industrialized phase of development as societies learn to mechanize and produce more wealth. Advanced industrialized economies have seen a substantial shift from the primary and
20 secondary sectors to the tertiary sector over the past century. Calculations suggest that 70 % of the workforce of the United States is now engaged in the service sector and less than 4 % in the primary sector.

In 1978, the Chinese government decided to enact economic reforms. The result was a move from a centrally planned economy to a model that was market based
25 and open to international trade. China opted to focus on the manufacturing sector, which is why "made in China" labels are so ubiquitous – in cheap plastic goods,

1 transform sth make sth change completely
3 numerous many
5 labour force *Arbeitskräfte*
7 extraction getting sth out of sth else
7 raw materials *Rohstoffe, -materialien*
8 forestry *Forstwirtschaft*
10 manufacturing *Herstellung, Produktion*
24 centrally planned controlled by the government
24 market based open to the influence of the market
26 ubiquitous found everywhere

29 per capita income *Pro-Kopf-Einkommen*

34 substandard poor quality

40 graduate student who finishes university with a qualification

42 outsourcing contract *Outsourcing-Vertrag*

45 solar technology *Solartechnik*

45 medical appliance instruments used by doctors

53 infrastructure *Infrastruktur*

56 knowledge-based economy an economy dominated by intellectual services

58 consultation offering specialist advice

61 wealth creation activities that help people make money

India concentrates on the service industries.

China concentrates on the manufacturing industries.

clothing and, increasingly, electronics. The resultant economic and social development has lifted more than 500 million people out of poverty. However, the per capita income is still considerably less than those of advanced countries, and it has the second largest number of poor in the world after India.   30

India, on the other hand, concentrated more on services. While agriculture is still the largest employer, its share of the country's GDP is declining. After the economic reforms of 1991, one of the industries that took off was the manufacture of pharmaceuticals. At first, India became known for making cheap, substandard copies of Western drugs and selling them to developing countries. But more   35 recently India has been gaining respect in this industry, as well as in other manufacturing industries.

Perhaps more significantly, the Indian economy has one of the fastest-growing service sectors in the world. It has exploited the fact that it is the largest English-speaking country in the world with over a million college graduates a year to   40 become a major exporter of IT and software services. India gets by far the most outsourcing contracts of any country in the world: contracts for IT services and services such as tuition, human resources, finance and accounting. With an eye to the future, India now plans to continue its development by focusing on new industries such as solar technology, LED lighting, small cars, and medical   45 appliances.

China's astonishing growth rate over the past decade is forecast to slow down, which is partly a result of the combination of low population growth and an aging population. This will result in many millions becoming less productive and thus not making a contribution to the state's resources. India, by contrast, looks likely   50 to surge ahead because of its younger population. However, much depends on sustained reforms and increased investment in education – particularly for women in rural areas – transport and other elements of infrastructure.

There is a further reason for optimism about the Indian economy. Analysts now believe that the economic model has a fourth, quaternary sector, which reflects   55 the emergence of our current knowledge-based economy. Activities in this sector include scientific research, education, information technology, information-generation and -sharing, and services such as consultation. This new sector might be called infotronics, as it merges information and electronics. The advanced economies have made huge investments here. In Australia, for example, the   60 quaternary sector accounts for almost half of all wealth creation. As the examples above show, India is already doing well here.   (758 words)

WORKING WITH THE TEXT

2 Copy and complete this grid with information from the text.

Sector	Social development stage	Process involved	Example professions
primary	agricultural	extraction of …	…
…	…	transformation of raw materials into goods	…
tertiary	post-industrial	…	…
…	infotronics age	…	…

3 Welche vier Folgen der chinesischen Wirtschaftsreformen von 1978 werden im Text genannt? Erstellen Sie eine Liste. Formulieren Sie vollständige Sätze auf Deutsch.

→ **EXAM PREPARATION**
Leseverstehen (p. 222)

S ▶ Doing comprehension tasks, p. 258

SPEAKING

4 Look at lines 5–22 of the text. Discuss with a partner: Why has the number of people working in mining and agriculture declined so much in advanced economies and not in developing economies? Explain your reasons.

WORKING WITH WORDS

5 Explain these expressions from the text

1 a global economic powerhouse
2 in all likelihood
3 future prospects
4 a substantial shift
5 a declining share
6 one of the industries that took off
7 with an eye to the future
8 to surge ahead

6 Complete this text with the words from the box.

development | economy | fastest-growing | growth | investor | labour force |
resource-rich | trade

Africa is a …[1] continent, as it contains much of the world's gold, diamonds and copper. Nevertheless, it is also the poorest inhabited continent on the planet. Yet surprisingly, it is also the …[2] continent with an economic growth rate of around 5.6 % a year. …[3] with international partners is expanding, literacy and education are improving, and many Sub-Saharan countries have the advantage of English language skills. These, combined with a cheap …[4], form positive foundations for dynamic …[5]. China is probably the main …[6] in Africa, as the use of African resources has been a major contributor to the Chinese …[7]. Any slowdown in China's growth would affect the future …[8] of the continent.

7 With a partner, discuss what the underlined idiomatic phrases mean. Use your dictionary if necessary.

1 Millions of people are <u>living on the breadline</u> as a result of austerity measures.
2 Sports cars with the most up-to-date equipment <u>cost an arm and a leg</u>.
3 Buying new software for office computers without training the workers how to use it is <u>money down the drain</u>.
4 We decided to stop going to the gym, as it <u>costs a fortune</u>.
5 It was my birthday, so I <u>splashed out</u> on a couple of X-Box games.
6 I can't go out this weekend, as <u>I'm broke</u> and only get paid next week.
7 The cost of buying a house in London has gone <u>through the roof</u>.
8 African farmers are lucky if they make enough <u>to get by</u>.
9 Many retired people in developing economies struggle to <u>make ends meet</u>.
10 In parts of Latin America, millions of poor families <u>live from hand to mouth</u>.

COMPETENCE TRAINING: ANALYSING CHARTS AND GRAPHS

S ▶ Interpreting charts and graphs, p. 263

8 Charts and graphs present statistical information visually, in a way that is easy to understand. There are different types, e. g. pie charts, bar charts, line graphs or tables. It is often helpful to use charts and graphs to support your explanations in a presentation.

Work in pairs. Each of you chooses one of the diagrams and approaches them according to the steps given below.

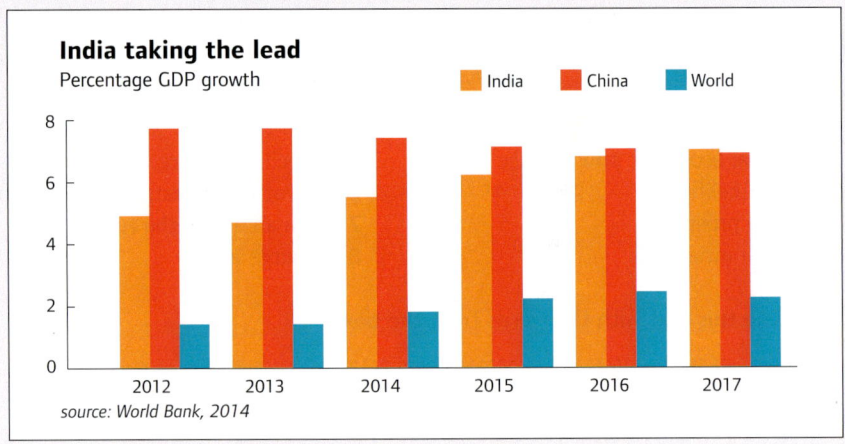

India taking the lead
Percentage GDP growth

source: World Bank, 2014

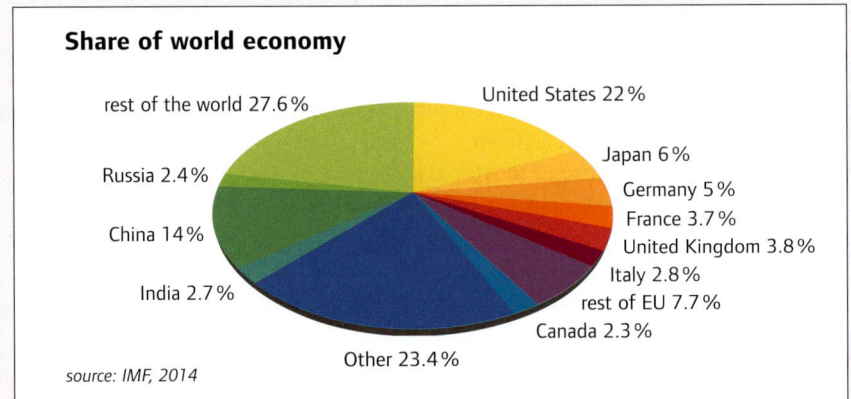

Share of world economy

source: IMF, 2014

> **LANGUAGE BOX 1**
> It is taken from /
> It contains data from … /
> It was published in …

> **LANGUAGE BOX 2**
> The bar/pie chart shows the different /
> compares the size/ number of …
> It deals with / is about …
> It compares … with …
> It shows … compared to …
> The chart is divided into segments, which show/ represent …
> Each segment represents …
> The bars show …

Step 1: Identify the type of diagram you are dealing with.

The following questions may help you when identifying a chart or graph:
1 What type of diagram is it: a pie chart, a bar graph, a line graph?
2 What is the source of the data?
3 What year is it from? Is it up to date?
Each of you tells the other what you know about your diagram (cf. Language box 1).

Step 2: Describe the chart or graph.

The following questions may help you when describing a chart or graph:
1 What is it about and what information does it give?
2 Does it show a development or does it compare or present things?
3 Does it use absolute figures or percentages?
Each of you tells the other what you know about your diagram (cf. Language box 2).

Step 3: Draw conclusions from the chart or graph.

The following suggestions may help you when drawing conclusions about a chart or graph (but not all of them need apply to each visual):

1 Find the most significant information. Typically, this will be in the form of a superlative (*highest/lowest; most/least; greatest/lowest,* etc.)

2 Compare and contrast key points to reveal the dominant trends. Typically, this will be in the form of a comparative (*better/worse, more/fewer, faster/slower*). Try to use contrast expressions such as *like/unlike, while/whereas, compared with*

3 Try to identify if there is a change. Typically, you can use verbs with adverbs like *has changed gradually/rapidly, has grown significantly, has risen/fallen dramatically*.

Discuss your diagrams together (cf. Language box 3).

> **→ LANGUAGE BOX 3**
>
> **verbs + adverbs:**
> increase/rise/decline/fall + gradually/rapidly/sharply/slightly/slowly/steadily
> **adjectives + nouns:**
> gradual/rapid/sharp/slight/slow/steady + increase/growth/rise/decrease/decline/fall/growth
> **comparisons:**
> whereas – while – on the one hand, … on the other hand, … – unlike – compared with
> **expressions:**
> There are big/vast/significant differences between …
> At the top/bottom of the ranking comes …
> The smallest/biggest segment / The segments representing
> … is twice / three times as high/much as …
> There are more than / nearly twice as many … as there are …

4 To check if you have understood your diagrams, both of you together decide which of the following statements are true or false:
   a There is still a big difference between the GDP per capita of India and China.
   b The combined share of the world economy of developing countries matches that of the USA.
   c Indian GDP is growing more than twice as fast as that of the rest of the world.
   d China and India will continue to grow at the same rate.
   e The GDP of the 4 largest EU countries is more than that of China.
   f Germany has the fourth largest economy in the world.

5 Write 4 more true or false statements about the information in your visual. Your partners must decide if they are true or false.

SPEAKING

9 Produce an uninterrupted five-minute discourse based on the graphics in task 8, relating the material to the changing world economy.

> **→ EXAM PREPARATION**
> *Kommunikationsprüfung (p. 224)*

WRITING

10 Explain the quotation below in relation to the text and give examples of significant changes in the world of work.

> **→ EXAM PREPARATION**
> *Textproduktion (p. 223)*

"Advanced industrialized economies have seen a substantial shift from the primary and secondary sectors to the tertiary sector over the past century." (ll. 18 –20).

S ▶ Writing an essay, p. 259

TEXT 4   The effect of automation on work

1 **a** Look at the pictures and match the comments to the jobs in the photos.

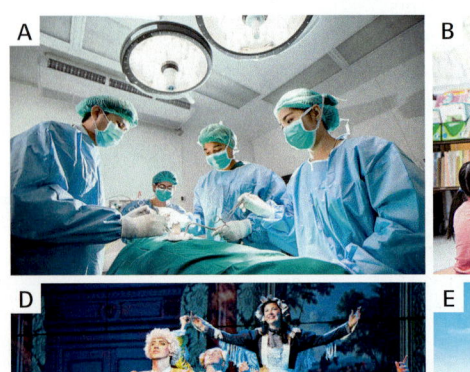

1 On stage things are pretty much as they always have been. However, with films it couldn't be more different. Many rely heavily on computer-generated images for special effects and so on these days – especially the blockbusters.

2 The basics of sitting in front of a camera in a studio haven't changed. What has changed is the speed of everything. Live links to reporters around the world and the ability to show stories filmed on mobiles are completely normal nowadays.

3 Even when the job is about working with nature, in fact there's a lot of science involved. Think of the fertilizers and pesticides we use, and the machines get better year by year to make the job easier – in theory at least.

4 We've come a long way since the days of propellers. Almost everything in the cockpit is fully automated and controlled by computer these days, so travel is safer than ever before. Passengers like to know there's a real person in charge, though.

b Write down some sentences like those above for the two jobs not described in 1, saying how technology has affected the job.

c Do you think robots and computers could ever completely replace any of these jobs?

Will your job still exist in 2025?

Jenna Awford

¹ carebot (here) robots that do the work of nurses
⁴ **redundant** not needed
⁴ **artificial intelligence** *künstliche Intelligenz*

From self-driving cars to carebots for elderly people, rapid advances in technology have long represented a potential threat to many jobs normally performed by people. But experts now believe that almost 50 per cent of occupations existing today will be completely redundant by 2025 as artificial intelligence continues to transform businesses.

5

A revolutionary shift in the way workplaces operate is expected to take place over the next 10 to 15 years, which could put some people's livelihoods at risk. Customer work, process work and vast swathes of middle management will simply "disappear", according to a new report by consulting firm CBRE and China-based Genesis. "Experts predict that 50 per cent of occupations today will no longer exist by 2025 as people will take up more creative professions," said Martin Chen, Chief Operating Officer of Genesis. "This means that jobs will evolve and so will real estate development."

Workspaces with rows of desks will become completely redundant, not because they are not fit for purpose, but simply because that purpose no longer exists, according to the report.

"The next fifteen years will see a revolution in how we work, and a corresponding revolution will necessarily take place in how we plan and think about workplaces," said Peter Andrew, Director of Workplace Strategy for CBRE Asia Pacific. A growing proportion of jobs in the future will require creativity, intelligence, social skills and the ability to leverage artificial intelligence. "And for most people that will be a route to happiness and fulfilment," the report states. "For many of us, artificial intelligence will be a tool to undertake tasks of a scale and complexity that were once unimaginable but which are now eminently possible and hugely rewarding."

The report – "Fast Forward 2030: The Future of Work and the Workplace" – is based on interviews with 200 experts, business leaders and young people from Asia Pacific, Europe and North America.

Data in the US suggests that technology already destroys more jobs than it creates, as GDP has been able to grow faster than employment since 2000. But the report states: "Losing occupations does not necessarily mean losing jobs – just changing what people do."

Growth in new jobs could occur as much through crowdsourced freelancers as within the bounds of the corporation, according to the research. "The biggest wild card will be the emergence of 20 to 40 person companies that have the speed and technological know-how to directly challenge major corporations," it states.

A 2014 report by Pew Research found 52 per cent of experts in artificial intelligence and robotics were optimistic about the future and believed there would still be enough jobs in the next few decades. The optimists envisioned "a future in which robots and digital agents do not displace more jobs than they create," according to Aaron Smith, the report's co-author. Microsoft's Jonathan Grudin told researchers that: "Technology will continue to disrupt jobs, but more jobs seem likely to be created. When the world population was a few hundred million people there were hundreds of millions of jobs. Although there have always been unemployed people, when we reached a few billion people there were billions of jobs. There is no shortage of things that need to be done and that will not change."

Oxford University researchers have ranked the occupations most in danger of being replaced by computers and robots, including telemarketers, insurance underwriters and watch repairers. Some of the least likely to be replaced are therapists, audiologists and choreographers.   (579 words)

From: Daily Mail Online, 8 November 2014

6 shift change

7 livelihood job

8 swathe large quantity

8 middle management *mittlere Führungsebene*

9 consulting firm business that offers specialist advice

12 evolve develop

13 real estate development the business of how buildings are built and used

14 **row** [rəʊ] line

15 fit for purpose suitable

17 corresponding *entsprechend*

21 leverage sth make good use of sth

23 **tool** helpful instrument

24 eminently very

25 **rewarding** *lohnend, bereichernd*

30 GDP *BIP (Bruttoinlandsprodukt)*

33 crowdsourced paid by online contributions

33 **freelancer** sb who works for themselves, not a company

34 within the bounds of inside

34 wild card sth unexpected and unpredictable

36 **know-how** skills and abilities

39 **decade** period of ten years

39 envision sth imagine sth

40 digital agent *digitale/r Händler/in*

42 disrupt sth cause an extreme change to sth

46 **shortage** lack

48 telemarketer *Telefonverkäufer/in*

48 insurance underwriter *Versicherer/in*

WORKING WITH THE TEXT

→ **EXAM PREPARATION**
Leseverstehen (p. 222)

S ▶ Doing comprehension tasks, p. 258

2 Entscheiden Sie, ob die Aussagen zum Text richtig oder falsch sind. Begründen Sie Ihre Entscheidung auf Deutsch in vollständigen Sätzen.

1 Within ten years half of all jobs that exist today may no longer exist.
2 Middle managers are less likely to be affected by the changes predicted.
3 It is expected that people will move to work that requires higher levels of personal creativity.
4 Workspaces with rows of desks will disappear as they have been shown to be inefficient.
5 Experts predict big organizations will find themselves being challenged by small companies.
6 It is expected that advances in technology will lead to large-scale unemployment.

3 Find words or expressions in the text that mean the same as these.

1 no longer necessary
2 a complete change
3 an increasingly large number
4 a source/cause of satisfaction
5 impossible to even think of
6 extremely satisfying
7 a period of ten years
8 a lack of, not enough of something

WORKING WITH WORDS

4 **a** Put these words in the right category so that they form collocations:

a great …   … experience   …load   …place
a low-paid …   find a …   lose your …   … satisfaction
a well-paid …   …force   out of …   …seeker
after …   full-time …   part-time …   …-sharing
apply for a …   leave …   … permit   …station

Expressions with 'work'	Expressions with 'job'
	a great job

b Complete these sentences with expressions from above in the correct form.

1 The number of people … has increased by 100,000 this year.
2 Companies value young people who have some relevant … .
3 The process of automation allows companies to reduce their … .
4 While people feel stressed when they have a heavy … , computers don't.
5 Companies will be smaller, so it will be rare to find 75 … in a single office.
6 Do you need a … to work in Japan as a European Union citizen?
7 I think it's a mistake to put salary before … when thinking of a career – life isn't just work.
8 Lots of teenagers have one or two … at the weekend to earn spending money.

LOOKING AT LANGUAGE

5 Decide which pair of words best completes the sentences on the next page.

fewer/less | greater/more | greatest/fewest | less/more | more/higher |
more/than | less/than | not as/as

1　People worry that … jobs will be lost … created as a result of automation.
People worry that more jobs will be lost than created as a result of automation.
2　In the past, the speed of technological change was … fast … at present.
3　Robotics is likely to have … impact on artistic jobs … on regular jobs.
4　Experts predict there will be … large companies in the future as they are … flexible than smaller organizations.
5　If the predictions are accurate, people will make … use of their creativity … of the time.
6　There may be … jobs, but unemployment will also be … because the world population will increase.
7　The jobs at … risk of disappearing are those that need … skills.
8　There is … chance that robots will replace teachers … other professions.

COMPETENCE TRAINING: WRITING AN INTRODUCTION TO AN ESSAY

S ► Writing an essay, p. 259

6 **A good introduction should:**
–　catch the readers' attention and make them want to read on;
–　let them know exactly what topic your text deals with.

You have to write an essay entitled:
"Discuss the advantages and disadvantages of the increasing use of technology in the world of work."

Here are 3 possible introductions.

A　Technology has radically changed how we live and work. Communication between people is faster and more reliable - and cheaper - than ever before, and access to information has improved enormously. Computers can perform tasks in an instant that previously required considerable effort for people. In this essay I will examine both the advantages and disadvantages of technology to workers and companies.

B　Is there any aspect of modern life that has not been influenced by technology? From the world of work to how we spend our leisure time, computers have opened up new possibilities. However, the same process that saves us valuable time and increases productivity at work has also resulted in job losses and made cyber crime possible. I will show that despite the negative sides, technology is a great help in the world of work.

C　Technology affects all areas of our life. It has been estimated that eight out of ten British companies are victims of computer crime. And yet most of us enjoy using the internet for communication and shopping. So technology is a good thing for us. But it can also be a bad thing.

1　Which do you think is the best introduction? Give reasons.
2　Which one(s) refer(s) to the topic in the task?
3　Which one(s) shows what the student is going to write about?
4　Which one(s) show that the student has understood the instruction *(Operator)*.
5　In your own words write an introduction to this essay.

WRITING

7 Discuss the advantages and disadvantages of the increasing use of technology in the world of work.

→ TIP BOX
Use all the information you have learned from this unit as well as your conclusions from task 6.

→ EXAM PREPARATION
Textproduktion (p. 223)

TEXT 5   Being a leader

1 Work in groups. Discuss what makes a good leader in these situations:

in a group of musicians | in a sports team | in family life | in politics | in the world of work | working with a group of classmates at school

CEO *Geschäftsführer/in*

¹⁰ **project sth** present sth in a particular way

¹⁰ **breezy** that seems relaxed and easy

¹¹ **game face** professional appearance

¹³ **the big picture** the entire perspective

¹⁶ **relentless** *unermüdlich, unablässig*

¹⁸ **coincidence** *Zufall*

²² **battle-hardened** having survived difficult experiences

²³ **embrace sth** positively accept sth

²³ **adversity** difficult situation

²³ **relish sth** positively enjoy sth

²⁷ **take ownership of sth** take over responsibility for sth

³⁰ **team player** sb who works well with others

³¹ **truism** something obviously true

³⁴ **ad hoc** (Latin) not planned

³⁶ **wow sb** impress sb

³⁷ **set sth aside** forget about sth

Five secrets of the world's top CEOs

Adam Bryant

Interviews I conducted with more than 70 chief executives and other leaders for my weekly column in the *New York Times* point to five essentials for success, qualities that most of those chief executives share and look for in people they hire. The good news is these traits are not genetic. They're developed through attitude, habit and discipline; factors within your control. They will make you a better employee, manager and leader. 5

1   Passionate curiosity

Many successful chief executives are passionately curious people. It is a side of them rarely seen in the media and in investor meetings, and there is a reason for that. In business, CEOs are supposed to project confidence and breezy authority. 10 Certainty is the game face they wear. But get them away from these familiar scripts and a different side emerges. They share stories about mistakes and failures. They ask big-picture questions. They wonder why things work the way they do and whether those things can be improved upon. They want to know people's stories, and what they do. 15

It is this relentless questioning that leads entrepreneurs to spot opportunities and helps managers understand the people who work for them, and how to get them to work together effectively. It is no coincidence that more than one executive uttered the same phrase when describing what, ultimately, is the CEO's job: "I am a student of human nature." CEOs are not necessarily the smartest people in the 20 room, but they are the best students.

2   Battle-hardened confidence

Some people embrace adversity, even relish it, and they have a track record of overcoming it. They have battle-hardened confidence. And because the best predictor of behaviour is past performance, many chief executives interview job 25 candidates about how they dealt with failure in the past. They want to know if somebody is the kind of person who takes ownership of challenges or starts looking for excuses.

3   Team smarts

At some point, the notion of being a team player became devalued in corporate 30 life. It has been reduced to a truism: I work on a team, therefore I am a team player. The most effective executives are more than just team players. They understand how teams work and how to get the most out of the group.

Companies increasingly operate through the use of ad hoc teams. Team smarts refers to the ability to recognise those players the team needs and how to bring 35 them together around a common goal. "Early on, I was wowed by talent, and I was willing to set aside the idea that this person might not be a team player," says

40 Susan Lyne, chairman of online fashion retailer Gilt Groupe. "Now, I need people who are going to be able to build a team, manage a team, recruit well and work well with their peers."

4 A simple mindset

Most senior executives want the same thing from people who present to them: be concise, get to the point, make it simple. Yet few people can deliver the simplicity that many bosses want. Instead, they mistakenly assume the bosses will be
45 impressed by a long PowerPoint presentation that shows how diligently they researched a topic, or that they will win over their superiors by talking more, not less.

If executives in positions of authority are clear about what they want, why can't they get the people who report to them to lose the "Power" part of their
50 presentations and simply get to the "Point"? There are a few likely explanations. A lot of people have trouble being concise. Another possible explanation is that a lag exists in the business world. There was a time when simply having certain information was a competitive advantage. Now, in the internet era, most people have easy access to the same information. That puts a greater premium on the
55 ability to synthesise, to connect dots in new ways and to ask simple, smart questions that lead to untapped opportunities.

5 Fearlessness

Are you comfortable being uncomfortable? Do you like situations where there's no road map or compass? Are you willing to make surprising career moves to learn
60 new skills? In other words, are you fearless? With the business world in endless turmoil, maintaining the status quo is only going to put you behind the competition. So chief executives speak with reverence about executives on their teams who are fearless.

(805 words)

From: The Guardian, 22 July 2011

[39] recruit hire people
[43] **concise** offering only the information that is necessary and important
[43] **get to the point** be direct
[45] diligent hard working
[46] win sb over convince sb
[52] lag time delay
[54] premium extra value
[55] synthesise combine ideas
[55] connect dots understand how things work
[56] untapped not yet explored
[61] turmoil state of confusion
[61] status quo (Latin) the situation as it is
[62] reverence deep respect

WORKING WITH THE TEXT

2 Which numbered section of the text mentions:

1. being a team player
2. being bold and brave
3. being concise and straight to the point
4. being curious and interested in everything
5. enjoying difficult challenges

3 On a scale of 1 (= I'm not good at this) to 10 (= this is me), how would you rate yourself for each of the five criteria in the article?

4 Complete these mini dialogues with the right expression.

get a word in edgeways | have a good word | have a word | have my word | in a word | right from the word go | take the words out of my mouth | word for word

1. "Did you find the presentation useful?"
   "… , no. I think it was a waste of time, and had nothing original in it at all."
2. "So what happened when you met him? Did you explain our new ideas?"
   "No. You know what he is like. He talked so much. I couldn't … "
3. "Excuse me, Kim. Can I … with you?"
   "Sure. When? Now?"

33

4 "It sounds like you all work well as a team despite never having worked together before."
   "Yes, we've all got on brilliantly … "

5 "Promise me that you will explain all the problems to our boss."
   "Of course, I will. You … "

6 "Investment in new technologies is not an option, it's essential for our success."
   "You … . That was exactly what I was going to say!"

7 "Is that really what she said? That our work is a perfect example of sloppiness and laziness combined!"
   "Yes, that's what she said … "

8 "He doesn't think very highly of our accountants, does he?"
   "You're right there. He doesn't … to say about them."

LOOKING AT LANGUAGE

G ▶ The simple present, p. 267
G ▶ The present progressive, p. 267

5 **a** **Explain why the underlined verbs are in the simple or continuous form in these sentences.**

1 I <u>know</u> why it <u>isn't working</u>. It's because it <u>doesn't work</u> in these temperatures.
2 What <u>are you thinking</u> about – about what <u>you were doing</u> this time last week?
3 What <u>does he think</u> about what <u>we did</u> last week?
4 I normally <u>live and work</u> in London, but at the moment <u>I'm working</u> in Barcelona on a new project.
5 <u>We're hoping</u> to meet a lot of business contacts next week at the trade fair.
6 <u>I hope</u> <u>he's meeting</u> a lot of people. The business needs it.
7 It <u>takes</u> a long time to learn a language. You <u>don't become</u> fluent in a week.
8 It's <u>taking</u> a long time, but <u>they're becoming</u> more fluent.
9 People <u>say</u> the situation <u>is changing</u>.
10 They <u>are saying</u> the situation <u>changes</u> every day.

b **Complete these sentences so they are true for you.**

1 In my opinion, one of the biggest problems young people are facing today is …
2 At school I study …
3 This week we are studying …
4 Most teenagers I know hope …
5 I'm hoping to … later this year.

SPEAKING

→ **EXAM PREPARATION**
Kommunikationsprüfung (p. 224)

S ▶ Interpreting pictures and cartoons, p. 262

6 **Produce an uninterrupted five-minute discourse based on the cartoon and relate it to the quotes about leadership.**

1 A boss creates fear, a leader confidence. A boss knows all, a leader asks questions.
   (Russell H. Ewing)
2 A good boss makes his men realize they have more ability than they think they have so that they consistently do better work than they thought they could.
   (Charles Erwin Wilson)

"I believe there are no bad leaders, only bad *followers*."

TEXT 6   Gender issues in the workplace

1 You're going to read the text "Why is it right and smart to empower women?" Before you read, do this quiz, and compare your results in class.

1	How much of the world's work is done by women?	25%	54%	66%	81%
2	How much of the world's food do women produce?	25%	50%	65%	75%
3	How much of the world's income do women earn?	10%	30%	45%	55%
4	How much of the world's property do women own?	1%	20%	30%	50%
5	What percentage of MPs globally are women?	5%	21%	42%	51%

Why is it right and smart to empower women?

Valbona Zeneli

While women perform 66% of the world's work and produce 50% of the food, they earn just 10% of incomes and own 1% of the property globally. And out of 197 countries, only 22 of them have women currently serving as heads of state, just 11.2%.

5　There is noticeable progress as well. Back in 1979, when the United Nations introduced the Convention on the Elimination of All Forms of Discrimination against Women, women comprised less than 6% of members of parliaments globally, compared with women's global parliamentary representation of 21.4% today, according to the Inter-parliamentary Union. However, this is still well short
10　of women's proportionate share of the population. The most advanced are the Nordic countries, where women account for 42.2% of the parliamentary representatives, followed by the Americas with 25% and Europe with 23%.

While political life has thus become more open, many political, legal, cultural and economic barriers still exist. However, over the past three decades, women have
15　made significant strides. We have slowly and steadily advanced, earning more of the college degrees, taking more of the entry-level jobs and entering more into the fields dominated by men.

In education, women outpace men in educational achievement, with 58% of college graduates. While two-thirds of women graduate in the humanities and the
20　arts, men continue to dominate in science with 60% of graduates. More girls than boys now complete their secondary education in 32 out of 34 OECD countries, accounting for around 60% of the total.

And yet, much more needs to be done. In particular, women are not making any real progress at the top of any industry. In business, the gender gap remains wide.
25　In the United States, for example, only 21 of the CEOs of Fortune 500 companies are women. Translation? When it comes to making the decisions that most affect our world, voices are not heard equally.

Women face real obstacles in the professional world: discrimination, sexism and barriers in society. They have to prove themselves to a far greater extent than men
30　do. A 2011 McKinsey report shows that men are promoted based on their potential, whereas women, on the other hand, are promoted based on past accomplishments.

empower sb give power to sb
[3] head of state *Staatsoberhaupt*
[5] **noticeable** clear
[6] convention *Übereinkommen*
[6] elimination act of removing sth
[6] **discrimination** *Diskriminierung, Benachteiligung*
[7] **member of parliament** *(Parlaments)Abgeordnete*
[9] **well short of** much less than
[10] proportionate *entsprechend, proportional*
[11] **Nordic** from northern Europe
[11] **account for sth** be a particular amount of sth
[15] **stride** step forward
[15] **slowly and steadily** gradually
[16] **entry-level** suitable for beginners
[18] **outpace sb** do better than sb
[19] the humanities *Geisteswissenschaften*
[28] **obstacle** Hindernis
[29] **prove yourself** show that you are good at sth
[31] **past accomplishments** good things that sb has already done

33 pivotal important to make things change

34 diversity range of differences

34 tap sth make use of sth

34 pool of human resources the total talent of everyone

38 prerequisite sth needed in advance

38 equitable society *gerechte/ gleichberechtigte Gesellschaft*

39 crucial absolutely necessary

40 fundamentally very significantly

40 sheer simple

43 degrading *entwürdigend*

46 override sth be more important than sth and therefore be used instead of it

47 ingrained that has existed for a long time and is difficult to change

48 perpetuation act of making sth continue

50 run rampant be very common

53 to sb's great discredit causing damage to its reputation

53 imprint sth make a mark so that sth lasts a long time

Why is further progress so pivotal? It's really simple. The basic laws of economics, not just many studies of diversity, tell us that if we tapped the entire pool of human resources and talent, our collective performance would improve. Global GDP could rise significantly. [35]

It sounds like such a cliché to say that women's economic empowerment is a prerequisite to sustainable economic development and equitable societies. And yet, it is far more than that. Crucially, it is not only a matter of improving the economy. It is also fundamentally a matter of sheer human justice and fairness. [40]

In nearly every country, women work longer hours than men and are paid less. Women in poor countries do more unpaid work, work longer hours in the informal economy and accept degrading working conditions. Moreover, in virtually every country, even the most advanced ones, domestic work still remains "invisible" work. [45]

In developing countries, customs and traditions still override formal legal protections. This happens via the deeply ingrained patriarchal and conservative character of society, as well as the not-so-accidental perpetuation of leadership myths that are still in existence. To make things even worse, domestic violence runs rampant in both rural and urban areas in these regions. Women are not [50] informed of their rights, and the vast majority of them do not even trust the very structures that should protect them.

To its great discredit, the media plays an important role in imprinting these stereotypes – and not just in developing countries. Far from it.

Politicians should do more to empower women. They should lead by giving women [55] more power. Women in power should support other women. Because, as President Obama said, "empowering women isn't just the right thing to do – it's the smart thing to do."

(659 words)

From: The Globalist, 7 March 2014

WORKING WITH THE TEXT

EXAM PREPARATION

Leseverstehen (p. 222)

S ▶ Doing comprehension tasks, p. 258

2 Entscheiden Sie, ob die Aussagen zum Text richtig oder falsch sind. Begründen Sie Ihre Entscheidung auf Deutsch in vollständigen Sätzen.

1 While women perform three quarters of the world's work, they only own a tenth of the world's property.
2 The increased number of women in parliaments around the world gives a true reflection of the global population.
3 In all college subjects, there are now more women graduates than men.
4 Men tend to be given better jobs in their companies depending on how their bosses view their potential.
5 In the developing world the law increasingly protects women from being oppressed by the traditional male-dominated way of life.
6 Newspapers and TV are responsible for some of the positive changes in the role of women in society throughout the world.

EXAM PREPARATION

Leseverstehen (p. 222)

S ▶ Doing comprehension tasks, p. 258

3 Im Text nennt die Autorin vier Beispiele, wie Frauen in der Arbeitswelt gegenüber Männern diskriminiert werden. Erstellen Sie eine Liste dieser Beispiele. Formulieren Sie vollständige Sätze auf Deutsch.

4 Discuss the following questions.

1 What does the title of the article mean?
2 Do you think the article has an equal focus on "right" and "smart"?
3 Which paragraph has the most surprising information, in your opinion?

COMPETENCE TRAINING: DEALING WITH UNKNOWN WORDS

S ▶ Dealing with unknown words, p. 255

5 a Match the different ways of dealing with new vocabulary with the examples.

Strategies	Example
1 Don't look up every new word.	a *prerequisite* (l. 38): the root of *prerequisite* is "require", so it must mean something is required before something can happen.
2 Decide if a word seems important in the text.	b the Convention on the *Elimination* of All Forms of Discrimination against Women (l. 6): discrimination is bad, so *elimination* must have to do with stopping or preventing it.
3 Try to work out the meaning of the word from the context.	c Many texts have technical vocabulary you will never use in real life. Don't waste time learning these words.
4 Look at the structure of the word, its prefix and suffix and so on.	d An *entry-level* job (l. 16) implies a job you get when you start at a company. It is the opposite of a top-level job; it's the sort of job you expect when you begin work as a junior.
5 Look at the root of the word and try to relate it to a word family.	e *discredit* (l. 53): *un-, de-, dis-, il-*, words are negative ideas. So *discredit* must be a negative idea. As *credit* means praise or approval, *discredit* means the opposite.
6 English is a very visual language. Try to see the picture painted by idiomatic expressions.	f If a word is repeated several times, or appears in the title of a text, or the first sentence of a paragraph, it is probably a key word.

b Without using a dictionary, decide what these words and expressions mean. Explain your reasons.

1 While looking for evidence of early settlement, pieces of <u>pottery</u> were <u>unearthed</u>.
2 As the fire spread through the <u>crops</u>, the farmhouse was soon <u>engulfed</u> in flames.
3 We need to <u>encourage</u> <u>multinationals</u> to <u>relocate</u> their factories.

LOOKING AT LANGUAGE

6 **a** Join the two parts of these sentences. Each one contains an expression of contrast.

1 While there are laws to protect the rights of women, …

2 Men get promotion based on their potential, …

3 In Arts subjects most graduates are women, …

4 There has been steady progress in closing the gender gap; …

5 There is less discrimination against women today …

6 Women make up nearly half the members of parliament in Nordic countries; …

a in Europe, on the other hand, the figure is just 25 %.

b however, more remains to be done.

c they are not always respected.

d whereas woman are judged on what they have done.

e unlike in sciences.

f compared with two or three decades ago.

b Work with a partner. Discuss how you could complete these sentences so they are true for you. Then compare your answers with another pair.

1 Nowadays I spend a lot of time … , whereas when I was younger …

2 When I'm in school, I … , unlike when I'm at home.

3 While I feel optimistic about … , I still worry about …

4 In some countries … . In Germany, on the other hand …

5 Compared with some of my friends, I …

6 Some people … , whereas I don't/can't/haven't.

7 In the winter … , while in the summer …

8 Many jobs … , however, some …

WORKING WITH WORDS

7 **a** Copy and complete this table

Noun	Verb	Adjective
…	…	accomplished
development	…	…
…	…	discriminatory
…	dominate	…
education	…	…
protection	…	…
representation	…	…
significance	…	…

b Complete this summary of the text using some of the words from the table.

There have been …¹ improvements in the position of women over the past decades, but …² still exists and more needs to be done to close the gender gap. The …³ of women in the world of politics has improved steadily in most parts of the world; likewise in …⁴, where over half of all college graduates are now women, although men are still …⁵ in science subjects. In the world of work, more jobs are open to women but barriers still prevent women from achieving success: for example women tend to be judged on what they have …⁶, whereas men are rewarded with promotion based on their potential. In many countries of the …⁷ world, there are few laws offering women …⁸ from problems such as domestic violence.

LISTENING

1.05

8 Sie hören ein Radiointerview über die Geschichte der Frauenbewegung. Beantworten Sie die Fragen auf Deutsch in Stichworten.

1 Welche Verbesserungen brachte das neue Gesetz von 1870 den Frauen?
2 Welche zwei Folgen hatten Pankhursts Versuch, die Wahlen zu stören?
3 Welche zwei bedeutsamen Veränderungen erreichten Frauen im Jahr 1918?
4 Was war an Constance Markiewicz so bemerkenswert?
5 Was genau erreichten die 187 Arbeiterinnen, die in 1968 im Ford-Werk in Dagenham in Streik traten?
6 Wie veränderte der „Sex Discrimination Act" von 1975 das Arbeitsleben von Frauen?
7 Welche zwei Beispiele bekannter Kämpfe werden genannt, die Margaret Thatcher führte?
8 Wie wird sich nach Meinung der Sprecherin die Rolle der Frau in der britischen Armee ändern?

> **EXAM PREPARATION**
> *Zentrale Klassenarbeit Hörverstehen (p. 224)*

DOING A RESEARCH PROJECT

9 Work in groups of six. Each student chooses one category from the table below. Look at the top local, national and international news stories in the media today for your chosen category, and answer the questions.

Categories	Questions
• politics • business • sport • fashion • crime • education	• Are there an equal number of stories about men and women? • Do stories include the same details about men and women (e.g. age, marital status, physical description, family details)? • Are there differences in whether they are presented as active, responsible, capable, professional and responsible? • Are their views presented in direct or indirect speech?

Report your findings to the group. Then exchange your findings with other groups.

TEXT 7 Globalization: its risks and opportunities

1 Work in groups. Read your extract and prepare an uninterrupted three-minute monologue that summarizes the key facts and gives your opinion on the positive and negative aspects of your text.

Partner A: Read "What is globalization?"
Partner B: Read "Reasons for globalization"
Partner C: Read "Transnational corporations"
Partner D: Read "History of globalization"

A What is globalization?
Globalization is the process by which the world is becoming increasingly interconnected as a result of increased trade and cultural exchange. Globalization has increased the production of goods and services, and also the interchange of world views, ideas and aspects of culture. The biggest companies are no longer national firms but multinational corporations with subsidiaries in many countries.

B Reasons for globalization
Several key factors have influenced the process of globalization. These include improvements in transport: cargo ships are now larger, which means that the cost of transporting goods between countries has decreased, while low-cost airlines make most places accessible. Similarly, improvements in communications such as the internet and mobile technology have resulted in better communication between people in different countries. Finally, global access to labour markets means companies try to produce goods and offer services more cheaply by using workers in parts of the world where wages are lower.

C Transnational corporations
Globalization has resulted in many businesses setting up or buying operations in other countries or outsourcing their work to where costs are lower. When a foreign company invests in a country, perhaps by building a factory or a shop, this is called inward investment. Companies that operate in several countries are called multinational corporations (MNCs) or transnational corporations (TNCs). The US fast-food chain McDonald's is a large MNC – it has nearly 30,000 restaurants in 119 countries. Internet companies are obviously transnational. Truly transnational corporations have a worldwide approach to marketing and often exploit tax advantages in different countries to their advantage.

D History of globalization
The Industrial Revolution made it possible to standardize production of household items while rapid population growth created sustained demand for commodities. Globalization in this period was decisively shaped by 19th-century imperialism. Steamships reduced the cost of international transport significantly and railways made inland transport cheaper. After the Second World War, the World Trade Organization and similar institutions were created to help with the reduction of trade barriers and the promotion of new trade agreements.

2 While reading the text below, match the missing final sentences to the paragraphs. You do not need all the sentences.

a When this happens, we naturally turn inwards, effectively reverting to our earlier evolutionary instincts, to a time when we relied on cooperation among families for our needs to be met.

b The dominance of English as a world language has led, some say, to the death of a number of local languages.

c And of course it means you can always find a cappuccino just the way you like it no matter where we wake up.

d For the first time in history, your morning cappucino is the same no matter where you are sipping it in Tokyo, New York, Bangkok or Buenos Aires.

e But that could change as resources become scarce.

f After all, why cooperate when there are no spoils to divide?

g This will happen at rates that exceed those at which they can be culturally integrated.

turn inwards focus on yourself
revert to sth go back to sth

spoils prizes for success

Does globalization mean we will become one culture?

Mark Pagel

Stroll into your local Starbucks and you will find yourself part of a cultural experiment on a scale never seen before on this planet. In less than half a century, the coffee chain has grown from a single outlet in Seattle to nearly 20,000 shops in around 60 countries. Each year, its near identical stores serve cups of near identical coffee in near identical cups to hundreds of thousands of people.
1 – ? –

Of course, it is not just Starbucks. Select any global brand from Coca-Cola to Facebook and the chances are you will see or feel their presence in most countries around the world. It is easy to see this homogenization in terms of loss of diversity, identity or the westernization of society. And, if diversity is a part of our psychological make-up, how will we fare in a world that is increasingly bringing together people from different cultural backgrounds and traditions? […]

Two factors looming on the horizon are likely to slow the rate at which cultural unification will happen. One is resources, the other is demography. Cooperation has worked throughout history because large collections of people have been able to use resources more effectively and provide greater prosperity and protection than smaller groups. **2** – ? –

This must be one of the most pressing social questions we can ask because if people begin to think they have reached what we might call 'peak standard of living' then they will naturally become more self-interested as the returns from cooperation begin to leak away. **3** – ? –

Related to this, the dominant demographic trend of the century will be the movement of people from poorer to richer regions of the world. Diverse people will be brought together who have little common cultural identity. **4** – ? –

At first, I believe, these factors will cause people to pull back from whatever level of cultural scaling they have achieved to the previous level. An example is the nations of the European Union squabbling over national versus EU rights and privileges. A more troubling example might be the rise of nationalist groups and political parties. […]

[1] **stroll into sth** walk casually into sth
[3] **outlet** shop
[10] **fare** get on, survive
[12] loom look threatening
[13] unification *Vereinigung, Vereinheitlichung*
[13] demography *Demografie, Bevölkerungsstatistik*
[15] **prosperity** wealth
[17] pressing urgent
[18] peak standard of living the highest possible quality of life
[19] **self-interested** motivated by your own personal concerns
[20] leak away escape
[25] scale Maßstab, Umfang, Skala
[26] **squabble over sth** argue about sth
[27] **troubling** worrying

30 resource-scarce having few natural resources

32 creak *ächzen, es kaum schaffen*

33 disengage from sth remove yourself from being involved in sth

34 harbinger a sign of sth bad that will happen

35 vigilant paying close attention to sth

36 grant sb sth give sb sth

41 decry sth criticize sth

47 **upheaval** great change

48 **setback** problem

49 **species** Spezies, Art, Gattung

Then, if the success of modern societies up to this point is anything to go by, new and ever more heterogeneous and resource-scarce societies will increasingly depend upon clear enforcement of cultural or democratic rules to maintain stability, and will creak under the strain of smaller social groupings seeking to disengage further from the whole.

One early harbinger of a sense of decline in the sense of social relatedness might be the increasing tendencies of people to avoid risk, to expect safety, to be vigilant about fairness, to require and to be granted "rights." These might all be symptoms of a greater sense of self-interest, brought about perhaps by declines in the average amount of "togetherness" we feel. **5**   – ? –

Against this backdrop the seemingly unstoppable and ever accelerating cultural homogenization around the world brought about by travel, the internet and social networking, although often decried, is probably a good thing even if it means the loss of cultural diversity: it increases our sense of togetherness via the sense of a shared culture. In fact, breaking down of cultural barriers – unfashionable as this can sound – is probably one of the few things that societies can do to increase harmony among ever more heterogeneous peoples.

So, to my mind, there is little doubt that this century is going to be a time of great uncertainty and upheaval as resources, money and space become ever more scarce. It is going to be a bumpy road with many setbacks and conflicts. But if there was ever a species that could tackle these challenges it is our own. It might be surprising, but our genes have created in us a machine capable of greater cooperation, inventiveness and common good than any other on Earth. **6**   – ? –

(771 words)

From: the website of the BBC, 18 November 2014

WORKING WITH THE TEXT

3 **a** Join the two parts of the sentences.

1 Jobs are at risk because they can be outsourced …
2 There is no doubt that some jobs are likely …
3 Low skilled jobs like hairdressers and waiters are difficult …
4 People who are highly skilled and in well paid jobs move …
5 Globalization tends to be driven by companies looking …
6 Working conditions in low wage economies are different …
7 The global market means the same products are available …
8 The rapid development of the internet has led …

a to where their work takes them already.
b to what we might find acceptable here.
c to maximize profits however they can.
d to buy everywhere in the world.
e to automate, and so are relatively safe.
f to migrate to cheaper parts of the world.
g to a region where wages and costs are lower.
h to huge changes in where and how we work.

b   Work in pairs. Which two statements in 3a do you think best summarize globalization, and why? What other advantages and disadvantages of globalization can you think of?

WORKING WITH WORDS

4   Exchange the underlined expressions with these words from the text, making sure you use the right form and the correct preposition, where necessary.

stroll | loom | prosperity | squabble | creak | strain | upheaval | setback

1   The children <u>argued about</u> who could use the internet.
2   We <u>walked slowly and casually</u> along the sea front.
3   The exam date <u>approached</u>, making me feel worried.
4   The country is enjoying a period of peace and <u>people generally have more money to spend</u>.
5   The old wooden door <u>made a noise</u> as it opened.
6   Our relationship is <u>not at all easy</u> due to both our workloads.
7   It caused a <u>dramatic change</u> to our lifestyle.
8   We had a <u>temporary problem</u> when the printer broke down.

VIEWING

5   a   Pre-viewing

You are going to watch a video about globalization. Which of these themes do you think the video will mention:

transport | unemployment | health and safety | consumer choice | politics | climate change | trade unions | the English language

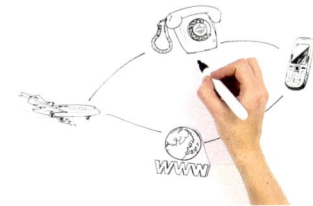

b   Viewing for detail
    Answer the following questions:

1   According to the video, which two types of networks improved due to technological advances?
2   In addition to goods (such as TVs), the video mentions four other exchanges that play a major part in globalization. List them.
3   Which three types of transport are mentioned in the text?

c   Viewing for information
    Answer the following questions:

1   Why does globalization not benefit workers in industrialized or developing countries?
2   Why is globalization putting pressure on the environment?
3   Do you agree with the conclusion that globalization is neither good nor bad? Why/why not?

SPEAKING

EXAM PREPARATION
Kommunikationsprüfung (p. 224)

S ▶ Interpreting pictures and cartoons, p. 262

6 Work with a partner: Partner A looks at this page; Partner B looks at File 1 on p. 216.

a Describe your cartoon to your partner, and explain to him or her what it says about globalization.

b Listen to you partner describe and analyse his or her cartoon, and then decide which one you both prefer, and why.

"The internet means we can organise anti-globalisation demos across the planet."

WORKING WITH WORDS

7 Complete these sentences by creating negative adjectives/adverbs from the verbs in the box, following this example: You can't stop it = it's unstoppable (un- + verb + -able or un- + verb + -ably)

control | do | put down | question | repeat | sustain | think | work

1 It's not possible to get every country to agree to something. It's just … .
2 This book is absolutely brilliant. I read it in one sitting. It's … .
3 However bad the situation gets, I can't imagine another world war. I find it … .
4 The agreement their company wanted was … . It could never have succeeded.
5 This is … the biggest problem facing us at the moment. There can be no doubt about that.
6 He wept … as he learned what had happened to his family.
7 What she said was … . It was very rude.
8 We can't keep using the world's resources at the same rate. It's … .

LISTENING

1.06

8 Sie hören eine Radiodiskussion zum Thema Globalisierung.
Vervollständigen Sie die unten stehenden Sätze auf Deutsch.

1 Pete behauptet, dass zwei Vorteile der Globalisierung darin bestehen, dass …
2 Mia hat das Gefühl, dass, egal wo man ist …
3 Pete sagt, dass es Betriebe aus zwei Gründen gut haben: erstens, …
4 Mia weist darauf hin, dass der Import von Gütern aus aller Welt Umweltprobleme mit sich bringt, da …
5 Mias Meinung nach haben es die Arbeiter in Entwicklungsländern schwer, da …
6 Pete ist der Meinung, Globalisierung fördere …
7 Mia behauptet, dass Einwanderung durch Globalisierung …

→ **EXAM PREPARATION**
Zentrale Klassenarbeit Hörverstehen (p. 224)

S ▸ Practising listening skills, p. 256

WRITING

9 Read the following statement about globalization. Write a comment on the statement, saying whether you agree or disagree with it.

Globalization does not benefit individuals. It only benefits companies.

→ **EXAM PREPARATION**
Textproduktion (p. 223)

S ▸ Writing an essay, p. 259

GIVING A PRESENTATION

10 Prepare a 10-minute presentation on globalization.
You decide which aspects you want to cover. You can use any material you have discussed in class. Here are some key ideas that may help you:

· sweatshops
· fair trade
· the clothes I wear
· the music I listen to, and how I listen to it

· outsourcing
· social media and their global impact
· working abroad – skills, languages, culture: what does one need today?

Remember to create handouts for the audience, decide what media you can incorporate and write prompt cards.

→ **EXAM PREPARATION**
Präsentationsprüfung (p. 225)

S ▸ Giving a presentation, p. 264

ENGLISH FOR WORK   Writing a CV

WARM-UP

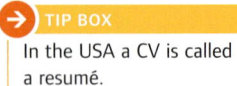

TIP BOX

In the USA a CV is called a resumé.

1 Decide whether the following statements about a British CV are true or false.

1 Include information about your family background and the number of brothers and sisters you have.
2 Mention your driving licence.
3 Attach a recent photo and put the date and your signature at the bottom of the CV.
4 Do not include your date of birth.
5 Mention at least three references: a personal one, an academic one, and a work-related one.
6 Avoid abbreviations and contractions.
7 Divide your CV into sections with headings.
8 Write the information in chronological order, with your most recent experience and school details last.
9 Don't just say how many years you have been studying English or what class you are in. Say if your level is fluent, conversational or basic.
10 List any foreign holidays you have had as these demonstrate your willingness to travel and your language ability.

INFO BOX

If you send your CV to an international company, don't assume that they will be familiar with the German educational system. Don't just translate the name of the type of school you go to. Explain it, or use an equivalent that the reader will be familiar with. The following may be of help:

Abitur	GB: A levels (in the plural, as you have one A level in each subject you take in the exam). Students usually take 3 or 4 A levels. USA: high-school diploma.
Mittlere Reife	GB: GCSE (General Certificate of Secondary Education). Students usually take 9–14 GCSEs. USA: no equivalent, so something like "Mittlere Reife (diploma given after 10 years of schooling)".
Realschule	GB: no equivalent, so "secondary school". USA: no equivalent, so "high school".
Gesamtschule	GB: comprehensive, but "secondary school" is also fine.
berufliches Gymnasium	GB: vocational sixth-form college. USA: no equivalent, so "high school".

WRITING A CV

2 a Which of these sections do not belong on a CV? What is the normal sequence for the sections of a CV?

education and qualifications | future ambitions | health status | interests and activities | personal details | personal profile | references | religion | skills | work experience

3 Look at Fabian's CV and answer these questions:

1   Where could he have underlined how reliable he is? What could he say to prove it?
2   Which parts of the CV indicate that Fabian could be suitable for work in an advertising agency?
3   What could Fabian add to show he is happy to work as part of a team?

Fabian Thiele

Personal details

Address:	Bachstrasse 6, 70145 Hornberg, Germany
Telephone:	+49 160 987654 (mobile)
Email:	f_thiele@e-mail.de
Nationality:	German

Personal profile

An excellent communicator with good organizational skills and a creative approach who works well under pressure.

Education and qualifications

2016	Abitur (equivalent to A levels) in the following subjects: Economics, English, German, Maths Average mark 2.1 (equivalent to B)
2013–16	Johann-Friedrich-von-Cotta-Schule (vocational sixth-form college) Hornberg
2013	Mittlere Reife (equivalent to GSCEs) in 9 subjects including Maths, English, German and Art
2008–2013	Raitelsburg Realschule (secondary school)

Work experience

August 2015	Internship at Creative Industries, Edinburgh. Main responsibilities included: welcoming visitors at reception, translating emails and documents into German, filing documents Skills gained: communication, team work, problem solving
August 2014	General office work at Pap-und-pier (office material distribution centre) Responsibilities included: filing, data entry on the computer, ordering office supplies Skills gained: working to tight deadlines, interpersonal

Skills	IT (Microsoft Word, Excel, Powerpoint) B1 level English with good fluency in speaking
Interests and Activities	Swimming and winter sports, travel, world cinema Voluntary work for "Art in Hospital" charity for sick children
Additional Information	Driving licence
References	Available on request

The future of Planet Earth

VA 2   1.07

climate change	*Klimawandel*
global warming	*Erderwärmung*
man-made	*von Menschen verursacht*
greenhouse gas	*Treibhausgas*
carbon dioxide (CO$_2$)	*Kohlendioxid*
release sth	*etw abgeben*
reduce sth	*etw verringern*
emission	*Ausstoß*
natural disaster	*Naturkatastrophe*
flooding	*Hochwasser*
drought [draʊt]	*Dürre*
impact	*Auswirkung*
heatwave	*Hitzewelle*
desertification	*Wüstenbildung*
water shortage	*Wasserknappheit*
melting of glaciers	*Gletscherschmelze*
rising sea levels	*steigende Meeresspiegel*
climate-change refugee	*Klimaflüchtling*
water supply	*Wasserversorgung*
urban population	*städtische Bevölkerung*
irrigate sth	*etw bewässern*
grain	*Getreide*
overpump sth	*etw trockenpumpen, etw abpumpen*
groundwater	*Grundwasser*
drinking water	*Trinkwasser*
sanitation	*sanitäre Anlagen*
water rationing	*Wasserrationierung*
finite natural resource	*begrenzte Naturressource*
pollution	*(Umwelt-)Verschmutzung*
exhaust	*Abgas(e)*
acid rain	*saurer Regen*
agribusiness	*Agrarindustrie, industrielle Landwirtschaft*
pollutant	*Schadstoff*
pesticide	*Schädlingsbekämpfungsmittel, Pestizid*
herbicide	*Unkrautbekämpfungsmittel, Herbizid*
contaminate the soil	*den Erdboden verseuchen*
animal waste	*tierische Abfallstoffe/Exkremente*
sewage	*Abwasser/Schmutzwasser*
toxic/poisonous	*giftig*
marine life	*Meereslebewesen*

BACKGROUND INFORMATION

Climate change

The vast majority of scientists agree that global warming is, at least partly, man-made. The main cause appears to be the greenhouse gases, particularly carbon dioxide (CO_2), that we are releasing into the atmosphere. Unless we act quickly to reduce greenhouse gas emissions, experts predict that 5 changing weather patterns will lead to an increase in natural disasters such as typhoons and hurricanes, flooding and drought. If global warming continues as predicted, it will also have a strong impact on human life. On the one hand, heatwaves will claim the lives of the sick and the elderly, and the desertification of farmland will cause food shortages. Water shortages 10 will increasingly become a source of international conflict. On the other hand, the melting of glaciers will cause rising sea levels, and coastal land and low-lying islands will disappear, creating climate-change refugees.

Water supply

Global warming is not the only reason why the threat to global water supply 15 is increasing. The global urban population is exploding, so more water is needed to irrigate land to provide food, particularly grain, for the megacities. This means that many countries are overpumping their groundwater supply, causing problems for billions of people who lack clean drinking water and proper sanitation. Droughts and water rationing will be the consequence 20 unless we raise awareness that water is a finite natural resource.

Pollution

Industry and transport are the main sources of air and water pollution: exhaust from our cars is one example of a pollutant which creates smog in cities and causes acid rain. Agribusiness is another source of pollutants: 25 farmers use pesticides and herbicides that contaminate the soil and the ground water while vast quantities of animal waste and sewage are produced. All of these pollutants are toxic/poisonous in some way. In the oceans, there are millions of tons of plastic garbage that are a danger to sea birds and marine life. 30

Waste disposal

Humans are producing more rubbish/trash than ever, and it all has to go somewhere. Some of it gets reused or recycled. Organic waste is biodegradable and can therefore be composted. Rubbish sent to landfill sites, on the other hand, takes a very long time to break down. Another disposal method is incineration, which pollutes the air. 35

Energy sources

40 The climate crisis is forcing us to re-examine how we generate our energy. It has become clear that our dependence on oil is not sustainable. Not only will we run out of it someday, but fossil fuel emissions are damaging the environment. The use of nuclear energy remains controversial: it is cheap
45 and clean compared to fossil fuels, but the risk of radioactive fallout and radiation is high, as the disaster in Fukushima shows, and the long-term problem of disposing of nuclear waste has not yet been solved. The search for ways to conserve energy and the search for alternative sources of energy, such as wind and solar power and other kinds of renewable energy, are
50 creating new economic opportunities.

Biofuels

Typical biofuels are made from crops such as corn and palm oil. They only release as much carbon into the atmosphere as they absorb when they grow. However, the West's current demand for biofuels to supplement diesel has
55 increased the rate of deforestation. Farmers (and others) have been cutting down forests at an unsustainable rate for a long time. Deforestation causes global warming, because forests, particularly tropical rainforests, absorb carbon dioxide; without the forests carbon dioxide levels increase. The destruction of these ecosystems also has other catastrophic consequences:
60 animal habitats are destroyed, which can lead to the extinction of species. However, biosphere integrity is not only vital for animals, as the examples of the oceans, rivers and forests clearly show.

waste disposal *Abfallentsorgung*
rubbish/trash *Müll*
reuse sth *etw wiederverwenden*
recycle sth *etw wiederverwerten*
organic waste *Biomüll*
biodegradable *biologisch abbaubar*
compost *kompostieren*
landfill site *Mülldeponie*
incineration *Abfallverbrennung*
pollute sth *etw verschmutzen*

energy source *Energiequelle*
climate crisis *Klimakrise*
generate sth *etw erzeugen*
dependence *Abhängigkeit*
oil *Erdöl*
sustainable *tragbar, nachhaltig*
fossil fuels *fossile Brennstoffe*
environment *Umwelt*
nuclear energy *Atomenergie*
radioactive fallout *radioaktiver Niederschlag*
radiation *Strahlung*
dispose of sth *etw entsorgen*
nuclear waste *Atommüll*
conserve sth *etw sparen*
alternative sources of energy *alternative Energiequellen*
wind power *Windkraft*
solar power *Solarenergie*
renewable energy *erneuerbare Energie(quellen)*

biofuel *Biotreibstoff*
crops *Anbaupflanzen*
corn *Mais*
palm oil *Palmöl*
carbon *Kohlenstoff*
absorb sth *etw aufnehmen, etw absorbieren*
deforestation *Entwaldung*
unsustainable *untragbar*
tropical rainforest *tropischer Regenwald*
ecosystem *Ökosystem*
habitat *Lebensraum*
extinction of species *Artensterben*

1 a Match words from box A to ones in box B to make collocations. They are all
highlighted words from the text.

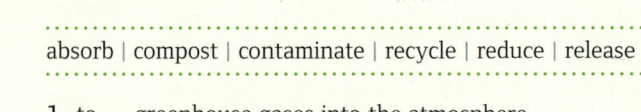

A		B	
carbon	climate	change	dioxide
fossil	global	energy	fuels
greenhouse	renewable	gases	shortage
water	nuclear	warming	waste

b Use each collocation in a sentence, showing what it means.

2 Complete the phrases using a verb from the box. The phrases are all highlighted in
the text.

absorb | compost | contaminate | recycle | reduce | release

1 to ... greenhouse gases into the atmosphere
2 to ... greenhouse gas emissions
3 to ... the soil with chemicals
4 to ... plastic garbage
5 to ... organic waste
6 to ... carbon dioxide from the atmosphere

3 Complete the sentences using a suitable noun form of the verbs in the box.
Use your dictionary to help you, if necessary.

conserve | contaminate | depend | dispose | emit | incinerate | irrigate | pollute

1 Most scientists agree that greenhouse gas ... are the main cause of the rise in
temperature in the atmosphere that we have been seeing since the middle of the
last century.
2 Exhaust from cars is one example of a ... that causes smog in big cities.
3 Agricultural chemicals and fertilisers don't just have negative effects on the quality
of the groundwater: they also result in the ... of the soil.
4 Plastic is an incredibly useful material, but its ... is an enormous problem.
5 The ... of non-recyclable garbage is problematic as it causes enormous amounts of
air pollution.
6 Unless we can develop cheap sources of renewable energy soon, our ... on fossil
fuels will cause global warming to continue.
7 We cannot increase our food supply without widespread ... of farm land, which
can lead to water shortage.
8 The ... of biosphere integrity, especially in our remaining rain forests, is vital for
the survival of human life and animal species.

4 Find highlighted words and phrases in the text that match these definitions.

1 a long period without any rainfall
2 dirty, waste water from houses and factories
3 highly poisonous or dangerous
4 that can be continued for a long time without damaging the environment
5 clearing trees and woods to use the land to grow crops (or build houses)

TEXT 1   The human impact on the Earth

1 **a** Work in small groups and copy the mind map below on a sheet of paper. Add factors that are necessary to support life on earth. Use your own ideas to add information to the mind map.

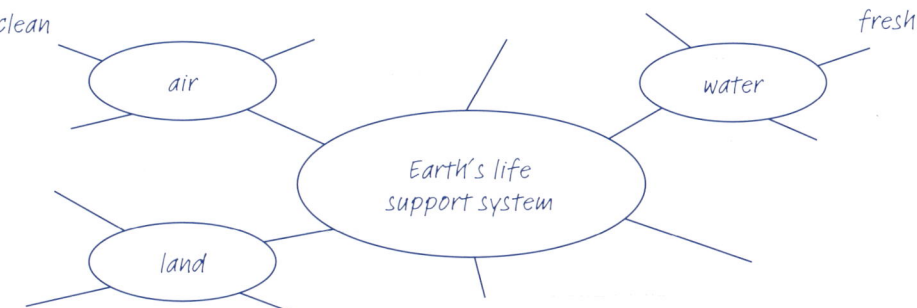

b Think of ways that humans are having an influence on these factors. Add them to your mind map in another colour.

c Compare your mind map with another group and add any ideas you have missed.

Life on Earth at risk

Oliver Milman

Humans are "eating away at our own life support systems" at a rate unseen in the past 10,000 years by degrading land and freshwater systems, emitting greenhouse gases and releasing vast amounts of agricultural chemicals into the environment, new research has found.

5   Two major new studies by an international team of researchers have pinpointed the key factors that ensure a livable planet for humans, with stark results.

Of nine worldwide processes that underpin life on Earth, four have exceeded "safe" levels – human-driven climate change, loss of biosphere integrity, land system change and the high level of phosphorus and nitrogen flowing into the
10 oceans due to fertiliser use.

Researchers spent five years identifying these core components of a planet suitable for human life, using the long-term average state of each measure to provide a baseline for the analysis.

They found that the changes of the last 60 years are unprecedented in the
15 previous 10,000 years, a period in which the world has had a relatively stable climate and human civilisation has advanced significantly.

Carbon dioxide levels, at 395.5 parts per million, are at historic highs, while loss of biosphere integrity is resulting in species becoming extinct at a rate more than 100 times faster than the previous norm.

20 Since 1950 urban populations have increased seven-fold, primary energy use has soared by a factor of five, while the amount of fertiliser used is now eight times higher. The amount of nitrogen entering the oceans has quadrupled.

[2] degrade sth damage sth
[2] **emit sth** *etw ausstoßen*
[3] **release sth** *etw freisetzen, etw ausstoßen*
[3] vast very large, enormous
[3] agricultural chemicals chemicals used for farming purposes
[5] pinpoint sth identify sth
[6] stark unpleasant
[7] underpin sth make sth possible
[7] exceed sth be greater than a particular amount of sth
[8] **human-driven** *von Menschen verursacht*
[9] nitrogen *Stickstoff*
[10] **fertiliser** *Dünger*
[11] identify sth find or discover sth
[11] core components the factors that are most important for sth
[13] baseline a starting point
[14] unprecedented that has never happened before
[18] **become extinct** *aussterben*
[19] norm situation that is usual or normal
[20] seven-fold seven times
[21] soar rise up suddenly
[21] by a factor of five five times
[22] quadruple increase by four times

51

24 hospitable to sth able to support sth

25 indicator a sign that shows sth is happening

25 shoot up rise up suddenly

28 go into overdrive start moving very quickly

29 resource *Ressource*

29 be confined to sth *auf etw beschränkt sein*

31 variability *Schwankungen*

33 evidence fact(s) that make you believe sth is true

33 tipping point point after which it is difficult to change sth

35 ice cap *Eiskappe*

37 robust strong and able to survive

41 core body temperature *Körpertemperatur*

41 evolve change and adapt to new situations

44 flawed containing a basic mistake

All of these changes are shifting Earth into a "new state" that is becoming less hospitable to human life, researchers said.

"These indicators have shot up since 1950 and there are no signs they are slowing down," said Prof Will Steffen of the Australian National University and the Stockholm Resilience Centre. Steffen is the lead author on both of the studies. 25

"When economic systems went into overdrive, there was a massive increase in resource use and pollution. It used to be confined to local and regional areas but we're now seeing this occurring on a global scale. These changes are down to human activity, not natural variability." [...] 30

"It's fairly safe to say that we haven't seen conditions in the past similar to ones we see today and there is strong evidence that there [are] tipping points we don't want to cross," Steffen said.

"If the Earth is going to move to a warmer state, 5-6 °C warmer, with no ice caps, it will do so and that won't be good for large mammals like us. People say the world is robust and that's true, there will be life on Earth, but the Earth won't be robust for us. 35

"Some people say we can adapt due to technology, but that's a belief system, it's not based on fact. There is no convincing evidence that a large mammal, with a core body temperature of 37 °C, will be able to evolve that quickly. Insects can, but humans can't and that's a problem." 40

Steffen said the research showed the economic system was "fundamentally flawed" as it ignored critically important life support systems.

"It's clear the economic system is driving us towards an unsustainable future and people of my daughter's generation will find it increasingly hard to survive," he said. "History has shown that civilisations have risen, stuck to their core values and then collapsed because they didn't change. That's where we are today." 45

(564 words)

From: The Guardian, 15 January 2015

WORKING WITH THE TEXT

→ **EXAM PREPARATION**

Leseverstehen (p. 222)

S ▶ Doing comprehension tasks, p. 258

2 Entscheiden Sie, ob die Aussagen zum Text richtig oder falsch sind. Begründen Sie Ihre Entscheidung auf Deutsch in vollständigen Sätzen.

r 7.10 **1** Recent research projects have identified four key processes that are necessary to support life on earth.

r 14-16 **2** Humans have done more damage to the environment in the last 60 years than in the previous 10,000 years.

r 17 **3** The amount of carbon dioxide in the atmosphere has never been higher.

4 The amount of nitrogen in the oceans has increased at a greater rate than the number of people living in cities.

x 20-22 **5** The negative influence on the environment has been caused by increased economic activity in a few parts of the world.

x **6** Prof. Steffen believes that humans will be able to use technology to adapt to an increase in the Earth's temperature.

r 39-42 **7** According to Prof. Steffen, the economic system is based on the wrong values so that life on Earth may soon not be sustainable.

3 Im Text gibt der Autor drei Beispiele, wie die Menschheit genau das ökologische System zerstört, das sie am Leben erhält. Erstellen Sie eine Liste dieser Beispiele. Formulieren Sie vollständige Sätze auf Deutsch.

→ **EXAM PREPARATION**
Leseverstehen (p. 222)

S ▶ Doing comprehension tasks, p. 258

SPEAKING

4 Look at lines 35–48 of the text again. Discuss with a partner whether humans will be able to adapt to climate change.

WORKING WITH WORDS

5 a Match a word from box A to a word in box B to make collocations from the text.

A	B
agricultural | biosphere | body | climate | fresh | global | greenhouse | regional | resource | urban	area | change | chemicals | gas | integrity | population | scale | temperature | use | water

b Complete the following text with collocations from 5 a.

Human-driven … is one of the four key factors that is making our planet inhospitable for future generations. Economic activity now takes place on a …, rather than just in a few … and this results in the emission of … that contribute to global warming. The growth of the large metropolis with its large … means that we can no longer sustain … in many areas and species are becoming extinct at an alarming rate. It is also increasingly difficult to supply … to many cities as many rivers are polluted by … If we do not limit our … and pollution, the planet will become increasingly inhospitable for mammals such as ourselves with a core … of 37 °C.

Mountain gorillas: in danger of extinction

6 Find words in the text for the following phrases used to describe figures.

1 parts in every million
2 at the highest levels in history
3 at a speed
4 over a hundred times quicker than
5 have grown seven times larger
6 has increased five times
7 800 % more
8 risen by four times as much

LOOKING AT LANGUAGE

7 Which words in the following sentences are adjectives and which are adverbs? Say which words they describe and what type of words they are describing.

G ▶ Adjectives and adverbs, p. 279

1 … a period in which the world has had a relatively stable climate and human civilisation has advanced significantly. (ll. 15–16)
2 … the research showed the economic system was "fundamentally flawed" as it ignored critically important life support systems. (ll. 43–44)
3 If the world is heading towards an unsustainable future, the next generation will find it increasingly difficult to adapt to the conditions.
4 The urban population has increased rapidly since 1950 and there is no sign of even a slight decrease in the years to come.
5 Most scientists are absolutely certain that greenhouse gases are contributing dramatically to unprecedented climate change.

DESCRIBING A DIAGRAM

8 Look at the diagram below and complete the sentences using words and phrases from the box.

climate change | clouds | droughts | emissions | energy | flooding | fossil fuels | global warming | greenhouse | human activity | radiation | sea levels | temperature rise

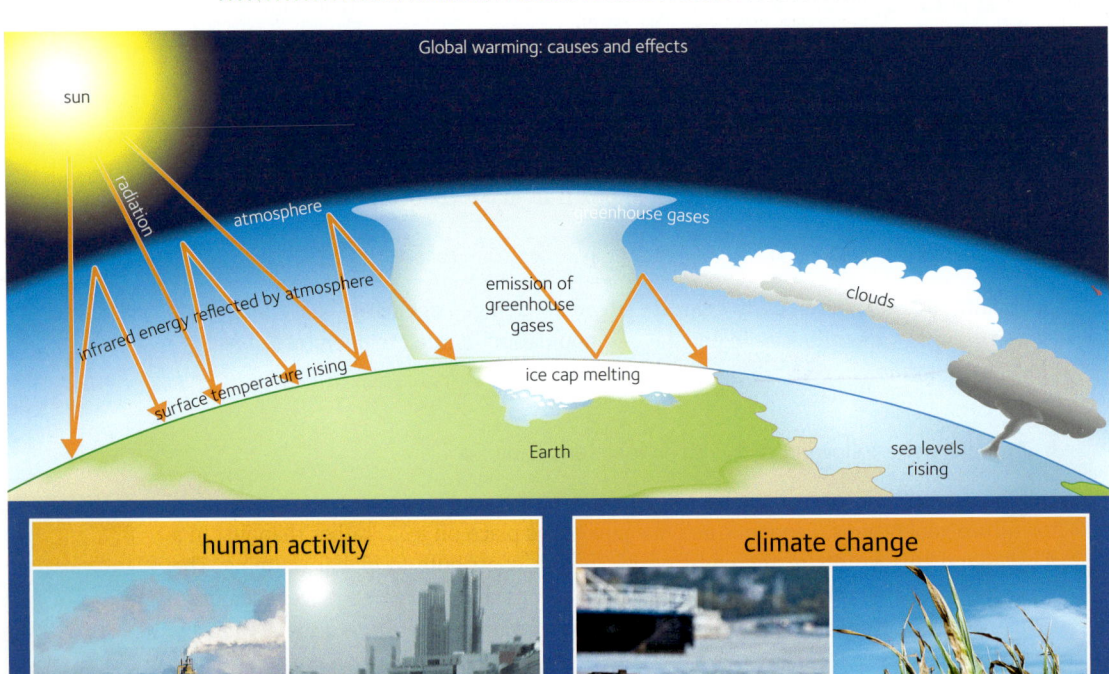

Global warming: causes and effects

sun

radiation

atmosphere

greenhouse gases

infrared energy reflected by atmosphere

emission of greenhouse gases

clouds

surface temperature rising

ice cap melting

Earth

sea levels rising

human activity

climate change

1 … from the sun passes through the Earth's atmosphere, where the energy is absorbed by the Earth's surface.
2 The Earth's surface then emits infrared … back into the atmosphere.
3 The Earth's atmosphere contains water vapour (i.e. …) and … gases, which reflect the energy back to Earth. It is this greenhouse effect that makes life on Earth possible.
4 However, burning … such as coal, natural gas and oil produces excessive … of greenhouse gases into the atmosphere.
5 The increased greenhouse gases in the atmosphere cause a … on the Earth's surface, which is what we call … .
6 The Earth's average temperature has risen by about 0.5 °C in the last century. The past 50 years of warming have been mainly attributed to … .
7 During the last 100 years, … around the world have risen by 10–20 cm.
8 Some predictions for the local effects of … include increasingly hot summers and …, but also intense thunderstorms and … .

SPEAKING

9 Use the diagram on p. 54 and the graph below to prepare a 3-minute monologue.

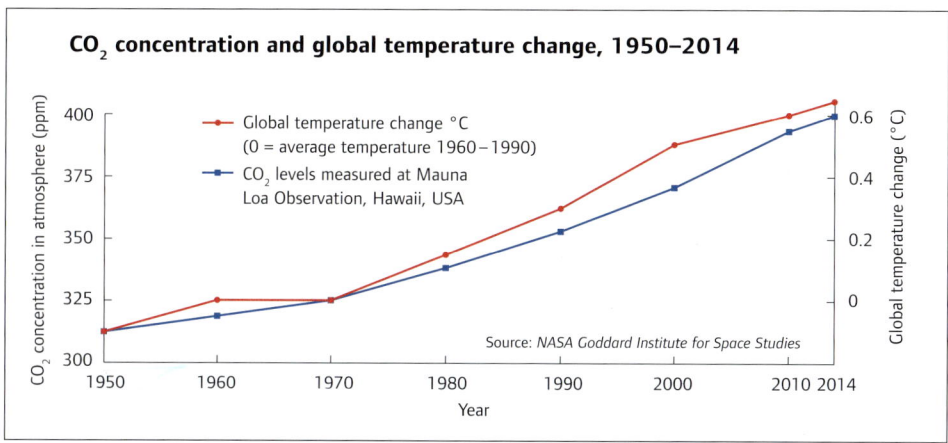

CO$_2$ concentration and global temperature change, 1950–2014

Legend:
— Global temperature change °C (0 = average temperature 1960–1990)
— CO$_2$ levels measured at Mauna Loa Observation, Hawaii, USA

Source: *NASA Goddard Institute for Space Studies*

Y-axis (left): CO$_2$ concentration in atmosphere (ppm) — 300, 325, 350, 375, 400
Y-axis (right): Global temperature change (°C) — 0, 0.2, 0.4, 0.6
X-axis: Year — 1950, 1960, 1970, 1980, 1990, 2000, 2010 2014

→ **EXAM PRACTICE**
Kommunikationsprüfung (p. 224)

S ▶ Interpreting charts and graphs, p. 263

→ **TIP BOX**

When giving your monologue:
· explain how the greenhouse effect works.
· point out how human activity is contributing to global warming.
· evaluate the consequences of climate change for life on earth.

S ▶ Writing an essay, p. 259

COMPETENCE TRAINING: STRUCTURING A PARAGRAPH

10 a Put the following sentences in order to create a paragraph about the causes of global warming.

a For example, there has been a rise of 0.6 °C in the average global temperature which corresponds exactly to the increase in the CO$_2$ concentration in the atmosphere since 1950.

b However, an excessive amout of greenhouse gases in the atmosphere is causing the Earth's temperature to rise significantly.

c Most scientists now agree that this temperature increase is caused by human activity, particularly during the last 50 years.

d The greenhouse effect is a core component of our life support system as the atmosphere traps radiation from the sun and warms the Earth's surface.

e The result is man-made global warming, which is now reaching a critical level for life on Earth.

f Without this effect, the Earth would be cold and inhospitable for human life.

b Look at each sentence above. What category does it fit into?

1 introducing the topic of the paragraph
2 introducing an idea or argument
3 developing an idea
4 giving an example
5 summing up the paragraph

c Now use the notes below to write a second paragraph on the effects of global warming on life on earth.

Global warming is causing climate change, but this does not mean that all regions of the world will be affected in the same way.
· melting ice caps – rising sea levels – flooding – low-lying coastal areas – islands
· more extreme weather phenomena – less rainfall – drought – extreme thunderstorms – hurricanes – colder winters
· climate change – planet less hospitable
· humans less able to evolve – adapt using technology?

TEXT 2   Earth's precious resources

 washing the car

 washing clothes

 having a bath/shower

 washing dishes

 cooking/drinking

 flushing the toilet

 cleaning the house

 personal hygiene

watering the garden

1 a With a partner, match the activities on the left to the pie chart about water consumption below. Can you agree on which activities use the most and which use the least water?

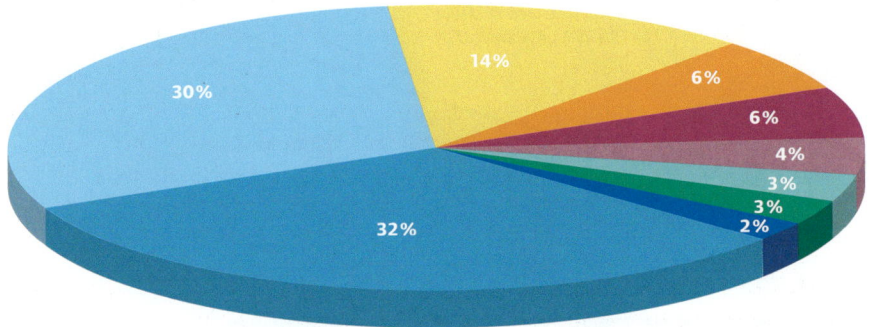

b Compare your answer with another pair. Now guess how much water the average German consumes per day for each activity.

c Compare your results in class. (Your teacher has the answer.) Is there anything you find surprising?

d Which countries in the world do you think use the most and least water per person/day? Do some research online and report back to the class.

The end for the glamorous world of LA swimming pools?

Rory Carroll

The Mojave desert stretches in all directions, sand and scrub as far as the eye can see, with no road or trail, no marker or signpost, to indicate that here, in the middle of a wilderness furnace, sits a swimming pool.

The pristine pool, five feet deep, five feet wide and 11 feet long, is no California mirage. It is an art installation.   5

An Austrian artist, Alfredo Barsuglia, created the sculpture, entitled Social Pool, and declared it open to the public. Before plunging in, you need to contact the MAK Centre for Art and Architecture in West Hollywood to request its secret GPS coordinates and a key to open the white cover. You must bring a gallon of water to replace evaporated water and return the key within 24 hours.   10

The installation is a critical commentary, among other things, on California's love affair with private swimming pools. "In a desolate and drought-hit area, a pool is something absurd," Barsuglia told the Observer. "Luxury goods are status symbols – things that are expensive but not important to survival."

With droughts in much of the western US triggering water rationing and intense   15
political battles, others are also wondering if private pools, long part of the
iconography of California, and especially Los Angeles, have become anachronisms.

---

¹ scrub *Gestrüpp*

³ furnace *Ofen*

⁴ pristine unused, completely clean

⁷ plunge in dive in

¹⁰ **evaporate** *verdunsten*

¹² desolate empty of people, unfriendly

¹² **drought-hit** suffering from long periods without rain

¹⁵ trigger cause sth to start, make necessary

¹⁷ iconography the images that you associate with sth

¹⁷ anachronism sth that is no longer up to date, old-fashioned

"The swimming pool's position as status symbol and sign of health, wealth and beauty has come into question with increasing public concern over pool security, code enforcement, liability, the rising costs of maintenance and a growing awareness of the finite nature of water as a natural resource," said Dick Hebdige, a media studies professor at the University of California, Santa Barbara, who wrote an essay for an exhibition about pools in southern California.

Pools are bottomless pits of wasted money and water as well as "potential lawsuits, floating rodent carcasses and summer algae blooms", said Hebdige. "The swimming pool and the gas-guzzling automobile are the twin booster icons of LA in its mid-century glory days as the city of a future that's no longer considered viable." […]

More than half of the state – 58 % – is now classified as experiencing "exceptional" drought, the harshest on a five-level scale. The entire state has been in "severe" drought since May, which has had the effect of melting ski runs, drying lakes and rivers, marooning boats, draining reservoirs, and turning farms to dust. Cemeteries are cutting back on grass. […]

Some cities have turned off fountains and rationed water until – unless – rains come. California has given local agencies the authority to fine those who waste water up to $500 a day. Environmentalists are depicting green lawns – another symbol of the middle-class dream – as reckless.

Against that backdrop, private swimming pools can appear indulgent, if not selfish. The average uncovered pool in LA loses about 20,000 gallons to evaporation per year.

Those with leaks can lose an additional 700 gallons daily, according to Hebdige. […]

Christopher Hawthorne, the *Los Angeles Times* architecture critic, said private pools represented a bold 20th-century effort to cleave the metropolis from the natural world, specifically the Pacific.

"Increasingly that brashness looks misplaced or antique; instead we seem at the mercy of forces beyond our control when it comes to water," he noted last month. "The swimming pool – like the surface parking lot, the freeway, the lawn and the single-family house – is rapidly fading as a symbolic and cultural marker of Los Angeles." […]

There are an estimated 1.1m pools in California. Thanks to two young academics, Benedikt Gross and Joseph Lee, we have a precise number for the LA basin: 43,123. They used satellite images, public databases and crowdsourcing to produce the digital map. […]

Beverly Hills, with 2,481, had the highest number per capita. Long Beach, with 2,859, and Rancho Palos Verdes, at 2,592, were also privileged. Two neighbourhoods, Watts and Florence, which are predominantly poor, Latino and African-American, had no backyard pools at all.

Drought notwithstanding, there is little sign that the artistic and environmental critique will signal a popular revolt.

Barsuglia, whose desert installation runs until 30 September, thinks private pools will probably endure as symbols of glamour and status: "Most people are aware of the fragility of the environment but only a few will change their way of living. That's one problem with the capitalistic democracy – nobody takes personal responsibility for society."   (718 words)

From: The Guardian, 6 September 2014

---

20 **code enforcement** making people stick to regulations
20 **liability** [ˌlaɪəˈbɪləti] *Haftung, Haftpflicht*
21 **finite** *begrenzt*
25 **rodent carcasses** *Nagetierkadaver*
25 **algae blooms** *Algenblüten*
27 **viable** [ˈvaɪəbl] that will be successful
29 **severe** extremely bad or serious
31 **maroon sth** *etw stranden*
31 **drain sth** remove all the water from sth
31 **reservoir** man-made lake where drinking water is stored
31 **cemetery** the place where dead bodies are buried
36 **reckless** without thinking about the consequences of an action
37 **indulgent** *maßlos*
39 **leak** hole where water can escape
41 **cleave sth** cut sth
43 **brashness** unpleasant, agressive behaviour
43 **misplaced** not right for a certain situation
43 **antique** very old, out of date
43 **at the mercy of sb/sth** not able to control sb/sth that is more powerful
56 **drought notwithstanding** despite drought

→ EXAM PREPARATION

Leseverstehen (p. 222)

S ▶ Doing comprehension tasks, p. 258

WORKING WITH THE TEXT

2 Entscheiden Sie, ob die Aussagen zum Text richtig oder falsch sind. Begründen Sie Ihre Entscheidung auf Deutsch in vollständigen Sätzen.

1 Alfredo Barsuglia criticizes private swimming pools in California because they are too expensive for most people.
2 The lack of water is not the only reason that private swimming pools in California have been called into question.
3 Local authorities are powerless to make people save water during the drought.
4 It's possible for a pool to lose thousands of gallons of water over the course of a year, even if it doesn't have a leak.
5 Pool ownership is equally spread across all social classes and ethnic groups.
6 Alfredo Barsuglia doesn't believe that private swimming pools will go out of fashion in Los Angeles in the near future.

→ EXAM PREPARATION

Leseverstehen (p. 222)

S ▶ Doing comprehension tasks, p. 258

3 Abgesehen von den privaten Schwimmbecken werden im Text vier Bestandteile des Traums der amerikanischen Mittelschicht genannt, die als Symbol für die Stadt Los Angeles in ihrer Blütezeit stehen. Erstellen Sie eine Liste der Bestandteile. Formulieren Sie vollständige deutsche Sätze.

WORKING WITH WORDS

4 Complete the sentences with a suitable abstract noun formed from one of the adjectives in the box.

authoritative | fragile | private | responsible | secure

1 Even though people are aware of the … of the city's water supply, they still continue to use their private swimming pools.
2 The city is trying to improve the … of its water supply by building a new aqueduct from the Colorado River.
3 Local councils have the … to fine people who continue to waste water.
4 Nobody takes personal … for the drought. Everyone just blames it on the weather.
5 People are more interested in enjoying pools in the … of their own backyards than worrying about the environment.

S ▶ Learning new vocabulary, p. 256

COMPETENCE TRAINING: LEARNING VOCABULARY

Learning vocabulary in word fields (groups of words and phrases related to one topic) is a good way to help you remember the vocabulary. You can do this using mind maps, index cards or by collecting vocabulary under headings.

5 Copy the table below and look at the text again. Find words and phrases related to the water crisis in southern California and add them under the suitable heading.

Word field: Water crisis in southern California
Words and phrases describing …

… the region	… the effects of the crisis
desert, sand, …	*melting ski runs, …*
… the use of water	… possible solutions
love affair with private swimming pools, …	*water rationing, …*

LOOKING AT LANGUAGE

6 **a** Which sentence below tells you that the drought is not yet over? Explain the difference between the two tenses.

G ▶ The simple past, p. 268
The present perfect, p. 269

a) Some cities turned off fountains and rationed water because of the drought.
b) Some cities have turned off fountains and rationed water because of the drought.

b Complete the sentences below with the correct form of the verb in brackets.

1 Los Angeles … (build) its first aqueduct in 1913, but water supply is still a huge problem as the city … (grow) enormously in size.
2 Only a few people … (travel) into the desert to see the swimming pool installation which the artist … (create) last year.
3 We … (have) a new swimming pool built 6 months ago. It … (lose) 5,000 gallons of water already, even though we keep it covered most of the time.
4 Two young academics … (publish) an atlas where you can see all of LA's private swimming pools. They … (collect) the data for their book from many sources.
5 The current drought … (make) it impossible for farmers in Imperial Valley, California, to supply water to the city of San Diego – even though they … (sign) a contract to do so fifteen years ago.
6 Hollywood filmmakers … (use) swimming pools to symbolize the American Dream hundreds of times since a body … (be) shown floating face down in a pool in the opening scene of the film *Sunset Boulevard*.

The California aqueduct

LISTENING

7 Sie hören ein Interview des Radiomoderators Walter Smith mit der Aktivistin LiAnn Delray über einen neuen Wassersparplan, das sogenannte "Dirty Car Pledge". Beantworten Sie die Fragen auf Deutsch in Stichworten.

→ EXAM PREPARATION
Zentrale Klassenarbeit Hörverstehen (p. 224)

S ▶ Practising listening skills, p. 256

1.08

1 Worum geht es bei „Dirty Car Pledge"?
2 Wie viel Wasser verbraucht jeder Bewohner von Los Angeles im Durchschnitt?
3 Wie viel Wasser verbraucht eine Autowäsche in einer Autowaschstraße?
4 Mit welchem konkreten Ziel wurde das „Dirty Car Pledge" ins Leben gerufen?
5 Wie ist die Kampagne angelaufen?
6 Was bekommen die Teilnehmer an der Aktion, wenn sie sich anmelden?
7 Worauf soll die Kampagne aufmerksam machen?
8 Warum ist Wassersparen ein derart wichtiges Thema in Südkalifornien?

GIVING A PRESENTATION

8 **a** Work in groups of four. Think of a simple idea, such as the Dirty Car Pledge, to save water. How could you make this into a water-saving campaign?

b In your group, present your campaign to the class. You can do this with a poster, a PowerPoint presentation or in the form of a radio or TV interview.

Here are a few ideas:
Brown Lawn Club – Dirty Window Society – Shower Not Bath Promise

c The class decides on the most original campaign idea. (You can persuade your family and friends to sign up for the campaign!)

→ EXAM PREPARATION
Präsentationsprüfung (p. 225)

→ TIP BOX
· Describe exactly what your idea involves.
· Decide what the aim of the campaign is.
· Think of an interesting way to persuade people to sign up for the campaign.

PETE   HDPE

V   LDPE   PP

PS   OTHER

TEXT 3   Polluting the environment

WARM UP ....

1 Carry out a quick class survey. Write the answers on the board.

How many people in the class …
· know where these symbols come from?
· know what all the symbols mean?
· know what at least one of the symbols stands for?
· know which of these items can be recycled?
· recycle plastic items a) always b) sometimes c) never?

2 Look in your pockets, handbag, school bag, locker, desk, etc. How many different items can you find that are made of plastic? Think about these questions in class:

· What would they be made of if they couldn't be made of plastic?
· What qualities make plastic so useful?
· What happens to these items when they are broken or finished with?

²³ gyre *Wirbel*

²⁵ disintegrate break into small parts

²⁹ circulate move in a circular direction

²⁹ current *Strömung*

²⁹ patch area (of land)

⁴² plankton small forms of animal and plant life in sea water

⁴³ microplastics very small pieces of plastic

⁴⁷ (sea) turtle *Meeresschildkröte*

⁴⁸ seal *Seehund, Robbe*

⁵² intestines *Eingeweide*

⁵⁴ marine to do with the sea and sealife

⁶¹ soak sth up absorb sth (esp. a liquid)

⁶⁴ food chain *Nahrungskette*

Plastics in the ocean: FAQs

1   — ? —
If you walk along any beach anywhere, the chances are that you will come across plastic bags, bottles and containers washed up on the shore. Almost all of this litter has been carelessly thrown away on land and washed out to sea. Every year 100 million tonnes of plastic are turned out by factories all over the world, but only 5% is recycled. Most plastic items are used once and then thrown away.

2   — ? —
Scientists have been collecting data over the last few years and have come up with a ballpark figure of 5.25 trillion plastic particles in the oceans weighing almost 270,000 tonnes. The facts speak for themselves.

3   — ? —
We just can't do without plastic because it is light-weight, comes in all shapes and sizes and is long-lasting but that's exactly what makes it such a big can of worms. Plastic doesn't ever go away, it breaks up on the shore, or in huge gyres in the oceans, into smaller and smaller pieces, eventually disintegrating into plastic particles or microplastics that are less than 5mm long.

4   — ? —
These are enormous areas where the ocean circulates in a slow current and vast patches of floating plastic rubbish collect in the centre, turning the ocean into a sort of plastic trash soup. There are five giant ocean gyres in the North Pacific Ocean, for example, or the Sargasso Sea in the Atlantic.

5   — ? —
Because of the influence of sunlight and the waves, a gyre acts like a gigantic washing-machine where the plastics rub together and break up into smaller pieces. Experts estimate that there are six kilos of plastic floating in these garbage patches for every kilo of plankton. A single 1-litre mineral water bottle could create enough microplastics to put one piece on every mile of beach in the entire world.

6   — ? —
Large pieces of plastic rubbish, such as six-pack can holders, can strangle sea birds, sea turtles or other sea mammals such as seals. The smaller pieces are eaten by fish, who mistake them for food. A dead turtle that turned up in Hawaii had over a thousand pieces of plastic in its stomach and intestines. It is estimated that over a million seabirds and one hundred thousand marine mammals and sea turtles are killed each year by eating or getting caught up in plastic rubbish.

7   — ? —
Well, yes it does actually. The direct effects of plastic trash on marine life are bad enough, but experts point out that plastic trash also soaks up some of the pollutants that are washing around the world's oceans. Small fish are eaten by larger fish and the microplastics gradually make their way up the food chain to humans. So any animal eating microplastics will also be taking in toxic chemicals too.

8   — ? —
The first thing you can do is find out what happens to plastic waste in your area. Then …

(568 words)

WORKING WITH THE TEXT

3 Match these questions (a–j) to the answers (1–8) from the website above. There are two more questions than you need.

a But that doesn't really affect me, does it? 7
b Doesn't the plastic trash just sink to the bottom of the ocean eventually?
c How much plastic are we talking about? 2
d I've got some old plastic CD cases. Where can I recycle them?
e OK, that sounds bad, but how does it affect marine life? 6
f So what goes on in a gyre? 5
g Sorry, you've lost me there. What is a gyre? 4
h Ugh! That makes me want to throw up! What can I do to help? 8
i Where does all the plastic trash in the oceans come from? 1
j Why don't we use other materials instead of plastics? 3

4 Explain to your partner in German what happens to plastic rubbish that is washed into the ocean and how it affects marine life and humans.

WORKING WITH WORDS

5 a Phrasal verbs are often used in less formal texts. Match 10 of the highlighted phrases in the questions and answers to the more formal verbs below.

1 disappear
2 discard sth
3 disintegrate
4 explain sth
5 ingest sth
6 manage without sth
7 occur
8 produce sth
9 transform sth into sth
10 vomit

b Look up the meaning of the other four highlighted phrasal verbs in your dictionary. Make a sentence with each of them.

6 Find six synonyms for *big/very big* and four synonyms for *trash* in the text.

7 a Match an idiomatic phrase from box A with the correct meaning from box B.

A	B
the chances are	a rough estimate
how much … are we talking about?	a serious, unpleasant problem
a ballpark figure	how much does this involve?
the facts speak for themselves	I don't understand you
a can of worms	it is very probable that
you've lost me there	that doesn't need any further explanation

b With a partner, discuss what the following idiomatic phrases mean. Use your dictionary if necessary.

a drop in the ocean | the elephant in the room | face the music | get to grips with sth | get to the bottom of sth | it beats me | light at the end of the tunnel | it's common knowledge

SPEAKING

→ **EXAM PRACTICE**
*Kommunikationsprüfung
(p. 224)*

8 Produce an uninterrupted 5-minute discourse, describing the photo and relating it and the quotation to ecological problems of our times.

The average American throws out 185 pounds of plastic every year. So while regulation may not be the sexiest approach to reducing waste, it's likely the most tenable. After San Jose, California, banned plastic bags in 2012, bag litter choking the city's storm drains dropped by almost 90 percent; it fell 60 percent in creeks and rivers. (Remember, those feed into the Pacific.)

LOOKING AT LANGUAGE

G ▶ The passive, p. 275

9 **a** Look at the first paragraph of the text. Which are passive sentence constructions? Give reasons why they are used instead of active ones.

> If you walk along any beach anywhere, the chances are that you will come across plastic bags, bottles and containers washed up on the shore. Almost all of this litter has been carelessly thrown away on land and washed out to sea. Every year 100 million tonnes of plastic are turned out by factories all over the world, but only 5 % is recycled. Most plastic items are used once and then thrown away.

b A Greenpeace scientist makes the following statements in an interview. Rewrite them using passive constructions, as in a formal report. Only use the *by*-agent when necessary.

1 Scientists have collected data proving that there are 5.25 trillion plastic particles in our oceans.
    Data has been collected proving that there are 5.25 trillion plastic particles in our oceans.
2 The researchers collected the plastic particles in large nets that they towed behind their ships.
3 A scientific journal published their data in 2014.
4 Circular ocean currents trap the plastic items in gyres.
5 The action of the sun and the waves break the plastics up into smaller pieces.
6 Fish absorb the plastic particles into the food chain.
7 Consumers currently recycle only 5 % of the world's plastics.
8 We use most plastic items once and then throw them away.
9 Plastic waste kills over 1 million sea birds every year.
10 Several countries will introduce a ban on plastic bags in the next few years.

2

VIEWING

10 You are going to watch a video about an unusual plastic recycling project in Lima, Peru.

a Before watching: Find Lima on a map (and look at the photo).

- What do you know about Peru? What problems do you think the country might face?
- What things do you think young people in Lima might want to do, but not be able to afford?

b While viewing: Work with a partner and make notes under the following headings:

Partner A: How the invention works	**Partner B:** The advantages of the project

disposable Wegwerf-
dry ice Trockeneis
fibre glass Glasfaser

c After viewing: Partner A explains how the invention works; partner B sums up the advantages of the project.

d Discuss the project in groups: Do you think this is a good project to help save the environment? Explain why or why not? Report your ideas to the class.

GIVING A PRESENTATION

11 Work in small groups. Each group chooses a different material and research some interesting facts and figures about recycling online. Then present them to the class.

electrical and electronic appliances | food and garden waste | glass | metal | paper | plastic | textiles

- If all cans in the UK were recycled, we would need 14 million fewer dustbins.
- Each UK family uses an average of 500 glass bottles and jars annually.
- Recycled paper produces 73 % less air pollution than if it was made from raw materials.
- Most families throw away about 40kg of plastic per year, which could otherwise be recycled.

→ **EXAM PREPARATION**
Präsentationsprüfung (p. 225)

WRITING

12 If the government wants to be serious about the environment, it must add higher VAT onto products that use plastic. This would make people think about what they are buying. Discuss.

→ **EXAM PREPARATION**
Textproduktion (p. 223)

S ▶ Writing an essay, p. 259

CREATING A WEBSITE

13 a In your group, create a webpage with the facts and figures you have found about your material. Design the webpage to make people think about recycling more.

b Look at all the webpages and rank them according to the following categories:

clarity | interesting information | design | overall effect

TEXT 4   Meeting our energy needs

WARM-UP

1.09

1 a Listen to a description of how fracking works. Follow the information the speaker gives and match the words from the box to the numbers on the diagram below.

fissures | fracking fluid | gas | shale rock layer | water, sand and chemicals | water table

   b Read the infobox and then explain the fracking process to your partner in German.

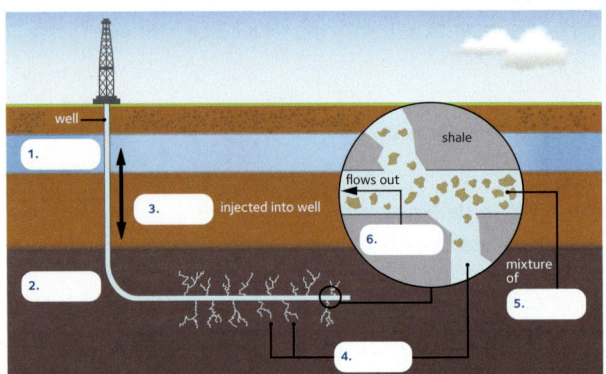

INFO BOX: FRACKING

Hydraulic fracturing, or 'fracking', is a technique used to recover methane gas from layers of shale rock. During the fracking process, a mixture of water, sand and chemicals (the 'fracking fluid') is injected into the gas or oil-carrying rock layer at very high pressure; this creates small cracks, or 'fissures', which allow the gas to flow out to the head of the well. The gas that is collected can be used for cooking, heating or to create electricity in power stations.

   c Discuss with your partner: what problems do you think fracking might create?

Spokane Jenny's environment blog

20 July 20..: Is fracking really the answer to all our energy problems?

Do you remember what the gas company executives said about fracking a few years ago? They said it was the answer to all our energy problems. They said it was going to be a 'bridge fuel' that would help us to reduce coal and oil emissions while we slowly change our energy supply to renewables. They said fracking caused half the emissions of coal. They said it would create new jobs. They said it was a green energy source.

OK, so now we have more than enough gas thanks to fracking and new jobs have been created, some of them in really depressed rural areas. But at what price? For example, what about all that toxic waste water that the process generates? It's polluting the ground water in some places and I'm certain the gas companies aren't telling us the whole story about the chemicals they use. They are so evasive.

I mean, why are we still talking about fracking and all those other fossil fuels? There is so much we can do to change to renewables – and they create jobs, too, folks! We really don't need to rely on shale gas as the short-term answer to our energy needs. Here in the Pacific North-west we're going to become America's first coal-free region over the next few years. We're cutting back on coal, using more renewable energy sources and we're working to increase energy efficiency … and that's the biggest problem in the USA. Across the nation, we've doubled our wind power to 60 gigawatts (enough to power nearly 15m homes), and we generate five times more solar power than we did just four years ago. So come on, let's get off fossil fuels and get onto renewables!

[5]
[10]
[15]
[20]

[2] executive manager

[4] bridge fuel source of energy to replace fossil fuels until more renewable energy sources can be used

[4] reduce sth *etw verringern*

[5] renewables *erneuerbare Energiequellen*

[12] evasive not giving a clear or definite answer to a question

[15] rely on sth depend on sth heavily

[15] shale gas the gas extracted from shale rock by fracking

[18] energy efficiency not wasting energy

Comments

Walt27, 20 July 20..: Hi, Jenny. I couldn't agree with you more. So-called "experts"
25   say that shale gas causes fewer greenhouse gas emissions than coal, but believe
me, shale gas is a far greater threat to climate stability than its supporters admit.
The process of fracking is dangerous enough – just look at those videos of burning
gas coming out of the water taps! And there is leakage from the gas distribution
network which emits huge amounts of methane into the atmosphere.

30   *SuziQ, 20 July 20..:* It seems to me, we need energy to keep the economy going
and fracking is one of the best ways of getting energy with less emissions than
coal. All forms of energy production have environmental consequences but do
you really want us to build more nuclear power stations? In my opinion, we can't
get enough energy from renewables so we need energy from fracking to keep the
35   emissions down. I reckon fracking is the lesser of two evils.

PhillyTheKid, 20 July 20..: I think Walt27 is just exaggerating. As SuziQ said, all
forms of energy production have environmental consequences, but fracking has a
lot more going for it, too. Before shale gas came on the market, we had a real
energy shortage, prices were high and we were at the mercy of countries like
40   Russia and Iran to provide gas and oil. Shale gas production in the USA was almost
non-existent ten years ago but by 2040 it could provide over half of our natural
gas needs – at a reasonable price. And we aren't the only ones: Australia,
Argentina, South Africa and China are looking at shale gas production as well.

MemphisDude, 20 July 20..: PhillyTheKid has got a really good point there.
45   Countries in Europe don't have to rely so much on Russian gas now because there
is more of it on the market and it is cheaper. That has to be a good thing, even if
there are a few problems. And all that gas is going to boost our economy because
we don't have to import so much energy any more. It really is going to create jobs
and economic growth.

50   *SpokaneJenny, 20 July 20..:* It might be good for the economy now, but I don't
believe that switching from one fossil fuel to another is going to help us stop
climate change. If we want to keep global warming under 2 °C, which is still going
to cause huge problems, we've got to keep our fossil fuel reserves under ground.
We can't afford to use them!   (742 words)

[28] **leakage** an amount of liquid or gas escaping through a hole in sth

[28] **distribution network** the system of pipes and pumping stations needed to deliver gas to consumers

[29] **methane** *Methangas*

[32] **consequence** sth that happens as a result of an action or a situation

[39] **shortage** *Mangel*

[39] **at the mercy of sb/sth** not able to control sb/sth that is more powerful

[47] **boost sth** make sth increase or become better

[51] **switch** change (from one thing to another)

drilling for shale gas

WORKING WITH THE TEXT

2   Entscheiden Sie, ob die Aussagen zum Text (Blog und Kommentaren) richtig oder
falsch sind. Begründen Sie Ihre Entscheidung in vollständigen deutschen Sätzen.

1 According to the experts that Spokane Jenny quotes, shale gas from fracking will make renewable energy sources unnecessary.

2 According to Jenny herself, the biggest problem in the USA is that too much energy is wasted.

3 Walt27 claims that fracking releases huge amounts of methane gas into the atmosphere.

4 SuziQ thinks that shale gas is preferable to nuclear power as a source of energy.

5 PhillyTheKid doesn't believe that fracking has any negative effects on the environment.

6 Jenny hopes that shale gas will help to keep global warming below 2 °C.

EXAM PREPARATION
Leseverstehen (p. 222)

S ▶ Doing comprehension tasks, p. 258

3 Copy the line below. Where would you place each of the comment writers?

in favour of fracking   against fracking

SpokaneJenny

S ▶ Mediating, p. 266

4 Copy the table below and make notes in German on the advantages and disadvantages of fracking.

Vorteile von Fracking	Nachteile von Fracking

WORKING WITH WORDS

5 a Copy the table below and find phrases in the blog and comments that you could write under the following headings:

Expressing an opinion	Agreeing with somebody	Disagreeing with somebody
It seems to me ...		

b Add phrases from the box below to the three headings.

Actually, I think (that) ... | I believe (that) ... | I couldn't agree more. | I feel (that) ... | If you ask me, ... | I'm afraid I can't accept that. | My view of the matter is ... | Oh, I don't agree. | That's exactly my own view. | That's quite right/true. | Well, as a matter of fact, ... | Yes, I agree. | Yes, that's just how I see it. | You must be joking!

LOOKING AT LANGUAGE

G ▶ Reported speech, p. 272

6 A reporter is interviewing a fracking company manager. Report what they say, using the reporting verbs in brackets in the past tense.

Reporter: "Is fracking going to be the answer to all our energy problems?" (ask)

Manager: "Shale gas has turned the energy market here upside down. It provided 25 % of all gas production last year." (reply | point out)

Reporter: "What is the fracking industry doing to improve safety?" (want to know)

Manager: "There has been some negative publicity in the last few months. We will do everything in our power to make sure that fracking remains a clean energy source." (admit | promise)

Reporter: "Will fracking create more jobs in the USA?" (inquire)

Manager: "Fracking has already created thousands of jobs. It will continue to boost our economy for the next ten years." (state | predict)

Reporter: "Don't you think it would be better to invest more money in renewable energy sources?" (ask)

Manager: "Alternative energy sources will never be able to supply our energy needs. Fracking is clean and green." (deny | insist)

The reporter asked (the manager) if fracking was going to be the answer to all their energy problems.

LISTENING

7 Sie hören ein Interview mit Fenella Williams, einer Umweltjournalistin, über die Zukunft von Fracking und Schiefergas.

1.10

EXAM PREPARATION
Zentrale Klassenarbeit Hörverstehen (p. 224)

S ▶ Practising listening skills, p. 256

Beantworten Sie die Fragen auf Deutsch in Stichworten.

1 Warum ist nach Aussage der Energieversorgungsunternehmen Schiefergas eine „grüne" Energiequelle?
2 Welche Argumente nennt Fenella Jones, um diese Aussagen zu entkräften?
3 Zu welchem Ergebnis kommt Fenella Jones beim Vergleich von Kohle und Schiefergas als Energiequelle für Kraftwerke?
4 Mit welchen weiteren Argumenten werben die Lobbyisten für Schiefergas bei den Regierungen in Europa und in den USA?
5 Welche Konsequenzen sieht Fenella Jones für den Fall, dass die Schiefergas-Lobbyisten Erfolg haben?
6 Welche Auswirkung hat die Fukushima-Katastrophe auf die Energie-Debatte gehabt?
7 Welchen Vorteil haben die Gasfirmen nach Aussage von Fenella Jones?

SPEAKING

8 Work in groups of four. Do you think shale gas from fracking is a green alternative energy source that should be used to replace coal, oil and nuclear power stations?

Discuss in your group and report what you said/thought back to the class.

Anja thought that …

Toni argued that …

Elvira insisted that …

WRITING

9 Explain the quotation in relation to the text and give examples of why fracking has helped the USA with its energy supplies.

"They said fracking was the answer to all our energy problems." (l. 3).

EXAM PREPARATION
Textproduktion (p. 223)

S ▶ Writing an essay, p. 259

TIP BOX
Go back to Task 4 and see what you listed there under advantages.

SPEAKING

EXAM PRACTICE

Kommunikationsprüfung (p. 224)

S ▶ Interpreting pictures and cartoons, p. 262

10 Work with a partner: Partner A looks at this page; partner B looks at File 2 on p. 216.

a Produce a five-minute uninterrupted discourse (monologue) based on the cartoon about the problems of securing energy.

b Now listen to your partner talk about his or her cartoon.

c Discuss for 10 minutes:

- Explain how both your cartoons relate to the current energy debate.
- Then, discuss the advantages and disadvantages of the four different energy sources shown in the cartoon below.

TIP BOX

While your partner talks about his or her cartoon, listen and take notes. When discussing both cartoons, sum up, comment on and discuss what your partner said.

TEXT 5   Climate change: running out of time

WARM-UP ....

"Global Warming", painting by Paul Cumes (2001), mixed media 183 x 137 cm

Earth's clock

Pat Moon

Imagine that the earth was shaped
Twenty-four hours ago,
Then at 6 a.m. rains fell from the skies
To form the seas below.
5   At 8 a.m. in these soupy seas
The first signs of life appeared.
The dinosaurs called seventy minutes ago
But at twenty to twelve disappeared.
Man arrived just one minute ago,
10   Then at thirty seconds to midnight,
Raised himself from his stooping stance
And started walking upright.
In the thirty seconds man's walked the earth,
See what he's managed to do.

15   Earth's clock continues ticking;
The rest is up to you.

[7] call come to visit
[11] stooping stance way of standing bent over

1 **a** Work in groups of four. Partners A and B, look at the poem; partners C and D look at the painting.

Partners A and B: Sum up the main idea of the poem in one sentence. Think about what the image of the clock means.
Partners C and D: Describe the painting and the style the painter uses. What effect of global warming does it show?

S ▶ Interpreting pictures and cartoons, p. 262

b Explain the poem/painting to the other partners. What point is the poet/artist trying to make?

c Discuss in your group of four which you find more effective: the poem or the painting? Report your findings to the class.

Miami Beach – a city affected by climate change

Robin McKie

¹ **tide** the regular rise and fall in the level of the sea

¹ surge move quickly and forcefully in a particular direction

⁴ **severe** extremely bad or serious

⁴ **hurricane** *Orkan*

⁵ batter sth hit sth hard and repeatedly, causing serious damage

⁶ sweep move quickly

⁶ storm drain pipes under the roads to gather rainwater

⁶ reverse sth change the direction in which sth moves

⁷ **flood sth** *etw (über)fluten*

⁷ gutter *Regenrinne, Rinnstein*

⁸ thoroughfare a main road

⁹ **pour** flow quickly and strongly

¹⁰ calamitous causing great damage to lives and property

¹⁰ inundate sth cover sth (esp. an area of land) with a large amount of water

¹¹ corrosive tending to destroy sth slowly by chemical action

¹¹ immerse sth cover sth with water

²⁰ corrode sth destroy sth slowly, esp. by chemical action

²⁰ rot sth *etw verrotten lassen*

²⁰ innards *das Innere*

²² bring about sth make sth happen

²⁸ **devastating** causing a lot of damage and destruction

²⁸ scenario a description of how things might happen in the future

³¹ generous *(here:) fast*

³² crane *Kran*

³² condominium *AE* an apartment building or group of houses

³² scaffolding *Gerüst*

³³ enclose sth cover sth, wrap sth

³⁴ be oblivious of sth not be aware of sth

³⁵ awash covered by water

⁴³ **be in denial** refuse to accept that sth unpleasant or painful is true

⁴⁵ mind-boggling very difficult to imagine or to understand; very surprising

Every year, with the coming of high spring and autumn tides, the sea surges up the Florida coast and hits the west side of Miami Beach, which lies on a long, thin island that runs north and south across the water from the city of Miami. The problem is particularly severe in autumn when winds often reach hurricane levels. Tidal surges are turned into walls of seawater that batter Miami Beach's west coast and sweep into the resort's storm drains, reversing the flow of water that normally comes down from the streets above. Instead seawater floods up into the gutters of Alton Road, the first main thoroughfare on the western side of Miami Beach, and pours into the street. Then the water surges across the rest of the island. [5]

The effect is calamitous. Shops and houses are inundated; city life is paralysed; cars are ruined by the corrosive seawater that immerses them. During one recent high spring tide, laundromat owner Eliseo Toussaint watched as slimy green saltwater bubbled up from the gutters. It rapidly filled the street and then blocked his front door. "This never used to happen," Toussaint told the *New York Times*. "I've owned this place eight years and now it's all the time." [10] [15]

Today, shop owners keep plastic bags and rubber bands handy to wrap around their feet when they have to get to their cars through rising waters, while householders have found that ground-floor spaces in garages are no longer safe to keep their cars. Only those on higher floors can hope to protect their cars from surging sea waters that corrode and rot the innards of their vehicles. [...] [20]

"There has been a rise of about 10 inches in sea levels since the 19th century – brought about by humanity's heating of the planet through its industrial practices – and that is now bringing chaos to Miami Beach by regularly flooding places like Alton Road," says Harold Wanless, a geology professor at the University of Miami. "And it is going to get worse. By the end of this century we could easily have a rise of six feet, possibly 10 feet. Nothing much will survive that. Most of the land here is less than 10 feet above sea level." [...] [25]

It is a devastating scenario. But what really surprises visitors and observers is the city's response, or to be more accurate, its almost total lack of reaction. The local population is steadily increasing; land prices continue to surge; and building is progressing at a generous pace. During my visit last month, signs of construction – new shopping malls, cranes towering over new condominiums and scaffolding enclosing freshly built apartment blocks – could be seen across the city, its backers apparently oblivious of scientists' warnings that the foundations of their buildings may be awash very soon. [30] [35]

Not that they are alone. Most of Florida's senior politicians – in particular, Senator Marco Rubio, former governor Jeb Bush and current governor Rick Scott, all Republican climate-change deniers – have refused to act or respond to warnings of people like Wanless [...], though Rubio [...] has made his views clear in speeches. "I do not believe that human activity is causing these dramatic changes to our climate the way these scientists are portraying it. I do not believe that the laws that they propose we pass will do anything about it, except it will destroy our economy," he said recently. Miami is in denial in every sense, it would seem. Or as Wanless puts it: "People are simply sticking their heads in the sand. It is mind-boggling." [...] [40] [45]

Philip Stoddard is particularly well-placed to judge what is happening to Miami. Tall, thin, with a dry sense of humour, he is a politician, having won two successive elections to be mayor of South Miami, and a scientist, a biology professor at Florida International University. […] "Another foot of sea-level rise will be enough
50 to bring salt water into our fresh water supplies and our sewage system. Those services will be lost when that happens," says Stoddard.

"You won't be able to flush away your sewage and taps will no longer provide homes with fresh water. Then you will find you will no longer be able to get flood insurance for your home. Land and property values will plummet and people will
55 start to leave. Places like South Miami will no longer be able to raise enough taxes to run our neighbourhoods. Where will we find the money to fund police to protect us or fire services to tackle house fires? Will there even be enough water pressure for their fire hoses? It takes us into all sorts of post-apocalyptic scenarios. And that is only with a one-foot sea-level rise. It makes one thing clear though:
60 mayhem is coming."   (788 words)

From: The Guardian, 11 July 2014

50 sewage system *Abwassersystem*
52 flush sth away *etw wegspülen*
54 plummet fall a long way very quickly
58 hose *Schlauch*
58 post-apocalyptic similar to, or related to, the end of the world
60 mayhem confusion and fear, caused by a sudden shocking event

WORKING WITH THE TEXT

2 Entscheiden Sie, ob die Aussagen zum Text richtig oder falsch sind. Begründen Sie Ihre Entscheidung auf Deutsch in vollständigen Sätzen.

1 Most of the flooding in Miami Beach occurs because of spring high tides.
2 The floods are caused by sea water flowing back through the drains and into the streets.
3 Scientists expect the sea level to rise between six and ten feet by the end of this century.
4 State politicians in Florida are very concerned about the effects of climate change.
5 Senator Marco Rubio believes that measures to curb global warming will help the economy.
6 If the sea level rises another foot, it will start to affect local water and sewage services in Miami.
7 People will only leave Miami when climate change starts to affect them financially.

→ EXAM PREPARATION
Leseverstehen (p. 222)

S ► Doing comprehension tasks, p. 258

3 Im Text werden drei Beispiele genannt, die die Gelassenheit der Bewohner Miamis angesichts der drohenden Hochwassergefahr verdeutlichen. Erstellen Sie eine Liste dieser Beispiele. Formulieren Sie vollständige Sätze auf Deutsch.

→ EXAM PREPARATION
Leseverstehen (p. 222)

S ► Doing comprehension tasks, p. 258

SPEAKING

4 Every year Miami is hit by hurricanes (cf. photos on this page of Hurricane Wilma, 2005). Discuss in small groups:

· Would you be worried if you lived in Miami? Why / Why not?
· Think of other examples of low-lying cities. What can they do to avoid the effects of rising sea levels? How realistic is this for Miami?

Report your ideas to the class

WORKING WITH WORDS

5 Complete the text on the following page with words from the box.

climate-change deniers | fresh water | low-lying | refugees | salt water | sea levels | severe | tides

While …[1] refuse to accept scientists' warnings about the consequences of global warming, for many people in …[2] coastal areas, climate change is already a reality. Rising …[3] are already causing problems in many islands in the Pacific and Indian Oceans. Due to high spring and autumn …[4], it is increasingly difficult to grow crops there as …[5] floods the ground. In addition, …[6] drought means less rainfall, so that …[7] supplies are becoming more and more limited. It is only a matter of time before the first climate-change …[8] arrive.

→ EXAM PREPARATION

Präsentationsprüfung (p. 225)

DOING RESEARCH AND GIVING A PRESENTATION

6 **a** Read these headlines and paragraphs.

Meet the first Pacific Island Town to Relocate Thanks to Climate Change

A small town on Taro Island – the capital of Choiseul Province in the Solomon Islands – is planning to relocate its entire population in response to climate change, Reuters reports. It's the first time that a provincial capital in the Pacific Islands will have done so.

World's first 'climate change refugee' has appeal rejected as New Zealand rules Ioane Teitiota must return to South Pacific island nation of Kiribati

Ioane Teitiota, from the South Pacific island nation of Kiribati, had hoped to be recognized as the world's first climate change refugee. His low-lying homeland is likely to be engulfed by waves by the end of this century – and to become uninhabitable long before then.

b Miami, Kiribati and the Solomon Islands are far away, but parts of Europe are also likely to be affected by rising sea levels. Do research on one area of the world and find out:

- why the area is vulnerable to climate change.
- the problems the population is facing.
- the ways people are dealing with new situation.
- In what way the two newspaper cuttings might be relevant to the area.

S ▶ Giving a presentation, p. 264

c Prepare a five-minute presentation on how that place or country is affected by climate change.

WRITING

7 Choose one of these activities:

1 Write a short poem on the effects of climate change. Imagine that you are one of the people affected, or express your own feelings about climate change.

2 A **haiku** is a short poem of only 17 syllables, written in three lines of 5, 7, then 5 syllables. Look at the examples below, then write your own haiku about climate change.

→ TIP BOX

Haikus often focus on images from nature, using simple and direct language.

"Global climate change" –
A long and abstract title
For a world in pain.

A beautiful day,
But don't spend your time outside:
High ozone levels!

TEXT 6   Unusual solutions

1 Work in groups of three.

a Discuss what the following terms might mean:

carbon cycle | carbon footprint | carbon offsetting | food miles

b Compare your ideas with the rest of the class.

c Each group member chooses one text. You have one minute to skim your text <u>and</u> write a short sentence telling your partners what it is about.

d Exchange your sentences with your partners. How do the terms in 1a relate to the texts?

New ideas to save the planet

1.11

Farming in the sky in Singapore

The island-state of Singapore has a population of 5 million people crammed into an area of just 715 km². The cityscape is a forest of high-rise residential tower blocks. Due to the lack of space, only 7% of the island's food supply is grown locally and the rest has to be imported. So it is only logical that Singapore has started to apply this vertical model to urban agriculture too.

A company called Sky Greens has developed a water-driven, rotating vertical farm that produces a new harvest of vegetables every 28 days. The system consists of a 9-metre high aluminium tower with shelves that rotate vertically once every 8 hours. Seeds are planted in pots on the shelves and the vertical rotation enables the plants to absorb sunlight on the way to the top. In keeping with Sky Greens' low-carbon philosophy, the system is powered by water which is eventually recycled to water the plants.

If set up on the roof of a residential tower block, retirees and homemakers could earn some extra income by maintaining these easy-to-use systems and selling the harvest.

Farming the seas

What do Scotland, Norway, Vietnam and Chile have in common? Thousands of miles of coastline and a desire to transform their ancient seaweed industry into a major source of biofuels. Biofuels are important as green alternatives to oil but many of them are produced from food crops, such as corn and sugar. The demand for biofuels drives up food prices in places where people are already starving. Biofuels also use vital freshwater resources, and the production of palm oil, a major source of biofuel, actually causes more CO_2 emissions than diesel.

---

³ cram sth *etw hineinstopfen*

⁴ cityscape the way a city looks

¹¹ **harvest** *Ernte*

¹² consist of sth be formed from sth

¹² rotate turn in a circular motion, like a wheel

¹⁴ **enable sth** make it possible for sth to happen

¹⁴ **in keeping with** *in Übereinstimmung mit*

¹⁷ retiree *Rentner/in*

²¹ **have in common** *etw gemeinsam haben*

²³ seaweed *Seetang*

32 **kelp** *Kelp, Seetang*

33 **convert sth into sth else** change sth to sth else through a chemical process

36 **cost-effective** giving the best possible profit in comparison with the money that is spent

37 **double whammy** *Doppelschlag, doppelte Ausbeute*

37 **money-spinning** *hoch profitabel, gewinnbringend*

38 **extract sth** take sth out through a chemical process

42 **poo** child's word for excrement

45 **biomethane** methane gas made from human, animal or plant waste

46 **unfit for human consumption** *nicht für menschlichen Verzehr geeignet*

55 **go to waste** not be used properly

55 **landfill site** *Mülldeponie*

56 **incineration plant** place where household waste is burnt

56 **anaerobic digestion** *anaerobe Faulung/Vergärung*

59 **domestic** relating to the home

60 **waste not, want not** *spare in der Zeit, so hast du in der Not*

Biofuel from seaweed does not have any of these problems. Kelp grows far more quickly than plants on land and converts sunlight into chemical energy far more efficiently. Modern cars can already use 10 % ethanol, or biodiesel, produced by crops grown on land. 35

Millions of pounds are being poured into research to make the process cost-effective. Scientists are looking for a double whammy: a money-spinning product – such as iodine or ingredients for cosmetics – that can be extracted first before the remainder is used to produce biofuel. It looks as if large-scale seaweed farming will soon become a reality. 40

Recycling waste from sewage farms

In Britain the first "poo bus", powered entirely by human and food waste, has gone into service. The bus runs on biomethane gas generated from household sewage and food that is unfit for human consumption. Engineers are confident that biomethane could offer a sustainable way of providing public transport services that don't cause damaging CO_2 emissions. 45 50

The biomethane for the "poo bus" comes from a sewage treatment plant in Bristol which processes roughly 75 million cubic metres of sewage waste a year – as well as 35,000 tonnes of food collected from private homes, supermarkets and food manufacturers. This food would otherwise literally go to waste in landfill sites or end up in incineration plants. Through a process known as anaerobic digestion, the waste can be turned into biomethane or fertilisers. 55

Biomethane gas can also be fed into the national gas network where it can be used for domestic heating and cooking. It could replace 10 % of the UK's national gas needs, giving the old idiom "waste not, want not" a whole new meaning. 60

(586 words)

WORKING WITH THE TEXT

2 Copy the table below and complete it with information from the text.

	Current problem	Solution to problem	Other advantages
Text 1	…	…	…
Text 2	…	…	…
Text 3	…	…	…

3 Work in small groups. The texts don't mention any disadvantages of the new ideas. What disadvantages or problems do you think there could be? Think, for example, about the costs of the projects, the technical difficulties that need to be overcome, or think of your own ideas.

WORKING WITH WORDS

4 a Match words or phrases from the text to the meanings (a–j).

1 harvest	a a plant that is grown for food
2 absorb sth	b materials that are no longer needed and are thrown away
3 biofuel	c an energy source from animal or plant waste
4 crop	d area where waste material is buried under the earth
5 convert sth	e giving the best profit compared to the money spent
6 cost-effective	f place where waste material is burned at high temperatures
7 waste	g the amount of grain, corn, etc. that a farm produces
8 sewage	h change sth from one form to another
9 landfill site	i take in a liquid or gas from the air
10 incineration plant	j used water and household waste

b Complete the following text with the words from 4 a. Some words have to be changed.

Oil and gas are expensive fossil fuels that are damaging to the environment and are non-renewable. Scientists are always looking for …[1] ways to …[2] other natural resources, such as seaweed or human …[3], into …[4] that could replace carbon-based energy sources. The …[5] that are currently used are desperately needed on the world food market. Seaweed has the advantage that it …[6] sunlight very efficiently and provides a quick …[7]. Biomethane gas could be created from food waste or from …[8]. The advantage here is that thousands of tons of food waste are dumped in …[9] every year or are sent to …[10].

5 Explain the meaning of the underlined words and phrases in your own words.

1 … a population of 5 million people <u>crammed into</u> an area of just 715 km^2.
2 … Singapore has started to <u>apply this vertical model</u> to urban agriculture too.
3 <u>In keeping with</u> Sky Greens' low-carbon philosophy, …
4 What do Scotland, Norway, Vietnam and Chile <u>have in common</u>?
5 Scientists are looking for <u>a double whammy</u>: …
6 … a <u>money-spinning</u> product
7 … food that is <u>unfit for human consumption</u>.
8 … giving the old idiom <u>"waste not, want not"</u> a whole new meaning.

LISTENING

1.12

6 Sie hören einen Bericht über den Umgang mit Lebensmittelabfällen in der Stadt Seattle. Vervollständigen Sie die unten stehenden Sätze auf Deutsch.

1 Die Stadt Seattle hat ein neues Gesetz erlassen, mit dem Ziel, …
2 Nach einer Einführungsphase müssen Hausbesitzer ein Bußgeld von $1 zahlen, wenn …
3 Nach Schätzungen der Stadtverwaltung wirft jede Familie …
4 Die Stadt möchte den Anteil an recyceltem Biomüll von …
5 Mit der neuen Müllverordnung hat die Stadt nicht vor, …
6 Das Ziel des neuen Systems ist vielmehr, darauf aufmerksam zu machen, …
7 Verhängte Bußgelder werden …
8 In den Recycling-Anlagen der Stadtwerke werden neben Papier auch …
9 Ab Juli werden Bußgelder auch verhängt, wenn …

→ **EXAM PREPARATION**
Zentrale Klassenarbeit Hörverstehen (p. 224)

S ▶ Practising listening skills, p. 256

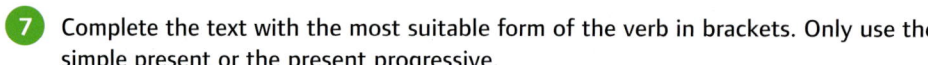

LOOKING AT LANGUAGE

G ▶ The simple present, p. 267
The present progressive, p. 267

7 Complete the text with the most suitable form of the verb in brackets. Only use the simple present or the present progressive.

Scientists …[1] (look) for ways to reduce CO_2 emissions and the use of biofuels …[2] (seem) to provide one possible solution. Biofuels …[3] (be) theoretically carbon-neutral because of the carbon cycle of plants, which …[4] (help) to support life on earth. This …[5] (be) one of the key factors in our life support system which excessive human activity …[6] (threaten). The carbon cycle …[7] (work) as follows: live plants …[8] (absorb) CO_2 from the atmosphere and …[9] (release) oxygen in return. The carbon is held in the plants until they …[10] (die), when it is released back into the atmosphere. Thus biofuels theoretically only …[11] (emit) as much carbon as they have absorbed while growing. However, farmers and large agricultural corporations in Indonesia, for example, …[12] (clear) vast areas of ancient rainforest and …[13] (plant) palm oil trees in their place. What is worse, in some regions they …[14] (also/dry) ancient peat bogs, which …[15] (contain) millions of tons of carbon in the form of decayed wood and plant material. Furthermore, they …[16] (destroy) the natural habitat of many endangered species, such as the Sumatran tiger. Indonesia …[17] (quickly/become) one of the world's largest sources of greenhouse gases. We …[18] (need) to do something to stop this urgently.

COMPETENCE TRAINING: USING LINKING WORDS

S ▶ Improving your writing skills, p. 260

When you are writing a composition, it is important to use linking words and phrases to structure your text and to make it easier for the reader to follow your arguments.

8 a Read the introduction and first paragraph of this composition and the teacher's comments. Rewrite them, incorporating the linking words and phrases.

But it makes sense to start by asking whether … Use this to introduce the topic.	Do biofuels from plant sources do more harm than good? Biofuels are one way in which many European countries are trying to meet their Kyoto Protocol obligations. <u>Are</u> biofuels really as environmentally-friendly as their supporters claim?
First of all, … Good for starting a list of arguments.	
on the one hand, … on the other hand, … Use this to contrast different ideas or arguments.	<u>We should make</u> the distinction between the different sources of biofuels: <u>there are those</u> biofuels that are created from specially-grown plants, such as maize or palm oil trees, <u>and there are those</u> which are won from naturally ocurring waste material, such as sewage and food waste. <u>It makes sense</u> to create biofuels from waste material rather than letting it go to waste.
There can be little doubt that … Useful for emphasizing a point.	

b Now add suitable linking words and phrases from the box to improve the structure of the rest of the composition.

although | as a result | because | despite | for example | furthermore | however | in conclusion | in my opinion

…[1], biofuels from palm oil trees are a completely different matter. The CO_2 emissions related to this type of biofuel are enormous …[2] they are planted on ground where rainforests have been cleared. The rainforests in Indonesia, …[3], contain millions of tons of carbon, which are released into the atmosphere when the forests are razed. …[4], where these rainforest are on ancient peat bogs, up to 15 metres deep, thousands of years of carbon deposits from decaying wood are released at one go.

…[5] one hectare of palm oil can save 6 tonnes of diesel CO_2 emissions per year, razing one hectare of rainforest releases 500–900 tonnes of of CO_2. …[6], it would take 80 to 150 years of palm oil production to offset the emissions caused by razing the forest.

…[7], it is clear that biofuels from plant sources do more damage than good …[8] the fact that they help to save some diesel emissions. …[9], we should do more to use waste material

WRITING

9 Now write your own composition about biofuels.

Biofuels are one form of energy that will help reduce our reliance on fossil fuels. Discuss the advantanges and disadvantages of biofuels.

EXAM PREPARATION
Textproduktion (p. 223)

S ▶ Writing an essay, p. 259

GIVING A PRESENTATION

10 Prepare a presentation on a new and/or unusual renewable energy source.

Choose one of the technologies listed below, or one of your own choice, and do further research on it. Present your results to the class.

· Explain how the technology works.
· Suggest some areas in which it could be applied.
· Evaluate how successful the technology is likely to be in the near future.

Remember to use pictures, graphs or anecdotes to make your talk more interesting.

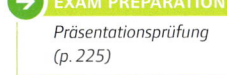
EXAM PREPARATION
Präsentationsprüfung (p. 225)

S ▶ Giving a presentation, p. 264

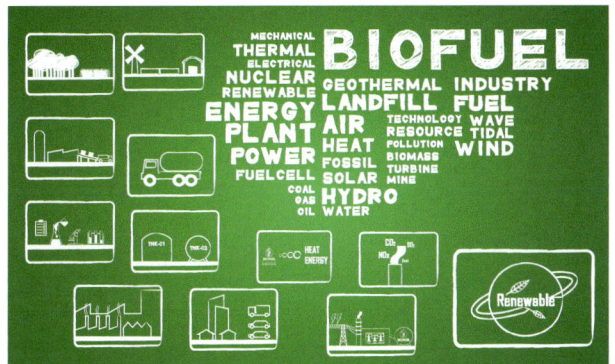

algae | bacteria | biofuel | geothermal energy | hydrogen fuel cell | landfill gas | piezoelectric effect | solar | wind | volcanoes

ENGLISH FOR WORK   Writing a covering letter

ANALYSING A JOB ADVERT

 1 Read the advert and note down under the headings below the information that is relevant if you want to apply for the job.

job description | skills and qualities required | necessary qualifications | application procedure

---

Internship: Audit Assistant (m/f)

Employer:
EMI Environment Management International

Posted: 14 May 20.

Ref: ERM395HR

Contact: Sandra Dixon, Human Resources Manager

Location: Manchester, UK

Position: Audit Assistant

Hours: Full time, 6-month contract

Apply with CV and covering letter.

EMI (Environment Management International) is one of the leading environment and sustainability consultants worldwide. We are offering a number of 6-month internships to school leavers.

Audit assistants will work closely with our sustainability consultants advising local firms. Responsibilities will include handling incoming and outgoing mail, maintaining databases and general research. Audit assistant interns may also attend sustainability meetings at local companies and contribute to creating our audit report.

We are looking for dynamic team players with excellent communication skills and the ability to work under pressure. The successful candidates will have completed a relevant course at a vocational school and have demonstrated an exceptional interest in environmental affairs.

Telephone interviews will take place in the next four weeks.

READING A COVERING LETTER

 2   a   Read Anika's covering letter below. Do you think she is suitable for the position of audit assistant at EMI? Explain why/why not.

Dear Ms Dixon

Audit Assistant Internship

I would like to apply for the position of Audit Assistant Intern as advertised on your company's website. I am presently attending a vocational sixth-form college in Stuttgart, Germany, and I expect to graduate in June. From October of next year I will be studying Environmental Technologies at the University of Applied Sciences in Berlin. I am seeking an internship during my gap year that will give me some practical experience of work related to climate change. I have always been interested in environmental issues. During the last summer vacation, I carried out voluntary work for our local herpetology society. I organized counting and mapping the toad and newt population in the fields around our town and I helped to create a database to monitor the numbers in future years.

I am a native German speaker, but I speak English with ease. I enjoy making new contacts and working with a wide range of people. In addition, I have good IT and communication skills and I am able to work under pressure. Travelling, particularly in the UK, is one of my hobbies.

The position offered would give me the opportunity to use my education and skills to the benefit of your company.

I enclose my CV and would appreciate the opportunity to talk to you on the phone to further discuss how I can be an asset to your company.

Yours sincerely

b Look at the information box below and identify the elements in Anika's covering letter.

INFO BOX

Essential parts of a standard covering letter

A covering letter (and your CV) should be adapted to show how your qualifications, interests and experience are relevant to the job advertised. A covering letter should contain the following points:
- your name and contact details
- name and address of the company
- salutation (name of specific person or "Dear Sir or Madam" if name is unknown)
- subject line (i.e. reference to job title)
- how you heard about the job/company
- explanation of your interest in the job
- how your experience and qualifications relate to the job
- suggestion of an interview or telephone call
- reference to enclosed CV (AE: resumé)
- formal close ("Yours sincerely" if addressed to a specific person; "Yours faithfully" if name is unknown)

WRITING A COVERING LETTER

3 Choose one of the jobs advertised below and write a suitable covering letter.

Entertainers/Animateurs

Sun-Splash.com is looking for young German speakers to train as all-round entertainers/animateurs at hotels in Majorca and Ibiza.

Starting date: 1 July 20_.

Requirements: Excellent English and some Spanish; fun-loving, outgoing personality with "can-do" attitude; physically top-fit and team player; previous experience a benefit but not required

Training: We'll teach you how to entertain, sing, dance and give classes to children

Terms: €500/month; board and lodging provided; flight to and from resort

Successfull applicants will be invited to a face-to-face interview and casting in Frankfurt.

Upload CV and covering letter here.

German-speaking tour guide

Location: Edinburgh, Scotland
Job type: Temporary, full-time

Salary: £1000 p.m.
Reference: RSJ015

Tour guides will accompany German-speaking coach tours in Edinburgh and Scotland. Responsibilities include providing information on sightseeing tours; helping with transport and accommodation issues; providing 24-hour assistance as necessary

Qualifications: fluent spoken English; friendly, helpful manner; excellent communication skills; well-groomed appearance; ability to be flexible

Send CV and cover letter for the attention of
Ms Margaret McQuarrie
Human Resources Dept,
Travel Scotland Ltd,
27 Highland Way,
Edinburgh EH1 3PQ

VA 3   2.01

lifetime *Lebensdauer*
defining force *bestimmende Kraft*
drive progress *den Fortschritt antreiben*
take sth for granted *etw als selbstverständlich erachten*
internal combustion engine *Verbrennungsmotor*
flushing toilet *Wasserspültoilette*
light bulb *Glühbirne*

labour market *Arbeitsmarkt*
working patterns *Arbeitsmuster, -modelle*

advance *Fortschritt*
life expectancy *Lebenserwartung*
keyhole surgery *minimalinvasive Chirurgie*
traumatic *traumatisch, traumatisierend*
recovery time *Genesungszeit*
X-ray *Röntgengerät*
genetic engineering *Gentechnik, -technologie*
controversial *umstritten*
screen sb *jdn durchleuchten, jdn überprüfen*
unborn *ungeboren*
genetic flaw *genetischer Defekt*
raise ethical questions *ethische Fragen aufwerfen*

overtake sb/sth *jdn/etw überholen*
mobile connectivity *mobile Verbindung*
social networking services *soziale Netzwerkdienste*
virtual world *virtuelle Welt*

BACKGROUND INFORMATION

A changing world

Each generation assumes that the word *technology* applies almost exclusively to the new technologies that have come into being during their lifetime. But since humans discovered fire, technology has always been a defining force that drives progress in the way we live. As new technology becomes part of everyday life, it is taken for granted and becomes in a sense invisible. Examples of technology that have transformed our lives include the invention of the wheel, the internal combustion engine, the flushing toilet and the electric light bulb, the television and, of course, the computer. Who knows what technological innovation might be the next to revolutionize life as we know it. 5 10

The social impact of technology

It's difficult to judge which new technological invention has had the greatest impact on society. One could argue for the telegraph and telephone, which both made communication easier; the washing machine, which reduced women's workload dramatically and allowed them to enter the labour market; the television or the internet, both of which have changed social interaction. Undoubtedly, technology has revolutionized working patterns over the past century. 15

Science and technology

20

Advances in science and technology have seen the creation of new medical drugs and treatments that have contributed to raising average life expectancy in developed countries. Keyhole surgery means that interventions are less traumatic and recovery times reduced, X-rays and ultrascans enable doctors to look inside the human body. Some areas, like genetic engineering, continue to be controversial. Screening unborn babies for genetic flaws may seem sensible, but it raises ethical questions about designer babies or parents choosing the sex of their children. 25

Technology and communication

In 2014 the smartphone market overtook the computer market, underlining a clear general preference for smaller handheld devices and mobile connectivity. Social networking services that supply the demand for connection, communication and sharing information have experienced huge success in a very short space of time. Facebook, Twitter, Instagram and Reddit have all rapidly gained hundreds of millions of users and generated incomes larger than those of many countries. All of them allow individuals to gain a little space in the virtual world. 30 35

Privacy and crime

Security services and internet companies collect data from the digital footprint we leave from web browsing and mobile communications. With new technologies come new temptations. With so much information about security and personal details online, new forms of crime involving phishing, identity theft, cyber bullying, hacking and malware have arisen that harm both individuals and companies on a vast scale each year. Policing the internet is proving difficult. Many feel that freedom of speech should not extend to allowing websites that teach disturbed people how to commit suicide, or fanatics how to make bombs. At the same time, technology has led to CCTV, satellite observation and drones that now monitor every aspect of life in the public domain. One justification for this unprecedented intrusion into individual privacy is the need to combat crime, and in particular global terrorism. The balance between security and freedom is one that is continually being adjusted.

The Digital Divide

It is common to divide the population into technophiles and technophobes. Many of the former proudly call themselves geeks. These are people who are keen to try out the latest gadgets and apps and are early adopters of technological innovations. They maintain a strong online presence that typically involves blogging, surfing, uploading and downloading and may even have created avatars for virtual reality gaming. The technophobes, on the other hand, tend to view technology with suspicion. The young generation who have grown up with the internet are referred to as digital natives, while older generations who have had to come to terms with new ways of communicating and learning are digital immigrants.

security *Sicherheit*
digital footprint *digitaler Fingerabdruck, digitale Spur*
identity theft *Identitätsdiebstahl*
cyber bullying *Cybermobbing*
malware *Schadsoftware*
on a vast scale *in großem Maßstab*
police sth *etw überwachen*
CCTV *Videoüberwachung*
satellite observation *Satellitenüberwachung*
monitor sb/sth *jdn/etw überwachen*
public domain *öffentlicher Bereich*
unprecedented *ohnegleichen*
intrusion *Eingriff, Eindringen*

technophile *Technikbegeisterte/r*
technophobe *Technikfeind/in*
geek *Computerfreak*
gadget *Gerät, technische Spielerei*
early adopter *frühzeitige/r Anwender/in*
technological innovation *technische Neuerung*
online presence *Internetpräsenz*
virtual reality gaming *PC-Spiele in virtuellen Realitäten*
digital immigrant *jd, der den Umgang mit Computern erst im Erwachsenalter erlernt hat*

1 a Match words from box A to ones in box B to make collocations. They are all highlighted words from the text.

A	B
combat	bullying
cyber	countries
developed	crime
digital	expectancy
life	footprint
technological	innovation
virtual	reality

b Use each collocation in a sentence, showing what it means.

2 Find an expression in the text which means the folliowing.

1 be invented
2 cause the most positive change
3 make people think about potential moral problems
4 become extremely popular
5 very rapidly
6 a person brought up in the age of digital technology

3 Complete the sentences using one of the verbs in the box, using the correct tense. Use your dictionary to help you, if necessary.

collect | gain | monitor | overtake | raise | transform

1 It is impossible to … the entire internet as there are millions of websites online.
2 The latest rocket explosion … questions about the future of space exploration.
3 Washing machines … the lives of women throughout the world.
4 The sales of ebooks are not expected to … the sales of real books.
5 Cookies are used to … data about the visitors to websites.
6 It is the hope of each start-up to … millions of new users in order to become successful.

4 Explain what each of the following is and how it is done.

1 cyber bullying
2 hacking
3 identity theft
4 malware
5 phishing

5 The text mentions successful social networking services (cf. ll. 32–36). Which other companies have been internet successes, and why?

TEXT 1   Housing and technology

WARM-UP

1   Look at the pictures and do the tasks below.

A

D

B

C

1   **Partner A:** Choose one type of accommodation from the photos. Make a list of its advantages and disadvantages. Without telling your partner which picture you are talking about, read the list.
Partner B: Decide which type of accommodation your partner is describing.
Then swap roles.

2   With your partner decide on the three most important things that make a house a home.

3   Imagine a friend has told you that technology plays little or no role in designing and buying houses. Think of as many examples as possible to prove him wrong.

3D-printed house you can download from the internet

Jonathan Owen

A modern take on traditional prefab housing may be the answer to Britain's housing crisis, with the launch of a two-bedroom home which anyone can put together in just a few days, according to experts. The first ever prototype of the WikiHouse 4.0 – which can be built for less than £50,000 – will be opened today,
5   outside the Building Centre, London, as part of this year's London Design Festival.

Made from blueprints which can be downloaded from the internet for free, the 68-square-metre wood-framed home has been built without involving teams of builders. It is the first time a two-storey house has been digitally cut and built using open source technology. And it took a small group of volunteers just eight
10   days to put together the component parts – which were manufactured using a form of 3D printing.

[1]   a modern take on sth   a modern version or understanding of sth

[1]   **prefab housing**   ready-made houses (that are quick and cheap to build)

[9]   open source technology   *Software, deren Quelltext offenliegt*

12 would-be hoping to be

15 spark sb's imagination cause sb to get excited about sth

19 host a disruptive debate start a debate intended to change things radically

20 landowner person who possesses land

25 on sb's behalf for or in the name of sb

45 price stability when prices remain unchanged for a long period

45 affordability state when prices are reasonable so people can manage to buy something

46 strategic policy advisor *Strategieberater/in*

The building has been designed so that would-be home builders can help themselves to plans and designs from the web, get the parts digitally "printed" and put them together themselves. Alastair Parvin, the co-designer of WikiHouse, said: "What we are trying to do with this installation is to spark people's imagination about how technology can now enable almost anyone to afford their own custom-built house without the need for conventional construction skills." He added: "We don't believe that WikiHouse is the only solution to the current housing crisis, but we do want to host a disruptive debate and challenge landowners, urban planners and policy makers to think differently about the barriers – such as land or building costs."

The question of who builds homes is important, according to Mr Parvin. "Since the industrial revolution the dominant idea from industry has been the assumption that if we want to produce homes they have to be provided by really large organisations who build them on our behalf." He argues that this traditional approach is being challenged by "the power of the web and the power of digital fabrication" and that new technologies "not only have the potential to change the way that we build but also who builds."

And people wanting to build their own WikiHouse 4.0 using the free designs which should go online later this year could save a small fortune in both time and money. A typical two-bedroom house can take around two months to build, costing some £97,500 to construct on average – double the amount of the WikiHouse.

The prototype home "opens up the potential of digital technology to change how we might design, make and construct buildings," according to Colin Tweedy, chief executive of the Building Centre, one of the partners in the WikiHouse project. And digital technology and the internet are combining to provide "an alternative collaborative way of working, bringing increased efficiencies", said Nina Tabink, a senior structural engineer at Arup, another partner in the project.

One in seven Britons would like to build their own home, according to the National Custom & Self Build Association, and a spokesperson said: "Anything that serves to open up the existing supply-driven housing model can only be a good thing and the Wikihouse's innovative approach certainly does that. We need people to take control of their own housing solutions – it is the only way to ensure long-term price stability and affordability for all."

James Hulme, a strategic policy adviser at the House Builders Association, said: "While products like this bring welcome innovation to the sector, potential customers need to bear in mind the high price of land must be added to the construction cost."

And Steve Turner, head of communications at the Home Builders Federation, said: "Ultimately what we need is more land to be made available to build the homes the country desperately needs and continued support for home buyers that in turn will enable the house building industry to maintain increases in supply."

(648 words)

From: The Independent, 12 September 2014

A 3D printed house that is being used as an office, Shanghai, China

15
20
25
30
35
40
45
50
55

WORKING WITH THE TEXT

2 Match the people and the summaries of their opinions.

1	Alistair Parvin	a	The high prices of housing can only be changed if more control is given to future buyers.
2	Colin Tweedy	b	All stages of house building can be improved, as has been illustrated by the example of the WikiHouse
3	Nina Tabink	c	Other costs such as the price of the land the house is built on must not be forgotten.
3	National Custom and Self-build Association spokesperson	d	New technology offers different ways of working together and of increasing efficiency.
4	James Hulme	e	The restrictions concerning land that can be built on must be lifted.
5	Steve Turner	e	Technology offering cheaper alternatives to the current situation needs to be explored.

3 Welche drei Vorteile beim Design des Gebäudes haben potenzielle Privathausbauer bei der Verwendung eines 3D-Druckers? Erstellen Sie eine Liste. Formulieren Sie vollständige Sätze auf Deutsch.

 **EXAM PREPARATION**

Leseverstehen (p. 222)

S ▶ Doing comprehension tasks, p. 258

WORKING WITH WORDS

4 **a** Change the underlined expressions into compound adjectives – remember, there are no plural forms in adjectives in English.

There is a new type of house <u>with two bedrooms</u>.
There is a new type of two-bedroom house.

1 It's a house <u>that costs fifty thousand pounds</u>.
2 This design is for a new house <u>that measures 68 square metres</u>.
3 Now house parts can be created by printing <u>in three dimensions</u>.
4 The WikiHouse had a construction time <u>of eight days</u>.
5 There can be delays <u>of two years</u> before planning permission is given to new houses.
6 City centre housing is expensive, so I have a drive <u>of one and a half</u> hours to get to work.
7 This design is too small for us because we are a family <u>with two adults and three children</u>.
8 We live in a block of flats <u>with ten storeys</u>.
9 Many people no longer have a traditional working week <u>of five days</u>.
10 There is a speed limit in this area <u>of thirty miles an hour</u>.

b Find more examples of compound adjectives in the text.

c Complete the sentences on the next page with one of these compound adjectives.

double-glazed | government-backed | hand-made | high-tech | long-term |
privately-owned | solar-powered

1 There is a movement back to … clothes and furniture, but they are much more expensive.
2 A lot of … housing is being constructed these days, which reduces the use of electricity from other sources.
3 Although it's quite cold here, many houses still don't have … windows.
4 The only … solution to our housing problem is to reduce the cost of flats and houses.
5 There is a new … scheme that makes it easier for young people to buy their first property.
6 A worldwide shortage of copper could have a devastating impact on … products.
7 The market in the UK is dominated by … homes rather than those provided by the council.

LOOKING AT LANGUAGE

G ► Modal auxiliary verbs, p. 271

5 Work with a partner. Decide which of the two modal verbs is most likely in each sentence and explain why.

1 The design plans <u>must</u>/<u>can</u> be downloaded from the internet for free.
2 Technology <u>will</u>/<u>may</u> enable more people to build their own homes more cheaply.
3 People who want to find out more about 3D design <u>might</u>/<u>should</u> go online.
4 Changing the current situation <u>can</u>/<u>must</u> only be a good thing.
5 The price of land <u>can</u>/<u>must</u> not be forgotten, as it adds considerably to the overall price.
6 Experts believe that self-build houses <u>may</u>/<u>would</u> be part of the solution.
7 A large number of people <u>will</u>/<u>would</u> like to build their own homes.
8 The Wikihouse gives us an idea of how the situation <u>can</u>/<u>might</u> change in the near future.

COMPETENCE TRAINING: DESCRIBING CHARTS AND GRAPHS

S ► Interpreting charts and graphs, p. 263

6 a Look at the expressions below and decide which can be used to describe Chart A, which Chart B, which both and which for neither of the charts.

compared with other countries | more or less the same | a big difference | outside London | large increase in price | loss of value | for a number of years | gradual rise | much more than | twice as much | twice as fast | remains constant

b Now formulate sentences using the phrases which you can use with the graphs.

A

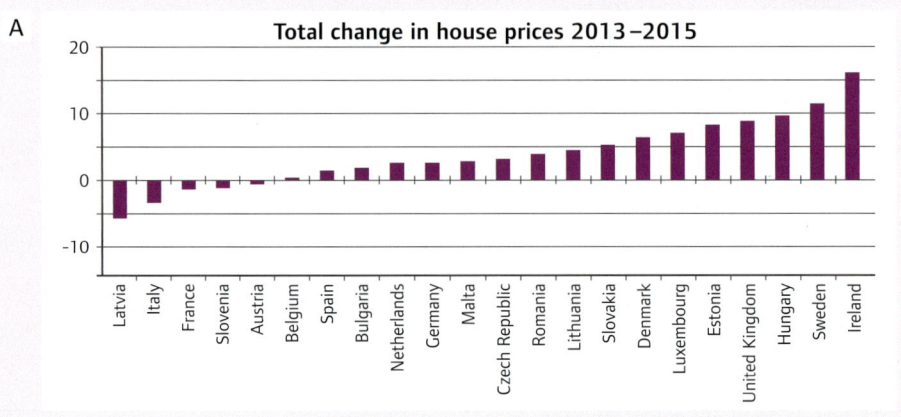

Total change in house prices 2013–2015

B

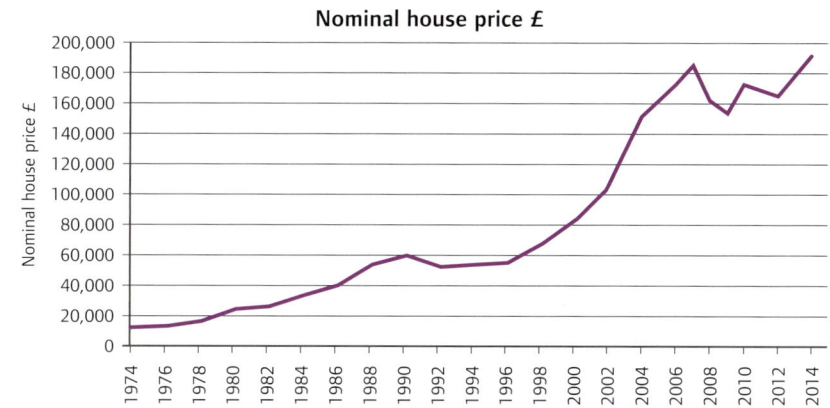

Nominal house price £

- In 1974, the average house price was £10,990.
- In 2014, the average house price was £188,810.

www.economicshelp.org
Source; Nationwide

SPEAKING

7 a Work in pairs. Partner A looks at the Chart A. Partner B looks at Chart B. Describe and analyse your chart to your partner.

b Then discuss your chart with your partner, explaining how technology might help us overcome housing problems in the future. You may make reference to the text.

→ **EXAM PREPARATION**
Kommunikationsprüfung (p. 224)

VIEWING / GIVING A PRESENTATION

8 a Watch the video and list all the new elements in "the house of the future" in the video. Which features do you find interesting, and which not?

b What advantages and disadvantages do you think "the house of the future" has?

c Prepare a short presentation about how you imagine the house of the future. Use ideas from the video and your own ideas.

3

→ **EXAM PREPARATION**
Präsentationsprüfung (p. 225)

S ► Giving a presentation, p. 264

Technology and materials

WARM-UP

1 Look at the pictures of people wearing different sorts of clothing in different situations. Decide

- what makes their clothes suitable for their situations.
- what different materials are used in the clothes, and why.
- what might make the clothes change over time.

2 With a partner, do the following tasks.

1 Make a list of how many different materials you can see in the classroom.
2 Explain the advantages of the objects being made of those materials (e.g. "The windows are made of glass. That lets the light come in, but keeps the cold out.").
3 Discuss how easy you would find it to live without the following: glass, plastic and wood.

3 Look at the headline of the text. Which materials do you think it will mention?

Why the story of materials is really the story of civilisation

Mark Miodownik

Everything is made of something. Take away concrete, glass, textiles, metal, and the other materials from our lives and we are left naked, shivering in a muddy field. We would quickly revert to animal behaviour without the stuff of our civilisation: what makes us human is our clothes, our homes, our cities, our things, which we animate through our customs and language. This becomes very apparent if you ever visit a disaster zone. Thus the material world is not just a display of our technology and culture, it is part of us, we invented it, we made it and it makes us who we are.

5

[1] **textile** *Textilie, Stoff*

[2] **shiver** *zittern*

[3] **revert to sth** become sth again

[5] **animate sb/sth** bring sb/sth to life

[6] **disaster zone** area affected by a disaster (e. g a fire or earthquake)

The fundamental importance of materials is made clear from the naming of ages of civilisations – the stone, iron and bronze ages – with each new era being brought about by a new material. Iron and steel were the defining materials of the Victorian era, allowing engineers to give full rein to their dreams of creating suspension bridges, railways, steam engines and passenger liners.

The 20th century is often hailed as the age of silicon, after the breakthrough in materials science that ushered in the silicon chip and the information revolution. Yet a kaleidoscope of other new materials also revolutionised modern living. Architects took mass-produced sheet glass and combined it with structural steel to produce skyscrapers that invented a new type of city life. Plastics transformed our homes and dress. Polymers were used to produce celluloid and ushered in a new visual culture, the cinema. The development of aluminium alloys and nickel superalloys enabled us to fly cheaply and accelerated the collision of cultures. Medical and dental ceramics allowed us to rebuild ourselves and redefine disability and ageing – and as the term "plastic surgery" implies, materials are often the key to new treatments used to repair our faculties (hip replacements) or change our features (silicone implants for breast enlargement).

Textiles are one of the earliest synthetic materials; when we wear a pair of jeans we are wearing a miniature woven structure, the design of which is older than Stonehenge. Clothes have kept us warm and protected for all of recorded history, as well keeping us fashionable. But they are hi-tech too. In the 20th century we learnt how to make space suits from textiles strong enough to protect astronauts on the moon as well as solid textiles for artificial limbs called carbon fibre composites.

The central idea behind materials science is that changes at invisibly small scales manifest themselves as changes in a material's behaviour at the human scale. It is this process that our ancestors stumbled upon to make bronze and steel, even though they did not have the microscopes to see what they were doing – an amazing achievement. When you hit a piece of metal you are not just changing its shape, you are changing the inner structure of the metal, which is why metals get harder when you hit them. Our ancestors knew this from experience but didn't know why.

Making is not just an economic activity, it is the equal of literature, performance or mathematics as a form of human expression. By eschewing material knowledge we cease to understand the world around us. We wring our hands about climate change or urban sprawl without any recognition that our ignorance of materiality might be the cause. We feel proud of the technological marvel that is a smartphone, and yet we upgrade – ditch one for a newer model – at the first opportunity.

The ages of civilisation are named after materials precisely because they transformed and shaped society. By distancing ourselves from the act of making, by buying and consuming stuff but never having any experience of their manufacture, the developed world finds itself not to be the illiterate society that education ministers fear, but an unmakerly society. In my view this practical ignorance is every bit as dangerous to a modern democracy as a lack of literacy.

(663 words)

From: The Guardian, 14 September 2014

---

10 era a period of history

11 bring about sth make sth happen

12 give full rein to sb/sth allow sb/sth to do what they want

13 suspension bridge *Hängebrücke*

13 passenger liner *Passagierdampfer*

14 hail sth as sth else call sth sth else

14 breakthrough an important new development

15 usher sth in make sth new happen

15 silicon chip *Siliziumchip*

20 aluminium alloy *Aluminium-legierung*

20 nickel superalloy *Nickel-Superlegierung*

21 accelerate sth make sth happen much faster

21 collision meeting of two things that are very different

22 dental ceramics *Zahnkeramik*

24 hip replacement *Hüftprothese*

25 feature *Merkmal*

25 implant ['– –] sth put inside sb's body

25 enlargement act of making sth bigger

27 miniature very small

27 weave sth (past: woven) *etw weben*

31 carbon fibre composite *Kohlefaserverbundwerkstoff*

33 at small scales having very small dimensions

34 manifest sth reveal sth, show sth

35 stumble upon sth find sth by accident

42 eschew sth ignore sth, not use sth

43 cease stop

43 wring your hands *die Hände ringen*

44 urban sprawl the spreading of an expanding city into the countryside

44 ignorance of materiality state of not knowing anything about the functions or properties of materials

45 technological marvel wonderful thing created by technology

46 ditch sth throw sth away

50 manufacture the industrial process of making something

51 unmakerly that has forgotten how to make things

89

WORKING WITH THE TEXT

EXAM PREPARATION

Leseverstehen (p. 222)

S ▶ Doing comprehension tasks, p. 258

4 Entscheiden Sie, ob die Aussagen zum Text richtig oder falsch sind. Begründen Sie Ihre Entscheidung auf Deutsch in vollständigen Sätzen.

1 The human-made environment we live in is what civilization is.
2 Many of the ages of civilization are named after a particular material.
3 Modern life is dominated by one single new material.
4 Textile woven structures are some of the oldest designs made by humans.
5 The clothes we wear have always reflected our technological knowledge.
6 An "unmakerly" society is one where people are more interested in using things than understanding them.

EXAM PREPARATION

Leseverstehen (p. 222)

S ▶ Doing comprehension tasks, p. 258

5 Welche drei Epochen der Frühzivilisationen werden im Text erwähnt, die nach Materialien benannt sind? Erstellen Sie eine Liste. Formulieren Sie vollständige Sätze auf Deutsch.

6 Explain the following statements from the text in your own words.

1 We would quickly revert to animal behaviour without the stuff of our civilisation. (ll. 3 – 4)
2 Iron and steel were the defining materials of the Victorian era. (ll. 11 – 12)
3 Th[is] development [...] enabled us to fly cheaply and accelerated the collision of cultures. (ll. 20 – 21)
4 The ages of civilisation are named after materials precisely because they transformed and shaped society. (ll. 47 – 48)

WORKING WITH WORDS

7 Rewrite these sentences using words from the list below.

breakthrough | disaster zone | enhance | shivering | stumble upon | upgrade

1 I was so cold. I just couldn't keep still.
2 Medical teams were quickly sent to the area where the earthquake happened.
3 This was a new and important discovery that completely changed our lives.
4 Some people think that surgery can greatly improve what they look like.
5 We found this fantastic new restaurant more or less by accident.
6 I've got a phone, but I want to change it for the newest model.

LOOKING AT LANGUAGE

8 **a** Add the missing prepositions to these sentences.

1 It's normal to feel proud ... achieving things that are difficult.
2 Last week was unusually hectic, but now things have reverted ... normal.
3 Understanding materials science allows us ... explain the problem of pollution.
4 People dream ... living on another planet.
5 Modern life has been revolutionized ... the new materials we use.
6 The key ... success is hard work.
7 Making mistakes is normal. The important thing is to learn ... experience.
8 ... my view, life without computers is unimaginable nowadays.

b Look at the text again and find more examples of "verbs + preposition" and "noun + preposition" combinations.

LISTENING

9 Sie hören das Radiomagazin „Science and Society today", in dem der Radio-sendungswissenschaftsexperte Mark Jones über eine neue Zeitepoche spricht. Beantworten Sie die unten stehenden Fragen auf Deutsch.

1 Wie hat menschliche Aktivität die Erde verändert?
2 Was bedeutet das Wort „Anthropozän" (*anthropocene*)?
3 Wann fing die anthropozänische Epoche an?
4 Welche Veränderungen fanden nach dem Zweiten Weltkrieg statt?
5 Welche Konsequenzen hat Luftverschmutzung für Menschen?
6 Wie haben sich die Ozeane durch die Luftverschmutzung verändert?
7 Was ist der „Giant Garbage Patch"?

2.02

> **EXAM PREPARATION**
> *Zentrale Klassenarbeit Hörverstehen (p. 224)*

S ▶ Practising listening skills, p. 256

GIVING A PRESENTATION

10 Research one of the following topics from either A or B and give a short presentation.

> **EXAM PREPARATION**
> *Präsentationsprüfung (p. 225)*

S ▶ Giving a presentation, p. 264

A	B
The Stone Age (a)	iron
The Bronze Age (b)	glass
The Iron Age (c)	plastic
The Age of Steam (d)	gold
The Space Age (e)	silicon
The Anthropocene Age (f)	textiles
Include this information:	Include this information:
1. When it started and finished	1. When the material was discovered or invented
2. What life was like during the period	2. The main properties and advantages of the material
3. The key materials that defined the period	3. The main uses of the material
4. Any problems associated with the period	4. Any disadvantages associated with the material

a

b

c

d

e

f

TEXT 3   GM foods

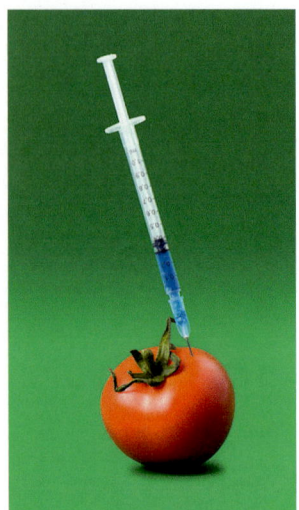

1 Copy and complete the questionnaire, then find who has the most different answers to you in class and discuss your answers.

1 = I couldn't agree more
2 = I agree to a large extent
3 = I agree to a certain extent
4 = I don't really agree
5 = I completely disagree

1	GM foods are safe: they're just another type of food.	1 2 3 4 5
2	We need GM food to feed the planet.	1 2 3 4 5
3	It is inevitable that one day we will all be eating GM food.	1 2 3 4 5
4	Studies may have shown that GM foods are safe, but we won't know about long-term problems for several generations.	1 2 3 4 5

Is a ban on GM crops more harmful than growing them?

Karl Mathiesen

12 inherently in itself
13 selective breeding *Auslese-züchtung, Selektionszüchtung*
20 yield result, production
20 plant molecular biologist *Pflanzenmolekularbiologe/in*
22 regulatory requirements *behördliche/gesetzliche Anforderungen*
24 be worth the risk *das Risiko wert sein*

The EU's ban on genetically modified (GM) crops may have caused more harm than good, according to the UK's chief scientist. Sir Mark Walport told MPs on the Science and Technology committee: "The consequence of inaction is that we are potentially, particularly in Europe, denying access to technologies that actually will potentially help feed people in ways that damage the environment less." 5

Only one GM crop is currently grown commercially in the European Union – the insect-resistant maize MON 810. Gaining approval for the cultivation of GM crops in the EU has been effectively impossible because each one requires a vote by member states. Many EU countries are sceptical of the technology. So even if a crop is approved by the European Food Safety Authority (Efsa) it is unlikely to 10
make it into commercial fields.

Scientists say GM is not inherently dangerous, essentially no different to the selective breeding that humans have engaged in for millennia and each crop should be assessed on its own merits. "It makes more sense to assess crops based on their individual characteristics and the farming practices that accompany them, 15
rather than the method by which they were produced," says Mark Downs, chief executive of the Society of Biology.

A study published in the journal PLOS One this year found "on average, GM technology adoption has reduced chemical pesticide use by 37 %, increased crop yields by 22 %, and increased farmer profits by 68 %". Jonathan Jones, a plant 20
molecular biologist at the Sainsbury Laboratory, says the tales of missed opportunity are legion because the regulatory requirements for GM crops are "far in excess of what's rational". The cost of the process, hundreds of millions of pounds, means very few crops are worth the risk of bringing all the way through.

25 In Europe, even well-resourced companies are turning away from the technology. A strain of blight-resistant potatoes was removed from the approval process by agrochemical giant BASF after it became clear that even if it was found to be safe by Efsa, it was likely be voted down by EU politicians. Jones says the GM potato could have saved millions. Blight costs UK potato farmers around £60m 30 every year in losses and the massive use of chemical sprays. Each hectare has £500 worth of fungicide dumped on it each season. There are similar stories for pest-resistant cabbages and broccoli as well as yellow-rust resistant wheat.

Efsa has not found any GM crops to pose a serious risk to human or animal health. But the cultivation of GM crops does raise legitimate environmental concerns. For 35 example, the cultivation of MON 810 maize, which produces a protein that harms the insects that eat it, could create a super pest strain with resistance to natural plant defences.

Walport joined Jones by suggesting the GM debate is a conflict between objective science and irrational belief. "We pretend that the debate about genetically 40 modified crops is a debate about science when the reality is actually that the science is very clear. It is really a debate about values. About people [with] strongly held personal opinions and beliefs [who] believe that there is something wrong in humans modifying nature."

Marco Contiero, Greenpeace's EU policy director on agriculture says many of the 45 scare tactics used against GM – for example the moniker "Frankenfoods" – are red herrings. He says GM technology is "absolutely brilliant" in highly controlled circumstances, but says there are serious, rational, empirical questions about the reality of GM cultivation in the wider environment. The benefits attributed to GM can only be seen as benefits if you accept a form of agriculture dominated by five 50 monolithic corporations and vast fields of single crops with a massive ecological footprint, he says. "However, it is imperative to achieve a paradigm shift from such kind of farming, which damages the environment in many different ways at local (e. g. agrochemical pollution) as well as international level (fostering climate change due to its reliance on fossil fuels) towards farming systems based on 55 agricultural diversity and biodiversity."   (666 words)

From The Guardian, 20 November 2014

26 strain a type
26 blight-resistant *resistent gegen Fäule*
27 agrochemical *agrochemisch*
30 **spray** *Spritzmittel*
32 yellow-rust *(Gelbrost) Schadpilz*
45 scare tactics things done to frighten people
45 moniker (usu. humorous) name
45 **red herring** sth irrelevant and misleading
47 empirical based on experience
50 monolithic huge and dominant
50 **ecological footprint** the impact your life and choices have on the environment
51 **imperative** absolutely necessary
51 paradigm ['pærədaɪm] shift *Paradigmenwechsel*
53 foster sth encourage sth, promote sth

WORKING WITH THE TEXT ....

2 Which paragraph(s) mentions:

1 GM as part of a long history of man's control of food sources
2 GM leading to the evolution of a pest that cannot be easily controlled
3 facts being overlooked in favour of subjective feelings
4 reservations about the role of big business in food production
5 regulation concerning GM foods being excessive
6 attempts to influence public opinion against GM foods
7 EU doing more harm than good concerning GM foods
8 each crop needing to be voted on by the EU countries
9 GM potatoes that might have been of great help

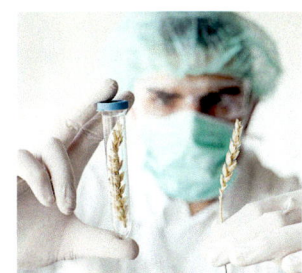

WORKING WITH WORDS

3 Match these adverbs from the text to their nearest meaning.

1 potentially (l. 4)   a at the present time
2 particularly (l. 4)   b that is the real situation
3 actually (l. 4)   c that is a probability
4 currently (l. 6)   d above all
5 effectively (l. 8)   e that is capable of becoming this
6 inherently (l. 12)   f by its nature
7 essentially (l. 12)   g having this result
8 likely (l. 28)   h in the most important sense

LOOKING AT LANGUAGE

G ▶ Adjectives and adverbs, p. 279

4 Rewrite the sentences using an adverb + past participle structure and making any other changes needed.

Foods which have had a genetic modification –> genetically modified foods.

1 I think it is a good idea to eat food which is produced in the local area.
2 The benefits of this have been proved by science.
3 The researchers are people who enjoy high levels of respect.
4 This type of food is available in a wide area.
5 We have done everything that it is possible for humans to do to avoid this problem.
6 It is so unusual to find problems like this that this is an exception.
7 This new model is a vast improvement on the previous ones.
8 Their marriage is a happy one.

SPEAKING

➔ **EXAM PREPARATION**
Kommunikationsprüfung (p. 224)

S ▶ Interpreting pictures and cartoons, p. 262

5 Describe and analyse the cartoon and relate it to the quotes by leading scientists about GM food.

"The genetic modification of food is intrinsically dangerous. It involves making irreversible changes in a random manner to a complex level of life about which little is known. It is inevitable that this hit-and-miss approach will lead to disasters."

"If it is left to me, I would certainly not eat it. We are putting new things into food which have not been eaten before. The effects on the immune system are not easily predictable and I challenge anyone who will say that the effects are predictable."

DOING A RESEARCH PROJECT

6 Choose one of the topics from the box and do some internet research on it, and report back to the class with your findings.

> obesity
> food miles
> GM foods
> famine
> fast food
> food additives and flavourings

WRITING

7 Write a composition about the topic you researched, taking all the aspects you found out about into account.

→ **EXAM PREPARATION**
Textproduktion (p. 223)

S ► Writing an essay, p. 259

SPEAKING

8 Work in groups of three. Discuss the advantages and disadvantages of GM foods.

1 **Partner A:** Use File 1 to present your opinion to the others.
2 **Partner B:** Turn to page 217 and use File 3 to present your opinion to the others.
3 **Partner C:** Listen to the opinions of Partners 1 and 2 and use File 4 on page 217 to ask questions and discuss further issues about GM foods.

> **File 1**
> **You are generally in favour of GM foods, although you realize there must be proper controls to ensure they are safe. Use these arguments:**
> · Millions of people starve to death each year. GM foods could prevent that.
> · More government controls could be imposed to ensure higher safety standards.
> · There's nothing new about modifying food - it's been done for centuries.
> · With the growing population of the world, we need new ways to feed everyone.

TEXT 4   Space exploration

WARM-UP

1 Make notes on one of these questions, then tell a partner your thoughts and ideas on the subject, giving at least one example to support your points.

A What makes science interesting or boring to study?
B How realistic is it to think people will live on other planets in our lifetime?
C What can we learn by exploring space?
D Do we spend too much money on space exploration?

Mission to colonise Mars

Carmen Fishwick

In 2022 four astronauts, picked from tens of thousands of applicants, will jet off on a one-way mission to Mars as part of the world's most expensive reality TV show. The £4bn project, founded in 2010 by engineer Bas Lansdorp, is set to recoup its costs by selling the broadcasting rights to the mission. "The biggest media event in the world," said Paul Römer, the co-creator of Big Brother and ambassador of the project, on the Mars One website. "Reality meets talent show with no ending and the whole world watching." 5

But the mission has been met by more than its fair share of sceptics. Funding issues, technological hurdles as well as the psychological challenges the astronauts will come up against have all come under scrutiny. If there's a problem, a call for help could take up to 22 minutes to arrive at Earth, and even then the fastest rocket would not arrive until six months later. 10

By 2015, 40 candidates will start their eight-year training programme where they will learn, amongst other essential skills, to deal with long periods of isolation. Here, some of the hopefuls explain why they're prepared to leave friends and loved ones behind for the chance to establish life on Mars. 15

Erica Meszaros, United States

Why did you apply for the Mars One mission?
I want to see the sun rise over a completely new horizon, in a completely new sky. I think that's worth any price. To me, the desire to explore a new world, a planet completely different from the one that every person who has ever lived has ever known, is intrinsic and essential to the human spirit. 20

How do you feel about leaving your family and friends behind?
It would be tough to have to say goodbye to my husband forever, tough in a way that hasn't really set in for me yet. We've been married for eight months. But he's always known that if space travel were an option, I'd be lining up, and he says that he would do everything in his power to get to Mars as well. My in-laws hate it, and my mom thinks it's a joke, but they're mostly concerned about losing the opportunity for grandchildren. 25

[1] **jet off** fly somewhere
[4] **recoup sth** get sth (esp. money) back
[8] **fair share** (here) quite a lot
[9] **hurdle** obstacle, problem
[10] **come under scrutiny** be examined critically
[14] **isolation** state of being completely alone
[22] **intrinsic** being an essential part
[24] **tough** difficult
[25] **set in** start to become clear
[26] **line up** queue
[27] **in-laws** your wife's or husband's parents

30

Josh Richards, Australia

What are you hoping to achieve by traveling to Mars?
I see it as the opportunity it is – an amazing chance to serve all of humanity by taking part in a project that will inspire generations to come. This isn't about what we might leave behind: it's about the potential for breathtaking scientific
35
discoveries and to recognise our species' incredible potential if we simply work together.

Ben Pearce, Canada

Why go all the way to Mars, why not become a scientist or an astronomer?
I've spent a couple of years working in the software industry, sitting at my desk
40
writing tedious code and I began to wonder: is this it? There are so many profound scientific questions that can be answered if we set out and explore the red planet.

Do you think you're psychologically prepared to leave your friends and family behind?
What gets me through the idea of leaving my friends and everyone I love forever
45
is the knowledge that this settlement is bigger than my relationships; bigger than anyone's relationships, because it will truly have an impact on the entire planet. I will also build new relationships with my crew because after all, they'll be my new family.

Rickard Feiff, Sweden

50
Do you have any reservations about Mars One overcoming technological problems?
The technology we have right now is enough to go there. There will always be a better ship, a better engine or a better habitat invented in the next decade. But it's the same on Earth, there are better cars, transportation and houses built
55
almost all the time, but we don't wait indefinitely to get a new TV because there might be a better one tomorrow. We go for what we want when we want it. Columbus could have skipped going west and waited a few hundred years for satellite technology to tell him what's was out there. He did not wait, nor should we.

(695 words)

Source: *The Guardian*, 10 September 2013

[33] **to come** in the future
[40] **tedious** boring
[40] **profound** deep and important
[45] **settlement** *Ansiedlung*
[55] **indefinitely** for ever
[57] **skip sth** not do sth deliberately

WORKING WITH THE TEXT

2 Who mentions:

	Erica	Josh	Ben	Rickard
Escaping from boring routine	…	…	…	…
Accepting risk	…	…	…	…
Being interested in new experiences	…	…	…	…
Contributing to science and knowledge	…	…	…	…
Enjoying adventure	…	…	…	…

Discuss the following questions with a partner:

1 What would you find difficult about leaving the Earth and living on Mars?
2 What sort of training do you think would be necessary for people going to live on Mars?
3 Do you think a reality TV programme about people living on Mars would be interesting or not, and why?

WORKING WITH WORDS

4 a Find a word or expression in the text that means.

1 chosen
2 get money from an investment back
3 people who doubt something is possible
4 people who apply to do something they want
5 the important people in your life
6 make a big difference
7 people who work as a team on a ship
8 natural living environment

b **Use the words from 5a to complete this text.**

If the Mars One TV needs to[1] ... after all their investment in this new space mission, it is going to be important to make sure that the 40 people finally[2] ... from the many thousands of[3] ... who apply are interesting to watch. That means that in addition to having the advanced skills needed to try to make a life in their new[4] ..., the hostile environment of Mars, people of the[5] ... will also have to be interesting personalities, and show their strengths and weaknesses. As they have all said goodbye to their[6] ... forever, it is likely there will be scenes of strong emotion, and that makes good TV viewing. The other question – whether the mission will have any real scientific value – is less clear. Many people are far from convinced. These[7] ... say that it is unlikely that a group of TV personalities (for that is what these Mars colonists will be) will do anything that will[8] ... our knowledge of space. What do you think?

COMPETENCE TRAINING: UNDERSTANDING A CARTOON

 When analysing a cartoon, it is important to know what the theme or subject of the cartoon is. If you can summarize the meaning of a cartoon in one sentence it will help you to identify the different elements that allow you to understand it.

Step 1: Look at the two cartoons on p. 99. Choose two of these sentences which you think best sum up each cartoon.

Colonizing planets is a great opportunity for us to develop.
Science enables us to discover new opportunities.
Through technology we can unlock the mysteries of life and the universe.
Science is a way of understanding our place in the universe.
Humanity is a dangerous species that has wrecked its planet.
If there were extraterrestrial life in the universe, it would hide from us.

Step 2: Discuss your choice with a partner.

Step 3: Write a caption for one of the cartoons. Remember it is a cartoon so it should be humorous.

SPEAKING

6 Produce an uninterrupted four-minute discourse on the two cartoons, describing and analysing them, and explaining what they say about science, our planet and space exploration.

EXAM PREPARATION
Kommunikationsprüfung
(p. 224)

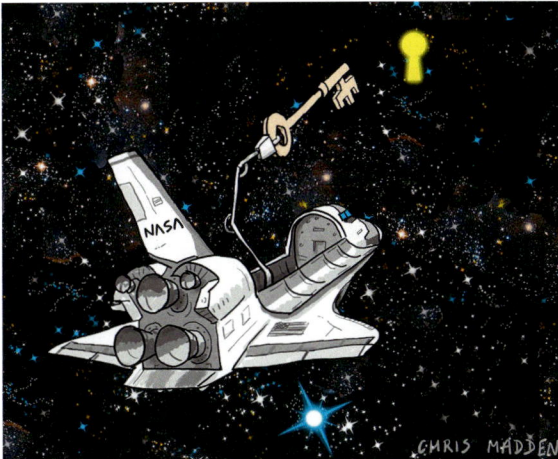

LOOKING AT LANGUAGE

G ▶ Conditionals, p. 276

7 **a** Match the sentence halves to make conditional sentences about the text.

1 If you want to apply to join the programme, ...
2 If things go wrong in space, ...
3 If you are chosen as one of the final crew members, ...
4 If the mission goes ahead, ...
5 Rickard says if you always wait until things are absolutely safe, ...
6 If you want to find out more about the mission, ...
7 If TV companies decide not to broadcast the programme, ...
8 Erica's husband knows that if she is given the chance to go into space, ...

a you'll probably never do anything in life.
b you'll need to send your CV to the company.
c the astronauts will have to wait a long time for help to arrive.
d you will have to go through years of training.
e the organisers will lose a lot of money.
f there could be huge benefits to our knowledge of the universe.
g she will definitely do it.
h you can check the information on the Mars One website.

b Complete these sentences so that they are true of you.

1 If I was part of the mission to Mars, the thing I'd find most difficult would be ...
2 If I told my friends and family I wanted to apply to join the mission, they would ...
3 If I had the chance to explore a new part of the world, ...

→ TIP BOX

Many English verbs end in
-ize or -ise (e.g. realize
and realise). The -ise
ending is only used in
Britain; the -ize ending is
used in the USA and also
in Britain. In this book
you will find both forms,
as the texts are from
different sources.

Exceptions:
· analyse (GB)
· analyze (USA)

Only -ise in both
countries:
· advertise, advise,
  compromise, improvise,
  surprise, televise

WORKING WITH WORDS

8 Rewrite the underlined expressions with one of these verbs in the appropriate form:

acclimatize | authorize | finalize | hospitalize | improvise |
prioritize | revolutionize | summarize | televise | memorize

1 The computer has <u>completely changed</u> the way we work.
2 You can't do everything, so you have to <u>decide what is most important</u>.
3 It takes a while to <u>get used to life in a new place</u>.
4 We haven't <u>completed</u> the arrangements for the programme.
5 The government <u>gave permission to</u> the company to go ahead with the mission.
6 The whole mission will be <u>shown on TV</u>.
7 I just want <u>to give a short version of</u> the key points of our discussion.
8 I didn't have time to prepare, so I <u>just made up</u> my speech.
9 I spent two hours <u>learning the text word by word</u>.
10 The people who were injured in the accident were <u>taken to hospital</u>.

WRITING

→ EXAM PREPARATION

Textproduktion (p. 223)

S ▶ Writing an essay, p. 259

9 "If humans need to use technology to escape from the world that technology has ruined, it is impossible to be optimistic about the future."

Discuss this line of reasoning in relation to space exploration.

DOING A ROLE PLAY

10 Work in groups of three. You are going to role-play a discussion between a space scientist, an explorer and a political activist about space exploration.

Space scientist: Look at File 1 below.
Explorer: Go to File 5 on page 217.
Political activist: Go to File 6 on page 217.

File 1
Space scientist
Your views are the following:
· Space exploration could provide us with the keys to the history of the universe.
· Understanding space means we will understand more about our world, too.
· The cost of space exploration is high, but the cost of NOT exploring space is higher, particularly if we need to leave the planet to survive.
· Space exploration has encouraged thousands of people to study maths and sciences, which has huge and positive results for world economies.
· Space exploration involves a great deal of international cooperation, which is one way of working towards and peaceful world.

TEXT 5 Technology and our privacy

1 Explain how these expressions relate to the pictures.

big brother | capture the moment | cut down on crime | great memories | obey the law | police state | public safety | reassure the public | road safety | spontaneous fun | warning

Worried about your privacy? Wait until the drones arrive.

Jemima Kiss

We live in an age increasingly shaped by our attitudes to, and our definition of, privacy. It is arguable whether the state of privacy itself has ever been more comprehensively and routinely challenged, and in many ways our changing relationship with technology is at the heart of this.

5 Reviewing the privacy controversies of the last few years reveals how far our sense of acceptable "inversion of privacy" has shifted. Take Facebook, its billionaire founder Mark Zuckerberg wallowing in the glory of his first decade in charge of one of privacy's biggest agents of change. Users first revolted when the site introduced the newsfeed – yet now it feels rather benign in terms of its
10 challenge to our sense of privacy, as well as being the main reason for visiting the site.

The boundary between the public and the private is porous: one person might be happy to overshare baby photos publicly, while another won't entertain being part of Facebook's semi-public "friends" discussion. Now that we have all largely
15 accepted the oversharing norm, Zuckerberg himself – who not so long ago claimed that privacy was over – seems curiously to have back-pedalled, introducing anonymous logins for some of Facebook's new apps.

Google has navigated a galaxy of privacy scandals. At one end of the spectrum, its Street View cameras have inadvertently recorded public sex acts, nose-picking,
20 and a naked man climbing in the boot of his car – and at the other end of the scale had to reassure consumers after a more prescient scandal about them sucking up personal information from unsecured wi-fi networks.

[6] **inversion** act of changing sth to its opposite (also an allusion to 'invasion of privacy')

[7] **wallow in glory** *sich im Ruhm sonnen*

[9] **benign** [bɪˈnaɪn] not dangerous

[12] **porous** *durchlässig*

[13] **overshare** make things public that should stay private

[13] **entertain sth** allow yourself to think about doing sth

[16] **back-pedal** reverse or undo sth

[19] **inadvertent** by accident

[21] **reassure sb** make sb feel less worried about sth

[21] **prescient** [ˈpresɪənt] *absehbar, voraussehbar*

[21] **suck sth up** *etw aufsaugen*

23 pledge promise

23 tech specs *technische Daten*

26 commitment promise, guarantee

27 acquisition buying or taking
possession of

39 rofl (abbr) rolling on the floor
laughing

44 social scrutiny *soziale Kontrolle*

52 snap sb take a photo of sb

52 venue a public place for an event

53 be under siege *belagert werden*

Google has pledged that Google Glass, its internet-connected tech specs, won't have image recognition switched on because of privacy concerns. "Well, never say never, but we have said we wouldn't do it," executive chairman Eric Schmidt said when I asked if that was a permanent commitment. And then there's last month's acquisition of Nest Labs, which makes ultra-smart gadgets for the home. Nest started with an internet-connected thermometer and then made a similarly wired-up smoke alarm; does this mean Google now has access to data inside your personal, physical space too?

Just as privacy isn't absolute, neither is trust. We find different levels of appropriate privacy or publicness and, as consumers, we need to trust a company only enough to give it our data. If the person using the site doesn't have any experience of revealing too much, or needing to keep some kind of issue private, that can't be a fair exchange to make. Schmidt used teenagers as an example.

"Teenagers are not legally an adult for a reason. My advice to parents would be to know their passwords and monitor what they are doing." He said that with a straight face, but it's a suggestion that will no doubt have the parents of teenagers rofling. [...]

All these developments are framed by the biggest technology story of the decade – that our online lives are accessed, monitored and stored by the UK and US security services. So we face surveillance in our online world, on our mobiles, on the street through CCTV and perhaps next in our own internet-connected smarthomes, plus social scrutiny of the parts of our lives we choose to display on social networks. Surely there can't be more to come?

Well, the next privacy scandal in waiting is the story of drones. Not military drones, but increasingly widespread use of drones for agriculture, disaster areas and emergencies, archaeology, forestry and property management, among others.

Drones are banned in London and can't be used below a certain height in residential areas. But how many uses could there be for a small, silent, fast, remote-controlled drone? How long before the first sunbathing politician is snapped on holiday? If the public is banned from a venue, or refused access to private land, or if a property is under siege from journalists, how long before a drone is used for high-quality aerial video? The next time you step outside and head off for some time alone, remember to look up.   (680 words)

From: The Guardian, 9 February 2014

WORKING WITH THE TEXT

2 a Go through the text and note down all the areas mentioned in which our privacy is being eroded.

b Decide which development you find most worrying.

WORKING WITH WORDS

3 a Complete this table based on words in the text.

	Noun	Adjective	Adverb
1	anonymity	…	…
2	argument	arguable	…
3	controversy	…	…
4	…	…	curiously
5	increase	…	…
6	…	private	…
7	residence	…	…
8	…	…	similarly

b Complete these sentences using words from above.

1 The threats to our … are becoming … serious.
2 Although there are restrictions on their use in … areas, drones are … the next big thing to worry about.
3 Companies like Facebook have been involved in some … decisions that have received lots of media attention.
4 Google's Street View turned out to be enjoyable for people with a sense of … about what other people were doing.
5 Although some companies offer … log-ins, it's almost impossible to keep your … on the internet. People can find out who and where you are quite easily.
6 Smart technology will mean that you are basically under surveillance more or less all the time at work, and … at home.

4 Complete these sentences with an "over–" or "under–" compound in the correct form.

over … | under …   come | cover | crowd | estimate | go | line | load | look

1 The number of CCTVs has been … – there are not as many as some people say.
2 As cities become more and more …, the level of crime goes up.
3 Society has … some profound changes as a result of our daily use of technology.
4 It's impossible to keep up to date with everything on the internet. We have a situation of information … now.
5 Companies have so much information on us as a result of our use of technology. This … the importance of being careful about what information you share online.
6 In addition to surveillance techniques such as CCTV, there are also police operating … in certain crime-ridden areas of town.
7 It's true there are problems with protecting privacy, but these can be … if you follow basic guidelines.
8 Because people are attracted by the convenience of technology, it is easy to … the threats to our privacy it can actually pose.

SPEAKING

EXAM PREPARATION

Kommunikationsprüfung (p. 224)

S ▸ Interpreting pictures and cartoons, p. 262

5 Produce an uninterrupted 5-minute discourse, in which you describe the cartoon and relate it to the short text and issues of privacy.

'CALL IT EXCESSIVE IF YOU LIKE, BUT NONE OF OUR GUESTS HAVE EVER PINCHED ANYTHING...'

The estimates for the number of CCTV cameras in the UK vary between 2 and 5 million. The vast majority of CCTV cameras are not operated by the UK Government, but by private companies, especially to monitor the interiors of shops and businesses. The total number of CCTV cameras operated by local governments was around 52,000 over the entirety of the UK. The average person on a typical day is seen by 70 CCTV cameras. The police use images from CCTVs in most cases of crime-solving nowadays.

EXAM PREPARATION

Kommunikationsprüfung (p. 224)

6 Using information from Topic 3, discuss the following statement with a partner.

"Advances in technology improve many aspects of life, but they also bring problems such as invasion of our privacy."

Partner A presents arguments supporting the first part of the quote.
Partner B presents arguments supporting the second part of the quote.

WRITING

EXAM PREPARATION

Textproduktion (p. 223)

S ▸ Writing an essay, p. 259

7 Explain the following quotation in relation to the text and give examples from history and literature of societies that have excessively monitored their citizens.

"All these developments are framed by the biggest technology story of the decade – that our online lives are accessed, monitored and stored by the UK and US security services." (ll. 40 – 42)

TEXT 6　Cyber crime

1　What are these people talking about?

1　"I always make a back-up just to make sure I don't lose anything."
2　"I never write them down. You could lose them, and then anything could happen."
3　"It always surprises me that so many people keep them in their back pockets. That's asking for trouble."
4　"I only left it unlocked for a minute, and that was enough. It's unbelievable!"
5　"I thought it was from a friend of mine, so I clicked it and opened it. What a mistake that was!"

First online murder will happen soon

Paul Peachey

Governments are ill-prepared to combat the looming threat of "online murder" as cyber criminals exploit internet technology to target victims, the European policing agency warned. In its most alarming assessment of the physical danger posed by online crime, Europol said it expected a rise in "injury and possible deaths" caused by computer attacks on critical safety equipment.

Police forensic techniques need to "adapt and grow" to address the dangers posed by the so-called "Internet of Everything" (IoE) – a new era of technological interconnectedness in which everything from garage doors to hospital health systems will be linked and controlled through computer networks.

The concept is behind the likely development of smart homes, cars and even cities, but police warned that the failure to protect devices properly could see them open to being hacked by outsiders to make money or to attack opponents. [...]

The former US vice-president Dick Cheney – who has a long history of heart problems – revealed last year that the wireless function had been disabled on his implanted defibrillator because of concerns that outsiders could hack the network and provoke a heart attack. The idea was used in US thriller series Homeland when Mr Cheney's fictional counterpart was murdered by a similar method. "Well, I was aware of the danger … that existed but I found it credible," he said in an interview last year. "Because I know from the experience we had and the necessity for adjusting my own device that it was an accurate portrayal of what was possible."

The Europol report also suggested the advent of new forms of extortion and blackmail through connected devices, including locking people out of their smart cars and homes before payment of a ransom. It said that new systems would increasingly rely on facial and speech recognition for security that were open to abuse without up-to-date security in place.

The opportunities for tampering with devices come amid predictions that tens of billions of devices will be connected to the internet within the next couple of decades, according to experts. [...]

Line numbers: 5, 10, 15, 20, 25

1 combat sth fight sth
1 loom *drohend anbahnen*
1 **threat** danger, menace
2 **exploit sb/sth** use sb/sth for your benefit
2 **target sb/sth** focus on sb/sth
3 assessment evaluation
3 **pose a danger** be dangerous
6 forensic techniques *gerichtsmedizinische Verfahren*
6 **adapt** change to suit sth
8 interconnectedness *Vernetzung*
12 **opponent** person or thing you are fighting against
16 defibrillator device that delivers electical energy to the heart
18 counterpart equivalent
22 advent beginning, arrival
22 extortion *Erpressung*
23 **blackmail** *Erpressung*
24 **ransom** money paid for the return of sb/sth
27 tamper with sth make changes to sth for bad reasons

31 render sth make sth different
32 vulnerability weakness, weak area
37 perpetrator person who does sth criminal
37 security breach a break in safety arrangements
39 abuse insults
43 quasi-underground *sozusagen im Untergrund*

"The IoE is inevitable. We must expect a rapidly growing number of devices to be rendered 'smart' and thence to become interconnected. Unfortunately, we feel that it is equally inevitable that many of these devices will leave vulnerabilities via which access to networks can be gained by criminals," according to the Europol threat assessment.   30

It said that flaws in one system were likely to be part of many more resulting in large numbers of victims. The complexity of technologies would make it hard to identify the perpetrators, it said. Security breaches already identified include the hacking of webcams. A couple in Texas reported that a hacker was able to shout abuse at a two-year-old after exploiting a flaw in their baby monitor.   35

The US health authorities ordered hospitals to improve security after identifying problems with 300 medical devices and amid reports that malware (malicious software) had slowed down monitors used for high-risk pregnancies.   40

"There's already this huge quasi-underground market where you can buy and sell vulnerabilities that have been discovered," said Rod Rasmussen, the president of US security firm IID. He said that while the first reported murder was yet to happen, "death by internet" was already a reality from online extortion and blackmail that has led to suicide. He said if his firm's prediction of an online murder did not come to pass in 2014, it would likely happen within the next few years.   45

"Someone could unlock your [smart] home and get in to cause harm," said Craig Spiezle, of the Online Trust Alliance, a US-based privacy and security organisation. With new technology "there's always someone in the background to exploit it", he said.   50

(661 words)

From: *The Independent,* 2 August 2015

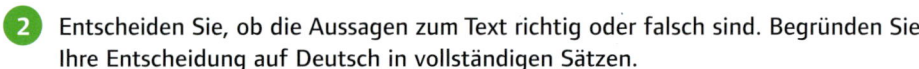

WORKING WITH THE TEXT

EXAM PREPARATION
Leseverstehen (p. 222)

S ▶ Doing comprehension tasks, p. 258

2 Entscheiden Sie, ob die Aussagen zum Text richtig oder falsch sind. Begründen Sie Ihre Entscheidung auf Deutsch in vollständigen Sätzen.

1 It is likely that people will be injured or even killed by computer attacks on safety equipment.
2 Someone hacked a computer that made former US Vice-President Cheney's implanted defibrillator stop working.
3 The hackers are inspired by TV programmes like Homeland.
4 It is expected that criminals will prevent devices from working and then extort money out of the owners so that they can use them again.
5 Hackers have been able to watch babies being born in a Texas hospital.
6 Most malware and hacking software can be bought at an underground market in the USA.

WORKING WITH WORDS

3   **a**   **Match words from A and B to form collocations.**

A	B
combat	access to
disable	crime
exploit	a danger
gain	a flaw
improve	a function
make	money
pose	security
target	victims

b   Use collocations in the correct form from the table above to complete this text.

As the Internet of Everything becomes a reality, it is likely that criminals will use the internet to ...[1] in new ways. Mostly, criminals are interested in ...[2] rather than causing physical harm. However, if they ...[3] to health equipment such as pacemakers they can ...[4] to life. Criminals generally work by trying to ...[5] in devices. The police and internet companies are of course trying to ...[6]. Individuals can also take action. In extreme cases, it may be a good idea to ...[7] on sensitive equipment so it cannot be tampered with. More practically, everyone can take steps to ...[8], such as making passwords more difficult to guess.

LOOKING AT LANGUAGE

4   **Complete these sentences so that they have the same meanings.**

1   Always change the default security settings on items such as mobiles and computers.
    It is strongly recommended that *you change the default security settings on items such as mobiles and computers.*
2   Don't write your passwords down on paper. It's asking for trouble.
    We were warned ...
3   It is highly likely that large numbers of people will be victims of cyber crime.
    It is predicted that ...
4   Unless you pay £1000 by tomorrow, you will find yourself locked out of your home.
    He threatened ...
5   It's a good idea to keep your internet security up-to-date at all times.
    You are advised ...
6   The hospital must improve security measures immediately, said the health authority.
    The health authority ordered ...
7   Some of the health equipment we use is vulnerable to hacking.
    He admitted ...
8   Because the technology is so complex, identifying cyber criminals will be very difficult.
    The article explained ...
9   One thing you can do to improve password security is to use a combination of letters and numbers.
    He suggested ...

LISTENING

2.03

→ EXAM PREPARATION
Zentrale Klassenarbeit
Hörverstehen (p. 224)

S ▶ Practising listening skills, p. 256

5 Sie hören ein Interview über Betrugsmaschen (sogenannte "scams"). Erläutern Sie, die drei beschriebenen Betrugsarten und erläutern Sie, wie diese ausgeführt werden. Kopieren Sie und vervollständigen Sie die Tabelle auf Deutsch mit Informationen aus dem Interview.

Art des Betrugs	Wie der Betrug funktioniert
…	…
…	…
…	…

SPEAKING

S ▶ Interpreting pictures and cartoons, p. 262

→ EXAM PREPARATION
Kommunikationsprüfung
(p. 224)

6 a Make notes on the cartoon below and find relevant passages in the text that relate to it.

b Produce a four-minute uninterrupted dialogue based on the cartoon. Describe and analyse the cartoon and relate it to the topic of the text.

"You know, you can do this all online now."

WRITING

→ EXAM PREPARATION
Textproduktion (p. 223)

S ▶ Writing an essay, p. 259

7 Explain the following quotation in relation to the text and give examples of things the government, the police and the individual can do to combat cyber crime.

"Governments are ill-prepared to combat the looming threat of 'online murder' as cyber criminals exploit internet technology to target victims." (ll. 1 – 2)

Mary Shelley

TEXT 7   Messing with life

WARM-UP

1 You are going to read an extract from a stage play about Frankenstein that was written a few years ago. You probably know a little about Frankenstein already. Combine the two parts to make statements.

1 The novel *Frankenstein* was first published …
2 A lot of people are surprised to learn that the novel was written …
3 Incredibly, the author started work on *Frankenstein* …
4 Parts of the story are set …
5 *Frankenstein* is not the name of the monster, but …
6 *Frankenstein* was originally written as a novel …
7 The monster is ugly because it was created …
8 Many people consider *Frankenstein* …

a to be the first science fiction story.
b from parts stolen from various dead bodies.
c in and around Geneva, where Shelley wrote the novel.
d while still in her teens.
e but has been turned into many films, and most recently a play.
f two centuries ago, in 1818.
g by a woman, the author Mary Shelley.
h of the scientist.

2 Look at the two different images of the monster.

· What do they have in common?
· What are the differences?
· Which do you prefer, and why?

left: A scene from the National Theatre's production of Nick Dear's *Frankenstein*, 2011

right: From the film *Frankenstein*, 1931

Frankenstein meets the monster

Nick Dear

Victor ascends Mont Blanc. A snowy wasteland, high in the Alps.
Victor: Are you here? Where are you? Are you here?
His cape billows in the howling wind. He has a stout stick.
                  Where are you? Show yourself, you monstrous thing!
5 *There is a sound like a great exhalation of breath, as the glacier shudders and shifts.*
Through the snowstorm the Creature is suddenly visible, standing very still on the ice. He makes a great leap towards Victor.

¹ ascend climb
³ cape *Umhang*
³ billow *sich aufblähen*
³ howl make a long loud cry like a wolf

8 muscular coordination *Muskelkoordination*

8 tissue *Gewebe*

9 suture *Naht*

10 grace elegance

11 swivel turn around quickly

11 **keep an eye on sb/sth** make sure you can see sb/sth

12 unsurpassed better or greater than any other

12 endeavour *Streben*

13 **sweat** *Schweiß*

14 **crawl** walk on your hands and knees

21 tattered torn and in pieces

21 journal diary

34 curtail sth end sth early

35 disarm sb take a weapon from sb

39 **duty** *Pflicht*

42 curse sth *etw verfluchen*

43 draw breath breathe

44 soil earth

44 clime country with a particular climate

45 archangel *Erzengel*

46 mournful very sad

46 gloom darkness

47 celestial from heaven

52 cast sb out throw sb out

53 bile *Galle*

57 refuge a place to hide

58 **whip sb** *jdn auspeitschen*

My God! Muscular coordination – hand and eye – excellent tissue – perfect balance! And the sutures have held! I failed to make it handsome, but I gave it strength and grace. 10

Victor circles the Creature. The Creature swivels to keep an eye on him.

What an achievement! Unsurpassed in scientific endeavour! God, the madness of that night – the heat, the sweat, the infusions, the moment when I saw it crawl towards me, and I – and I –

Creature: You ran away. 15

Victor: What?

Creature: You abandoned me.

Victor [stunned]: It speaks!

Creature: Yes, Frankenstein. It speaks.

Victor: You know my name? 20

The Creature hands Victor the tattered journal.

My journal!

Creature: Why did you abandon me?

Victor: I was terrified – what had I done?

Creature: Built a man, and given him life – 25

Victor: Well, now I have come to take it away –

Creature [laughs]: Oh, have you?

Victor: I have come to kill you!

Creature: To kill me? Why then did you create me?

Victor: To prove that I could! 30

Creature: So you make sport with my life?

Victor: In the cause of science! You were my greatest experiment – but an experiment that has gone wrong. An experiment that must be curtailed!

Victor runs at him and attacks him with his stick, but the Creature swiftly disarms him and throws him to the ground. 35

Creature: Be still, genius! I have a request.

Victor: Damn you, you can't have requests!

Creature: Oh, I can! Listen to me. It's your duty.

Victor: I've no duty to a murderer. 40

Creature: If I'm a murderer, you made me one.

Victor: You killed my brother! You did it, not me! – I curse the day when you drew breath. Since then I've lived in darkness.

Creature: 'Is this the region, this the soil, the clime,
Said then the lost Archangel, this the seat 45
That we must change for Heaven, this mournful gloom
For that celestial light?'

Victor [astonished]: That's *Paradise Lost*! You've read *Paradise Lost*?

Creature: I liked it.

Victor: Why? You saw yourself as Adam? 50

Creature: I should be Adam. God was proud of Adam. But Satan's the one I sympathise with. For I was cast out, like Satan, though I did no wrong. And when I see others content, I feel the bile rise in my throat, and it tastes like Satan's bile.

Victor: But this is remarkable! You are educated! And you have memory! 55

Creature: Yes, I use it to remember being hunted like a rat, running from human places, finding refuge in the woods. I use it to remember being beaten and whipped. And I was good, I wanted to be good!

Victor: Then why did you kill William?

60	Creature:	I wished to see you, and you came. Would you have come otherwise? If I had killed half of Ingolstadt, would you have come?
	Victor *[subdued]*:	Did no one show you kindness?
65	Creature:	There was an old man. He taught me many things. But he was blind, he never saw my face. He never knew I looked like this! After a year, after he'd described to me the seasons, and I'd watched them go round, one, two, three, four – when I was one year old, he said they'd take me in. The son, and his wife. A beautiful wife.
	Victor:	What happened?
	Creature:	You know what happened.
70	Victor:	Oh, God, I do.
	Creature:	I burned them. In a fire.
	Victor:	Do you feel no remorse?
75	Creature:	Remorse? When I walk through a village, the children throw stones. When I beg for food, they loose their dogs. What is the function of remorse?
	Victor:	I'm sorry, I –
	Creature:	Sorry? You're sorry? You caused this! This is your universe!
	Victor is silent.	
80		Frankenstein. Here is my request. I wish to be part of society. But no human being will associate with me. But one of my own kind – one just as deformed and horrible – she would understand – she would –
	Victor:	What, I –
	Creature:	I want a female. Built like me.
	Victor:	A female?
85	Creature:	You alone have the power to –
	Victor:	Create another brute – another monster? No, I will not, I –
	Creature:	It is my right!
90	Victor:	You have no rights. You are a slave. You want me to make you a female, so the pair of you can be wicked together? No, I will not. Torture me as much as you like, I'll never consent!
	Creature:	I will not torture you. I will reason with you. Isn't that what we do? Have a dialogue?
	Victor:	There is no dialogue with killers!
95	Creature:	Yet you'd kill me if you could! Why, you have just tried! So why is your killing justified, and mine is not?
	Victor:	I won't argue with you! My God, I'm halfway up a mountain, debating with a – a –
	Creature:	A living creature!
100	Victor:	A nothing, a filthy mass of nothing! I am your master, and you should show respect –
105	Creature:	A master has duties – you left me to die! I am not a slave. I am free. If you deny my request I will make you my enemy, I will work at your destruction, I will dedicate myself, I won't rest until I desolate your heart! *[Pause.]* I apologise. I did intend to reason. I am capable of logic. I do not think what I ask is immoderate? A creature of another sex, but as hideous as I am. If you consent, we'll disappear for ever. We'll go to the wilds of South America, and we'll build our little paradise, and live there in peace. And no human being will see us again. What do you say?
110	Victor:	I am amazed. You've learnt so much, so fast!
	Creature:	Are you proud of me?
	Victor:	Proud? No!

¹¹⁶ **yearn** want sth desperately

¹¹⁹ **detestation** hatred

¹²¹ **facilitate sth** make sth possible

¹²² **mate** a partner to share your life with

¹²⁴ **intellect** ability to think logically

¹²⁵ **inconsistent** *widersprüchlich, unstimmig*

¹²⁶ **infuriating** making you very angry

Creature:	Why not?
Victor:	Because your logic is flawed.
Creature:	Is it?
Victor:	You say you'll go abroad and disappear, yet you also say you yearn to be accepted by society. But won't you grow tired of exile? Won't you return, and try once more to live among people, only to meet with their detestation? Because that is what you will meet with. But now, when you run wild, there will be two of you, and double the destruction. Why should I facilitate this?
Creature:	Because I am lonely! Every creature has a mate. Every bird in the sky! Even you are to be married! Why am I denied the comforts you allow yourself? A moment ago you were amazed at my intellect, but now you harden your heart. Please, do not be inconsistent, I find it infuriating! All I ask is the possibility of love.

115

120

125

(1177 words)

From: Frankenstein, 2011

WORKING WITH THE TEXT

➔ **EXAM PREPARATION**
Leseverstehen (p. 222)

S ▶ Doing comprehension tasks, p. 258

3 Entscheiden Sie, ob die Aussagen zum Text richtig oder falsch sind. Begründen Sie Ihre Entscheidung auf Deutsch in vollständigen Sätzen.

1 Frankenstein taught the monster to speak.
2 Frankenstein considers his experiment a failure.
3 The creature holds Frankenstein responsible for his mistakes.
4 The creature has never been accepted by humans.
5 The creature killed for pleasure.
6 Frankenstein thinks that making a companion for the monster is not a good solution.

4 Find 4 examples of emotions expressed by the characters in the scene. Whose emotions seem more natural?

5 Answer the questions.

1 This is the first meeting of the two central figures. What makes it so important?
2 What do the two figures want?
3 Who learns most in the scene?
4 What does the scene tell us about the responsibility of scientists?
5 What makes each character a monster? In your opinion, who is more monstrous?

6 Choose 5 of these themes and explain where they feature most prominently in the scene.

revenge *Rache*

Humans have a great desire to create.
Scientists have moral responsibilities.
The desire for revenge is natural.
Humanity has a great capacity for learning.
The family is central to a happy life.
The imagination of human beings is a powerful tool.

Justice is central to a functioning society.
Judging by appearances is dangerous.
Language makes us human.
A human being is a social being not made for solitude.
Humanity is in a struggle to control nature.
Reason can control the emotions.

WORKING WITH WORDS

 7 a Copy the table and put these expressions in the right box according to whether they take "do" or "make". Then translate them into German.

a mistake | a promise | something wrong | your best | a job | an effort | what's best | a threat | your duty | good | a mess | well | progress | everything possible | the most of sth/it | friends | a noise | nothing | research | a difference

make ...	do ...	German

b Use some of the expressions from 7a to complete these sentences. Then explain whether the sentences refer to Frankenstein or the creature, and say why. Sometimes more than one answer may be possible.

1 As a scientist, I obviously ... a great deal of ... before I carried out this experiment. *Frankenstein*: As a scientist, I obviously *did* a great deal of *research* before I carried out this experiment.
2 I just want to ... with someone like me, so I have someone I can spend time together with.
3 I was wrong. I ... and now I regret it.
4 Nothing is easy. To succeed you have to ... in this life.
5 At first it was hard to hear the monster I had created because the wind ... such ...
6 My situation is awful, but I want to ... it. Otherwise my life will have been nothing but a waste.
7 I will ... you this ... : I will leave you alone, but on the condition that you create someone for me.
8 My work was unique; nobody had managed to achieve anything like this. I wanted to ... to science, and to the world. That's why I did it.

SPEAKING

8 Explain the connection between Frankenstein and the topics below, and discuss whether we can learn something from the story of Frankenstein.

GM foods | nuclear weapons | robotics | space exploration

WRITING

9 The original story of *Frankenstein* does not have a happy ending. Write an alternative version which ends well for both Frankenstein and the creature.

10 Discuss how relevant the themes of *Frankenstein* are to today's world.

EXAM PREPARATION
Textproduktion (p. 223)

S ▶ Writing an essay, p. 259

ENGLISH FOR WORK   Having an interview

WARM-UP

2.04

1 Listen to three different people talking about job interviews they attended recently.

a   What questions were they asked?

b   What were the good and bad points of each interview?

c   Who do you think made the most positive impression, and why?

INTERVIEW TIPS

2 Work in pairs. Complete this list of tips for interviews. Compare your answers with other pairs.

INFO BOX

Do

Appearance	First impressions count, so make sure you …
Preparation	To avoid a last minute rush, the night before you should check …
Knowledge	When going to interview for any company, you must find out …
Interview	Prepare answers for typical questions like … Treat the interviewers … It's not just about your experience, it's about what you can … Think of questions to ask about the company like …

Don't

Behaviour	You will probably be seated, so … You have to be in control of your body, so …
Language	Don't use …
Topics	Avoid talking about …
Character	The company is looking for a strong candidate, so don't … They will ask you about your strengths and weaknesses, but try to …
Experience	While everyone will try and show that they have experience, never …
Speaking	When an interviewer is speaking, never …

INTERVIEW QUESTIONS

 a Choose the correct preposition to complete these interview questions. Then answer them.

Yours skills

1 What do you consider your key strengths that are relevant ... this job?

Your work history

2 What previous experience do you have that is similar ... the job you have applied for?

Your ambitions

3 Where do you see yourself ... five years' time?

The employer

4 What do you know ... our company?

The job

5 What do you think the main challenge ... the job will be?

Teamwork

6 What can you contribute ... our team?

Dealing with problems

7 How do you react when you are ... pressure?

8 Can you give us an example of a time when you were faced ... a difficult situation?

Your personality, interests and activities

9 How might your friends describe you ... one word?

b Add one more question to each section above.

c Discuss what the interview wants to find out about you with each question. What would be a good/bad answer to each question.

ROLE PLAY

 Work in pairs. Choose one of the jobs below (or invent one that you would find interesting) and role-play the job interview.

Banking data input administrator _____
_____ We need computer literate staff to help with all aspects of office administration and international communications in our bank.

Educational software developer
You'll develop & manage the virtual learning environment & support learners in the use of our game-based learning technologies.

Customer service and sales advisor
Mobile phone sales staff needed for busy city-centre shop.

GM food laboratory analyst
Data analyst required for agricultural science company.

VA 4   2.05

class system *Klassensystem*
working class *Arbeiterschicht*
middle class *Mittelschicht*
upper class *Oberschicht*
privileges *Privilegien*
inherited wealth *geerbtes Vermögen*
social mobility *soziale Mobilität*

multiculturalism *Multikulturalismus*
immigrant *Einwanderer/-in*
colony *Kolonie*
racism *Rassismus*
overrun sth *etw überschwemmen*
Commonwealth *Gemeinschaft der Länder des ehemaligen Britischen Weltreichs*
immigrate *einwandern*
immigrant background *Migrationshintergrund*
urban *städtisch*
multicultural *multikulturell*
expand *sich erweitern*
attract sb *jdn anlocken*
suffer racial discrimination *unter Rassendiskriminierung leiden*
abuse *Beschimpfung*
originate from *stammen aus*
religious extremist *religiöse/r Extremist/in*
treat sb with suspicion *jdm mit Misstrauen begegnen*
threat *Bedrohung*

ethnically diverse *ethnisch vielfältig*
Native American *amerikanische/r Ureinwohner/in*
settler *Siedler/in*
slave *Sklave/in*
plantation *Plantage*
slavery *Sklaverei*
mistreatment *schlechte Behandlung*

foundation *Gründung*
Declaration of Independence *Unabhängigkeitserklärung*
discriminate against sb *jdn diskriminieren*
ethnic diversity *ethnische Vielfalt*
melting pot *Schmelztiegel*

BACKGROUND INFORMATION

The class system in the UK

Britain is often thought of as a country with a system of three distinct classes: the working class, traditionally working in manual labour or factories; the middle class, characterized by office jobs and professional careers; and the upper class, enjoying all the privileges of private education and inherited wealth. Increased social mobility and changing work patterns have meant that these traditional categories have become outdated. 5

Multiculturalism in Great Britain

Beginning in the1950s, many immigrants came to Britain from its former colonies like India and the West Indies. Some Britons felt their country had become overrun with immigrants, and incidents of racism became common. In 1983 laws were passed which made it harder for people from Commonwealth countries to immigrate to Britain. 10
Today about 13 % of the population of the United Kingdom was born abroad. Most people with immigrant backgrounds live in London or one of the other large cities, making urban Britain very multicultural. 15
Since the European Union expanded in 2004 to include several Eastern European states, workers from these countries have been attracted to Britain by its liberal employment rules for EU citizens.
Immigrants from the West Indies or African countries often suffered racial discrimination, but in recent years the focus for abuse has turned towards the Muslim minority, who originate mostly from Pakistan and Bangladesh. A small minority of religious extremists has meant that Muslim Asian families, many of whom have lived in the UK for several generations, are now treated with suspicion and are seen as a threat to the British way of life. 20 25

The United States – a nation built by immigrants

The USA was ethnically diverse from the very beginning. The land was originally home to various Native American tribes. In the 17th century, settlers started to arrive from European countries, particularly Britain, but also Holland, France and Spain. As their numbers grew, they brought in slaves from Africa to work on cotton and tobacco plantations, and they forced the natives off their tribal lands. Slavery and the mistreatment of the Native Americans are sources of bitterness and shame in the USA even today. 30
Ever since its foundation in 1776 with the Declaration of Independence, the USA has been a destination for wave after wave of immigrants from all over the world, each one feared and discriminated against by the immigrants that came before them. In their hearts, however, Americans know that their country is a nation of immigrants, and the USA welcomes them like no other. The enormous ethnic diversity in American society has led the country to be called a "melting pot" – where diverse peoples come together to create one 35 40

common American national identity. However, many Americans now prefer to think of their country as a "salad bowl" – where diverse cultural heritages can live side by side.

45 Ethnicity in modern America

Whereas European immigrants were able to enjoy "Life, Liberty and the pursuit of Happiness" on their arrival in the USA, African-Americans have had a long struggle for equality, even after slavery was finally abolished in 1863. They continued to suffer from segregation, particularly in the southern
50 states, economic oppression and racial discrimination. It wasn't until 1964 that these "Jim Crow" laws were finally struck down as a result of the Civil Rights movement under leaders such as Dr Martin Luther King.
Hispanics recently overtook African-Americans as the largest ethnic minority, and they are the fastest-growing ethnic group in the USA. They
55 often face prejudice and many Americans want stricter immigration control because they feel that immigrants – particularly Mexicans – are taking jobs away from blue-collar workers. Mexicans make up the largest number of illegal immigrants to the USA, many of them illegally crossing the long border.
60 White Americans still make up most of the American upper class, but members of other races are clearly moving up in society. The most notable example was the election of Barack Obama as US president. The USA has extreme wealth and extreme poverty but, according to "The American Dream", even a dishwasher can become a millionaire.

65 Gender equality

Women make up 50 % of the population, but women's rights are not guaranteed in many countries in the world. Women still don't have equal economic or political opportunities in most countries. Feminism has done a lot in western countries to close the gender gap but it will be a long time
70 before gender stereotypes are a thing of the past.

Non-ethnic minorities

Minority groups, such as the mentally or physically disabled are protected in Britain by equal opportunity legislation. The situation for gays and lesbians has also improved in recent years. Before 1967, homosexual activity was
75 illegal in Britain. Civil partnerships for gays and lesbians have been possible since 2004 and same-sex marriage became a reality in 2014. Homosexuality is still rejected on moral or religious grounds by many conservative
80 politicians, particularly in the United States.

---

national identity *Nationalbewusstsein*
salad bowl *Salatschüssel*

pursuit of happiness *das Streben nach Glück*
African-American *Afro-Amerikaner/in*
struggle *Kampf*
equality *Gleichberechtigung*
abolish *abschaffen*
segregation *Rassentrennung*
economic oppression *wirtschaftliche Unterdrückung*
"Jim Crow" laws *Gesetze zur Rassendiskriminierung*
strike down *aufheben*
Civil Rights movement *Bürgerrechtsbewegung*

Hispanic *Hispano-Amerikaner/in*
ethnic minority *ethnische Minderheit*
prejudice *Vorurteil*
immigration control *Grenzkontrolle*
blue-collar *in Arbeiterberufen*
illegal immigrant *illegale/r Einwanderer/in*
move up in society *gesellschaftlich aufsteigen*
poverty *Armut*
the American Dream *der Amerikanische Traum*

gender equality *Gleichberechtigung der Geschlechter*
women's rights *Frauenrechte*
equal opportunities *Chancengleichheit*
feminism *Feminismus*
close the gender gap *geschlechtsspezifische Unterschiede beseitigen*
gender stereotype *geschlechtsspezifisches Klischee*

minority *Minderheit*
mentally/physically disabled *geistig/körperlich behindert*
equal opportunity legislation *Gleichbehandlungsgesetz(e)*
gay *schwuler Mann*
lesbian *lesbische Frau*
homosexual *homosexuell, gleichgeschlechtlich*
civil partnership *eingetragene Lebenspartnerschaft*
same-sex marriage *gleichgeschlechtliche Ehe*
homosexuality *Homosexualität*
on moral/religious grounds *aus moralischen/religiösen Gründen*

1 Find highlighted words and phrases in the text that match these definitions.

1 special rights or advantages that a particular person or group of people has
2 no longer useful because of being old-fashioned
3 unfair treatment of people who belong to a different race
4 unfair, cruel or violent treatment of somebody
5 person or thing that is likely to cause trouble or danger, etc
6 person who is owned by another person and is forced to work for them
7 connected with people who do physical work in industry
8 a fixed idea or image that many people have of a particular type of person or thing, but which is often not true in reality

2 a Match words from box A to ones in box B to make collocations from the text.

A	B
class	background
immigrant	system
immigration	control
gender	gap
women's	group
minority	legislation
equal opportunities	rights

b Use each collocation in a sentence, showing what it means.

3 Complete the sentences using a suitable noun form of the verbs in the box.

discriminate | employ | immigrate | legislate | mistreat | segregate | suspect

1 Many Native Americans are still bitter about the … of their ancestors as the United States expanded westwards across the continent.
2 The descendants of African slaves suffered racial … in many southern states until the "Jim Crow" laws were struck down.
3 After World War II many … from the West Indies came to seek work in Britain.
4 The new arrivals to the UK often found … in factories or driving buses.
5 The Muslim minority in the UK is sometimes treated with … following terrorist attacks by religious extremists.
6 The "Jim Crow" laws were supposed to make African-Americans in the southern USA "equal but separate", but they were, in fact, just another form of racial … .
7 Equal opportunities … has made it easier for mentally and physically disabled people to find work in the UK.

G ▶ Adjectives and adverbs, p. 279

4 a Change these adjective-noun collocations into adverb-adjective collocations.

1 ethnic diversity   – *ethnically diverse*
2 social mobility
3 mental disability
4 physical abuse
5 racial prejudice

b Work with a partner. Write sentences for your partner, using the adjective-noun collocations. Your partner then rewrites the sentence using the adverb-adjective collocation.

The USA enjoyed <u>ethnic diversity</u> right from the very beginning.
The USA was <u>ethnically diverse</u> right from the very beginning.

TEXT 1   The class system in the UK

WARM-UP ....

1   Look at the photo and do the following tasks with a partner.

- Say what jobs you think the people in the photo have.
- Who do you think probably left school at 16? Who left at 18?
- Which of them probably did further training or went to university?
- Rank the jobs according to how much you think each person earns.
- Which jobs would you consider "working class", which "middle class", which "upper class"?

Compare your list with another pair and explain your answers. Do you agree?

2   With the other pair, make a list of the factors that you think determine "social class".

The new seven social classes in the UK

People in the UK now fit into seven social classes, a major survey conducted by the BBC suggests.

It says the traditional categories of working, middle and upper class are outdated, fitting 39 % of people.

5   It found a new model of seven social classes ranging from the elite at the top to a "precariat" – the poor, precarious proletariat – at the bottom.

More than 161,000 people took part in the Great British Class Survey, the largest study of class in the UK.

Class has traditionally been defined by occupation, wealth and education. But this
10   research argues that this is too simplistic, suggesting that class has three dimensions – economic, social and cultural.

The BBC Lab UK study measured economic capital – income, savings, house value – and social capital – the number and status of people someone knows.

The study also measured cultural capital, defined as the extent and nature of
15   cultural interests and activities.

---

5 **range from sth to sth else** cover a variety of different things from sth to sth else

5 **elite** a small group of people in a society, etc. who are rich, powerful and influential

6 **"precariat"** (from: precarious proletariat) people at the bottom end of the social scale, who have an uncertain (= precarious) economic status

9 **occupation** job

10 **simplistic** making sth seem less complicated than it really is

12 **economic capital** how much money in total you have available

12 **savings** the money you save in a bank

13 **social capital** the amount and type of friends you have

14 **cultural capital** the amount of cultural activities you take part in

15 **extent** *Umfang*

¹⁷ **distinct from sth** clearly different and separate from sth

¹⁹ **established** respected or well-known because it has existed for many years

²⁰ **gregarious** *gesellig*

²² **distinctive** having characteristics that makes sth different and easily noticed

²² **prosperous** rich and successful

²³ **distinguished by sth** *durch etw gekennzeichnet sein*

²³ **isolation** the state of being alone or lonely

²⁴ **apathy** the feeling of not being interested in sth

²⁵ **affluent** rich, well-off

²⁸ **deprived** without enough food, money, education, etc. to live a happy and comfortable life

³⁰ **emergent** new and still developing

³⁷ **at the opposite extreme** *am anderen Ende der Skala*

⁴⁰ **conventional** normal, traditional, usual

The new classes are defined as:

- Elite – the most privileged group in the UK, distinct from the other six classes through its wealth. This group has the highest levels of all three capitals

- Established middle class – the second wealthiest, scoring highly on all three capitals. The largest and most gregarious group, scoring second highest for cultural capital

- Technical middle class – a small, distinctive new class group which is prosperous but scores low for social and cultural capital. Distinguished by its social isolation and cultural apathy

- New affluent workers – a young class group which is socially and culturally active, with middling levels of economic capital

- Traditional working class – scores low on all forms of capital, but is not completely deprived. Its members have reasonably high house values, explained by this group having the oldest average age at 66

- Emergent service workers – a new, young, urban group which is relatively poor but has high social and cultural capital

- Precariat, or precarious proletariat – the poorest, most deprived class, scoring low for social and cultural capital

The researchers said while the elite group had been identified before, this is the first time it had been placed within a wider analysis of the class structure, as it was normally put together with professionals and managers.

At the opposite extreme they said the precariat, the poorest and most deprived grouping, made up 15% of the population.

The sociologists said these two groups at the extremes of the class system had been missed in conventional approaches to class analysis, which have focused on the middle and working classes.

Professor of sociology at Manchester University, Fiona Devine, said the survey really gave a sense of class in 21st-century Britain. […]

PRECARIAT This is the most deprived class of all with low levels of economic, cultural and social capital. The everyday lives of members of this class are precarious.

TRADITIONAL WORKING CLASS This class scores low on all forms of the three capitals although they are not the poorest group. The average age of this class is older than the others.

EMERGENT SERVICE WORKERS This new class has low economic capital but has high levels of "emerging" cultural capital and high social capital. This group are young and often found in urban areas.

TECHNICAL MIDDLE CLASS This is a new, small class with high economic capital but seem less culturally engaged. They have relatively few social contacts and so are less socially engaged.

NEW AFFLUENT WORKERS This class has medium levels of economic capital and higher levels of cultural and social capital. They are a young and active group.

ESTABLISHED MIDDLE CLASS Members of this class have high levels of all three capitals although not as high as the Elite. They are a gregarious and culturally engaged class.

ELITE This is the most privileged class in Great Britain. They have high levels of all three capitals. Their high amount of economic capital sets them apart from all other classes.

"It shows us there is still a top and a bottom, at the top we still have an elite of very wealthy people and at the bottom the poor, with very little social and cultural engagement," she said.

"It's what's in the middle which is really interesting and exciting, there's a much more fuzzy area between the traditional working class and traditional middle class.

"There's the emergent workers and the new affluent workers who are different groups of people who won't necessarily see themselves as working or middle class.

"The survey has really allowed us to drill down and get a much more complete picture of class in modern Britain."

The researchers also found the established middle class made up 25 % of the population and was the largest of all the class groups, with the traditional working class now only making up 14 % of the population.

They say the new affluent workers and emergent service workers appear to be the children of the "traditional working class," which they say has been fragmented by de-industrialisation, mass unemployment, immigration and the restructuring of urban space.

Researchers asked a series of questions about income, house value, savings, cultural and leisure activities and the occupation of friends. They were able to determine a person's economic, social and cultural capital scores from the answers and analysed the scores to create its class system.   (684 words)

From: the website of the BBC, 3 April 2013

46 engagement being involved with sth

48 fuzzy *unscharf*

59 fragment sth break sth

60 de-industrialisation
Deindustrialisierung

60 restructuring the act of organizing sth in a new or different way

---

WORKING WITH THE TEXT ....

3 Entscheiden Sie, ob die Aussagen zum Text richtig oder falsch sind. Begründen Sie Ihre Entscheidung auf Deutsch in vollständigen Sätzen.

1 The new Great British Class Survey has categorized people into seven new classes according to occupation, wealth and education.
2 A person's "cultural capital" can be determined from how often they take part in cultural activities and what sort of events they are.
3 The "established middle class" is the most culturally interested group according to the new survey.
4 The "traditional working class" group contains a lot of older people who own their own homes.
5 Previous surveys of class have concentrated mainly on the upper and working classes.
6 The "emergent service workers" and the "new affluent workers" now identify much more closely with the middle classes.
7 Immigration, redevelopment of inner-cities and changes in the job market have led to a decrease in the numbers in the "traditional working class".

EXAM PREPARATION
Leseverstehen (p. 222)

S ▶ Doing comprehension tasks, p. 258

4 Im Text werden drei Faktoren genannt, die als Grundlage für die Umfrage verwendet wurden. Erstellen Sie eine Liste dieser Faktoren und erklären Sie, was man darunter versteht. Formulieren Sie vollständige deutsche Sätze.

EXAM PREPARATION
Leseverstehen (p. 222)

S ▶ Doing comprehension tasks, p. 258

5 Match the statements to one of the "new" seven social classes.

"We have loads of friends and there's always someone round our house at the weekend. Our jobs allow us a little luxury every now and then, but we can't spend, spend, spend all the time. We have to keep something left over for the mortgage and the school fees."

a

"In the old days, everyone in our street worked at the car factory. The factory closed down years ago and our kids had to find other jobs. It's just not the same around here any more."

b

"Me? Got any hobbies? You must be joking? If there's any money left over at the end of the week, we have a few drinks in the pub."

c

"I work hard at my job ... programming takes a lot of time, but it pays good money. I don't have any time for going out with friends, and theatre and stuff like that doesn't interest me."

d

"We go skiing in Switzerland and we spend the summer in the Bahamas. Yeah, we can afford that – and the opera and dinner parties. We send our kids go to the right schools, of course, and get good jobs. We know the right people, so that's no problem."

e

"My job doesn't pay all that much, but I have masses of friends and we do loads of stuff together ... parties, gigs, you name it, there's always something going on."

f

"Yes, I work hard and play hard ... at the end of a working week I love to go out with my friends, but we don't just go to the pub, we go to concerts and plays as well, you know. Thank God I can afford it on my salary."

g

SPEAKING ....

6 a Discuss in groups: Is there a similar class system in Germany?

Think about the influence your family background has on …
· your choice of future job.
· the cultural or sporting events you like to attend.
· the circle of friends you socialize with.

b Report your findings to the class.

WORKING WITH WORDS

7 **a** Complete the table with adjectives derived from the nouns and verbs. The adjectives are all in the text.

G ▸ Adjectives and adverbs, p. 279

Noun	Adjective	Verb	Adjective
economy	…	prosper	…
society	…	interest	…
culture	…	excite	…
wealth	…	establish	…
privilege	…	deprive	…

b What are the two adjectives from *economy*, *interest* and *excite*? Write three sentences to show the difference in their meaning.

LOOKING AT LANGUAGE

8 Complete the sentences with a suitable adverb and adjective form of the words in brackets.

G ▸ Adjectives and adverbs, p. 279

1 The middle class is usually thought to be the most *socially active* group in society. (*active · social*)
2 The upper class, on the other hand, is said be very … . (*cultural · active*)
3 The working class was always considered the most … . (*deprived · economical*)
4 This conventional analysis of class is … and the categories it uses are … . (*high · simplistic /outdated · total*)
5 A recent survey of social, cultural and economic capital has shown up some … facts about social classes in Britain. (*absolute · fascinating*)
6 The new analysis has painted a … picture of class to the traditional one. (*complete · different*)
7 For example, the elite is still … but there is a new category, the precariat, which is … . (*enormous · rich /desperate · poor*)

LISTENING

2.06

9 In der Radiosendung „The World Today" hören Sie ein Interview mit Wendy Cheun von der World Development Bank über die wachsende Mittelschicht in der ganzen Welt. Vervollständigen Sie die unten stehenden Sätze auf Deutsch.

→ EXAM PREPARATION
Zentrale Klassenarbeit Hörverstehen (p. 224)

S ▸ Practising listening skills, p. 256

1 Laut UNO und OECD zählt jemand zur Mittelschicht, wenn er/sie …
2 Wer mehr als genug verdient, um sich und seine/ihre Familie zu ernähren, kann …
3 Im Verhältnis zur Mittelschicht in Nordamerika wird 2030 die Mittelschicht in Asien …
4 China besitzt nicht nur den größten Automarkt der Welt, sondern ist auch …
5 Mit geschätzten 450 Millionen Menschen in der Mittelschicht im Jahre 2030 wird Indien …
6 Wenn sich die Entwicklung in den nächsten Jahrzehnten fortsetzt, werden Verbesserungen der Lebensstandards eintreten, ähnlich denen…
7 In den letzten 20 Jahren hat der weltweite Wirtschaftsboom erreicht, dass …
8 Eine neue, selbstbewusste Mittelschicht wird wahrscheinlich Folgendes fordern: …

COMPETENCE TRAINING: STRUCTURING AN ESSAY

10 An essay should follow a logical structure, with an introduction to the topic of the essay, the main part (or "body") of the text, and a conclusion. The introduction and conclusion should each be one paragraph. For the body of the text you will need several paragraphs: each main argument for or against should be presented in a separate paragraph. Always save the most important argument until last to make the most impact.

a Look at these notes for an essay on the statement below. Match the missing items (a–h) to the numbers.

"There is no such thing as social class. Anybody can become anything they want, as long as they work hard and follow their dream."

Essay structure:

Introduction:	• reference to statement • example of "classless society", e. g. …^{1} • question for essay: …^{2}
Arguments for:	• some societies v. traditional and class-conscious: e. g. …^{3} – v. difficult to climb ladder for social/religious reasons – …^{4} • poor people have limited access to education – …^{5} – poor/immigrant families have less access to / time for extra activities, books, cultural events
Arguments against:	• social mobility easier now in most societies – …^{6} • film, music, sport: …^{7} – examples?? • further education now open to all; …^{8}
Conclusion:	• sum up the arguments • state your own opinion

a accent in UK a sign of background
b cost of university fees, e. g. in UK/USA
c does this apply everywhere?
d Indian caste system
e more opportunities to become rich and famous
f not just for middle and upper classes
g royalty marry commoners
h USA: "dishwasher to millionaire"

b **Compare your answers with a partner. Add your own ideas and arguments, if you wish.**

WRITING

11 **Write a comment on the following statement.**

There is no such thing as social class. Anybody can become anything they want, as long as they work hard and follow their dream.

EXAM PREPARATION
Textproduktion (p. 223)

S  Writing an essay, p. 259

TEXT 2 Minorities in Britain

Muslims observe Friday prayer at the London Central Mosque, April 2015

WARM-UP

1 **a Discuss these questions with a partner:**

1 Which different cultures can be found in your region or neighbourhood?
2 Do you have social contact with people of other cultures? If so, where?
3 How important are the following aspects in your culture? Explain why?

caring for elderly relatives | charity | daily religious practice | financial/professional success | respect for parents | romantic love | tolerance

b Report your ideas to the class.

What is it like to be a Muslim in Britain today?

We asked Muslim bloggers to share their own experiences and opinions about living as a Muslim in Britain today. […]

1   – ? –

Sadiya Ahmed, 40, lives in London. In 2010, she founded Everyday Muslim, a
5 *project creating an archive of British Muslim life, education and culture. […]*

Today, global events have transformed what being a Muslim means from a private to a public experience. We are faced with divisive and worrying questions from our children asking, "What does Jihad mean?" or "What is a Shia or a Sunni?" Why or how these questions have been created is debatable. What I do know is
10 being Muslim in essence can never change, only the political rhetoric that surrounds it.

To be a Muslim is a deeply personal and spiritual sense of being that is individual to every Muslim. Of the Sunnah teachings, my favourite is to smile. Smiling is considered a form of charity in Islam and epitomises what being a Muslim means
15 to me. […] Growing up as a Muslim in London was a unifying experience expressed through actions of kindness and consideration for neighbours, the elderly and each other – regardless of faith.

6 transform sth change sth completely

7 divisive causing people to disagree with each other

9 debatable questionable

10 in essence *im Wesentlichen*

10 rhetoric speech or writing that is intended to influence people

12 spiritual connected with religion

14 epitomise sth *etw verkörpern*

16 consideration quality of being sensitive to other people's wishes and feelings

2   – ? –

Fatima Adam […] left France eight years ago as a result of racism and islamophobia she experienced there. […]

How extraordinary it was, when I arrived in London eight years ago to discover women wearing headscarves at the town hall, in airports or in shopping centres. I felt it was not only acceptable, but also normal to be Muslim. It does not seem a big deal to have Muslim MPs in Britain.

My sister sent me a text message earlier this year to let me know she had seen a woman wearing a headscarf working in a clothes shop in the heart of Paris. I am French, so for me that was such news – it marked a sign of progress.

I feel free to be Muslim here. There are facilities available in some work places to perform daily prayers, I can attend diverse religious lectures and activities in locations shared with non-Muslims – such as universities.

3   – ? –

Hira Amin, 27 lives in London. She is completing a PhD at Cambridge University […].

The condescending remarks I receive for following a religion. I have actually had people say to me: "I don't believe in religion, I believe in science." As if I believe in Mickey Mouse! Just because I believe in God does not make me a less rational human being. The prevalent belief that science answers all questions is astonishing. As western philosophers of science point out, science cannot answer questions surrounding the issues of morality, meaning and purpose. Science can only study the physical world, not the metaphysical. Religious people do not reject science; we believe there is more to life than just physical matter. It is interesting to note that this issue is specifically European, as the US – the most practising Christian country in the industrialised world – has greater respect for religion.

4   – ? –

Shaista Aziz is a freelance journalist and stand-up comedian […] living between Islamabad, Pakistan and the UK. […]

Given the amount of time the media spends discussing "the Muslims" most people remain ill informed and ignorant about Islam and Muslims. Of course there is a correlation?

Headlines are sensational or distorted and reporting is often deeply racist. This impacts directly on the lives of British Muslims across the UK. Some of the stories that are emerging are painful and disturbing. Visible Muslim women in particular are bearing the brunt of Islamophobic abuse – verbal and physical – on the streets, at schools and colleges, in the office and online. […]

5   – ? –

Muhammad Akhter, 32, is a doctor in Essex. […]

Muslims have made contributions to British society in many ways: culinary, fashion, economic and medical. Yet this is still a young community finding its feet. We have many internal problems to contend with (illiteracy, sectarianism and identity crises to mention a few) and a few external ones that have a tendency to grab the headlines. None are insurmountable, but sometimes they can feel that way.

65 The Muslim community can be an innovative, socially conscious and energising presence in British society, creating and developing deep links to many of the rapidly growing economies of the world. On the other hand, it could slide into being a persecuted, marginalised and mistrusted minority that is a drain on resources and social cohesion. How things turn out will depend not only on whether we are able to move forward in a way that allows us to remain true to our faith and still be productive British citizens, but also on whether the wider

70 community will allow us the time and space to do so.

6 – ? –

Asif Iqbal, 32, lives in Keighley, Yorkshire and works for Sainsbury's as an IT Analyst. […]

75 I would say I am a British citizen because I was born here and grew up around the culture and values of the majority of Britons. However, I am familiar with my origin and would not disregard this to be more "British" in terms of my values, lifestyle or beliefs. I would not proudly be called "British", but this is not due to arrogance or ignorance; it's simply due to the prejudiced view of certain people living in Britain who feel that this is not "our" country because we have a

80 somewhat different lifestyle and upbringing to theirs.

We are free to live how we want within the boundaries of the UK law but are we not free to choose what is morally right for us? There is more to being British than looking, sounding and dressing a certain way. We can still be educated, successful, socially active and know the A to Z of royal history. As Britons we share some

85 values and recognise that there are commonalities between us which bring us together. Why do people refuse to accept differences if the one thing Britain prides itself upon is being multicultural?   (1190 words)

From: *The Guardian*, 9 July 2014

63 innovative introducing new ideas or ways of doing sth

63 energising providing new energy

66 **persecute sb** treat sb in a cruel and unfair way, esp. because of their race, religion or political beliefs

66 **marginalise sb** put sb in a position in which they have no power

66 **mistrust sb** not trust sb

67 social cohesion *sozialer Zusammenhalt*

76 disregard sth treat sth as unimportant

76 **values** beliefs about what is right and wrong

78 **prejudiced** having an unreasonable dislike of sb/sth, especially based on race, religion, sex, etc.

80 **upbringing** *Erziehung*

81 boundary border

82 **moral** concerned with principles of right and wrong behaviour

85 commonality *Gemeinsamkeit*

WORKING WITH THE TEXT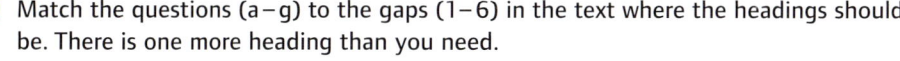

2 Match the questions (a–g) to the gaps (1–6) in the text where the headings should be. There is one more heading than you need.

a Do you consider yourself to be British? Why or why not?
b Have you ever experienced intolerance or abuse because you are a Muslim?
c How do you feel the media depicts Muslims and Islam and how does this affect you?
d What are the best aspects of being a Muslim in Britain today?
e What are the worst aspects of being a Muslim in Britain today?
f What contributions do you think Muslims have made to British society?
g What does it mean to you to be Muslim?

3 Which person(s) mention(s) which aspects of Muslim life in Britain?

a media stereotypes of Islam/Muslims
b the spiritual aspect of Islam
c the practice of Islam in daily life
d discrimination against Muslims
e the positive contributions of Muslims to British society
f problems within the Muslim community
g the question of identity of British Muslims

4 Answer these questions on the text.

1 What aspect of Islam does Sadiya Ahmed remember from her childhood?
2 Why does Fatima Adam prefer living in Britain to living in France?
3 Why does Hira Amin think Europe has less respect for religion than the USA?
4 How does Shaista Aziz say Muslims are affected by the way the media report stories concerning Islam?
5 What, according to Muhammad Akhter, are the options facing the Muslim community in Britain today?
6 Does Aziz Iqbal feel proud to be British? Why (not)?

SPEAKING

5 Work in small groups and discuss the following questions.

· What negative aspects of life as a Muslim in Britain does the text mention?
· Is the situation for Muslims different (for example, better or worse) in Germany?

WORKING WITH WORDS

6 Rewrite these sentences replacing the underlined phrases with a word from the box.

arrogance | charity | experience | ignorance | Islamophobia | morality | values

1 A group of young men shouted racial abuse at him. It was a terrible thing to happen to him.
2 Acts of kindness, such as giving to your neighbour, are an important part of Islam.
3 Fear and hatred of Muslims is a fact of life in many European countries.
4 Science is not able to answer questions of what is right or wrong, or about the meaning of life.
5 I'm not prepared to give up my ideas of what is important just because I live in a different country.
6 His proud, unpleasant behaviour came from his belief that he was more important than other people.
7 She couldn't believe their lack of knowledge about some of the basic beliefs of Islam.

Mosque in England

SPEAKING

7 Work with a partner and do the following tasks. (Partner A look here; Partner B look at File 7 p. 218.)

1 Look at your bar chart carefully and make notes. Prepare to present your findings to your partner.
2 Describe and analyse your bar chart to your partner.
3 With your partner, compare the two charts and discuss how they relate to the debate about the integration of ethnic minorities.

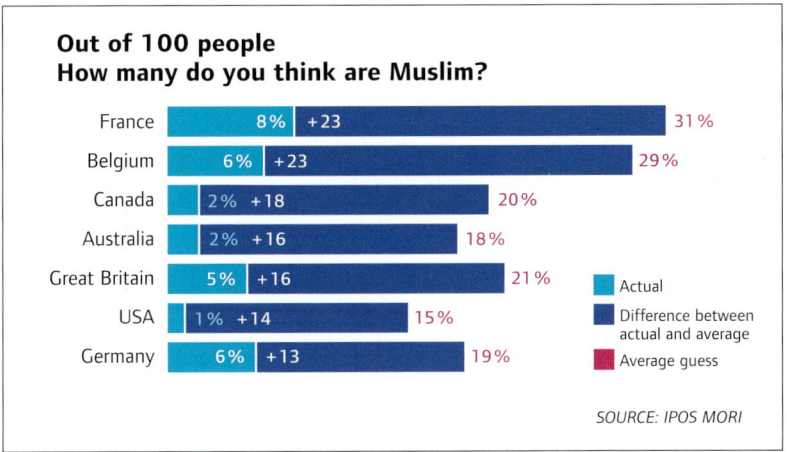

Out of 100 people
How many do you think are Muslim?

	Actual	Difference between actual and average	Average guess
France	8%	+23	31%
Belgium	6%	+23	29%
Canada	2%	+18	20%
Australia	2%	+16	18%
Great Britain	5%	+16	21%
USA	1%	+14	15%
Germany	6%	+13	19%

■ Actual
■ Difference between actual and average
■ Average guess

SOURCE: IPOS MORI

→ **EXAM PREPARATION**
Kommunikationsprüfung (p. 224)

S ▶ Interpreting charts and graphs, p. 263

WRITING

X **8** Explain the quotation below in relation to the text and give examples of the discrimination Muslims might experience in Western countries. Also think of possible solutions.

"There is more to being British than looking, sounding and dressing a certain way. […] Why do people refuse to accept differences if the one thing Britain prides itself upon is being multicultural?" (ll. 86–87)   *100 words*

→ **EXAM PREPARATION**
Textproduktion (p. 223)

S ▶ Writing an essay, p. 259

TEXT 3   Civil rights in the USA

1 The photo shows a famous milestone on the long road to equality for African-Americans. Look at the photo with a partner.

a What do you think is happening in the photo?

b When and where do you think the photo was taken?

c Choose one of the people in the photo and describe what they are feeling.

d What basic right is the person in the middle of the photo exercising?

e Why do you think this event was significant?

f What do you think the terms "segregation" and "desegregation" mean?

The long road to equality

a "We hold these truths to be self-evident, that all men are created equal, that they are endowed by their Creator with certain unalienable Rights, that among these are Life, Liberty and the pursuit of Happiness."

b "For fifteen years I have resided in Washington, and while it was far from being a paradise for colored people, when I first touched these shores, it has been doing its level best ever since to make conditions for us intolerable. As a colored woman I might enter Washington any night, a stranger in a strange land, and walk miles without finding a place to lay my head. Unless I happened to know colored people who live here or ran across a chance acquaintance who could recommend a colored boarding house to me, I should be obliged to spend the entire night wandering about. Indians, Chinamen , Filipinos, Japanese and representatives of any other dark race can find hotel accommodations, if they can pay for them. The colored man alone is thrust out of the hotels of the national capital like a leper."

c "Our flag is red, white and blue, but our nation is a rainbow – Red, Yellow, Brown, Black and White – we're all precious in God's sight. America is not like a blanket – one piece of unbroken cloth, the same color, the same texture, the same size. America is more like a quilt – many patches, many pieces, many colors, many sizes, all woven and held together by a common thread. The White, the Hispanic, the Black, the Arab, the Jew, the woman, the Native American, the small farmer, the businessperson, the environmentalist, the peace activist, the young, the old, the lesbian, the gay and disabled make up the American quilt."

d "I am the son of a black man from Kenya and a white woman from Kansas. I was raised with the help of a white grandfather who survived a Depression to serve in Patton's Army during World War II and a white grandmother who worked on a bomber assembly line at Fort Leavenworth while he was overseas. I've gone to some of the best schools in America and lived in one of the world's poorest nations. I am married to a black American who carries within her the blood of slaves and slaveowners – an inheritance we pass on to our two precious daughters. I have brothers, sisters, nieces, nephews, uncles and cousins, of every race and every hue, scattered across three continents, and for as long as I live, I will never forget that in no other country on Earth is my story even possible."

[line numbers: 5, 10, 15, 20, 25, 30]

---

1 hold sth to be self-evident consider sth to be obvious and needing no further explanation

2 be endowed with sth naturally have sth (e.g. a particular quality)

2 unalienable that cannot be taken away from you

5 do your level best make a great effort

6 intolerable completely unacceptable

9 chance acquaintance sb you meet by chance

10 boarding house cheap and basic hotel

10 be obliged to do sth be forced to do sth you do not want to do

13 thrust sb push sb suddenly or violently in a particular direction

13 leper Aussätzige/r

15 precious loved or valued very much

15 blanket Decke

17 quilt a colourful blanket made of many small pieces of cloth

17 patch a small piece of cloth

18 weave sth (past: woven) etw weben

18 thread Faden, Garn

20 environmentalist sb who works or protests to protect the environment

20 peace activist sb who works or protests for peace

21 disabled Behinderte/r

24 Patton George S. Patton (1885–1945), US World War II general

25 bomber assembly line factory for making bombers

25 Fort Leavenworth military base in Kansas

28 inheritance Erbe

30 hue colour

e "The democratic doors of equal opportunity have not been opened wide to Negroes. In the Deep South, Negro youth is offered only one-fifteenth of the educational opportunity of the average American child. The great masses of Negro workers are depressed and unprotected in the lowest levels of agriculture and domestic service, while the black workers in industry are barred from certain unions and generally assigned to the more laborious and poorly paid work. Their housing and living conditions are sordid and unhealthy. They live too often in terror of the lynch mob; are deprived too often of the Constitutional right of suffrage; and are humiliated too often by the denial of civil liberties."

f "I had crossed the line of which I had so long been dreaming. I was free; but there was no one to welcome me to the land of freedom, I was a stranger in a strange land, and my home after all was down in the old cabin quarter, with the old folks, and my brothers and sisters. But to this solemn resolution I came; I was free, and they should be free also; I would make a home for them in the North, and the Lord helping me, I would bring them all there."

g "I'm black, I don't feel burdened by it and I don't think it's a huge responsibility. It's part of who I am. It does not define me."

35 domestic service working as a servant in sb's home
37 assign sb to sth give sb a particular job to do
37 laborious involving hard work
38 sordid dirty and unpleasant
39 **right of suffrage** the right to vote
40 **humiliate sb** make sb feel ashamed or stupid and lose the respect of other people
40 denial refusal to allow sb to have sth they have a right to expect
40 **civil liberties** the rights people have under a constitution
44 old folks old people
45 solemn resolution *feierlicher Beschluss*
48 burden sb make sb carry a heavy responsibilty

WORKING WITH THE TEXT

2 a Work with a partner. Look at the dates, photos and texts below and match them to the quotations above. Say which clues in the text help you to decide.

1776 The Declaration of Independence

This document was one of the first to insist equal rights for all. While it did not refer to slaves, it did become a source of inspiration to abolitionists in the 19th century.

1850 Harriet Tubman

Born a slave, she managed to escape to Pennsylvania. She organised the "Underground Railroad", which helped many slaves escape to Canada.

1906 Mary Church Terrell

Born the daughter of former slaves, she was one of the first African-American women to earn a university degree. She became an activist for civil rights.

1938 Mary McLeod Bethune

She was an educator and civil rights activist who founded a private school for African-American students. She was an adviser to President Roosevelt.

1984 Jesse Jackson

A preacher and civil rights activist, he twice stood as a candidate for the Democratic presidential nomination in the 1980s.

2000 Oprah Winfrey

Probably the most influential talkshow host in the USA, she is also an important media mogul.

2009 Barack Obama

In 2009 he was inaugurated as the 44th President of the USA, becoming the first African American to hold the post.

131

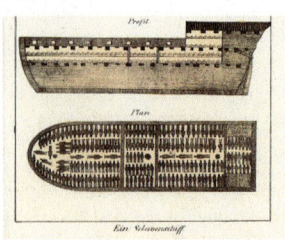

A slave ship

Slaves picking cotton

A lynching

b Compare your answers with another pair. Do you agree?

c Make a list of the forms of discrimination mentioned in the texts that African-Americans have experienced.

WORKING WITH WORDS

3 a Match words from box A to words from box B to make collocations.

A	B
civil	civil rights	economic	equal	living	race	racial	universal		activist	conditions	discrimination	liberties	relations	suffrage	opportunity	oppression

b Now use your answers from 3a to complete this text.

The history of …[1] between White Americans and descendents of former slaves has been marked by …[2]. Although slavery was formally abolished by the Emancipation Declaration of 1863, the …[3] of many African-Americans in the south of the USA continued to be extremely poor for decades and they suffered a great deal of …[4]. They were also denied …[5] and so were unable to vote in elections. It was not until the 1960s, when …[6] such as Dr Martin Luther King and Rosa Parks began their peaceful protests that …[7] for African Americans became a real possibility. African-Americans are now active in all areas of American society, but even 50 years later …[8], when compared to the white population, is still a long way off and discrimination is a fact of life for many African-Americans.

VIEWING

4

4 You are going to watch a video about people who took part in a Civil Rights march in Selma, Alabama, in 1965.

a Before watching: Think about the social and living conditions of Black Americans in the Deep South in the 1960s, and collect ideas on the board.

- What forms of discrimination do you think they faced?
- What forms of protest were available to them?

b While watching: Make notes on the following questions.

- What were the marchers protesting about?
- What was the response of the authorities?
- Where did most of the marchers come from?
- How would you describe the attitude of the marchers?

c After viewing: Discuss your reaction to the video.

- Do you find any of the speakers hard to understand? Why? Does that affect the impact of the video?
- What similarities can you find with the situation in the photo in the warm-up?

Marching on Selma

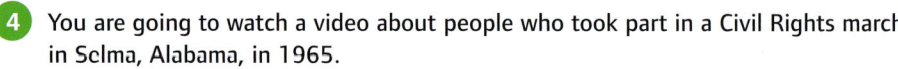

Marching on Washington

LOOKING AT LANGUAGE

5 Rewrite this political speech replacing the underlined phrases with "the + adjective" forms, as in the example.

"I dream that one day people who are old and young people will be able to live together in harmony. In my dream, people with lots of money and people without any money are working together to eliminate poverty. I see a vision where people with disabilities and those who can't see have access to every public building in this fair city. I can see a city where people without homes and people without employment prosper together, where those who are strong help weak people, people who are sick and those who are lonely in the long march to a better future."

I dream that one day the old and ...

GIVING A PRESENTATION

→ EXAM PREPARATION
Präsentationsprüfung (p. 225)

S ▶ Giving a presentation, p. 264

6 Choose one name or historical event from the list below OR one of the people quoted in the text (pp. 130–131). Prepare a five-minute presentation about this person/event, explaining how they fit into the history of the Civil Rights Movement in the USA.

- the slave trade
- the Underground Railroad
- The Emancipation Proclamation
- Jim Crow laws
- lynching/lynch justice
- Rosa Parks
- the March on Washington
- Martin Luther King

Rosa Parks

CREATING A TIMELINE

7 Using the information from the presentations, the whole class can now create a timeline showing the road towards equality in the USA.

- Make a long poster to hang on the wall around the class. Use photos, quotes and short texts from your presentations to illustrate each event or personality on the timeline.
- Make sure that the events are in the correct chronological order.
- Look for recent events in the news that illustrate the current situation for African-Americans in the USA.

Martin Luther King

TEXT 4   Hispanics and the American Dream

WARM-UP

epitome [ɪ'pɪtəmi] perfect example of sth

crock sth that is not true

I am the epitome of what the American Dream basically said. It said you could come from anywhere and be anything you want in this country. That's exactly what I've done.
Whoopi Goldberg (actress)

The American dream is a crock. Stop wanting everything. Everyone should wear jeans and have three T-shirts, eat rice and beans.
Bill Hicks
(comic and social critic)

I have spent my life judging the distance between American reality and the American dream.
Bruce Springsteen (singer)

The American Dream is one of success, home ownership, college education for one's children, and have a secure job to provide these and other goals. *Leonard Boswell (politician)*

1 Work in small groups and discuss the following questions.

- What do you understand by the term "The American Dream"? How would you define it?
- How do the quotes and the photos relate to "The American Dream"?
- Do you think "The American Dream" is mainly just that, a dream, or do you think it can become reality?

2.07

Hispanics' faith in the American Dream is still unbroken

faith strong religious belief
[1] **on the road** *unterwegs*
[3] **painter and decorator** sb whose job is painting buildings, walls, etc.
[8] **graduate** successfully complete a university course

When Venezuelan-American Luis Herrera gets home from a week on the road – sometimes in the early hours of the morning – his wife Maria is always waiting up for him in their small house in Trenton, New Jersey. Luis now works as a painter and decorator all over New Jersey and Pennsylvania and his small one-man business makes just enough money to keep his family and pay off the house.

On the living-room wall, there's a photo of Luis and Maria's daughter Marisa holding her diploma from NY City University – the first person in the Herrera family to graduate from college. The second came only a year ago, when their younger daughter Sara graduated from Penn State University.

5

When Luis gets home and looks at the photos, he knows that all the sacrifices he and Maria have made over the years have been worth it.

"It hasn't been easy," he reflects, thinking about some of their earlier difficulties. "We couldn't speak a word of English. It was all so that our kids could succeed in America."

The Herreras are typical of the attitude of many Hispanic immigrants to the USA. They are determined to succeed and have enormous faith in the power of hard work and education to raise their family from humble beginnings to a comfortable lifestyle. In fact, the faith of Hispanic families in the American Dream is far greater than that of Whites or African Americans – as a recent national survey by the Washington Post and the University of Virginia shows.

The Hispanics' positive attitude is partly due to the fact that poor immigrants start with nothing and expect to make huge sacrifices in order to provide a better life for their families. They look to a brighter future consisting of a better and safer place to raise their kids and a higher standard of living for their family – all earned through hard work and education. They may be in bad shape today, but they have faith that things will improve.

According to the survey, 64% of Hispanics believe that a college diploma is a major part of the American Dream, compared to only half of Whites and African Americans. Moreover, six out of ten believe that their children will enjoy a better lifestyle than they do – a percentage matched by African Americans, but more than double the number of Whites who think their kids will climb the ladder even higher.

Problems

The Herreras' journey began in Caracas, Venezuela more than 25 years ago. They were high-school sweethearts who got married as soon as they graduated. Luis wanted to become an accountant and Maria a teacher, but neither of them could afford to continue their education – and Maria soon became pregnant. Luis ended up driving a taxi instead and after a couple of years, they took the decision to leave their beloved country and make a new start – for the sake of their children – in the USA.

"I was very frustrated," Luis recalls. "But I had a cousin in Philadelphia and he told me there was lots of work available."

They ran into difficulties right from the start. Their first unfurnished one-room apartment cost $700 a month. Neither of them could read English so they never knew if the mail contained an overdue notice or the threat of eviction. Luis' first job as a taxi driver hardly paid the rent and he suffered ethnic slurs from passengers in silence.

Their girls accepted the change as a new adventure. They quickly picked up the new language, started making progress at school and bringing home good grades. They were different from some Hispanic classmates, who didn't take classes seriously and were in danger of dropping-out.

Maria and Luis raised their children in a strict but loving way – and the two girls grew up in the knowledge that their parents had sacrificed everything for their success. However, Luis didn't like them socializing in the unfamiliar, liberal society of their new home.

10 sacrifice *Opfer*
12 reflect think about sth
16 determined *entschlossen*
17 humble *bescheiden*
21 attitude the way that you think and feel about sb/sth
23 consist of sth be formed from sth
25 be in bad shape not be healthy or economically successful
31 climb the ladder rise socially
36 accountant *Buchhalter/in, Steuerberater/in*
41 beloved loved very much
41 frustrated feeling annoyed because you cannot achieve what you want
43 unfurnished without any tables, bed, chairs, etc.
45 overdue notice *Mahnung*
45 threat *Bedrohung*
45 eviction the act of forcing sb to leave a rented flat
46 slur insult
51 drop out leave High School or college without graduating
54 socialize meet and spend time with people in a friendly way, e.g. at a party
54 unfamiliar unknown

58 **hang out** spend a lot of time somewhere or with friends
62 **take sth for granted** *etw als selbstverständlich ansehen*

"I was always worried that something would happen to them. I never slept until they came home," Luis said. "What good are a big house and a big car if your kids end up taking drugs and hanging out with gangs?"

"I would get straight A's, and he still pushed me to work harder," Marisa adds. "It was really hard to take his advice, but now I understand. Our parents came here for us. If we had failed, they would have failed as well."

"Some Americans don't see the great advantages they have here. They take things for granted," says Sara, now aged 23 and studying for a PhD in psychology. "Our parents taught us that if we want someting, we have to work for it." (792 words)

60

WORKING WITH THE TEXT

→ **EXAM PREPARATION**
Leseverstehen (p. 222)

S ▶ Doing comprehension tasks, p. 258

2 Entscheiden Sie, ob die Aussagen zum Text richtig oder falsch sind. Begründen Sie Ihre Entscheidung auf Deutsch in vollständigen Sätzen.

1 Marisa Herrera is the only person in the family who has a university degree.
2 Many Hispanic immigrants to the USA believe that they can improve the living standards of their family by working long hours and succeeding at school.
3 Most African-Americans don't believe that their children will enjoy a higher standard of living than they currently do.
4 Luis and Maria Herrera left their home country because they could not achieve their dreams there.
5 Marisa and Sara Herrera had a difficult time at school in the USA and were in danger of dropping out.
6 Marisa Herrera thinks that her parents were too strict with her.

→ **EXAM PREPARATION**
Leseverstehen (p. 222)

S ▶ Doing comprehension tasks, p. 258

3 In dem vorliegenden Text werden vier Gründe genannt, warum Einwanderer aus Lateinamerika optimistisch in die Zukunft blicken. Erstellen Sie eine Liste dieser Gründe. Formulieren Sie vollständige deutsche Sätze.

WORKING WITH WORDS

4 **a** Find adjectives in the text that go with these nouns to make collocations.

attitude | beginnings | future | lifestyle | sacrifices | standard of living | work

positive attitude, …

b Use the collocations from 4a to write a short paragraph explaining Hispanic immigrants' attitude to the American Dream.

5 a You can *take a decision* or *make a decision*, but which of the words and phrases in the list are only used with "make" and which with "take"?

Copy the table below and write the phrases in the correct list.

… a big difference   … enough money
… a huge sacrifice   … good progress
… a new start   … sb's advice
… after your father   … sth for granted
… drugs   … sth seriously

make	*a decision (BE)*
	…
take	*a decision (AE)*
	…

b Work with a partner. Write five sentences for your partner that use the verb "make" or "take" and one of the phrases from the list above. Leave out the phrase, so that your partner has to guess what it is. Partner A: write phrases with "make"; Partner B: write phrases with "take".

They made … to leave their home country and emigrate to America.
– They made a decision to leave …

LOOKING AT LANGUAGE

6 Complete the text with the correct *-ing* form or *to*-infinitive form of the verb in brackets.

G ► The gerund and infinitive, p. 276

The Herrera's decided …[1] (leave) Venezuela because they both couldn't afford …[2] (continue) their education after high school. They didn't enjoy …[3] (live) in the USA at first but they refused …[4] (let) their problems stop them from …[5] (follow) their dream. Maria practised …[6] (speak) English with her daughters but she badly missed …[7] (meet) her friends and family in Caracas.
Luis encouraged his daughters …[8] (work) hard at school and he admits to sometimes …[9] (put) a lot of pressure on them to achieve good grades. He didn't allow them …[10] (go) to parties because he was trying …[11] (keep) them away from drugs and other bad influences.
Maria and Luis don't regret …[12] (leave) Venezuela and they expect …[13] (see) their daughters living the comfortable lifestyle they never had. Their girls have promised not …[14] (let) them down.

WRITING

7 Read the following quote from Ted Cruz, a US Republican senator. Write a comment on the statement, saying whether you agree or disagree with it.

EXAM PREPARATION
Textproduktion (p. 223)

"We need to remain a nation that doesn't just welcome but that celebrates legal immigrants who come here seeking to pursue the American Dream."

S ► Writing an essay, p. 259

TEXT 5   Gender equality

1 **a** Before reading the text, discuss in small groups what you understand by the following terms.

feminism | gender equality | gender stereotypes

b Report your findings to the class.

Gender equality is your issue too

Emma Watson

¹ launch sth start sth

² galvanize sb to do sth *jdm den Anstoß geben etw zu tun*

³ advocate sb who speaks in favour of sb/sth

⁴ tangible able to be touched and felt

⁷ synonymous with the same meaning

¹² gender-based *geschlechtsspezifisch*

¹² assumption belief that something is true although there is no proof

¹³ bossy always telling people what to do

¹⁵ sexualize sb make sb seem sexually attractive

¹⁵ certain elements of the press (hier:) *die Boulevardpresse*

Today we are launching a campaign called "HeForShe." […] This is the first campaign of its kind at the UN: we want to try and galvanize as many men and boys as possible to be advocates for gender equality. And we don't just want to talk about it, but make sure it is tangible.

I was appointed six months ago and the more I have spoken about feminism the   5
more I have realized that fighting for women's rights has too often become synonymous with man-hating. If there is one thing I know for certain, it is that this has to stop.

For the record, feminism by definition is: "The belief that men and women should have equal rights and opportunities. It is the theory of the political, economic and   10
social equality of the sexes."

I started questioning gender-based assumptions when at eight I was confused at being called "bossy," because I wanted to direct the plays we would put on for our parents – but the boys were not.

When at 14 I started being sexualized by certain elements of the press.   15

When at 15 my girlfriends started dropping out of their sports teams because they didn't want to appear "muscly."

When at 18 my male friends were unable to express their feelings.

20 I decided I was a feminist and this seemed uncomplicated to me. But my recent research has shown me that feminism has become an unpopular word. Apparently I am among the ranks of women whose expressions are seen as too strong, too aggressive, isolating, anti-men and, unattractive.

Why is the word such an uncomfortable one?

25 I am from Britain and think it is right that as a woman I am paid the same as my male counterparts. I think it is right that I should be able to make decisions about my own body. I think it is right that women be involved on my behalf in the policies and decision-making of my country. I think it is right that socially I am afforded the same respect as men. But sadly I can say that there is no one country in the world where all women can expect to receive these rights.

30 No country in the world can yet say they have achieved gender equality.

These rights I consider to be human rights but I am one of the lucky ones. My life is a sheer privilege because my parents didn't love me less because I was born a daughter. My school did not limit me because I was a girl. My mentors didn't assume I would go less far because I might give birth to a child one day. These 35 influencers were the gender equality ambassadors that made me who I am today. They may not know it, but they are the inadvertent feminists who are changing the world today. And we need more of those.

And if you still hate the word, it is not the word that is important but the idea and the ambition behind it. Because not all women have been afforded the same rights 40 that I have. In fact, statistically, very few have been.

In 1995, Hilary Clinton made a famous speech in Beijing about women's rights. Sadly many of the things she wanted to change are still a reality today. But what stood out for me the most was that only 30 per cent of her audience were male. How can we affect change in the world when only half of it is invited or feel 45 welcome to participate in the conversation?

Men – I would like to take this opportunity to extend to you a formal invitation. Gender equality is your issue too. Because to date, I've seen my father's role as a parent being valued less by society despite my needing his presence as a child as much as my mother's.

50 I've seen young men suffering from mental illness unable to ask for help for fear it would make them look less "macho" – in fact in the UK suicide is the biggest killer of men between 20 – 49 years of age; eclipsing road accidents, cancer and coronary heart disease. I've seen men made fragile and insecure by a distorted sense of what constitutes male success. Men don't have the benefits of equality 55 either.

We don't often talk about men being imprisoned by gender stereotypes but I can see that they are and that when they are free, things will change for women as a natural consequence. If men don't have to be aggressive in order to be accepted, women won't feel compelled to be submissive. If men don't have to control, 60 women won't have to be controlled.

Both men and women should feel free to be sensitive. Both men and women should feel free to be strong … It is time that we all perceive gender on a spectrum not as two opposing sets of ideals. If we stop defining each other by what we are not and start defining ourselves by what we are, we can all be freer and this is 65 what HeForShe is about. It's about freedom. […]   (850 words)

22 isolating separating sb socially from other people
25 male counterpart *männliches Pendant*
32 **sheer privilege** *absolutes Privileg*
35 **ambassador** *Botschafter/in*
36 **inadvertent** done by accident
39 **afford sb with sth** provide sb with sth
41 **women's rights** *Frauenrechte*
44 **affect sth** cause sth; bring about sth
45 **participate in sth** take part in sth
46 **extend sth to sb** give/offer sth to sb
51 **suicide** *Selbstmord*
52 **eclipse sth** make sth seem unimportant by comparison
53 **coronary heart disease** *koronare Herzerkrankungen*
53 **fragile** easily broken or destroyed
53 **distorted** changed out of shape, so that it is no longer true
54 **constitute sth** be considered to be sth
54 **benefit** advantage
59 **feel compelled to do sth** feel that you have to do sth
59 **submissive** willing to accept sb else's authority without question
61 **sensitive** able to understand other people's feelings
62 **perceive** understand or think of sth in a particular way

WORKING WITH THE TEXT

2 a Work with a partner. Partner A: make a list of "gender-based assumptions" about women that the text mentions; Partner B: make a list of "gender-based assumptions" about men from the text.

   b Exchange the ideas you have noted down with your partner.

WORKING WITH WORDS

3 Find words in the text that match these definitions. (They are in the same order as in the text.)

1 a belief that sth is true although there is no proof for it
2 polite behaviour towards sb that you think is important
3 sth that you are proud and lucky to have the opportunity to do
4 an experienced person who advises and helps sb with less experience
5 sth that you want to do or achieve very much
6 to take part in or become involved in sth
7 weak and easily broken or destroyed
8 a result of sth that has happened
9 willing to accept sb else's authority without question

4 Explain the <u>underlined</u> phrases from the text in your own words.

1 fighting for women's rights has too often <u>become synonymous with man-hating</u> (ll. 6–7)
2 I started <u>questioning gender-based assumptions</u> (l. 12)
3 I think it is right that <u>socially I am afforded the same respect</u> as men. (ll. 27–28)
4 I've seen men made fragile and insecure by <u>a distorted sense of what constitutes male success</u>. (ll. 53–54)
5 It is time that we all <u>perceive gender on a spectrum</u> not as two opposing sets of ideals. (ll. 62–63)

5 a What are the opposites of these words? (They are all in the text.) Copy the table and write them in the correct column.

able | attractive | comfortable | complicated | equal | equality | popular | secure

im-	in-	ir-	un-

   b Add the opposites of these words to your table. Find at least two more entries for each column.

effective | famous | human | perfect | personal | possible | regular | relevant | responsible | sensitive

LOOKING AT LANGUAGE

6 Rewrite these sentences using either a present or past participle to replace the underlined words.

1 I've seen young men <u>who suffer</u> from mental illness.
I've seen young men suffering from …
2 I've seen men <u>who have been made</u> insecure by gender stereotypes
I've seen men made insecure by …
3 Many men believe that any work <u>that involves</u> cooking is for women only.
4 I have several actress friends <u>who have been turned</u> into sex objects by the media.
5 I know many female film stars <u>who are paid</u> only a fraction of their male counterparts.
6 I know many male film stars <u>who are defined</u> by their macho appearance.
7 I would like to pay tribute to the many gender ambassadors <u>who help</u> to make the world a better place.
8 Gender stereotypes are a problem <u>that affects</u> both men and women.

G ▸ Relative clauses and contact clauses, p. 280

LISTENING

7 Sie hören eine Präsentation des *Global Gender Gap Report*, der jedes Jahr vom Weltwirtschaftsforum veröffentlicht wird. Hören Sie die Präsentation und beantworten Sie die Fragen auf Deutsch in Stichworten.

1 Welche zwei Faktoren werden vom *Global Gender Gap Report* gemessen?
2 Welche Faktoren in einem Land werden vom *Global Gender Gap Report* <u>nicht</u> gemessen?
3 Welche Länder befinden sich an der Spitze der Rangliste?
4 Welcher Nachteil entsteht für ein Land, in dem die weibliche Bevölkerung nicht am Wirtschaftsleben teilnimmt?
5 Welche zwei Fragen in Bezug auf Gleichberechtigung stellen sich jetzt für die Länder an der Spitze der Rangliste?
6 Welche Schritte müssen die Länder in der Mitte und am Ende der Rangliste unternehmen?

🎧
2.08

EXAM PRACTICE
Zentrale Klassenarbeit Hörverstehen (p. 224)

S ▸ Practising listening skills, p. 256

SPEAKING

8 **a** Work in groups of four. Collect reasons why the distribution of wealth and resources between men and women might be unequal.

b Discuss the reasons in your group: Do some of them only apply to industrialized countries or only to developing countries? Or do they all apply to any society?

c Report your findings to the class.

GIVING A PRESENTATION

9 Choose an English-speaking country and research on the Internet how this country performed in the original 2005 report and the most recent report. Present your findings to the class, describing how the country's gender gap has developed between 2005 and now.

EXAM PREPARATION
Präsentationsprüfung (p. 225)

S ▸ Giving a presentation, p. 264

SPEAKING

EXAM PREPARATION
*Kommunikationsprüfung
(p. 224)*

S ▶ Interpreting pictures and
cartoons, p. 262

10 Work with a partner: Partner A looks at this page; Partner B looks at File 8 on p. 218.

a Produce a five-minute uninterrupted discourse based on the cartoon about gender assumptions.

b Listen to you partner describe and analyse his or her cartoon

c Discuss whether you think the cartoons are relevant to today's society and what changes might be made to improve the situation of women.

DOING A ROLE PLAY

11 Work with a partner. Partner A is a Hollywood film producer, Partner B is a famous female film star (or her male agent). Look at the information in the chart below and agree a salary for your next film. The film producer wants to pay as little as possible, the star (or her agent) wants to earn the same amount as the male stars.

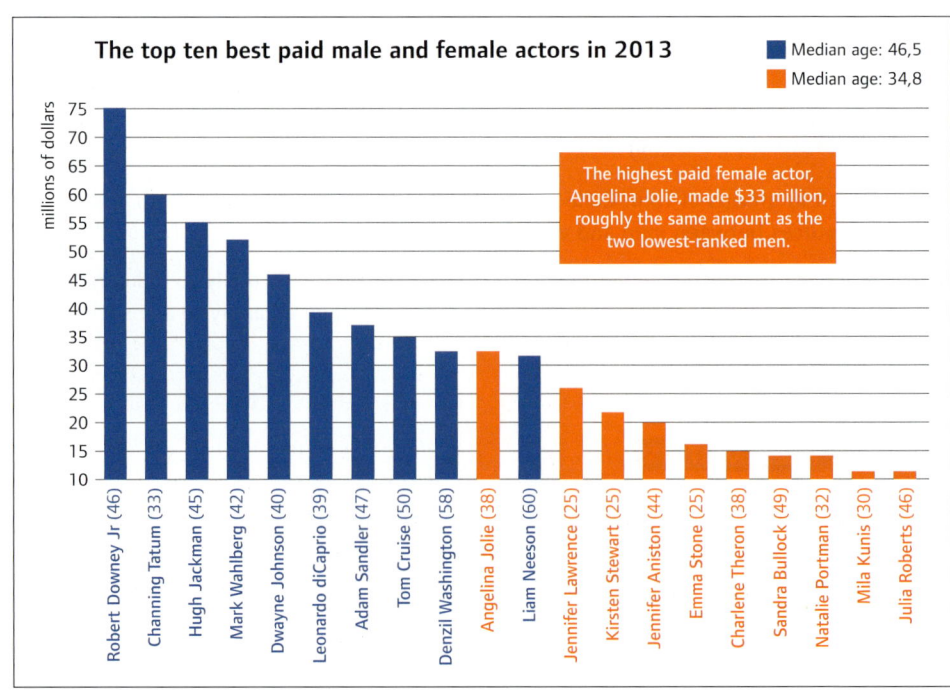

TEXT 6 Gay rights

WARM-UP

1 **Work in small groups and answer these questions.**

- What is discrimination?
- Why do people discriminate against other people?
- What personal characteristics may cause discrimination?
- What are the signs that someone is being discriminated against?
- What can you do if you are being discriminated against.

Note down your answers, as you will need them later.

The anguish of coming out

Darren Devine

Former Wales rugby captain Gareth Thomas has revealed the depth of his anguish over the gay taunts he suffered after coming out five years ago.

In his new autobiography Proud, Thomas tells how the reaction of Castleford fans after he came out in 2009 was the "manifestation of my worst nightmare". Thomas, who came close to killing himself while grappling with his sexuality, was then a Crusaders rugby league player and turned out for the club against Castleford at the Tigers' ground, the Jungle, in March 2010.

Fans berated Thomas with homophobic chants during the fixture and the club was later fined £40,000.

Thomas, 40, said: "This wasn't 'banter'. It wasn't the ranting of an isolated homophobe. It was an abusive chant taken up by a couple of hundred people in a crowd of just under 6,000, who stood on the steeply banked terraces and had decided to belittle me and everything I stood for.

"It didn't happen once, but three times. Castleford officials would later claim two of the chants were drowned out by public address announcements. They weren't – they were replayed on a tape loop in my brain for the rest of the match, and for months afterwards.

"Even today, I need only close my eyes to recall the braying ignorance of those cowards, who sought refuge in anonymity and sheer weight of numbers. It was a form of mass bullying which made bile rise to my throat."

The book also features a moving collection of letters Thomas, from Bridgend, received after coming out. One from a social worker told of a promising young rugby league player whose life spiralled out of control as he struggled to reconcile himself to his sexuality. By 18 he had stopped playing rugby and was having problems with drink and the police. He later suffered a "total mental breakdown"

2 anguish severe unhappiness
2 taunt insult
3 **come out (of the closet)** no longer hide the fact that you are homosexual
6 manifestation a sign that sth exists
8 grapple with sth struggle with sth
8 **sexuality** feelings and activities connected with a person's sexual desires
9 turn out (for a team) play a match for a team
12 berate sb speak angrily to sb
12 homophobic chants *schwulen-feindliche Gesänge*
13 fixture match
14 banter friendly jokes
14 ranting loud and angry comments
14 isolated *einzelne/r*
15 homophobe sb who has a strong dislike/fear of homosexuals
16 steeply banked terraces *steile Zuschauertribüne*
17 belittle sb make sb seem unimportan
20 tape loop *Tonbandschleife*
22 bray make a noise like a donkey
23 **coward** sb who has no courage
24 seek refuge in sth look for protection / hide somewhere
24 **anonymity** state of remaining unknown to most other people
24 **bullying** use of strength or power to frighten or hurt weaker people
24 bile *Galle*
27 spiral out of control *außer Kontrolle geraten*
27 reconcile yourself to sth make yourself accept an unpleasant situation because it is not possible to change it

30 bouts a short period of an illness

32 resume sth start doing sth again

34 strike a chord einen Nerv treffen

34 **stuck in the closet** unable to admit to being homosexual

37 hideous ugly, horrible

37 selfish only thinking of oneself

38 deception the act of deliberately making sb believe sth that is not true

39 motivational making sb want to do sth, especially sth that involves hard work

40 pretence Anschein

42 self-pity Selbstmitleid

and experienced "major bouts of depression". But the letter tells how Thomas' coming out "had a huge impact on him" and he intended to start playing rugby again. It reads: "Suddenly he seems to think that he can resume his life after seven years of what he describes as 'hell'. I have no doubt he can. Your story has struck a huge chord with many people who are stuck in the closet, limiting their potential to be happy."

Early on in the book Thomas, who knew he was gay from his late teens, admits he was "hideously unfair" and "terribly selfish" towards his ex-wife Jemma by maintaining the deception. [...]

The 6ft 3in retired sports star, who now spends his time giving motivational talks to youngsters, writes: "The pretence of a normal marriage kept my secret safe. Jemma was getting nothing out of the arrangement. I was being hideously unfair, terribly selfish, yet, at the moment of crisis, I was consumed by self-pity: '****. People are going to know something's wrong now. Everything I have hidden so well for so long is going to be discovered. For the first time in my life, I'm on my own'."

(547 words)

From: the website of WalesOnline, 11 September 2014

WORKING WITH THE TEXT

➔ **EXAM PREPARATION**

Leseverstehen (p. 222)

S ► Doing comprehension tasks, p. 258

2 Entscheiden Sie, ob die Aussagen zum Text richtig oder falsch sind. Begründen Sie Ihre Entscheidung auf Deutsch in vollständigen Sätzen.

1 Gareth Thomas decided to reveal he was gay after fans shouted abuse about him during a match.
2 Six thousand people chanted homophobic abuse at him during the match in Castleford.
3 Castleford club was fined £40,000 because of the chants aimed at Gareth Thomas.
4 Gareth Thomas could still hear the chants ringing in his head months after the incident.
5 Gareth Thomas suffered from depression because of his sexuality when he was a teenager.
6 His autobiography has inspired other gay people to come out of the closet.
7 Gareth Thomas got married to keep his sexuality a secret from his friends and colleagues.
8 He was more concerned about how his wife would react to his secret than about what would happen to him when he came out.

SPEAKING

3 Discuss these question in groups of four and report your findings to the class:

· How many examples of gay sports stars can you think of?
· Do you know any openly gay people in the world of film or politics?
· Why do you think sexuality is still a problem in many areas?
· Why are there pressures on gay people in the public eye to hide their sexuality?

WORKING WITH WORDS

4   **a**   **Find words in the text that match these definitions. (They are in the same order as in the text.)**

1   how you behave as a result of sth that has happened
2   having a strong dislike of gay people
3   rude and offensive
4   lack of knowledge or information about sth
5   try very hard to do sth when it is difficult or there are lots of problems
6   showing signs of being good or successful
7   state of feeling very sad and without hope
8   qualities that exist and can be developed

b   **Complete this paragraph with words from 4 a.**

Chester was a young man with a …[1] career as a professional footballer ahead of him. However, in his early 20s he started to …[2] with serious bouts of …[3]: not because he was gay but because he was afraid of what the …[4] of some of the fans and other players might be if he came out of the closet. Crowds at football matches were often …[5] towards players from visiting teams, but he was much more scared of …[6] chants if they knew that he was gay. He read Gareth Thomas' autobiography and was amazed at the …[7] of a section of the crowd about how their insults could hurt him. However, Gareth's example gave him the strength to realize his own …[8] and fulfill his dream.

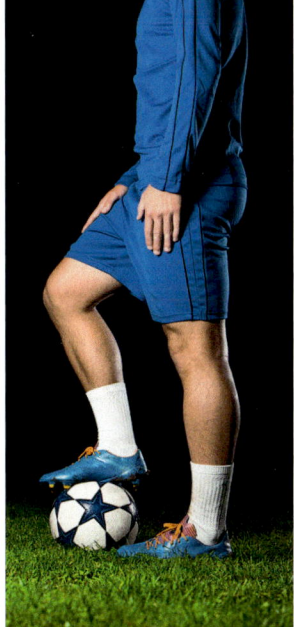

5   **Like all languages, English has many idioms.**

"To come out [of the closet]", meaning "to publicly say that you are gay", is an example from the text of an idiomatic expression.

Complete the sentences below with suitable idiomatic phrases from the box and explain what they mean. (You may have to make small changes.) Are there similar phrases in German?

as fit as a fiddle | blow the whistle | call the tune | face the music | jazz sth up | ring a bell | sing a different tune | strike a chord

1   I didn't believe him at first, but what he said … and I changed my mind.
2   Mark Simmonds? The name … but I can't picture his face at all.
3   My grandmother is eighty-eight but she's still … .
4   My outfit is really boring. I need something … a little.
5   I can't go on lying to my friends and family about what I did. I think it's time … .
6   My boss, likes to think he's in charge of our department, but it's actually his secretary who … .
7   He used to hate teachers, but he's … now that he's married to one.
8   It was one of the employees who … on the company, once she realized how much illegal business they were involved in.

LOOKING AT LANGUAGE

G ▸ Relative clauses and contact clauses, p. 280

6 Rewrite these sentences using a participle construction. (Use the words in brackets.)

1 The campaign for same-sex marriage in the USA began in the 1970s. However, it has only become successful in the last 10 years. (*Despite* …)
Despite beginning in the 1970s, the campaign for same-sex marriage in the USA has only been successful in the last 10 years.

2 Gay activist Harvey Milk was elected to San Francisco's Board of Supervisors in 1977. He was assassinated a year later. (*After* …)

3 The AIDS crisis broke out in 1981. Many activists turned their attention towards AIDS prevention. (*Following* …)

4 Wisconsin became the first state to outlaw discrimination based on sexual orientation in 1982. The state still didn't allow same-sex marriage until 2014. (*Having* …)

5 Gay activists put pressure on the Pentagon. The Pentagon implemented a "don't ask, don't tell" policy towards gays in the military in 1993. (*Pressured by* …)

7 Ellen DeGeneres came out on her TV sitcom in 1997. More than 40 million people watch the show. (… *with* …)

8 The Massachusetts Supreme Judicial Court ruled in favour of same-sex marriage in 2003. This paved the way for same-sex couples to legally marry in the state a year later. (… *thus* …)

9 Same-sex marriage is now legal in the whole of the USA but it is still hotly-debated. (*Despite* …)

WRITING

→ EXAM PREPARATION
Textproduktion (p. 223)

S ▸ Writing an essay, p. 259

7 Read the following quote from the Supreme Court of the USA when it legalized same-sex marriage. Write a comment on the statement, saying whether you agree or disagree with it.

Marriage embodies a love that may endure even past death. It would misunderstand these [gay] men and women to say they disrespect the idea of marriage. Their plea is that they do respect it, respect it so deeply that they seek to find its fulfillment for themselves. They ask for equal dignity in the eyes of the law.

DOING A PROJECT ....

8 You are going to prepare an information leaflet or brochure for fellow students, advising them of their rights in case they are discriminated against for any reason, i.e. because of sexuality, race, religion, etc.

a Read the start of a website for teenagers about discrimination. Complete it with the missing words.

against the law | bullying | characteristic | disability | discriminated against | gender | negative discrimination | respect | respectfully | sexual | unfairly | upset

What is discrimination?
Discrimination is about being treated differently to everybody else because of something about you that somebody else doesn't …[1].

What is discrimination?
Everybody has the right to be treated fairly and …[2], but when you discriminate against somebody, you choose to treat somebody differently based on a particular …[3] they possess. If somebody is treated badly or …[4] merely because of that characteristic, it's known as …[5].

Here are some common reasons why people are …[6]
- their sex or …[7]
- if they have some form of …[8]
- their race
- their age
- their …[9] preferences.

Discrimination is often linked with …[10] and harassment (when somebody behaves in a way that is intended to disturb or …[11] another person). It's actually …[12] to be discriminated against in many areas of public life, for example the workplace, education, housing and government services, and also when accessing goods, services and facilities.

b Look at the notes you made in answer to the "warm-up" questions on page 143. Use your notes and internet research to write two extra sections for the website:
- Signs of discrimination
- What to do if you think you're being discriminated against

c Bring your information together in the form of a flyer, brochure or poster to attract the attention of your fellow students.

ENGLISH FOR WORK Telephoning

LISTENING AND TAKING NOTES

2.09

1 a Pia Durnfeld is from Germany and is working as a volunteer receptionist at StreetHelp, a charity for homeless people in Manchester.

Listen to a telephone call. Pia has made a note of the conversation, but there are four mistakes. Listen and correct the mistakes.

> **Telephone message**
> Name of caller: *James Whittaker*
> Company: *The Stookpad Printing Company*
> For: *Jenny Chalmers*
> Department: *Marketing Department*
> Date: *12 August*
> Time: *10.12 a.m.*
> Message: *Mr Whittaker will call again tomorrow.*

2.10

b Now listen to two more telephone calls. Imagine you are Pia. Make notes of the conversations so you can tell your boss about them later.

TELEPHONE PHRASES

2 a Work with a partner. Copy and complete the list of phrases. Listen to the conversations again and add one more phrase for each situation.

> **→ LANGUAGE BOX**
>
> **Basic telephoning language**
>
> **Introducing yourself**
> · Good morning/afternoon. *(Name of company/organisation)*. This is *(name)* speaking.
> · Hello. My name's *(name)*. I'm calling from *(name of company/organization)*.
>
> **Offering help**
> · How can I help you?
>
> **Asking for help**
> · Could you put me through to *(name)*, please?
>
> **Putting the caller through**
> · Just one moment, please. I'll put you through.
>
> **Asking for more information**
> · Could you tell me what the call is about, please?
>
> **Checking information**
> · Could you spell that / your name for me, please?
>
> **Saying that the call isn't possible**
> · I'm sorry, but Mr/Ms …'s line is engaged at the moment. Would you like to try again later?
> · Mr/Ms … is in a meeting all morning. Can I put you through to someone else?
>
> **Replying**
> · No, thanks. I'll try again later.
> · Yes, please. Could you ask him/her to call me back.
>
> **Ending the call**
> · Thank you for calling. Have a nice day.

b Which phrases would a caller say, and which phrases a receptionist? Which might both of them say?

Telephoning in English

· When telephoning in English, it is important to be polite. English speakers often use phrases such as *Could … ?, May …?, I'm sorry, but …, I'm afraid …* when speaking to business partners on the phone.

Saying telephone numbers

0	is "oh" or "zero"
00	is "double oh" or "zero, zero"
0123	is "oh-one-two-three" or "zero-one-two-three", not "~~zero-one-twenty-three~~"

BEING POLITE

3 Work with a partner. Read one of these sentences out loud. Your partner has to say it in a more polite way. Then change roles.

1 I need to talk to Jamie Michaels in the Purchasing Department.
2 Put me through to Liam Hargreaves now.
3 Wait. I'll connect you.
4 Why are you calling?
5 Mr Smalling isn't here. What do you want to do?
6 Ask Ms Westlake to call me back.
7 I don't understand. Spell your name for me.
8 What's your telephone number?
9 Tell him I will try again later.
10 Goodbye.

ROLE-PLAY

4 Work with a partner. Role-play telephone calls to the charity StreetHelp using information from the table below. Change roles after each conversation.

Caller's company	Caller wants to speak to … (choose one)	Reason why person is unavailable (choose one)	Caller decides to … (choose one)
Housing Department, City Council	Jenny Chalmers, Advertising Department	in a meeting	call back later
Customer Services, Barclays Bank		not in the office	leave a message
Marketing Department, Jaguar Cars	Bob Williams, Planning Department	line engaged	ask to speak to someone else
Production Department, Unigate Foods Ltd	Susan Lee, Finance Department	on holiday business trip	ask for the person to call back when available

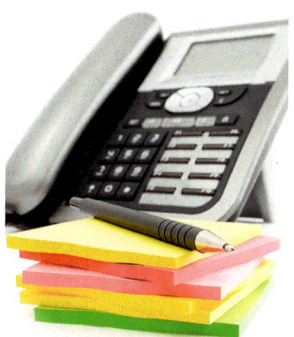

Britain – tradition and change

VA 5   2.11

leave sb/sth behind *etw/jdn überflügeln*
overseas *Übersee-, im Ausland*
shipbuilding industry *Schiffbauindustrie*
shape sth *etw formen*
reign *Herrschaft, Regentschaft*
claim sth *etw beanspruchen*
settlement *Siedlung*
source of wealth *Vermögensquelle, Wohlstandsquelle*
sugar plantation *Zuckerplantage*
slave trade *Sklavenhandel*
spice *Gewürz*
War of Independence *Unabhängigkeitskrieg*

self-governing *selbstverwaltet*
head of state *Staatsoberhaupt*
Indian mutiny *indischer Aufstand*
steamship *Dampfschiff*

Sea power and the first period of Empire

Spain and Portugal were the pioneers of European exploration of the world
in search of new trade routes. England and France, determined not to be left
behind, also began to establish overseas colonies and trade networks. This
rush for power depended on good navigation and large fleets of ships
supported by a big shipbuilding industry, and resulted in many of the   5
conflicts that have shaped the history and geography of the modern world.
During the reign of Elizabeth I (1558–1603), land was claimed in North
Carolina and Newfoundland by explorers such as Walter Raleigh. However,
problems of supplies meant colonies were not successful until the early 17th
century, when settlements in North America were founded, followed by   10
settlements in the Caribbean, which rapidly became a great source of wealth
thanks to sugar plantations and the slave trade. Private companies such as
the East India Company both traded in spices and gained land in Asia, thus
expanding the Empire. The War of Independence (1776–1783) ended
British rule in the American colonies, although Canada remained a British
settlement, and marked the end of the first period of Empire.   15

The second period of Empire

The second period of Empire is marked by a change of focus towards Asia,
the Pacific and later Africa. In 1770 James Cook claimed Australia, which
became a destination for prisoners. As the colony developed, Australia
became profitable for wool and gold. For a time Melbourne was the richest
city in the world. New Zealand was claimed by the British in 1840. These   20
colonies achieved self-governing status, and later full independence, but still
regard the Queen as Head of State, as does Canada.
The period between 1815 and 1914 is known as Britain's "imperial century".
The British government formally took control of India in 1857 after the
Indian mutiny. India was "the jewel in the crown" of the Empire because of   25
its size, location and important natural resources. In Africa, colonies were
established in Nigeria, Kenya, South Africa, Rhodesia – now Zimbabwe –
Gambia and Ghana. During this period, which roughly corresponds to the
reign of Queen Victoria, around 26 million km² of territory and 400 million
people were added to the British Empire, which explains why it was said   30
that "the sun never sets on the British Empire".
New technologies such as the steamship and the
telegraph became integral parts of the
administration of this vast empire.

The end of the British Empire

The cost of two world wars was immense. Although victorious, Britain was
35 in effect bankrupt in 1945 and could no longer afford to administer or
defend the Empire. The decision was made to give independence peacefully
to any country that requested it. In 1947 India was given independence, and
the Muslim state of Pakistan was created, though this partition resulted in
massive population exchanges and led to violence and the loss of about a
40 million lives. The last major colony of Hong Kong was handed over to the
Chinese in 1997.

Britain's role in the world today

As the Empire slowly disappeared, the Commonwealth came into being. The
Commonwealth is a voluntary intergovernmental organization of 53 member
states, most of which were part of the British Empire. The Queen is the
45 symbolic head of the Commonwealth, though the members are free and
equal and have no legal obligation to one another. The organization aims to
promote democracy, human rights, free trade and peace. The parliamentary
systems and systems of law, police and civil service of member states tend to
be modelled on their British equivalents. The Commonwealth Games, the
50 second largest sporting event after the Olympics, takes place every four
years. Until the 1960s, the citizens of former colonies could enter Britain
with a British passport as British Commonwealth citizens.
The British wartime Prime Minister, Winston Churchill, described Anglo-
American cooperation as "the Special Relationship". This recognizes their
55 shared language, culture and history, and the high degree of cooperation
between them in economic and industrial activity, defence technology and
intelligence sharing. They have worked closely as NATO partners and as
allies in conflicts such as the two world wars, the Korean War, and more
recently in the Gulf War and the "War on Terror". The UK still describes its
60 relationship with the United States as its most significant bilateral
partnership, but foreign policies on both sides have undergone considerable
changes since 1945. The rise of China has resulted in America turning more
of its attention to the Pacific Rim and away from Britain and the EU.
The UK has an ambivalent relationship with the EU. While most business
65 people are Europhiles in favour of closer ties with Europe, there is a strong
eurosceptic tradition among politicians of the left and right, and many of
them are in favour of Britain becoming completely independent from
Brussels. When promoting the idea of a United States of Europe to form a
bloc that could stand up to Stalin's Russia, Churchill did not intend Britain to
70 play a significant role in it. Britain did not apply to join the European
Economic Community (EEC) at first. It was only in 1973 that Britain joined
the EU. Britain decided against adopting the euro in 2002, and it remains to
be seen if Britain will stay in the EU.

1 Find the highlighted expressions that have these meanings:

1 special rights or advantages that a particular person or group of people enjoys
1 someone who has been found guilty of breaking the law
2 without enough money to pay what is owed
3 the government departments that administer a country
4 the few people who have the greatest power in a country
5 British people who want more independence from the EU
6 to resist/oppose
8 official separation (e.g. of a country) into different independent parts
9 connected with (normally distant) foreign countries
10 a group of countries that cooperate closely as a result of shared views

2 Find the word partnerships from the text in this grid.

plantation	weapons	trade	shared
currency	slave	natural	policy
human	networks	*sugar*	trade
resources	foreign	nuclear	rights

sugar plantation

3 The text mentions three British monarchs.

· Who are they?
· Do some internet research to find 10 facts about them.
· Write a list of key similarities and differences between them.

4 Britain, Germany, France, Portugal and Belgium all had colonies. Copy the grid below and fill it with information about two of their colonies.

European country	former colony	continent	natural resources	year of loss/ independence	official language(s)
Germany	*Namibia*	*Africa*	*uranium*	*1915/1990*	*English*
Belgium	...	...	...	...	...
Britain	...	...	...	...	...
France	...	...	...	...	...
Portugal	...	...	...	...	...

TEXT 1   Immigration

WARM-UP

1   Complete the chart of push and pull factors behind migration using items from the box below and others you can think of.

lack of basic services | high level of personal danger | high crime | higher employment | more affluence | better services | good climate | safer, less crime | political stability | lower risk from natural hazards | crop failure | drought or flooding | poverty | war | risk of persecution

Push factors (reasons why people want to leave an area)	**Pull factors** (reasons why people want to move to a particular area)

Who do we let in?

Douglas Murray

It is the easiest thing in the world to say who should come to Britain and why. But if there are people who should be coming here, then surely there are others who should not? It is through our unwillingness to address the second part of this question that our problems arise.

5   All polls show a majority of the British public want immigration reduced. But our politicians do not know what to do about it. One answer is to be honest. So let's have that discussion. There are those who like to pretend that immigrants consist solely of technology entrepreneurs. In reality almost nobody is opposed to letting in highly skilled workers, especially from first-world countries. They benefit us 10   and cause little to no societal trouble.

Mass immigration from second-world countries (Eastern Europe) is more of a mixed bag. There is an argument that these immigrants do the jobs 'we' don't want to do. But to support this you have to see no problem in importing people to do jobs so that our domestic working class don't have to work. And financial 15   benefits? Most studies show the real-term economic benefits of such immigration to be negligible.

Then there is the 'third world'. This is the part of the debate we ought to be thinking about most. But our fear of racism means it is the issue we now talk about least. Yet the countries from which mass immigration has caused real trouble 20   are all third-world countries: Bangladesh, Pakistan, Somalia and Jamaica, for instance. (Cue the obvious but necessary disclaimer – no this doesn't mean every person from these countries is a problem.).

Today it is almost impossible to find anyone, even of the left, who thinks that transplanting whole Kashmiri villages to the North of England in the 1960s was a 25   good idea. Brought in to do low-paid, low-skilled jobs which then disappeared, their children don't even have their parents' opportunities. Stuck in areas with few prospects, the religion their parents often sought to escape becomes – predictably enough – the dominating factor in their lives. Did anybody in favour of immigration factor that in during the 1960s? No. Does anybody factor in the

3 unwillingness not wanting to do something
4 arise occur, happen
5 poll *Meinungsumfrage*
7 pretend imagine that sth is true
10 societal connected with the organization of society
12 mixed bag partly good, partly bad
15 benefits advantages
15 real-term real
16 negligible almost nothing
21 cue *Stichwort*
21 disclaimer *Einschränkung, Richtigstellung*
24 transplant sb/sth move sb/sth from one place to another
26 stuck fixed
27 seek (past: sought) try
27 predictable that could be known before
27 dominating factor most important part
29 factor sth in *etw berücksichtigen, etw miteinbeziehen*

31 fiscal issue a financial/economic problem
32 better off in a better position
34 lawless where there is no law
35 influx arrival in great numbers
36 diverse having different ethnic groups
39 asylum seeker Asylsuchende/r
40 constitute sth make up sth, represent sth
41 advocate sb who speaks in favour of sb/sth
42 continuously without stopping
44 give sanctuary to sb jdm Zuflucht gewähren
45 meld sth together mix sth
45 well supply
50 botch sth make a mess of sth
53 turn out end up
55 gamble risk

multi-generational issues mass migration raises today? No. Experts discuss immigration solely as a fiscal issue. But it isn't. It is also a societal one and a moral one. Nobody doubts most Somalis are better off here, but are our lives better for having them here? We pretend that Somalis from one of the most dangerous and lawless countries on the planet become secular democrats once they are in Acton. And we like to say that the vast influx of families from the Indian subcontinent simply makes East London more 'diverse'. Sure. But it has also brought Bangladesh-style political corruption and Pakistan's religious wars to areas such as Tower Hamlets. 30 35

Finally, wrapped up in all of this, are genuine asylum seekers. These are the people who get a double dose of bad luck. Though they constitute the tiniest percentage of immigrants to the UK, the advocates and apologists for mass immigration continuously use them as examples. In doing so they make a terrible mistake. Very few people who want stricter border controls object to genuine asylum seekers being given sanctuary in this country. But when the mass economic migration of recent decades is melded together with asylum, the well of public tolerance for genuine asylum seekers is poisoned. One reason France may take in twice as many asylum seekers as the UK each year is that France takes in less than a quarter of the net economic migrants each year that we do. 40 45

Only two things really matter on immigration: who you take in, and in what numbers. We refuse to discuss the former and our governments botch the latter. In the years after 1681 Britain took in roughly 50,000 Huguenots – an extraordinary occurrence. But that is equal to a normal six weeks of immigration in 21st-century Britain. Perhaps this will all turn out beautifully. Perhaps everyone will integrate every six weeks as well as those French Protestants did over centuries. Or perhaps they won't. But what a gamble to take with a country. 50 55

(703 words)

From: The Spectator, 8 November 2014

WORKING WITH THE TEXT

→ **EXAM PREPARATION**
Leseverstehen (p. 222)

S ▶ Doing comprehension tasks, p. 258

2 Entscheiden Sie, ob die Aussagen zum Text richtig oder falsch sind. Begründen Sie Ihre Entscheidung auf Deutsch in vollständigen Sätzen.

1 Immigrants from Eastern European countries are generally welcome because there are insufficient numbers of British workers to do the sort of jobs they do.
2 There is little debate about third-world immigration because the topic is associated with sensitive issues.
3 The children of immigrants in the north of England have better career opportunities than their parents.
4 According to the writer, diversity caused by immigration has positive and negative elements.
5 Many people don't know the difference between asylum seekers and immigrants.
6 Immigration has only been an issue in recent times.

3 Explain in your own words what these sentences mean:

1 "(Highly skilled workers) benefit us and cause little to no societal trouble." (ll. 9–10)
2 "Experts discuss immigration solely as a fiscal issue. It isn't. It is also a societal and moral one." (ll. 30–31)
3 "What a gamble to take with a country." (l. 55)

WORKING WITH WORDS

4 Find a word or expression in the text that means the same as the following.

1 talk about a topic
2 imagine or claim something is true
3 minimal, not significant
4 opportunities for the future
5 not surprisingly
6 rush of people/things arriving
7 people in favour of something
8 approximately

LOOKING AT LANGUAGE

5 a A common metaphor is "life is a journey". Complete these sentences with the missing words. Then explain what they mean.

at a crossroads | at the end of the tunnel | dead-end | high flyer | in the way | on the road | short cuts | side-tracked | turning back

1 The last year has been very difficult for us, but there's light … now, and we hope things will improve.
2 He's …: He has to decide whether to stay here or move to another country for work.
3 She's feeling a bit better now after the operation. It looks like she's … to recovery.
4 There are no … to success. You have to put in a lot of hard work.
5 It took me hours longer than I expected because I got … . My sister needed some help with her computer. Sorry about that!
6 Lots of people work in … jobs with no prospects.
7 There's no … now. I've made my decision and I am going to stick to it.
8 Ambitious people don't let anything get … of their success.
9 She's a … . She's the youngest person to get promoted to the board and I see her ending up as the CEO.

b Which metaphors are similar in German?

LISTENING

2.12

6 a Sie hören eine Radiosendung über Briten, die im Ausland leben. Beantworten Sie die Fragen auf Deutsch in Stichworten.

1 Wie viele Briten leben im Ausland?
2 Welche Art von Briten zieht heutzutage ins Ausland?
3 Warum ziehen nur wenige Briten nach Spanien?
4 Was hat Kalifornien britischen Auswanderern zu bieten?
5 Warum ist Australien für Briten so attraktiv?
6 Welches Land ist besonders gut dabei, Kontakt mit seinen Bürgern im Ausland aufrechtzuerhalten?
7 Warum können sich Briten in Commonwealthländern gut integrieren?

b What surprised you most about what you heard?

c Do you know anyone who chose to live and work abroad? Where did they go, and why?

→ **EXAM PREPARATION**
Zentrale Klassenarbeit Hörverstehen (p. 224)

S ► Practising listening skills, p. 256

EXAM PRACTICE
Kommunikationsprüfung (p. 224)

SPEAKING

7 Work in pairs. Partner A, look at the first graph. Partner B, go to File 9 (p. 219).

a Prepare a short monologue on your graph.

Over 6 decades, where migrants came from
Top 10 countries of birth of British residents

1951		1981		2001		2011	
Ireland	492,000	Ireland	580,000	Ireland	473,000	India	694,000
Poland	152,000	India	383,000	India	456,000	Poland	579,000
India	111,000	Pakistan	182,000	Pakistan	308,000	Pakistan	482,000
Germany	96,000	Germany	170,000	Germany	244,000	Ireland	407,000
Russia	76,000	Jamaica	164,000	Bangladesh	153,000	Germany	274,000
USA	59,000	USA	106,000	Jamaica	146,000	Bangladesh	212,000
Canada	46,000	Kenya	100,000	USA	144,000	Nigeria	191,000
Italy	33,000	Italy	93,000	S.Africa	132,000	S. Africa	191,000
Australia	31,000	Poland	88,000	Kenya	127,000	USA	177,000
France	30,000	Cyprus	83,000	Italy	102,000	Jamaica	160,000
Top ten total	1,126,000	Top ten total	1,949,000	Top ten total	2,285,000	Top ten total	3,367,000
Others	774,000	Others	1,251,000	Others	2,315,000	Others	4,133,000
Total 1.9 m		Total 3.2 m		Total 4.6 m		Total 7.5 m	

b After listening to your partner, discuss what you have learned from the two graphs.

WRITING

8 Choose one of the visuals from task 7. Find the same information for Germany. Write a text comparing and contrasting the situation in the UK and Germany.

PRESENTATION

EXAM PREPARATION
Präsentationsprüfung (p. 225)

S ▶ Giving a presentation, p. 264

9 Work in groups of 4. Each person chooses one of the following types of migrant:

asylum seekers | economic migrants | refugees | illegal immigrants

Research your chosen group and prepare a presentation that provides this information:
· An explanation of this type of migrant
· Reasons why they migrate
· Where they come from
· Typical destination countries
· Problems they face in their host countries

EXAM PREPARATION
Textproduktion (p. 223)

S ▶ Writing an essay, p. 259

WRITING

10 Discuss the pros and cons of immigration control.

TEXT 2 The Legacy of the British Empire

WARM-UP

1 Look at the map showing the growth of the British Empire and discuss whether the statements are true or false or not given.

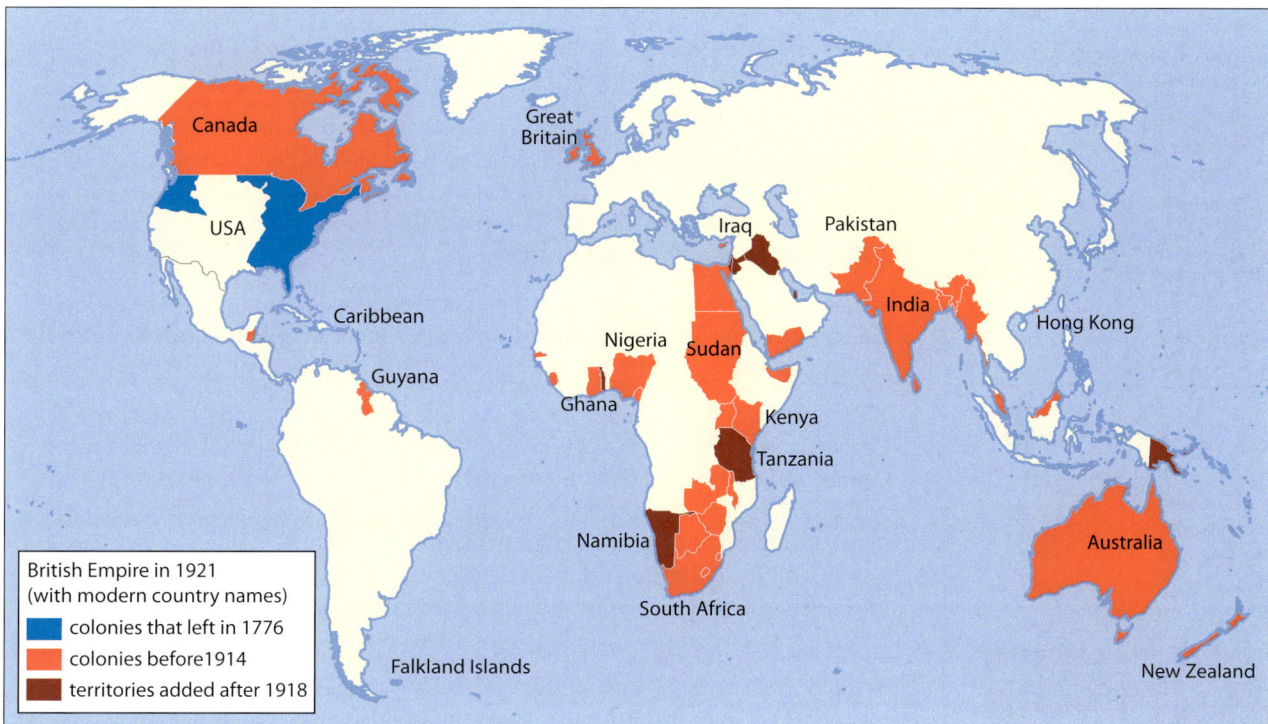

British Empire in 1921
(with modern country names)
- colonies that left in 1776
- colonies before 1914
- territories added after 1918

1 The British Empire had a presence on every continent.
2 The Empire was at its greatest extent after the First World War.
3 India was the last country to come under British rule.
4 China was once part of the British Empire.
5 Some countries freed themselves from British rule before 1900.
6 The British Empire expanded most easily in regions where English was already spoken.
7 About a fifth of the globe formed part of the British Empire at one time.
8 For most of its history India was a British colony.

2 Work in groups. Discuss these questions, then report back to the class.

1 In addition to the British, the Romans, Portuguese, Spanish, French, Austro-Hungarians, Turks and Russians all had empires, as did the Mongols, different Chinese dynasties and the Japanese, and the Aztecs and the Zulus - and many others. To what extent do you think it human nature to want to build an empire?
2 None of the empires mentioned above exist today. Why do you think that is?
3 Do you think there will ever be another empire? Why/why not?

2.13

³ dominion colony with its own government
⁹ profound very significant
¹² ideal Wertvorstellung
¹³ common law (geltendes) Recht
¹⁵ source of income Einkommensquelle
¹⁷ scattered verstreut
²⁴ crumble break up
²⁷ surge sudden increase
³³ successive following one after the other
³⁸ ambiguous unklar, zweideutig

The sunset of the British Empire

At the height of its power in the 19th and early 20th centuries, so much of the earth was under Britain's control that it was said that "the sun never set on the British Empire". The British Empire numbered 57 colonies, dominions, territories and protectorates and extended from Australia to Canada and from India to South Africa. It has been calculated that 20 percent of the world's population and 25 percent of the world's total land mass were once governed from London. After the Second World War, however, the unavoidable conclusion was that the sun was slowly but surely slipping toward the horizon.

The British Empire brought profound changes to the world. Its colonial aspirations resulted in the creation of the United States, the main superpower since the end of World War One; it led to the formation of the nation of India, which is the largest democracy in the world; and it spread British ideals of freedom, democracy and common law well beyond its shores.

The darker side of British history includes deliberately corrupting an entire nation, China, with opium for the sole purpose of exploiting the drug as a source of income, and subjugating people throughout the world in an arrogant and racist manner.

What remains of the Empire today are a few scattered islands largely in the Caribbean and the South Pacific. The Commonwealth of Nations, which was formed in 1949, comprises 53 mostly former British territories. Despite a population of 3.2 billion, which is nearly a third of the world population, and its rather grand claims to be the largest association of countries united by language, history, culture and shared values of democracy, human rights and the rule of law, the Commonwealth is more or less just a peaceful monument to the Empire.

The power of the Empire started to crumble when the Japanese army took Singapore during the Second World War and advanced its guns to within range of the borders of India and Australia. Japan showed that non-European powers could defeat Western powers, and the end of the war saw a surge of nationalist spirit demanding independence. The withdrawal from India in 1947 heralded the definitive end of Britain as a colonial power. Shortly afterwards, Dean Acheson, the US Secretary of State, remarked, "The British are finished". The United States quickly displaced the United Kingdom as the main stabilizing power in the West, and took on the lion's share of policing the world and defending the West's values. Successive British governments gave independence to most of the colonies, with the city-state Hong Kong being handed back to China in 1997 – perhaps the final nail in the coffin of the Empire.

Acheson also said later, "Great Britain has lost an Empire and has not yet found a role." Despite its lack of power, Britain still today acts as though it is a leading power. It has an ambiguous relationship to the EU, it claims a "special relationship" with the USA, and it still feels it is the leading nation in the Commonwealth. Other powers on the world stage today – the United States, China and Russia – may be justified in viewing the British claim to a continuing influence despite its rapid decline since 1945 as a left-over relic from another age.

Perhaps one of the nation's problems is that the word "Great" is still attached to Britain. It may take another generation to realize the word is related to geography and not to greatness. Indeed, as an independent Scotland becomes more likely, the political unity of the British Isles themselves is under threat, and Great Britain as a country may cease to exist.   (600 words)

5

10

15

20

25

30

35

40

45

WORKING WITH THE TEXT

3 Entscheiden Sie, ob die Aussagen zum Text richtig oder falsch sind. Begründen Sie Ihre Entscheidung auf Deutsch in vollständigen Sätzen.

1 The British Empire stretched around the whole world.
2 The British Empire banned the opium trade in China.
3 The present-day Commonwealth consists largely of small islands scattered around the world.
4 The British Empire can be said to have ended when the Japanese invaded India and Australia.
5 The USA took over the position of most powerful nation in the world once Britain went into decline.
6 The future of Great Britain is uncertain due to the Scottish independence movement.

➔ **EXAM PREPARATION**
Leseverstehen (p. 222)

S ▸ Doing comprehension tasks, p. 258

4 Erstellen Sie eine Liste mit den drei wichtigsten Veränderungen, die das britische Weltreich mit sich gebracht hat. Formulieren Sie vollständige Sätze auf Deutsch.

➔ **EXAM PREPARATION**
Leseverstehen (p. 222)

S ▸ Doing comprehension tasks, p. 258

WORKING WITH WORDS

5 **a** Look at the words on the left and match them to their meanings on the right.

1	profound	a	only
2	spread	b	beliefs that are important
3	sole	c	expand
4	values	d	the act of taking sth. out of sth.
5	claim	e	the biggest part
6	crumble	f	a right that sb believes they have to sth.
7	withdrawal	g	extremely significant
8	the lion's share	h	break into small pieces

b Decide which words or phrases from 5a best complete these sentences.

1 No empire lasts for ever. Sooner or later, they all …
2 Britain became rich partly because … of resources from the colonies were used to benefit Britain.
3 Losing its empire has had … consequences for Britain, forcing it to seek a new role on the world stage.
4 Britain's … to the Falkland Islands is disputed by Argentina.
5 Following the end of the Cold War, the USA became the … superpower.
6 The Indian subcontinent was partitioned into India and Pakistan following the British … .
7 The English language … around the globe as the British Empire gained more colonies.
8 The British and Americans have many shared …, like the belief in freedom of speech and democracy.

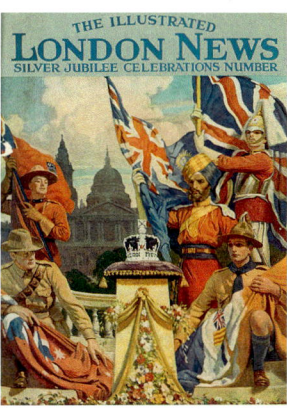

LOOKING AT LANGUAGE

6 **a** Complete these sentences using the idioms connected with animals.

1 We were working in pairs, but I did …
2 This information is true. You can trust me. I got it from …
3 I didn't realize it was a secret. Sorry if I let …
4 I really didn't feel comfortable there. I was like …
5 It was great meeting up again. I hadn't seen him for …
6 I love this music. I could listen to it until …
7 I spent all day in vain looking for a 3D-printer. It was …

a the cat out of the bag.
b the cows come home.
c donkey's years.
d the horse's mouth.
e the lion's share of the work.
f a wild goose chase.
g a fish out of water.

b Discuss what the sentences mean.

c To what extent do the qualities of each animal make the expressions appropriate?

d Which animal expressions are similar in German?

VIEWING

5

7 **a** Watch the video. Then copy the table and make notes about the facts on the left.

1	King Henry VII	…
2	1607	…
3	1815	…
4	400 million	…
5	1922	…
6	1997	…

b What examples are given of the continuing influence of the British Empire?

SPEAKING

→ **EXAM PRACTICE**
Kommunikationsprüfung (p. 224)

8 Produce a five-minute uninterrupted monologue on the graphs and quotation on p. 163, explaining reasons for different views on the British Empire.

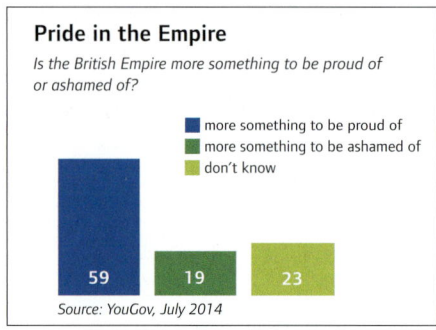

Pride in the Empire
Is the British Empire more something to be proud of or ashamed of?

- more something to be proud of
- more something to be ashamed of
- don't know

59 19 23

Source: YouGov, July 2014

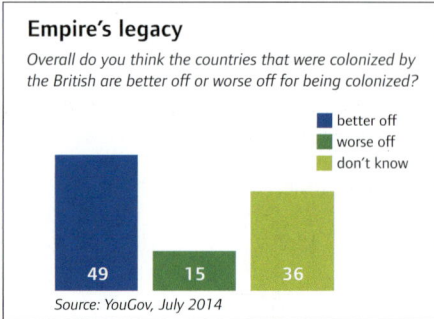

Empire's legacy
Overall do you think the countries that were colonized by the British are better off or worse off for being colonized?

- better off
- worse off
- don't know

49 15 36

Source: YouGov, July 2014

"Britain gave us democracy, the rule of law, an independent judiciary and a free press. It built railways, canals, and harbors, but it could not bring about an industrial revolution. It could not raise economic growth or lift people out of poverty. It could not avert famines. The truth is the British rule in India was economically incompetent. It just did not know how to "develop" a country. Had it known it, Britain could have gained much from having a larger market for its manufactures. It introduced modern education and helped create a small middle class, but it did not educate the mass of the people."
Gurcharan Das (Indian writer)

GIVING A PRESENTATION

9 Choose one of these countries that once belonged to the British Empire. Prepare a presentation that includes the following information:

Australia | Canada | India | Ireland | Jamaica | Nigeria | New Zealand | South Africa

- when it became part of the British Empire
- why Britain wanted the country to be part of the Empire
- the history of the country after becoming part of the British Empire
- when and how it gained independence
- current relationship with Britain

→ **EXAM PREPARATION**
Präsentationsprüfung (p. 225)

S ► Giving a presentation, p. 264

WRITING

10 Choose one of the photos and write a short creative text, e.g. a dialogue between the people in the photos, the thoughts of one of the people, a diary entry or a letter, which reveals something of the relationship between the people involved.

After the hunt

Queen Victoria and her Indian servant Abdul Karim

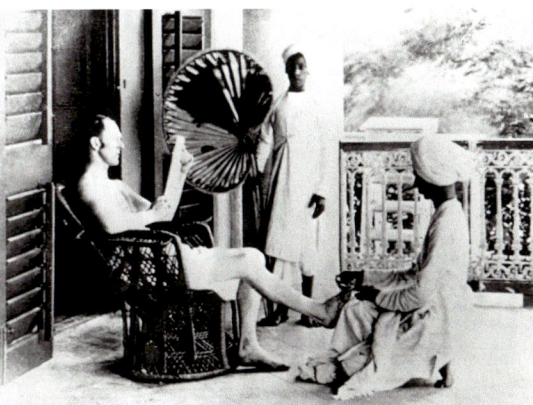

Reading the newspapers

11 Explain the following quotation in relation to the text and give examples to support the statement.

"The British are finished" (l. 30)

→ **EXAM PREPARATION**
Textproduktion (p. 223)

S ► Writing an essay, p. 259

TEXT 3   Britain's future influence

1 Look at the pictures and discuss the different sorts of "power" represented in the pictures and how they can influence people's lives.

2 You are going to read a text about different sorts of power. Before you read, discuss these questions.

1 Why do countries want to have influence over others?
2 In what ways can a country influence another country?
3 How many different ways can a country try to exert a positive influence on the world?
4 Name two countries and explain how they exert power and/or influence in the world.

Britain is losing its grip on soft power

Indra Adnan

lose your grip on sth lose your power over sth
[2] **deliver sth** provide sth
[4] House of Lords *Oberhaus*
[4] select committee *Sonderausschuss*
[7] **shift** move
[9] **conduct sth** perform sth, do sth
[9] **diplomacy** *Diplomatie*
[9] **internet-driven** caused by the internet
[11] **set** group
[12] **challenge sth** test sth, put strain on sth
[13] **enhance sth** improve sth
[14] **meaningful** important
[14] **engagement** involvement
[15] **proceed** continue

It is almost 25 years since the American academic Joseph Nye first introduced his distinction between hard power – force delivered through guns and money – and soft power – influence delivered through attraction and relationship. Yet Friday saw the first House of Lords select committee report on soft power – and its significance for Britain, as the Lords put it, "in a now almost totally transformed international scene".   5

Not only has economic power shifted unmistakably towards the south and east of the planet, says the report, but international relations – which used to be conducted entirely through diplomacy – are equally transformed. An internet-driven connectivity – between states as well as between institutions, groups and   10
non-state actors of all kinds – has led to a new set of political relationships and identities, which could challenge traditional loyalties to either the US or Europe in the future. The Lords suggest that we should greatly enhance the capacity for meaningful engagement at all levels, including with online opinion formers, adding: "The UK cannot simply proceed as before."   15

Internationally, Britain is seen to have a deep, historic understanding of soft power. The BBC successfully frames international events on British terms, broadcasting in every major language. The British Council, British Museum and other arts institutions make cultural contributions worldwide. The royal family and the mother of parliaments offer a picture of a stable, working democracy. And London's spectacle as a well-connected, multicultural city suggests Britain is a microcosm of the globe. We are attractive to the rest of the planet, however different it looks from the inside.

Yet we are behind the curve in articulating a soft power agenda in our politics. Many BRIC and Scandinavian countries shape their foreign policies around explicit soft power goals. For example, China has opened 327 of a projected 1,000 Confucius Institutes, encouraging a philosophical understanding of its civilisation. India's investment in Bollywood has changed our view of it as a global agent: we now think of that great dance scene in Slumdog Millionaire before we remember the poverty. Finland sends monitors to join the Red Cross in the Ukraine – not just for humanitarian aid, but specifically to get closer to the people, to understand their wishes. All Nye's acolytes want to show themselves to the world as non-threatening and engaged, as attractive poles of influence.

Yet, through what the report calls absent-mindedness and neglect, Britain is weakening rather than bolstering its soft power institutions. Twenty-five countries have launched English-speaking world-affairs news outlets: we have cut funding to the BBC World Service, closing 22 bureaus (including the Ukraine) since 2011. Instead of harnessing institutions such as these, which reliably attract goodwill and trust, the Coalition government under David Cameron placed a commerce-oriented advertising campaign proclaiming "Britain is great" at the heart of its operations.

The report recommends that we hold a national debate on our traditional reliance on the military to make our presence felt in the world. While it wants to defend a role for armies in the arena of global security, the report makes a strong case for a more explicit balance between hard and soft responses to events, described by Nye as smart power. The Lords argue that such a debate would require a degree of popular education about how our international relationships are actually forged, and why these should matter to ordinary citizens.

National narratives – the story we tell the world about ourselves – are key. Evidence from nation-branding experts such as Simon Anholt suggests behaviour that is proactively friendly to the global community is rewarded with trust. And trust is the corridor for any influence a modern state wants to have in the world.

The Lords say that aggressive debates on immigration policy, widely reported in mainstream and social media, will have caused us a loss of soft power over the past two years. In a pre-publication interview, Lord Howell said: All witnesses who came before us … said the visa policy and some of the handling of immigration policy was creating a blot, creating a 'nasty Britain' feeling. Not only will that drive tourism and business away from us, it will give us less credibility in bigger discussions about the direction of globalisation over coming decades.

This is not a simple tasklist for the Foreign Office. The entire government has to think about Britain in this new global environment. How does the UK retain its trust and influence of the past? How does it proceed into a future where the edges of statecraft have become softer and more porous than ever before? (779 words)

From: The Guardian, 31 March 2014

WORKING WITH THE TEXT

3 a Complete these sentences in your own words.

1 Soft power is different from traditional "hard power" because …
2 The House of Lords report on soft power states that the UK must change the way it thinks of international relations because …
3 Examples of the positive image Britain projects include …
4 The report states that Britain does not compare well with how some countries are improving their soft power, because …
5 It is important to project a friendly image internationally because …
6 The problem with recent news coverage of immigration in the UK is …

b Explain these sentences from the text in your own words.

1 London's spectacle as a well-connected, multicultural city suggests Britain is a microcosm of the globe. (ll. 21–22)
2 Trust is the corridor for any influence a modern state wants to have in the world. (l. 52)

4 Work in pairs. The text ends with the two questions.

1 How does the UK retain its trust and influence of the past? (ll. 61–62)
2 How does it proceed into a future where the edges of statecraft have become softer and more porous than ever before? (ll. 62–63)

Discuss possible answers. Compare your answers with another pair.

→ EXAM PRACTICE

Kommunikationsprüfung (p. 224)

SPEAKING

5 Produce a five-minute uninterrupted monologue on the two visuals below, explaining how soft power works and why some countries make use of it effectively.

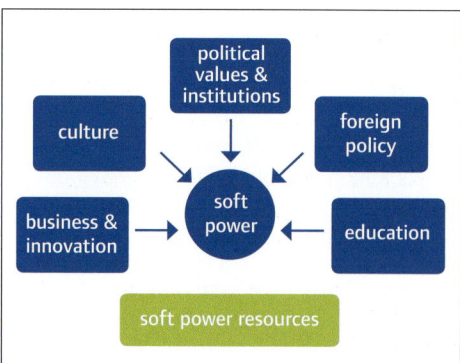

soft power index, 2015

Rank	Country	Rank	Country
1	UK	9	Sweden
2	Germany	10	Netherlands
3	USA	11	Denmark
4	France	12	Italy
5	Canada	13	Austria
6	Australia	14	Spain
7	Switzerland	15	Finland
8	Japan	16	New Zealand

WORKING WITH WORDS

6 **a** Join the two parts of these sentences.

1 All governments are worried about loss
2 Climate change is a great cause
3 Lack of resources and unemployment are causes
4 I've got a terrible sense
5 If the negotiations fail, there is a risk
6 Many people rely on the media for their view
7 She has a great understanding
8 The USA fears that the balance

a of concern to scientists.
b of direction. I always get lost.
c of influence in the world.
d of people and can get along with anyone.
e of poverty throughout the world.
f of power is changing in favour of China.
g of what is happening in the world.
h of war.

b Find examples in the text of this common English structure:
noun + of + (the) noun (e. g. House of Lords, set of relationships).

7 Complete these sentences with the missing words. Then describe situations in which you might hear them.

answer | convincing | inspired | no | right | talks | way | will

1 Might is … .
2 Money … .
3 I was … by the book.
4 She made a … argument.
5 Where there's a …, there's a … .
6 I won't take "…" for an … .

LOOKING AT LANGUAGE

8 Rewrite the sentences using a passive infinitive structure following the example.

G ▶ The passive, p. 275

People think Britain has a deep understanding of soft power
Britain is thought to have a deep understanding of soft power.

1 People believe that soft power is an important element of international influence.
2 Everyone knows that the way the media report immigration stories has an affect on how the UK is perceived abroad.
3 They say that the royal family provides a positive image of tradition in the UK.
4 People think that the situation is getting worse.
5 Everyone assumes that this is the century that sees China rival the US as the number one global power.
6 People often claim that European power is in decline.
7 They reported that figures were lower than before.
8 They consider that the Prime Minister is in a strong position.

165

MEDIATING

9 Read the information about the British Council and use it to write a short summary in German about the work of the British Council and its contribution to British soft power.

The British Council was founded to create a friendly knowledge and understanding between the people of the UK and the wider world. We call this work cultural relations.

We work in over 100 countries, connecting millions of people with the United Kingdom through programmes and services in the English language, the Arts, Education and Society. We believe these are the most effective means of engaging with others, and we have been doing this work since 1934.

Our work in English aims to bring high quality language materials to every learner and teacher who wants them. In developing and post-conflict countries we teach English and train teachers through radio, web and TV broadcasts. We offer over three million UK examinations worldwide, helping people gain access to trusted qualifications to support their career and study prospects.

Our work in Education and Society helps transform national education systems, builds more inclusive and open societies and increases young people's opportunities. We encourage international students to come and study in the UK, and British students to experience life abroad.

Our work in the Arts involves the very best British and international artistic talent. We help increase audiences for international work in the UK and for UK work globally. We bring artists together and support the development of skills and policy in the arts and creative industries.

In these ways, the British Council builds links between UK people and institutions and those around the world, helping to create trust and lay foundations for prosperity and security around the world.

From: the website of the British Council

EXAM PREPARATION
Textproduktion (p. 223)

S ► Writing an essay, p. 259

WRITING

10 Discuss Britain's role in the world, taking into consideration its past history as an empire and its present membership of the UN, the EU, the Commonwealth and NATO.

World leaders at a G7 summit meeting

TEXT 4 Britain and Europe

1 a You are going to read a text about British attitudes towards Europe. Before you read, predict which of these expressions will be in the text, and say why/why not.

fish and chips | ethnic minorities | European legislation | political institutions | abolish the monarchy | think of themselves as Europeans | a common currency | middle-class people | get on fine with them | terrible food | foreign language | trade with China

b Scan the text quickly to see if you were right.

British attitudes to Europe

Michael Skey

Britain and Euroscepticism seem to go together like fish and chips. Polling data consistently show that Britain is the most Eurosceptic country in Europe, with only around 25 % of people attached or fairly attached to the EU (compared with a European average of around 45 %) while over 70 % of Brits said they were 'not very' or 'not at all' attached (the European average is just over 50 %).

My own research was interested in the experiences and attitudes of members of the ethnic majority living in England. I conducted 21 group interviews with members of this group, and asked them general questions such as; 'what do you dis/like about living here', 'what are the biggest challenges facing the country' and so on. This type of research isn't meant to be representative of the population as a whole given the relatively low numbers of people involved, but is able to explore people's views. I also asked about Europe and their responses can be categorised into four broad themes; antagonistic, disinterested, pragmatic, positive.

It's perhaps not surprising to learn that a good number of the people I spoke to were antagonistic towards the EU and the project of European integration. They raged against the perceived impact of European legislation and the challenge it presented to British social and political institutions and often made reference to stories they had read or heard in the media.

The second group, the disinterested, did not see European issues as relevant to their own lives and often struggled to think of themselves as European. The following extract, which involves a group of twenty-somethings in north London, offers an illustrative example.

Interviewer: What about Europe, do you consider yourself European at all?

Katie: No. When I think of Europe, I think of other countries.

Fiona: Funnily enough, when I was staying with relatives in America they, like, [...] class me in Europe and that was weird at the time because I hadn't really thought of myself as European.

5

10

15

20

25

2 **consistently** always

11 as a whole in total

11 given when you consider this

13 **antagonistic** very negative

13 **disinterested** with no particular interest in something

17 **rage against sth** be angry with sth

18 make reference to sth mention sth

22 **extract** short passage

22 **twenty-something** people aged 20–29

23 illustrative helpful

26 **funnily enough** surprisingly

30 prompt sth cause sth

31 engagement contact

33 rooted staying in the same place

35 welcome sth feel positive about sth

42 conversion rate exchange between currencies

43 lose out get a bad deal

51 regardless of sth when sth does not matter

52 happen to be may be

55 enunciate sth express sth

55 outward looking *außenorientiert*

57 eschew sth ignore sth, not use sth

58 allegiance sense of belonging to a group

59 cosmopolitan with experience of different cultures

62 mark sb/sth out make sb/sth appear different

63 undertake sth do sth

This example points to the importance of travel in exposing people to new ways of thinking about their own sense of identity and place, often prompted by engagements with other people and cultures. While increasing numbers are becoming more mobile, we should not, of course, forget that many continue to remain relatively rooted, whether through choice or lack of opportunities.

The views of the first two groups can be usefully contrasted with those who either talked about Europe in more pragmatic terms or welcomed greater integration and identified strongly as European. This was often because they had travelled extensively and saw the benefit of having, for example, a common currency and passport and reduced border controls, or as a positive development, uniting people with shared tastes and values.

Dennis: … I think we should take up the euro.

Kay: Yeah … because it's a lot cheaper when you're going on holiday and you're having to pay stuff in Europe and there's a conversion rate and personally and financially you lose out

A good example of how these changes are being welcomed by some comes in the following extract from an interview I carried out with a group of middle-class people based in the south-east of England

Andrew: We're looking at, y'know, the countries of Europe divided vertically. You've got, sort of, y'know, English people, Dutch people, French people, Belgian people, and I almost believe it's not like that, it's, it's almost a horizontal division. When you go abroad you meet people who have similar values and interests and … um … hobbies as yourself and you get on with those people, regardless of national identity, so …, you find people of a similar nature who happen to be Dutch or French or German and you'd get on fine with them, better than you would with people who happen just to be English.

Andrew enunciated the most outward looking perspective of all those I interviewed by focusing on horizontal commitments, that link people by virtue of value, taste and lifestyle, in the process eschewing the more narrow, vertical allegiances most closely associated with the nation. This group represented, at least in part, the ideal of the cosmopolitan – able and willing to engage with others, in this case Europeans. Their views and experiences offer an important challenge to distinctly national ways of thinking about the world. One further point is worth making here. Members of this group were marked out by being able to speak at least one foreign language having undertaken university-level studies in Europe and by having family members living abroad.   (779 words)

From: the blog "British Politics and Policy" of the London School of Economics

WORKING WITH THE TEXT

→ **EXAM PREPARATION**
  Leseverstehen (p. 222)

S ▶ Doing comprehension tasks, p. 258

2 Entscheiden Sie, ob die Aussagen zum Text richtig oder falsch sind. Begründen Sie Ihre Entscheidung auf Deutsch in vollständigen Sätzen.

1 Over two-thirds of British people are indifferent to or against the European Union, while just a quarter of the population thinks the EU is a good idea.

2 Skey's research is important because it is representative of the majority of British people.

3 Fiona understood straight away why her relatives in the USA referred to Britain as part of Europe.

4 Kay likes the idea of a common currency because it would make life easier for her when she's abroad.

5 Andrew thinks that there are too many differences for people from different European countries to truly understand each other.

6 One thing that all those who had positive views on Europe had in common was that they spoke at least one foreign language.

3 Im Text nennt der Autor vier Dinge, die Menschen, die sich eher als Europäer fühlen, als positive Beispiele europäischer Integration empfinden. Erstellen Sie eine Liste dieser Beispiele. Formulieren Sie vollständige Sätze auf Deutsch.

EXAM PREPARATION
Leseverstehen (p. 222)

S ▶ Doing comprehension tasks, p. 258

SPEAKING

4 a Discuss with a partner which of the following statements you agree with most.

1 Travelling is a great way of learning about other countries and cultures. But it also teaches you about yourself and your own culture.

2 I don't see the point of travelling at all. These days, you can find all the information you want about a place by using the internet from the comfort of your own home.

3 Holidays are so stressful! When I get back I always feel I need another holiday, just to recover!

4 Everyone thinks their own ideas and way of life are normal. When you go abroad, you realize that your way of doing things is just one way, and that there are other ways of doing things.

5 Why travel? I have everything I need right here – family, friends, home.

b How have travel and the ability to speak other languages influenced your view of other countries?

5 a Make a list of the advantages and disadvantages of learning about another culture in these different ways. Discuss your list with another pair.

Advantages of learning about other cultures by travelling	Advantages of learning about other cultures by reading and research
Disadvantages of learning about other cultures by travelling	**Disadvantages of learning about other cultures by reading and research**

b Use the information to make a five-minute presentation outlining different ways of learning about a culture, and giving your opinion on the topic.

EXAM PREPARATION
Präsentationsprüfung (p. 225)

S ▶ Giving a presentation, p. 264

WORKING WITH WORDS

6 Check the meaning and use of these words from the text. Then complete the sentences with the right form of the appropriate option.

funnily enough | given | happen to | regardless | think of yourself as

1 We play football every Friday, … of the weather.
2 You're from London? …, I was there last weekend.
3 I like to … a reasonable person with a balanced outlook on life.
4 … how important it could be for our future, I think we should have a debate about Europe.
5 Do you … know which country is most pro-European?
6 I think Britain should be part of the Eurozone, … of what other people say.
7 If you … be in the city centre, could you get me something from the shops?
8 Even in Germany a large percentage of the population … German rather than as European.
9 It's not surprising many people are unsure about Europe, … the stories in the news.
10 I was talking to some friends about Berlin this morning. I turned on the TV just now and … there was a programme about Berlin.

7 Decide which preposition completes the expressions in the boxes. Check by looking back at the text.

– ? –	– ? –	– ? –	– ? –
I see myself … British.	my view … the situation	… various reasons	It is divided … sections.
I work … a teacher.	my way … thinking		I changed pounds … euros
	a lack … opportunities		
	people … a similar nature		

– ? –	– ? –	– ? –	– ? –
I'm open … new ideas.	I was encouraged … him	I must focus … this.	I have nothing … common with him.
It's not relevant … my life.	I was welcomed … my colleagues	… several occasions	I am interested … his story.
		I get … well with him.	
		I went … holiday.	

LOOKING AT LANGUAGE

8 a Complete these sentence beginnings following the prompts so they are true of
you.

As someone who has been abroad several times, … (what did I learn?)
*As someone who has been abroad several times, I know from personal experience
that travel is a great way of learning about other cultures.*

1 As someone who lives in a big/small place, I … (how has this influenced your
opinion of other places?)
2 As someone who lives in Germany, I … (how does this influence how you react to
things?)
3 As someone who is about to leave school, I … (what worries you about the
future?)
4 As someone who is learning English, I … (how do you hope English could be
useful in the future?)
5 As someone who does/doesn't smoke/drink/drive, I … (how does this influence
your spending/daily routines etc?)
6 As someone who is (not) very interested in … , I … (how does your interest
affect your life?)

b Compare your answers with other students. Who has the most similar/different
answers to you?

9 Work with a partner: Partner A looks at this page; Partner B looks at File 10 on
p. 219.

a Produce a five-minute uninterrupted discourse based on the cartoon about
Britain and its role in the European Union.

b Listen to you partner describe and analyse his or her cartoon.

c Discuss how you see the future role of Britain in Europe.

EXAM PREPARATION
*Kommunikationsprüfung
(p. 224)*

S ▶ Interpreting pictures and
cartoons, p. 262

COMPETENCE TRAINING: INTERPRETING CHARTS ....

10 A chart just presents information, but so often you have to interpret the chart in order to understand more about the information it is presenting. Look at the chart below.

a In one sentence say what the chart shows.
b Look at the chart and state four pieces of information you find interesting.
c Which countries are at the top of the chart, and which countries are at the bottom of the chart?
d Look at the nationalities that have a similar feeling towards being an EU citizen as the British. What strikes you most about them?
f Now go beyond the chart and explain:
  • why one does not hear about Italy wanting to leave the EU.
  • why Greece is at the bottom.
  • why Luxembourg is at the top.
  • why people in France and Germany have different views of themselves as EU citizens.
g Now write a short statement on what you can say about the chart.

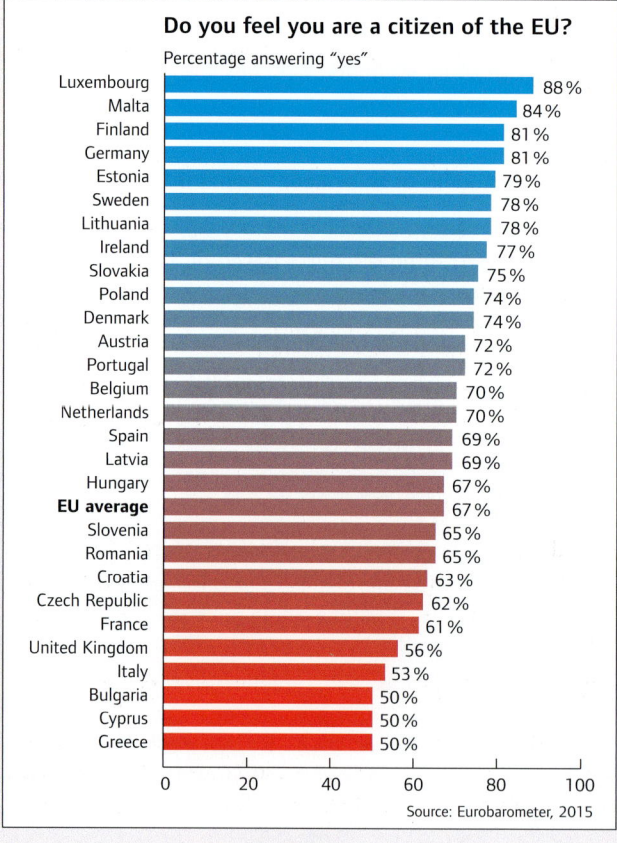

Do you feel you are a citizen of the EU?
Percentage answering "yes"

Country	%
Luxembourg	88%
Malta	84%
Finland	81%
Germany	81%
Estonia	79%
Sweden	78%
Lithuania	78%
Ireland	77%
Slovakia	75%
Poland	74%
Denmark	74%
Austria	72%
Portugal	72%
Belgium	70%
Netherlands	70%
Spain	69%
Latvia	69%
Hungary	67%
EU average	67%
Slovenia	65%
Romania	65%
Croatia	63%
Czech Republic	62%
France	61%
United Kingdom	56%
Italy	53%
Bulgaria	50%
Cyprus	50%
Greece	50%

Source: Eurobarometer, 2015

EXAM PREPARATION
Textproduktion (p. 223)

S ▶ Writing an essay, p. 259

WRITING ....

11 Comment on the statement that Britain would be better off outside the EU and the EU would be better off without Britain.

TEXT 5   Britain's role in the world

1 Make word partnerships from the words in the boxes. Then use the answers to complete the sentences.

World	British	Nations	Empire	Industrial
United	War	States	Revolution	Cold

a The … began in Britain and fundamentally changed the world of work. It saw the mass production of goods and textiles in factories and mills.

b The … was established in 1945 to promote peace and international cooperation.

c Historians say the … started when explorers claimed land for England in the Americas in the late 16th century.

d The First … saw the emergence of the … as a superpower. Throughout the … it remained in opposition to the Soviet Union.

2 **a** **Work in pairs. Using the internet or dictionaries, correct the mistakes in these sentences that contain abbreviations. Careful – there are spelling, grammar and vocabulary mistakes, too!**

1 NATO stands for North American Treaty Organization.
2 UN stands for United Nationalities. It is based in Washington.
3 You can say the US or the USA. The United States are a big country.
4 FDI is foreign direct income, and means the money that is invested into a country from abroad.
5 GDP is an economical term that stands for Gross Domestic Population.
6 G8 refers to the leading industrial economies of the world: Canada, China, French, Germany, Italy, Japan, Russia, the UK and the USA.
7 OECD is the Organization for Economic Countries and Development.
8 BRIC stands to Brazil, Russia, Indien and Cameroon - emerging markets whose economies are likely to develop significant this century.

b **Compare your answers with another pair.**

c **You are going to read an article with the title "Britain's place in the global economy". Before you read: All the abbreviations in 2 above occur in the text. Discuss what the text might say about them.**

Britain's place in the global economy

The British economy, and its place in the wider global economy, has shifted dramatically from the early days of British sea exploration in the 16th century, through the Industrial Revolution of the 18th and 19th centuries, to the global world of today.

5   In the 19th century, the rapidly industrialising UK was one of the world's most open economies, with trade climbing to half of its overall national income – compared to 35–40 % in France and Germany and around 10 % in the United States. Britain exported mainly manufactured goods – specialising in textiles, shipping and iron – while importing raw materials from the Empire and other
10   resource-rich countries. It also was the source of almost half of the world's foreign

8 **textile** *Textilie, Stoff*

9 shipping manufacture and operation of ships

9 **raw materials** *Rohmaterialien*

10 foreign direct investment *Direktinvestitionen im Ausland*

direct investment (FDI) at the outbreak of the First World War, while receiving less than 2 % itself, and had one of the world's highest rates of net emigration.

Whereas in the 19th century Britain forced openness through industrial dominance and naval power, through the 20th century openness became increasingly secured and influenced through multilateralism, regionalism and the setting of international rules. Once trade with the Empire and Commonwealth began to fade in importance after the Second World War, membership of the European Union and its predecessors became the centrepiece of Britain's global trade policy.

Today, the UK economy is diverse and one of the largest and most prosperous on the planet with a GDP per capita that puts it 3rd among the world's ten largest economies. The bulk of the economy is service-based: from the large and world-beating financial and insurance industry, through professional, technical and support services to the smaller but internationally renowned cultural sector. And, contrary to popular belief, the UK still makes, shapes and builds things too: its manufacturing sector is the 9th largest in the world; construction is the other large non-services sector; while the oil & gas sector remains crucial in strategic terms.

Britain remains a trading nation. Over 65 % of its GDP is linked to trade – higher than that in many other large advanced economies including France (57 %), Italy (59 %) and Japan (31 %). The UK has particular export strengths: for example, it is the second-largest exporter of services in the world after the United States; OECD data indicates that the UK's comparative advantage lies in chemicals, transport equipment and food & drink.

For an island nation covering 0.16 % of the world's land area and with 0.9 % of its population, British influence around the world remains extensive. It has a permanent seat on the United Nations Security Council helping to shape global affairs; it is a major force in the world's most powerful military alliance, NATO; its economy is the 6th largest in the world, underpinning its leadership roles in both the G 8 and G 20; it is a leading member of the European Union, the wealthiest trading bloc in the world; the economy is diverse with export successes in manufacturing and services; and it is both a major recipient and significant source of global investment.

But the world is changing and so too is Britain's place in it. Growth in China and India is shifting the economic centre of gravity to the East – a process accelerated by the worst financial crisis in the developed world since the Great Depression. Although Britain will undoubtedly remain a prosperous nation, the coming decades will see its weight in the world economy fall back as today's emerging powers – the BRICs and other countries such as Mexico and Indonesia – take their places among the world's largest economies. The rise of emerging nations is also changing the nature of global trade, with the emerging world exploiting a comparative advantage in lower labour costs in labour-intensive sectors.

Closing off from this world is not how the UK will create and keep the jobs it needs to pay for public investment and provide a decent standard of living for all its citizens, or maintain its status as a global leader. We must decide if the best way to be outward-facing and globally competitive lies in continuing to use and influence the EU to maximise integration and interdependence with economies all over the world or, instead, in attempting to reverse this process and return to a system of bilateral ad hoc arrangements.

60 The choices the UK makes will fundamentally affect its future. One thing is clear: the process of globalisation will continue, and even accelerate, whatever we decide.   (733 words)

From: the website of the CBI

60 **fundamentally** very significantly

Leseverstehen (p. 222)

S ▶ Doing comprehension tasks, p. 258

WORKING WITH THE TEXT

3 Entscheiden Sie, ob die Aussagen zum Text richtig oder falsch sind. Begründen Sie Ihre Entscheidung auf Deutsch in vollständigen Sätzen.

1 In the 19th century Britain earned considerably more from international trade than the USA.
2 Openness to world trade has become less important to the UK now that the EU is its major trading partner.
3 Despite the decline of trade with former Empire and now Commonwealth countries, Britain's economy is still one of the largest in the world.
4 Manufacturing has replaced the service industries as the main element of the British economy.
5 British influence on the world stage is not in proportion to the size of the country.
6 Britain is unlikely to remain a wealthy country as the economies of the emerging nations develop.

4 Make a list of all the facts and figures mentioned in paragraphs 4–6 (ll. 20–43), then find similar information for Germany and compare the two countries.

5 Explain these expressions from the text.

1 … rapidly industrialising UK was one of the world's most open economies. (ll. 5–6)
2 (Britain) had one of the world's highest rates of net emigration. (l. 12)
3 (Britain's) world-beating financial and insurance industry (ll. 22–23)
4 Contrary to popular belief, the UK still makes, shapes and builds things too. (l. 25)
5 Growth in China and India is shifting the economic centre of gravity to the East. (ll. 44–45)

WORKING WITH WORDS

6 Work in pairs. Use a dictionary to find what the abbreviations in these sentences mean.

1 I worked all night because he had told me to send him all the documents ASAP.
2 There was a great programme on the BBC about UFOs.
3 If we don't find an ATM soon, I have no idea how we'll pay for the taxi.
4 The house was so different from before. I could tell he'd done a lot of DIY.
5 The bill was wrong because they'd forgotten to include the VAT.
6 We had hoped more people would RSVP to our invite to the BBQ.
7 He was stopped by the police for driving at 80mph on the M1.
8 We knew she had a high IQ because she had done well in all her tests.

LOOKING AT LANGUAGE

7 a **Join the two parts of these sentences.**

1 By the end of last century, Britain's status in the world …
2 The Industrial Revolution profoundly changed the world of work; …
3 While openness in trade was achieved by cooperation and agreement between countries in the twentieth century, …
4 By the end of last century, there were already signs that …
5 Britain wanted and needed to do more business with Europe …

a the economies of China and India had improved considerably.
b because trade with the former countries of the Empire had declined.
c had changed a great deal.
d force had been used in the nineteenth.
e before that, most people had worked on the land, and factories had not existed.

G ▸ The past perfect, p. 270

b **Work in pairs. Ask and answer these questions.**

1 By the age of thirteen, what had you already learned to do?
2 How many different things had you done by nine o'clock this morning?

GIVING A PRESENTATION

→ **EXAM PREPARATION**
Präsentationsprüfung (p. 225)

S ▸ Giving a presentation, p. 264

8 **Work in groups. Choose one of these countries:**

Brazil | China | France | Germany | India | Russia | USA

Research and give a presentation that compares and contrasts their economy with the British economy. Consider the following:

• culture
• GDP
• imports and exports
• investment
• labour costs
• manufacturing
• size and population
• technology

2.14

LISTENING

→ **EXAM PREPARATION**
Zentrale Klassenarbeit Hörverstehen (p. 224)

S ▸ Practising listening skills, p. 256

9 Sie hören eine Radiosendung, in der zwei Politiker, Mike Smith und Harriet Clarke, über Entwicklungshilfe diskutieren. Erläutern Sie die jeweils vier Argumente für und gegen Entwicklungshilfe, die die beiden Politiker anführen. Schreiben Sie die Tabelle ab und vervollständigen Sie diese auf Deutsch mit Informationen aus der Radiosendung.

Argumente für Entwicklungshilfe	Argumente gegen Entwicklungshilfe

TEXT 6   Accepting new arrivals

WARM UP

1   a   Put these expressions in the correct category.

seagulls crying | traffic roaring | people chatting | ferries loading and unloading | fish frying | waves breaking | wind howling | builders working | rain falling | people walking | women wearing perfume | people smoking | puddles forming | dogs barking | a radio playing | doors opening and closing

mainly sights	mainly sounds	mainly smells

b   What sights, sounds and smells do you associate with a port?

2   There are hundreds of thousands of refugees in Europe. Brainstorm with a partner where refugees are housed. Think also of where else they might be housed.

The port

Lawrence Bradbury

On a coastal ledge backed by high white cliffs,
which are not white but rising green,
reticulated cast iron balconies bleed rust
down the pale frontage of hotels,
5   which are not hotels but emergency accommodation
housing short stay clients,
who are not clients but the subjects of the money, agents, chance,
their own tenacity
which bore them through tight conduits with Europe's roaring freight
10   to this safe country,
which is not safe but undecided,
so it stalls them
on this doorstep backed by high green cliffs
like sour milk
15   while it supervises slumping mounds of forms
handwritten
with versions of their lives laid out
precisely as required
showing the unique chronology
20   of their horrors
which are not horrors but the usual inhumanities, banal,
classifiable,
which gets the clients nowhere,
which is here
25   where the wind gnaws at the gantries and the ferries, like sudden building sites,
come up too close.
This is no emergency. It is the routine of the port.   (161 words)

The Forward Book of Poetry, 2009

¹ coastal on the coast
¹ ledge *Felsvorsprung, Kante*
³ reticulate form into squares like a net
³ **bleed** lose blood
³ **rust** *Rost*
⁴ frontage front part
⁵ **emergency accommodation** *Notunterkunft*
⁶ **short stay** for a short period
⁷ **agent** *Makler/in*
⁸ tenacity *Hartnäckigkeit*
⁹ bear (past: bore) carry
¹⁰ tight narrow
¹¹ conduit ['kɒndjuɪt] (here:) passage
¹² stall sb/sth delay sb/sth
¹⁴ **sour** sauer
¹⁵ **supervise sth** check sth
¹⁵ slump fall
¹⁵ mound small hill
¹⁷ lay sth out (past: laid) reveal sth
²¹ **inhumanity** cruel behaviour
²² classifiable *klassifizierbar*
²⁵ gnaw at sth chew away at sth

WORKING WITH THE POEM

3 Answer the questions.

1 Who are "the clients"? How do they differ from normal clients in hotels?
2 Explain in your own words the reasons for these "corrections" in the poem:
  · the cliffs are not white but green
  · hotels are emergency accommodation
  · the country is not safe but undecided
  · horrors are usual inhumanities
  · here is nowhere
  · this is not an emergency but routine
3 Look at the punctuation of the poem. It is made of just three sentences. What effect does this create?
4 What information is likely to be required on the forms the people have to fill in? Why are there mounds of forms?
5 Why is "tenacity" the only quality that people have? What other qualities do you think people in their situation need?

4 Work in groups. Discuss whether the author presents a positive or negative image of a) immigrants, b) the host country. Report back to the class.

WORKING WITH WORDS

5 Complete the sentences with these words from the text in the correct form.

agent | bleed | building site | doorstep | emergency | roar | undecided

1 Everything is very convenient here. I have everything I need right on the ….
2 This is more than serious, it's a/an …. Call an ambulance.
3 Footballers don't negotiate their salaries. They have a/an … to do that for them.
4 I cut myself when I was shaving this morning. It … a lot.
5 They stood on the bridge and watched the traffic … past on the motorway.
6 It's very noisy at the moment because of the … next door.
7 I don't know who to vote for in the election. I'm ….

LOOKING AT LANGUAGE

 a We often add emphasis to what we say by using an extreme word. Add the appropriate word to complete these sentences.

agony | aggressive | awful | chaotic | disaster | exorbitant |
freezing | impossible | shocked | tiny

1 It wasn't just a little cold. It was …
2 It was more than difficult. It was …
3 I don't think impolite is how I would describe him. He was extremely …
4 A problem is not how I would term it – it was a … .
5 I was more than surprised. I was completely … .
6 No, I don't think it was just bad. I think it was …
7 It wasn't small. It was …
8 The price wasn't expensive. It was …
9 Come on, it wasn't just a little painful – I was in … .
10 I'd say it was more than busy. It was completely … .

b Work in pairs. Make a list of as many different ways as possible to replace the underlined words in these sentences with words that are similar. Compare your lists with another group.

1 We had a <u>nice</u> time.
2 They're really <u>nice</u> people.
3 Your holiday sounds <u>nice</u>.
4 The view was really <u>nice</u>.
5 That's a <u>good</u> idea.
6 Yesterday was a <u>bad</u> day for me.
7 It's a <u>big</u> problem.
8 I had <u>a lot of</u> problems.

WRITING

 Choose one of these tasks.

1 Write a poem or short story with one of these titles:
A nice day
A nice place
A nice person
2 Imagine you are one of the "clients" in the poem. Write your story including details of why you left your home, how you travelled to the UK, and what happened after you arrived.

ENGLISH FOR WORK
Intercultural Communication 1

WARM-UP

1 **a** Discuss what the intercultural problem could be in each of these situations.

1 A Japanese business woman gives you her business card. You have run out of cards, so ask her for one of hers, and write your details on the back of her card and give it to her.

2 You are invited to a restaurant by a Chinese company. During the meal you take the opportunity to give more details about the business deal you have discussed before.

3 You developed an advertising campaign to promote your glasses in Thailand. To be fun and memorable, you show animals wearing them.

4 A Saudi businessman has offered you a cup of coffee. You have just had one, so say no.

5 Your Italian colleague is half an hour late for a meeting she agreed with you. When she arrives, you comment on this and say you can only stay for ten minutes as a result.

6 A Greek colleague has explained something to you, and asked your opinion. You put your hand up, palm towards him, to indicate you need a bit more time to think.

7 A group of Indian business men and women greet you with hands together and say "namaste". You do the same to show respect to their culture, then go round the group shaking everyone's hand.

8 You feel a little cold in a Russian office as the heating doesn't seem to be working, so you keep your coat on and put your hands in your pockets.

2.15

b Listen to this discussion about the importance of intercultural awareness and check your answers. Which two are not mentioned?

LISTENING

2 Decide which comments best complete this grid.

What the British say	What the British mean	What others understand
I hear what you say.	Oh dear! I don't like what he is saying and want to end the conversation.	He accepts my point of view
With the greatest respect …	…	They are listening to me
That's not bad.	…	That's not all that good.
Quite good.	…	It's quite good, but could be better.

I would suggest …	…	Keep my idea, but consider their ideas if I want to.
Oh, by the way,/ incidentally,	…	This is not very important.
I was a bit disappointed that …	…	It's ok but not that important.
Very interesting.	…	They are impressed
I'll bear it in mind.	…	They'll probably do it.
I'm sure it is our fault.	…	Why do they think it is their fault?
You must come for dinner.	…	I will get an invitation soon.
I only have a few minor comments.	…	Great! Basically they like what I've done.
Perhaps you could think about some other options.	…	They want me to adjust a few things.

1 Your idea is worthless.
2 Very good indeed.
3 A bit disappointing.
4 I'm just being polite.
5 Do what I say, or else.
6 Please change this completely.
7 There's no way I am going to do what you said.

8 I think what you said was stupid.
9 What on earth is this?
10 I am really annoyed.
11 You obviously had no idea what we wanted.
12 Please start it all again.

3 a Copy the sentences below and underline the different words or expressions that 'soften' the negative ideas in these sentences.

1 There might be a slight delay with finishing this, unfortunately.
2 I'm afraid the meeting didn't go exactly as we had planned.
3 There were one or two problems with the launch of our new technology.
4 I think it might be a good idea to look at a couple of alternatives before we decide which programme to install.
5 Do you think we should perhaps contact another supplier for a quote on this?
6 I'm afraid I haven't quite had time to finish the report.
7 It's unlikely that we will be able to give you a better deal than what we have already offered.
8 I take your point, but I'm afraid I don't think we'll be able to do what you are suggesting.

b Work in pairs. Use "softeners" and/or rewrite these sentences to make them more acceptable.

1 That's not acceptable.
2 You're wrong.
3 We can't have a meeting on the date you suggest.

4 We're not ready.
5 The quality of this product is poor.
6 I don't agree with what you said.

181

The USA: a fading superpower?

VA 6   3.01

settler *Siedler/in*
colonist *Siedler/in, Kolonist/in*
Puritan *Puritaner/in*
work ethic *Arbeitsmoral*
religious faith *Glaube*
colony *Kolonie*
Declaration of Independence *Unabhängigkeitserklärung*
constitution *Verfassung*
Founding Fathers *Gründerväter*
Revolutionary War *Revolutionskrieg*

pioneer spirit *Pioniergeist*
Wild West *Wilder Westen*
Native American *amerikanische/r Ureinwohner/in*
tribe *Stamm*
reservation *Reservat*

civil war *Bürgerkrieg*
secession *Abspaltung, Sezession*
slavery *Sklaverei*
cotton *Baumwolle*
plantation *Plantage*
Confederacy *Konföderation, die Konföderierten Staaten von Amerika*
Union *Union, die Nordstaaten*
abolish sth *etw abschaffen*
African-American *Afroamerikaner/-in*
Civil Rights Movement *Bürgerrechtsbewegung*
immigration *Einwanderung*
emigrate *auswandern*
escape poverty *der Armut entfliehen*
religious persecution *Verfolgung aus religiösen Gründen*
melting pot *Schmelztiegel (der Kulturen)*
national identity *Nationalbewusstsein, nationales Selbstverständnis*

BACKGROUND INFORMATION

Ideological beginnings

The first settlers to America came from Europe in the 17th century, either to seek a new life or religious freedom. Among the first colonists were Puritans from England whose way of life was guided by Biblical law and their belief in hard work. The "work ethic" and religious faith still play an important role 5 in American society and politics today.

In the 1760s, the thirteen original colonies on America's eastern coast started to protest against unpopular British taxes and other laws. In 1776, representatives of the colonies signed the Declaration of Independence, which stated that "all men are created equal". The authors of this document 10 and the Constitution (1787) became known as the Founding Fathers of the United States. It was the first time that any colony had ever broken away from its "mother country". Against all the odds, the Americans won this Revolutionary War against Britain. Their victory reinforced their belief that the foundation of their nation was part of God's plan. 15

The 19th century expansion

During the 19th century many Americans believed that the United States was meant to extend across the continent from the Atlantic to the Pacific. The pioneer spirit of the USA encouraged families to settle the Wild West. The US government acquired the land by fighting over it with the Mexicans, 20 by buying it from other countries, or by stealing it from the Native Americans. In the course of the century, the traditional way of life of the Native American tribes was all but destroyed and they were forced to resettle on reservations, often made up of barren or unfertile land that was hundreds of miles from their tribal homeland. 25

The Civil War

In 1860–61, eleven southern states declared their secession from the USA. The main reason for this was because they wanted to keep slavery. The practise of keeping slaves from Africa to work on cotton or tobacco plantations was still widespread in the South and seen by many there as an 30 economic necessity. A civil war raged between the Confederacy (the southern states) and the Union (the northern states). The Union won in 1865 and slavery was abolished and the slaves were set free. However, it would be another hundred years before African-Americans achieved full equality with the Civil Rights Movement of the 1960s. 35

The years following the Civil War were marked by huge waves of immigration, especially from Ireland, Italy, Germany and Russia. Many Irish, for example, emigrated to escape poverty and famine; others, such as Jews, were fleeing from religious persecution. Up to 1 million people per year emigrated to the USA during this period, giving rise to the notion of the USA as a "melting 40 pot", where all nationalities could come together to create one American national identity.

The Great Depression and World War II

The numbers of immigrants dropped significantly in the 1930s and 1940s as
45 the USA suffered from the Great Depression following the Wall Street Crash
of 1929. The Japanese attack on Pearl Harbor, Hawaii, in December 1941
forced the USA into the Second World War. The mobilization of troops and
the general war effort effectively ended the Depression years. After the war,
new waves of immigrants from Asia and Latin America moved to the USA in
50 search of the American Dream. The Hispanics are now the largest ethnic
minority in the USA and the debate on nationality has now moved on to
whether the USA should be described as a "salad bowl", where each
immigrant group keeps its ethnic identity, rather than immerse itself into
one monolithic culture.

55 ## The USA as a superpower

Ever since the Second World War, the USA has been the world's superpower,
but this position has not been unchallenged. The Cold War saw the USA in
constant competition with the Soviet Union until the fall of Communism.
Despite the failure of the Vietnam War, this was a time of great prosperity
60 for the USA. With its dynamic economic system and diverse population, the
USA became the world leader in science, medicine, space exploration,
entrepreneurship, entertainment, digital communication and many other
areas. It also maintained the world's most powerful military.
The first two presidents of the 21st century, George W. Bush of the
65 Republican Party and Barack Obama of the Democratic Party, personify the
division of the nation into what some call the "two Americas". On the one
side are conservative politicians, who believe in traditional "family" values
and on the other side are liberal groups. These divisions run along the same
lines for many questions that are hotly-debated in the USA today, such as
70 gun control, health care and same-sex marriage.
The terrorist attack on the World Trade Center in New York on 11 September
2001 – usually referred to as "9/11" – has had a deep effect on the American
psyche. Following the attack, President Bush launched the so-called "War
on Terror". This led to invasions of Afghanistan and later Iraq. Many
75 Americans protested against these interventions and were in turn accused of
being unpatriotic and "not supporting the troops". To prevent terrorist
attacks, the US security agencies have been carrying out mass
electronic surveillance, which has come under a lot of criticism at
home and abroad.
80 The subprime mortgage crisis of 2007–2008 led to the worst
financial crisis since the Great Depression and to the national
debt rising significantly. With the continuing increase in
Chinese economic power, we may see the USA lose its status as
superpower.

Great Depression	*Weltwirtschaftskrise (von 1929)*
immigrant	*Einwanderer/in*
Wall Street Crash	*Börsenkrach (von 1929)*
war effort	*Kriegsanstrengungen*
the American Dream	*der Amerikanische Traum*
Hispanic	*Hispano-Amerikaner/in*
salad bowl	*Salatschüssel*
ethnic identity	*ethnische Identität*
monolithic culture	*erstarrte, nicht wandlungsfähige Kultur*

superpower	*Supermacht*
Cold War	*Kalter Krieg*
Soviet Union	*Sowjetunion*
Vietnam War	*Vietnamkrieg*
prosperity	*Wohlstand*
economic system	*Wirtschaftssystem*
diverse population	*vielfältige/ multikulturelle Bevölkerung*

Republican Party	*republikanische Partei*
Democratic Party	*demokratische Partei*
value	*Wert*
gun control	*Reglementierung von Waffenbesitz*
health care	*Gesundheitswesen, medizinische Versorgung*
same-sex marriage	*gleichgeschlechtliche Ehe*
terrorist attack	*Terroranschlag*
9/11	*11. September (2001)*
War on Terror	*Antiterrorkrieg, Bekämpfung des Terrorismus*
intervention	*Eingreifen, militärische Intervention*
unpatriotic	*unpatriotisch*
security agency	*Sicherheitsbehörde*
mass electronic surveillance	*elektronische Massenüberwachung*
national debt	*Staatsverschuldung*

1 **a** Copy and complete the table with suitable verbs and nouns. A member of each word family is in the text. Use your dictionary for help if necessary.

verb	noun (person)	noun (abstract)
settle	…	…
enslave	…	…
…	immigrant	…
…	…	competition
entertain	…	…
…	invader	…

b Write four sentences of your own showing how the words are used.

2 Complete these sentences using a suitable form of the verbs in the box.

abolish | achieve | carry out | escape | launch | prevent | protest | rebel | seek | set

1 The 13 original colonies … against the unpopular British government in London.
2 Many immigrants came to the USA to … a new life.
3 Irish immigrants came to … poverty following the Great Famine.
4 President Abraham Lincoln wanted to … slavery in the southern states.
5 At the end of the Civil War, the slaves in the southern states … free.
6 African-Americans only … full equality before the law in the 1960s.
7 Following 9/11, the USA … an invasion of Afghanistan.
8 Many Americans … against the war in Iraq.
9 The US security agencies … mass surveillance of digital communications.
10 We are told that surveillance is necessary to … terrorist attacks in future.

3 Which adjectives from the text complete these collocations?

1 … minority/identity/diversity/group
2 … identity/debt/interest/security/unity
3 … necessity/system/power/growth/decline
4 … way of life/values/costume
5 … freedom/persecution/education/fanatic

4 Which highlighted phrases in the text match these definitions?

1 the group of people who wrote the Constitution of the USA
2 the document which started the Revolutionary War
3 the war fought between the northern and the southern states of the USA from 1861 to 1865
4 the war of independence between the thirteen British colonies in America and Britain
5 American people whose ancestors came from Africa.
6 the belief that America offers everyone the chance of a good and successful life through hard work
7 the people who were the original people living in America
8 the campaign in the 1950s and 1960s for equal rights for African-Americans

TEXT 1   My homeland America

WARM-UP

1 **a** Which of the state or city names belong in the song titles below?

Alabama | California | L.A. | Vegas | Memphis | New York | Philadelphia | San Jose

1 Dionne Warwick: Do you know the way to ––?––
2 The Doors: ––?–– Woman
3 Lynyrd Skynyrd: Sweet Home, ––?––
4 The Eagles: Hotel ––?––
5 Sting: An Englishman in––?––
6 Marc Cohn: Walking in ––?––
7 Bruce Springsteen: The Streets of ––?––
8 Katy Perry: Waking up in ––?–– !

b How many other songs can you think of with American place names in the title or in the lyrics? Work in groups and make a list. See which group can put together a list of 10 songs fastest.

c Compare your lists in class: What is it about American place names that make people want to write songs about them? (Try putting together a list of 10 songs with either German or British place names.)

2 **a** The USA is a land of contrasts. Look at these two photos and discuss the contrasting images of the USA that they show.

b What places do <u>you</u> think of when you think of the USA? Find two photos and explain to the class what aspect(s) of the USA they represent for you.

c In class, make a top 10 of your USA photos and stick them on the board. What impression of the USA does this photo collage give?

Lee Greenwood performing in Nashville, 2013

God bless the USA
3.02

Lee Greenwood

If tomorrow all the things were gone,
I'd worked for all my life.
And I had to start again,
with just my children and my wife.

I'd thank my lucky stars,   5
to be livin here today.
'Cause the flag still stands for freedom,
and they can't take that away.

And I'm proud to be an American,
where at least I know I'm free.   10
And I won't forget the men who died,
who gave that right to me.

And I gladly stand up,
next to you and defend her still today.
'Cause there ain't no doubt I love this land,   15
God bless the USA.

From the lakes of Minnesota,
to the hills of Tennessee.
Across the plains of Texas,
From sea to shining sea.   20

From Detroit down to Houston,
and New York to L.A.
Well there's pride in every American heart,
and its time we stand and say.

That I'm proud to be an American,   25
where at least I know I'm free.
And I won't forget the men who died,
who gave that right to me.

And I gladly stand up,
next to you and defend her still today.   30
'Cause there ain't no doubt I love this land,
God bless the USA.

And I'm proud to be and American,
where at least I know I'm free.
And I won't forget the men who died,   35
who gave that right to me.

And I gladly stand up,
next to you and defend her still today.
'Cause there ain't no doubt I love this land,
God bless the USA.   40

(261 words)

From: You've Got a Good Love Comin', 1984

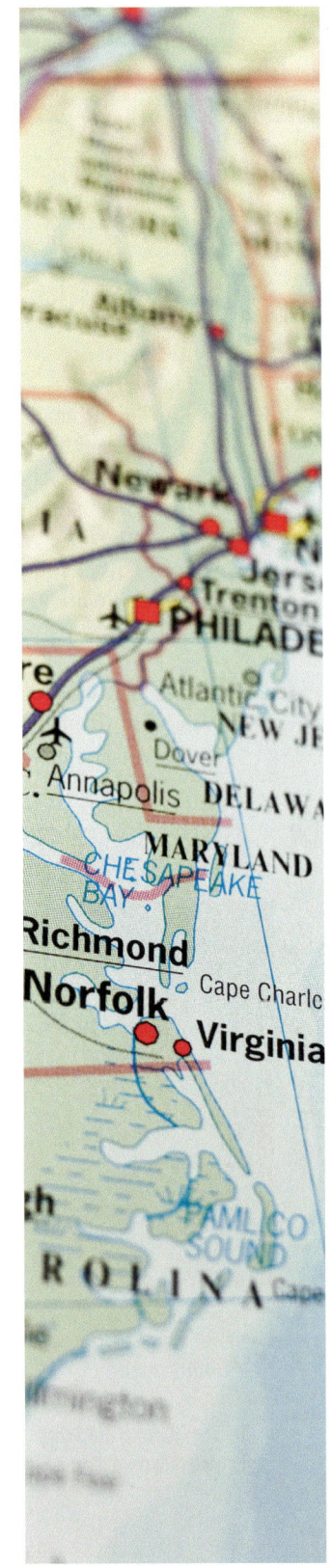

Bruce Springsteen performing in Hershey, 2014

[4] cover up try to stop people knowing the truth about sth

[9] in a jam in a difficult situation

[18] refinery *(Erdöl-)Raffinerie*

[19] **if it was up to me** *wenn's nach mir ginge*

[20] V.A. (U.S. Department of Veterans Affairs) *US Behörde, die sich um die Belange von Kriegsveteranen kümmert*

[22] Khe Sahn battle area in Vietnam in 1968

[22] Viet Cong communist army in Vietnam War

[27] penitentiary prison

Born in the U.S.A.

3.03

Bruce Springsteen

Born down in a dead man's town
The first kick I took was when I hit the ground
You end up like a dog that's been beat too much
Till you spend half your life just covering up

Born in the U.S.A.   5
I was born in the U.S.A.
I was born in the U.S.A.
Born in the U.S.A.

Got in a little hometown jam
so they put a rifle in my hand   10
Sent me off to a foreign land
to go and kill the yellow man

Born in the U.S.A.
I was born in the U.S.A.
I was born in the U.S.A.   15
I was born in the U.S.A.
Born in the U.S.A.

Come back home to the refinery
Hiring man says "son if it was up to me"
Went down to see my V.A. man   20
He said "Son, don't you understand now"

I had a brother at Khe Sahn fighting off the Viet Cong
They're still there, he's all gone

He had a woman he loved in Saigon
I got a picture of him in her arms now   25

Down in the shadow of penitentiary
Out by the gas fires of the refinery
I'm ten years burning down the road
Nowhere to run ain't got nowhere to go
                                                                     30
Born in the U.S.A.
I was born in the U.S.A.
Born in the U.S.A.
I'm a long gone Daddy in the U.S.A.
Born in the U.S.A.   35
Born in the U.S.A.
Born in the U.S.A.
I'm a cool rocking Daddy in the U.S.A.

From: Born in the USA, 1984

LOOKING AT THE TEXTS

 a Work with a partner. Each choose the lyrics of one of the songs and make notes on the following questions.

1 What places does the song mention? What image do they give of America?
2 What reason does the song give for going to war?
3 How do the people at home treat war heroes and veterans?

b Share your notes with your partner. What contrasting picture of American patriotism do the songs present? Explain your answers.

SPEAKING

 a Both songs are very popular in the USA. Which one can you relate to more? Give reasons. Could you imagine singing either song about Germany. Say why (not)?

b The "Pledge of Allegiance" below is an important part of many public ceremonies in the USA, including school assemblies and sports competitions. Why do you think patriotism (to a town, city, state, or to the United States) plays such an important role in the USA?

"I pledge allegiance to the flag of the United States of America, and to the republic for which it stands, one nation under God, indivisible, with liberty and justice for all."

GIVING A PRESENTATION

5 Each bring a favourite song about the USA to class. Play a (short) extract of the song and explain what it says to you about the USA and why you like it. Afterwards, you can vote on your "Top 10 Songs About the USA".

TEXT 2 Economic dream or nightmare?

WARM-UP

  a Which of the places in the photos do you associate with these industries or services? Can you locate the places on the map on the inside cover of this book?

1 space exploration
2 computer industry
3 crop-growing agriculture
4 film industry

5 banking and financial services
6 oil industry
7 the old industrial heartland
8 cotton-growing agriculture

Silicon Valley

Dallas

The Corn Belt

The Cotton Belt

Cape Canaveral

Wall Street

The Rust Belt

Hollywood

b What other products do you associate with the American economy?

c What challenges do you think the American economy faces?

The end of the American Dream?

Michael Cohen

During the 2012 presidential election, Republican nominee Mitt Romney regularly liked to joke that President Obama wanted the US economy to look "more like Europe". In the context of modern American politics, few insults are more stinging. To be European is to be somehow effeminate, irresolute and, perhaps worst of all,
5 socialist. It's the opposite of the "rugged individualism" and "exceptional nature" of the uniquely American experiment in self-government.

But, as a sobering *New York Times* article last week made clear, America could have a lot to learn by looking to Europe. According to the *New York Times*, the American middle class – the linchpin of the country's phenomenal postwar
10 economic growth – can no longer call itself the richest in the world. "While the wealthiest Americans are outpacing many of their global peers," says the NYT, "across the lower- and middle-income tiers, citizens of other advanced countries have received considerably larger raises over the last three decades." America's poorest citizens lag behind their European counterparts; 35 years ago, the opposite
15 was true.

[1] nominee *Kandidat/in*
[3] insult *Beleidigung*
[3] stinging hurtful
[4] effeminate *unmännlich, weibisch*
[4] irresolute not able to make a decision
[5] rugged *rau, robust*
[5] **individualism** the belief that individuals rather than the government should make decisions about their lives
[7] sobering making you feel serious and think carefully
[9] linchpin *wesentliche Stütze*
[11] outpace sb grow faster than sb
[11] **peer** person of the same age or social status
[12] tier level
[14] lag behind sb not do as well as sb else

16 wake-up call event that makes people realize there is a problem

17 malaise *Missstand*

23 tenacious *hartnäckig*

27 disquieting worrying

30 counterintuitive the opposite of what you would expect

30 swagger walk in a proud and confident way

31 sense of moral purpose *moralisches Empfinden*

33 **stable** solide, stabil

34 **technological capability** the ability to use technology to one's advantage

35 **fall behind sb** not do as well as sb else

37 granted *zugegeben*

38 wreak havoc cause a huge amount of damage or chaos

39 ostentatious expensive and showy, in a way that is meant to impress

43 abdicate your responsibilities fail to perform a duty

43 tilt the scales toward sb give sb an unfair advantage

44 **affluent** wealthy

45 **obligation** duty, responsibility

45 **social safety net** *soziales Netz*

46 vulnerable weak and easily hurt

47 go the way of sth (here:) disappear in the same way as sth

47 VCR video cassette recorder

48 indifference lack of interest

52 **prosperity** wealth

53 **health benefits** *Kranken-versicherungsleistungen*

54 **retirement benefits** *Renten-versicherungsleistungen*

54 creature comforts all the things that make modern life more comfortable

56 suburbanite sb who lives in a suburb and enjoys that lifestyle

57 bounty sth provided in large amounts

58 nostalgic portrayal *verklärte Darstellung*

This was yet one more wake-up call about the reality of America's continuing economic malaise. Ask Americans if the country is on the right track – 60 % say no. Satisfied with the way things are going in America – only 25 % say yes. Still think you're a member of the middle class – only 44 % feel so confident. Forty per cent self-identify as lower-class, a 15-point jump since 2008. Among young people, the numbers are even more depressing. Those who place themselves in the lowest tier have doubled in just the past six years. [20]

While a majority of Americans tenaciously continue to hold dear the American Dream – that long-standing American ideal that if you work hard anything is possible – more and more people are reporting that the opportunity for social advancement feels increasingly out of reach for them and their children. Indeed, it is hard to think of a more disquieting trend in American society than the fact that those in their 20s and 30s are less likely to have a high school diploma than those between the ages of 55 and 64. [25]

All of this must seem counterintuitive to foreign audiences. The US swaggers along on the world stage with a certainty and sense of moral purpose that no other country can match. Blessed with practically limitless national resources, a dynamic and diverse population, a relatively stable political system and innovative technological capabilities that other nations can only dream of, how can so many Americans be falling behind – and how can the nation's leaders allow it to happen? [30] [35]

The answer is disconcertingly simple: we chose this path.

Granted, no one actively set out to attack the middle class in America. There wasn't some evil plan hatched behind closed doors to wreak socio-economic havoc. But the decline of the American middle class, the ostentatious wealth of the so-called 1% and the crushing economic anxiety of the growing number of poor Americans have happened in plain sight. [40]

It is the direct result of a political system that has for more than four decades abdicated its responsibilities – and tilted the economic scales toward the most affluent and well-connected in American society. The idea that government has an obligation to create jobs, grow the economy, construct a social safety net or even put the interests of the most vulnerable in society above the most successful has gone the way of transistor radios, fax machines and VCRs. Today, America is paying the price for that indifference to this slow-motion economic collapse. [45]

It wasn't always like this.

Once, Americans lived in a country where it wasn't just the biggest boats that floated high on a rising economic tide. In the years after the Second World War, America was defined by an unprecedented period of economic prosperity. Jobs were plentiful and well-paying, with generous health and retirement benefits. New creature comforts, from refrigerators and washing machines to televisions and cars, were suddenly available. Americans became homeowners and eventually, if they were lucky, suburbanites. Perhaps most important, those at the bottom of the economic ladder shared in the bounty as much as those at the top. [50] [55]

Life back then was never as idyllic as nostalgic portrayals of postwar America would suggest (this was particularly true if you were a minority or a woman). But it was also true that Americans enjoyed the type of economic security that current generations can only dream of.   (735 words) [60]

From: The Guardian, 26 April 2014

WORKING WITH THE TEXT

2 Entscheiden Sie, ob die Aussagen zum Text richtig oder falsch sind. Begründen Sie Ihre Entscheidung auf Deutsch.

1 Politicians in the USA admire the political system and the social achievements of European countries.
2 The enormous economic success of the USA after the Second World War was due to working class Americans.
3 Within the last few years, the number of Americans who consider themselves to be "lower class" has increased.
4 America's confident presence on the international stage is in stark contrast to the economic development of the majority of Americans.
5 During the last 40 years, the various governments of the USA have always made it a priority to create jobs.
6 In the years following the Second World War, all the social classes in the USA were able to profit from the economic boom in one way or another.

→ **EXAM PREPARATION**
Leseverstehen (p. 222)

S ▶ Doing comprehension tasks, p. 258

3 In dem vorliegenden Text werden vier Vorteile genannt, die die USA hat und von denen der Rest der Welt nur träumen kann. Erstellen Sie eine Liste dieser Vorteile. Formulieren Sie vollständige deutsche Sätze.

→ **EXAM PREPARATION**
Leseverstehen (p. 222)

S ▶ Doing comprehension tasks, p. 258

WORKING WITH WORDS

4 Rewrite the following sentences, replacing the underlined phrases with expressions from the box. You may have to change the form of the verb.

be a wake-up call to | lag behind | on the right track | out of reach | outpace their global peers | pay the price for sth

1 The richest 1 % of Americans have <u>got richer faster than anybody else in the world</u> in the last 25 years.
2 America's lower classes <u>have now been overtaken by</u> their counterparts in Europe.
3 Only 40 % of Americans think that their country is <u>heading in the right direction</u>.
4 The recent survey <u>has got the attention of</u> the government about its weak economic policy.
5 Many Americans now feel that a better life for their children is <u>completely impossible</u>.
6 American society is now <u>suffering badly from</u> the economic policies of the last 30 years.

5 Complete the text with the adjective form of the word in brackets. All the adjectives are in the text.

G ▶ Adjectives and adverbs, p. 279

The …[1] (phenomenon) economic growth in the USA after World War II was made possible by a …[2] (dynamism) workforce, many of them immigrants, working hard under …[3] (exception) circumstances, …[4] (confidence) of providing a better life for themselves and their children. Jobs were …[5] (plenty) and well-paid, often with …[6] (generosity) health and retirement benefits. The economy was technologically …[7] (innovation) and the system of government …[8] (stability) in comparison to many other countries. Looking back, the post-war years now seem …[9] (idyll), as many Americans today find the current economic situation …[10] (depression) and only a small …[11] (affluence) minority enjoys the economic security that people had 50 years ago.

LOOKING AT LANGUAGE

6 Rewrite the sentences using the verbs in brackets. You will need to use verb + object + to-infinitive as in the example.

1 Americans think their government should do more for the middle classes. (want/help)
Americans want their government to help the middle classes.
2 The advisers told the politician to look at Europe as an example. (ask/study)
3 Immigrants know that their families will have a hard time when they arrive in the USA. (expect/suffer)
4 Globalization made the company shut down its American factories. (force/close)
5 The President said that Congress should remember the unemployed. (warn/forget)
6 The pioneers made sure that their children had skills they could use in the Wild West. (teach/rely on)
7 His mother was unhappy when he got a job in the automobile factory. (not want/start)
8 She told him that he should get a college education first. (advise/go)
9 Government policies have made it easy for the rich to become richer. (allow/get)

3.04

LISTENING

EXAM PREPARATION
Zentrale Klassenarbeit Hörverstehen (p. 224)

S ▶ Practising listening skills, p. 256

7 Sie hören ein Interview von Michel Dobson von Radio South-East 7 mit der Professorin Jean Daly über ihr neues Buch „What Makes Americans Tick?". Jean Daly nennt vier Grundbegriffe, die wichtig sind, um die amerikanische Mentalität zu verstehen. Erläutern Sie diese Grundbegriffe, gegebenenfalls mit Beschreibung aus dem Text. Schreiben Sie die Tabelle ab und vervollständigen Sie sie auf Deutsch mit Informationen aus dem Interview.

Grundbegriff	Beschreibung

GIVING A PRESENTATION

EXAM PREPARATION
Präsentationsprüfung (p. 225)

S ▶ Giving a presentation, p. 264

8 Choose one of the events named below and prepare a short talk about it. What was the significance of the event for the economic development of the USA?

1865	End of the American Civil War.
1869	First transcontinental railroad completed.
1876	Alexander Graham Bell patented the telephone.
1914	Henry Ford opened first production line.
1927	*The Jazz Singer:* the first motion picture with sound.
1929	Wall Street Crash; start of the Great Depression.
1931	Empire State Building opened.
1933	Franklin D. Roosevelt's New Deal.
1941	USA declared war on Germany and Japan.
1945	The atom bomb dropped on two Japanese cities.
1955	Disneyland opened in Anaheim, California; first McDonald's opens.
1969	Apollo 11 moon landing.
1975	Microsoft Corporation founded.
2004	Facebook launched.

TEXT 3   Living on the rez

WARM-UP

1 What do you know about "Native Americans"? What words, people or events do you associate with them? Think about the questions below and collect your ideas on the board.

- What happened to the Native Americans as the United States of America spread across the continent towards the Pacific Ocean?
- What happened to their traditional way of life?
- Where does any information you have about Native Americans come from? How are/were they portrayed?
- Where do the descendants of the original tribes now live?

Custer's Last Stand, 1876

The Trail of Tears, 1838

Reservation in New Mexico

Native American casino on a reservation

Fighting the food desert with junk food taxes

3.05

In December 2014, Berkeley, Calif., became the first city in the U.S. to pass a soda tax measure. But the measure that the Navajo Nation Council has just signed into law goes even further. The Healthy Diné Nation Act is the first in the U.S. to tax not only sugary beverages but also snacks, sweets and baked or fried goods of
5 "minimal nutritional value."

250,000 people live in the Navajo Nation, a 27,000-square-mile reservation extending into Utah, Arizona and New Mexico. *Focus News* went to Window Rock, the capital of the Navajo Nation, to speak to Dana Washington, a community health worker.

10 **Focus** Dana, could you explain first of all what exactly the Healthy Diné Nation Act is?

food desert area, region where healthy, fresh food is not available
[1] soda (AE) *soft drink*
[2] measure *Maßnahme*
[4] beverage any kind of drink (except water)
[5] nutritional value *Nährwert*

Washington Well, "Diné" is just another name for Navajo. As of April 1, all junk food and snacks, like cheese puffs, sodas and energy drinks sold inside the Navajo Nation will have an extra 2-cent sales tax on top of the 5-cent sales tax already on most goods sold here. And fresh produce, such as fruit and vegetables, are now tax-free.

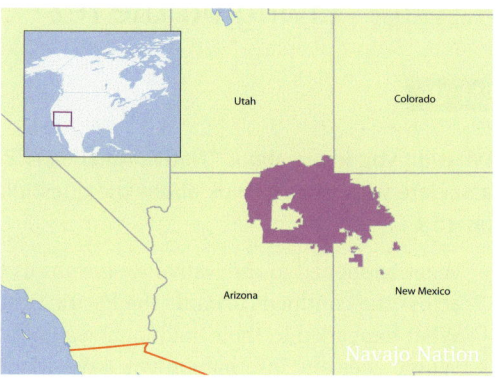

Focus What were the reasons behind this tax measure?

Washington For many years, health workers and volunteers have been seriously concerned about diabetes and obesity rates on the reservation and have been a campaigning for taxes on junk food and sodas. Some 10 percent of Navajo Nation residents have diabetes, and another 30 percent are pre-diabetic, according to the figures from the Indian Health Services. The obesity rate within the reservation ranges between 26 and 60 percent.

Focus What do you think is the cause of these alarming rates?

Washington The figures are partly due to the fact that the reservation is a food desert … and the U.S. Department of Agriculture has identified it as such. This means that there is a prevalence of unhealthy foods in the area, over 90 percent of the inventory of most local stores in fact, and there is only a limited number of places to shop for food of any kind. For example, there are only 10 full-service grocery stores on the entire Navajo reservation. And if you compare a grocery store on the reservation with one in Phoenix belonging to the same company, you'll see they have much more healthy foods available in Phoenix compared to here.

Focus So how much money is the Healthy Diné Nation Act going to raise?

Washington We don't know how much revenue the tax will generate between now and 2020, when it expires, but it could be as much as $3 million a year. Those funds are earmarked for health and wellness programs on the reservation, like gardening and nutrition education. So besides the reasons for introducing the tax we benefit financially.

Focus And the reasons are …?

Washington This is the start of making people aware that we are living in a food desert — something that's not normal – and show how difficult it is to buy healthy food on the reservation. We also wanted to improve the availability of these foods in our local markets and to improve people's access to them. By lifting the tax on fruits and vegetables, we also hope to raise demand for fresh groceries. More than half the Navajo members surveyed in 2012 said they traveled to off-nation stores to purchase groceries; some even said they needed a 240-mile round trip to buy fresh vegetables and meat. Now we will have the chance to buy healthy foods that are cheaper and re-create our grocery stores.

15

20

25

30

35

40

45

50

55

Focus Do you think the measures are going to have an effect on peoples' eating habits? Won't people who are addicted to sugar and junk food pay any price to get what they want?

Washington There's no precedent for a junk food tax anywhere in the U.S., so we don't know what effect it will have. But the campaign organizers faced a lot of pressure from the beverage industry to drop the soda tax proposal. They don't want people drinking less soda. I just hope that the tax will go back into the community for more education and raise peoples' awareness about what they eat.

60

Focus Thank you for the interview. (693 words)

[59] precedent *vergleichbarer Fall, Beispiel*

[61] proposal *Vorschlag, Antrag*

WORKING WITH THE TEXT

2 Read the text and answer these questions.

1 What measures does the Healthy Diné Nation Act include?
2 What percentage of the inhabitants of the Navajo reservation are affected by diabetes or are overweight?
3 What are the characteristics of a "food desert"?

3 In dem vorliegenden Text werden drei Ziele hinter der Idee des „Healthy Diné Nation Act" genannt. Erstellen Sie eine Liste dieser Ziele. Formulieren Sie vollständige deutsche Sätze.

 EXAM PREPARATION
Leseverstehen (p. 222)

S ▶ Doing comprehension tasks, p. 256

WORKING WITH WORDS

4 Which nouns from the text match these definitions? They are in the same order as in the text.

1 an official action that is done or taken to achieve a particular aim
2 any type of drink except water
3 things that have been grown, especially on a farm
4 state of being dangerously overweight
5 how much customers want to buy a product or a service
6 the state of being able to be bought, got, found, etc.

5 a How good is your American English? Match the American words on the left to their British equivalents on the right. Then find the German term.

	American		British	German	
1	cellphone	a	bill	1	
2	check	b	garden	2	
3	elevator	c	lift	3	
4	faucet	d	mobile	4	
5	gas	e	pavement	5	
6	pants	f	petrol	6	
7	sidewalk	g	soft drink	7	
8	soda	h	tap	8	
9	yard	i	trousers	9	

195

b **What is the British spelling of these American words?**

1 center	5 favorite	9 mom
2 color	6 harbor	10 neighbor
3 cozy	7 liter	11 program
4 inquiry	8 math	12 tire

c **If an American asks for the following, what would a British person ask for?**

1 eggplant	5 potato chips	9 downtown
2 drugstore	6 cookie	10 candy store
3 one-way ticket	7 front desk	11 restroom
4 crosswalk	8 principal (of a school)	12 vacation

LOOKING AT LANGUAGE

G ► The future, p. 270

6 **Ranger Williams is a teenager on the Navajo reservation. Complete what he says using a suitable form of the future.**

"I live on the 'rez' and if you want, I …[1] (tell) you something about my life. I live with my mom and dad and I go to high school in Chinle, that's a town in the north of the 'rez'. I play on the Chinle High School basketball team, the Wildcats. We …[2] (play) against the Window Rock Fighting Scouts on Saturday. I want to become a physiotherapist so I …[3] (take) extra math and biology next year. There's no course for that on the 'rez', so I …[4] (have to) go to Flagstaff. My mom and dad can't afford the fees for university, so I hope I …[5] (get) a scholarship to play on the basketball team. My dad works in a bar in Flagstaff because there aren't enough jobs on the 'rez'. He …[6] (come) home at the weekend to watch the game. Lots of people are unemployed on the 'rez' and we …[7] (have) huge alcohol and drug problems soon if they don't create some new jobs. Lots of my friends are overweight already because they don't eat properly. They …[8] (find) it difficult to get a job if they don't finish high school. Hey, I've gotta go – my mom needs some pizzas for dinner. I …[9] (drive) to the store to get them for her. I'd better be quick. It looks like there …[10] (be) a thunderstorm soon."

3.06

LISTENING

EXAM PREPARATION
Zentrale Klassenarbeit Hörverstehen (p. 224)

S ► Practising listening skills, p. 256

7 **Sie hören ein Radiobericht von Radio South-East 7 über Stahlbauarbeiter aus dem Mohawkstamm. Vervollständigen Sie die unten stehenden Sätze auf Deutsch.**

1 Neben vielen der bekanntesten New Yorker Wolkenkratzern haben die Mohawks auch …
2 Das Indianerreservat Kahnawake befindet sich 6,5 Autostunden nördlich von New York, …
3 Zu dem „Iroquois League" gehören 45.000 Mitglieder in Kanada und …
4 Der Stamm der Mohawk lebt in dieser Region …
5 Die Arbeiter des Mohawk-Stammes machten bei der Dominion Bridge Company auf sich aufmerksam, weil …
6 Zu seinem Höhepunkt in den 1950er Jahren arbeiteten …
7 Mohawks sind für diese gefährliche Arbeit besonders gut geeignet, weil …
8 Außer der gefährlichen Arbeit an einem Wolkenkratzer gibt es zudem den Nachteil, dass …
9 Heutzutage hat die Arbeit in der Baubranche Konkurrenz von …

GIVING A PRESENTATION

8 Choose one of the tribes, people or events and prepare a short 3-minute presentation.

→ **EXAM PREPARATION**
Präsentationsprüfung
(p. 225)

S ▸ Giving a presentation, p. 264

Tribes

Apache
Cherokee
Cheyenne
Iroquois
Navajo
Sioux

· Where were they originally from?
· When was the first contact with settlers?
· Where do the tribe live now?

People

Crazy Horse
Geronimo
Pocahontas
Sacajawea
Sitting Bull
Tecumseh

· What tribe did they belong to?
· What are they famous for?

Events

Indian Removal Act
Trail of Tears
Sand Creek Massacre
Custer's Last Stand
Wounded Knee Massacre
Navajo Code Talkers

· When did the event take place?
· What was the significance of the event?

SPEAKING

EXAM PRACTICE

Kommunikationsprüfung (p. 224)

S ▶ Interpreting pictures and cartoons, p. 262

9 Work with a partner and do the following tasks:

a **Partner A:** Look at the cartoon below.
Partner B: Look at the cartoon in File 11 on page 220. Describe the cartoon to your partner and analyse the point the cartoonist is trying to make.

b Compare the two cartoons and discuss their message with regard to the history of the Native Americans in the USA.

c Present your findings to the class.

WRITING

10 Use the information in this unit to describe the history of the Native American tribes since the European settlement of the USA and the situation of Native Americans in the USA today.

TEXT 4 Hyphenated Americans

 a What do you think the origins of these festivals might be? Which countries or cultures do you think they originate from? Collect ideas together on the board.

b Which of these festivals could you experience or take part in where you live? Explain why this is possible (or not possible).

c All these celebrations take place in American cities. Do you think they are typically American celebrations? Why (not)?

St Patrick's Day

Columbus Day

Mardi Gras

Thanksgiving

Kwanzaa

Cinco de Mayo

Stop Being Indian-American!?!

Parthiv N. Parekh

Listen up, immigrants of Indian origin! Y'all close down all the Indian grocery stores and restaurants in the United States. Stop watching those mushy, melodramatic Bollywood movies on American soil. No need to subscribe to those Indian TV channels, or follow Indian media. Playing Indian music at home that you grew up on? Shame on you! You are now an American! You must sever all ties to your roots, traditions and heritage!

Absurd? But that is precisely what Louisiana Governor Bobby Jindal recently suggested. […] "I do not believe in hyphenated Americans. […] My dad and mom told my brother and me that we came to America to be Americans – not Indian-Americans. […] If we wanted to be Indians, we would have stayed in India." […]

It is one thing to say immigrants must do more to assimilate. I am right there with Jindal up to this extent of the thought. Many Indians come to America only to

5

10

[1] Y'all (AE sl) you all
[2] mushy embarrassingly emotional
[3] subscribe to sth *etw abonnieren*
[5] Shame on you! *Pfui (Teufel)!*
[5] **sever all ties to sth** have nothing to do with sth
[6] **roots** *Wurzeln*
[6] **heritage** history, traditions and culture of a country or society
[7] governor *Gouverneur/in (eines US-Bundesstaates)*
[7] Bobby Jindal republican politician, governor of Louisiana
[8] **hyphenated Americans** Americans who refer to their country, e.g. Italian-American

13 cocoon yourself *sich einkapseln*

17 host country *the country to which people emigrate*

19 disown sb/sth *decide that you no longer want to be connected with sb/sth*

21 sensibilities *a person's feelings*

22 advocate sth *support sth*

24 disqualify sb *prevent sb (from doing sth) because they have broken a rule or are not suitable*

25 fabled *legendär, sagenumwoben*

26 certify sb (as sth) *give sb an official document proving that they are qualified (as sth)*

26 affiliation *connection with a political party or religion*

28 traitor *Verräter/in*

34 embrace a culture *sich eine Kultur bereitwillig zu eigen machen*

42 melting pot *Schmelztiegel*

43 beeline *Luftlinie, kürzester Weg*

45 conceivable *denkbar*

46 engagement (with sth) *being involved with sth*

48 offensive *causing offence*

49 pander to sb/sth *try to please sb/sth, even if this is not acceptable*

52 band around sth *gather around sth*

53 quintessential *representing the perfect example of something*

54 crux *the most important part of a problem or issue*

56 have a stake in sth *have a part or share in sth that is important to you*

Bobby Jindal

cocoon themselves in their native environment. Geographically, they may have moved here, but practically and psychologically they exist in a self-created, mini-India. That's a loss for both the immigrants and the host country.

But then, for Jindal to suggest that one must also go on to disown their native roots, heritage and culture is a slap in the face for both Indian and American sensibilities.

What exactly is Jindal asking us to do or not do when he advocates dropping the "Indian" part of our hyphenated lives? Is there, according to him, a certain code by which one is considered a "true," unhyphenated American? What disqualifies me from being that fabled American? What behaviors and practices are approved to be certified as a true American? Does affiliation with a Hindu temple or with a Mosque disqualify me? Can I attend one of those loud Indian weddings before I will be shouted down as a traitor?

Jindal offers, "I am not suggesting for one second that people should be shy or embarrassed about their ethnic heritage." Make up your mind, sir. You are saying don't be shy of your heritage, but are you also suggesting wipe it out entirely – don't be hyphenated?

"I am explicitly saying that it is completely reasonable for nations to discriminate between allowing people into their country who want to embrace their culture, or allowing people into their country who want to destroy their culture, or establish a separate culture within," offers Jindal further […].

So, which American culture does he want everyone to embrace? Do African-Americans subscribe to the same "American" culture as Jewish Americans? Does subscribing to a monolithic White Anglo-Saxon Protestant culture makes one an ideal American? […]

Jindal may argue, if the original European settlers could melt into the American melting pot, why can't newer immigrants? But history tells us there wasn't exactly a beeline to the melting pot. Initially, there were enclaves of English, Spanish, Portuguese, Irish and other settlers. There were attempts to preserve their native cultures. And it is conceivable that they would have succeeded if the technology of the times [had] allowed 24/7 engagement with the cultures they left behind, as is the case today.

The Governor's disgraceful comments are equally offensive to American sensibilities. If he can hear himself over his blind need to pander to the far right, he might see how much he sounds like the Taliban when he says people should fall in step with a singular culture of the land. The very notion that countries should band around such a monolithic culture seems like a concept that belongs to the Middle Ages. How quintessentially un-American is such a notion! Isn't the very crux of being American that you are free to practice whichever cuisine, culture and religion that you wish – so far as it is ethical and moral?

Granted, good citizenship also requires assimilation so that one has a stake in and contribution to the commons. But, as stressed earlier, there is a vast difference between encouraging assimilation and asking immigrants to wipe out their customs and heritage. It's not as if I will somehow not be able to enjoy and appreciate a good episode of House of Cards on television if I am doing it over

15

20

25

30

35

40

45

50

55

60

chai and samosa instead of coke and popcorn. Or that being Hindu will prevent me from pledging allegiance to the country I chose to live in, not only for the rest of my life in, but that, in all likelihood, will be the motherland of my descendants. […]

65   If Jindal does not believe in hyphenated Americans, is he now going to campaign against Cinco de Mayo celebrations? Saint Patrick's Day Parades? Kwanzaa? Passover?! Ultimately, this is not just about righteousness, but also about deciding which is a more desirable society: one that is bland, insular, parochial and monolithic. Or, one that is dynamic, diverse, colorful and inviting (such as … well, the United States of America)?   (818 words)

From: The Huffington Post, 30 January 2015

[62] **pledge allegiance to sb/sth** promise to support sb/sth

[67] **Passover** important Jewish festival

[67] **righteousness** the feeling that what you are doing is morally right

[68] **bland** without taste, boring

[68] **insular** only interested in your own culture

[68] **parochial** only concerned with small issues in your own area

WORKING WITH THE TEXT

2   Entscheiden Sie, ob die Aussagen zum Text richtig oder falsch sind. Begründen Sie Ihre Entscheidung auf Deutsch.

1   The author believes that Governor Bobby Jindal's suggestions are sensible.
2   Bobby Jindal's parents did not want their sons to be Indian-Americans.
3   The author thinks that all Indian-Americans have adapted well to American society.
4   According to the author, Governor Jindal is insulting both established Americans and new immigrants with his statement.
5   Governor Jindal says that the USA should only let in immigrants who are fully prepared to embrace American culture and values.
6   The author accepts that the White Anglo-Saxon Protestant culture is the ideal for all new immigrants.

→ EXAM PREPARATION
Leseverstehen (p. 222)

S ▶ Doing comprehension tasks, p. 258

3   In dem vorliegenden Text nennt der Autor fünf Aktivitäten, die Inder laut Governor Jindal nicht mehr machen dürfen. Erstellen Sie eine Liste dieser Dinge. Formulieren Sie vollständige deutsche Sätze.

→ EXAM PREPARATION
Leseverstehen (p. 222)

S ▶ Doing comprehension tasks, p. 258

SPEAKING

4   Discuss in small groups. Who do you agree with more: the author of the article or Governor Bobby Jindal? Explain your reasons to the class.

WORKING WITH WORDS

5   Explain the underlined phrases from the text in your own words.

1   "I do not believe in hyphenated Americans." (l. 8)
2   Many Indians come to America only to cocoon themselves in their native environment. (ll. 12–13)
3   That's a loss for both the immigrants and the host country. (ll. 16–17)
4   Does subscribing to a monolithic White Anglo-Saxon Protestant culture make one an ideal American? (ll. 38–40)
5   … if the original European settlers could melt into the American melting pot, why can't newer immigrants? (ll. 41–42)

6 Replace the <u>underlined</u> verbs in the following sentences with verbs from the box. They are all taken from the text.

....
assimilate | disown | embrace | pledge | preserve | sever | subscribe to
....

1 Governor Jindal wants Indian-Americans to <u>cut</u> all their ties to their Indian homeland.
2 He thinks they should <u>deny</u> their native roots to become better Americans.
3 He says that the country should only <u>welcome with open arms</u> those immigrants who are prepared to <u>become part of the culture</u>.
4 Bobby Jindal wants immigrants to <u>join in</u> a monolithic White Anglo-Saxon Protestant culture and <u>promise</u> allegiance to the USA.
5 The author says that immigrants have always tried to <u>keep</u> their native cultures.

LOOKING AT LANGUAGE

G ▶ tenses, pp. 267 – 269

7 Look at the sentences. Say in each case which of the underlined verb forms is correct: the simple form, the progressive form, or both forms?

1 Rani Banerjee <u>has lived</u> / <u>has been living</u> in Los Angeles since 2005.
2 She <u>emigrated</u> / <u>was emigrating</u> from Mumbai in India with her parents when she was 12 years old.
3 Rani <u>has studied</u> / <u>has been studying</u> electronic engineering at UCLA for the last three years.
4 She currently <u>studies</u> / <u>is</u> currently <u>studying</u> for her final exams.
5 After graduation, she <u>spends</u> / <u>is spending</u> 6 months in India with her uncle's family in Mumbai.
6 She <u>feels</u> / <u>is feeling</u> that she should get to know her own culture better before she <u>starts</u> / <u>is starting</u> her working life in the USA.
7 Her parents <u>try</u> / <u>are trying</u> to introduce her to suitable unmarried young men from the Indian community in LA, but Rani <u>doesn't want</u> / <u>is not wanting</u> an arranged marriage.
8 "I <u>don't get</u> / <u>I'm not getting</u> married until I meet someone I love," she <u>says</u> / <u>is saying</u>.
9 "I <u>love</u> / <u>I'm loving</u> Indian traditions," she adds, "but this is one I <u>go</u> / <u>I'm going</u> to ignore."

Hindu temple, Nebraska

EXAM PRACTICE
Kommunikationsprüfung (p. 224)

S ▶ Interpreting charts and graphs, p. 263

SPEAKING

8 Work with a partner and do the following tasks. Partner A looks here; partner B looks at File 12 on p. 220.

a Look at your bar chart carefully and make notes. Describe and analyse your bar chart to your partner.

b Compare your two bar charts and discuss the consequences of further immigration to the USA.

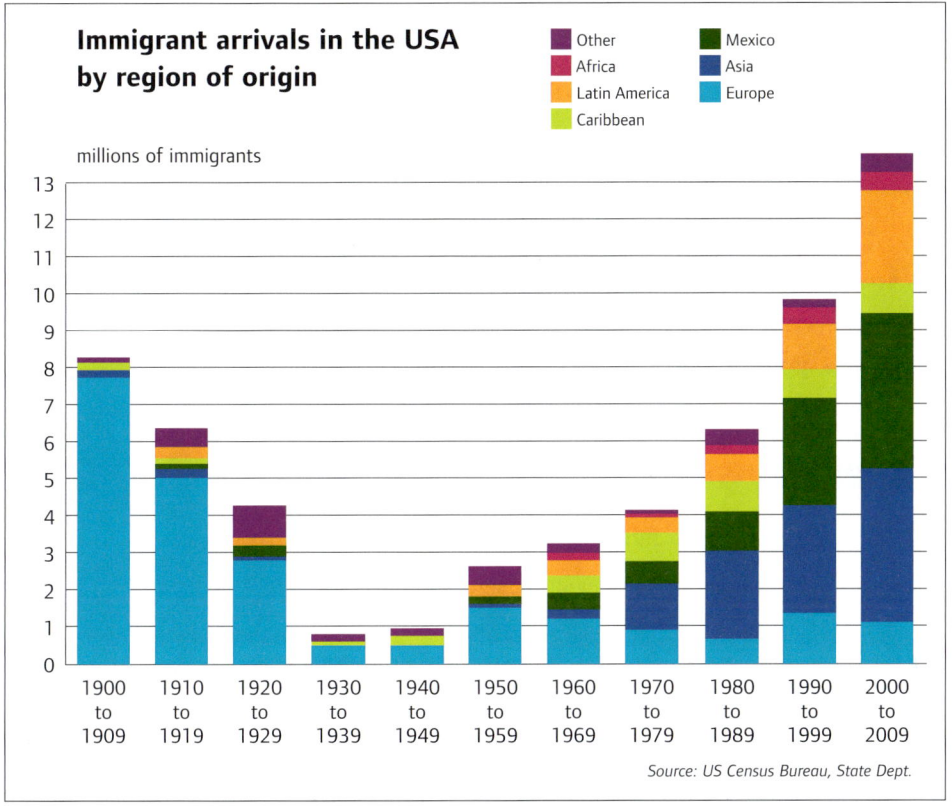

Immigrant arrivals in the USA by region of origin

Legend: Other, Africa, Latin America, Caribbean, Mexico, Asia, Europe

millions of immigrants

x-axis: 1900 to 1909, 1910 to 1919, 1920 to 1929, 1930 to 1939, 1940 to 1949, 1950 to 1959, 1960 to 1969, 1970 to 1979, 1980 to 1989, 1990 to 1999, 2000 to 2009

Source: US Census Bureau, State Dept.

WRITING

EXAM PREPARATION
Textproduktion (p. 223)

S ▶ Writing an essay, p. 259

9 a Explain the following quotation in relation to the text and describe how waves of immigration to the United States have contributed to its ethnic diversity and cultural identity.

"Isn't the very crux of being American that you are free to practice whichever cuisine, culture and religion that you wish – so far as it is ethical and moral?" (ll. 53–55)

b Comment on the following statement.

"Immigration without integration is a recipe for disaster."

TEXT 5 "From my cold, dead hands"

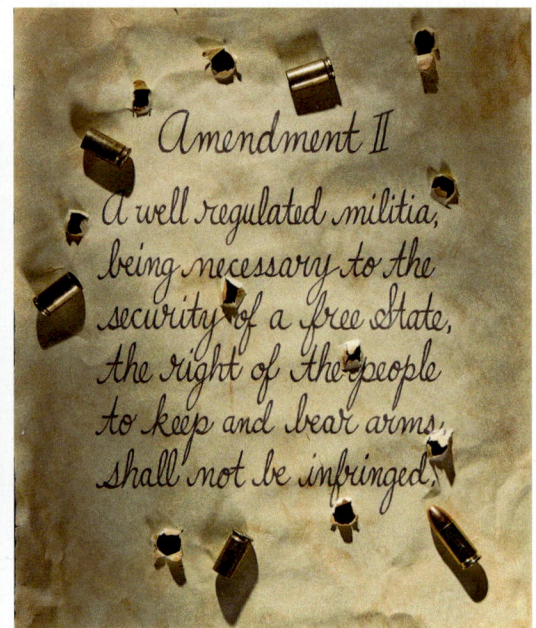

Father and daughter hunting (top left); Charlton Heston at an NRA convention (bottom left)

WARM-UP

1 Work in small groups and do the following tasks.

a Match these places and events. Use the internet for help if necessary.

1	Tombstone, Arizona, 26 October 1881	a Assassination of Dr Martin Luther King
2	Chicago, Illinois, 14 February 1929	b Assassination of President John F Kennedy
3	Dallas, Texas, 22 November 1963	c Execution of 6 members of a rival gang on St Valentine's Day, presumed to have been carried out by members of Al Capone's gang
4	Memphis, Tennessee, 4 April 1968	d Gunfight at the OK Corral between town marshalls from the Earp family and cowboys from the Clanton family
5	Columbine, Colorado, 20 April 1999	e Mass shooting of 21 elementary pupils and 6 members of staff at Sandy Hook Elementary School.
6	Newtown, Connecticut, 14 December 2012	f Massacre of 12 high-school students and one teacher by two fellow students.

b On 15 December 1791, the Bill of Rights, which contained ten amendments to the US Constitution, was adopted. The Second Amendment reads as follows:

infringe (on) sth
etw beeinträchtigen

> "A well regulated Militia, being necessary to the security of a free State, the right of the people to keep and bear Arms, shall not be infringed."

Why do you think owning firearms (= guns) is considered such a basic right by millions of Americans?

rifle Gewehr

c "From my cold, dead hands" is a slogan used by the National Rifle Association (NRA) in the USA: what do you think it means?

Viewpoints on US gun laws

Following a mass shooting at Sandy Hook Elementary School in Newtown, Connecticut, in 2012, another debate took place about US gun laws. The following people expressed their views on the issue.

Keith Garman, criminologist, Pennsylvania

3.07

Any killer who sets out to massacre people in a school or shopping mall commits the crime in the knowledge that he'll be caught and spend the rest of his life in prison – if he's in a state without the death penalty. Many of them commit suicide or deliberately allow themselves to be shot by police. There are no laws that can prevent this kind of thing.

These are men – and it's almost always men – who are willing to die in order to kill large numbers of people. Almost all mass shootings are planned for days and sometimes even months in advance. People who do this are going to be able to evade legal controls on the sale of firearms without difficulty.

At the moment the federal background check only applies to guns sold by registered dealers. If you buy a gun from a private person there is no requirement for a federal background check. In most states, if you buy a gun from a friend or relative you're not subject to a background check.

Linda dos Santos, former Republican congresswoman and talk show host

It can't be "business as usual". We must force our politicians to protect our children. Parents should no longer take "no" for an answer from Washington when the topic turns to gun control.

We see real violence on TV every day – from college campuses in Virginia, to movie theatres in Colorado – and it's being caused by a poisonous mixture of our violent popular culture, a growing crisis in our mental health and the proliferation of combat-style weapons.

Millions of parents are rightfully angry with the gun lobbyists and their cynical lawyers who hide behind their twisted readings of our Bill of Rights.

The government is obsessed, and rightly so, with how to prevent the next terrorist attack being launched from a desert training camp in Afghanistan, but perhaps they should start obsessing about how to stop the next attack on a shopping mall, a movie theatre, a college campus, or in our children's first grade classes.

Gus Berggruen, Firearm Owners Association of Michigan

What do you want to do? Force law-abiding private citizens to give up their guns? That would be wholly unconstitutional as the Supreme Court has already ruled on this issue.

Nobody in the gun-owning community is going to give up their firearm freedoms just because a few individuals misuse those freedoms. That's just not going to happen in the US.

We should start focussing on the real problem. Who are these guns owned by? Mass shootings like Newtown and all other mass shootings, clearly involve individuals who are mentally deranged.

---

4 criminologist scientist who studies crimes and criminals

5 commit carry out (e. g. a crime)

7 death penalty *Todesstrafe*

13 evade sth avoid sth

14 background check *Nachforschungen, polizeiliche Überprüfung*

17 be subject to sth be likely to be affected by sth

24 mental health psychological well-being of a person

24 proliferation increase in numbers

25 combat-style weapon gun etc. that can be used in wars

26 lobbyist sb who tries to influence politicians or the government and persuades them to support or oppose changes in the law

27 twisted reading *einseitige Auslegung*

27 Bill of Rights name given to the first 10 amendments to the US Constitution (1789–1791), that includes the "right to bear arms"in the Second Amendment

28 be obsessed with sth be always worrying about sth in a way that annoys other people

33 law-abiding *unbescholten*

34 unconstitutional *verfassungswidrig*

34 rule on an issue give a decision in a legal dispute

37 misuse not use properly

41 mentally deranged   mentally ill

⁴⁵ gun show *Waffenmesse*
⁴⁶ **purchase** sth that you have bought
⁴⁷ **obtain sth** get sth
⁵⁵ **modification** slight change to an existing plan/design
⁵⁷ **partial** related to only a part of sth
⁵⁸ **grim** unpleasant and depressing
⁶² **concealed weapon** gun etc. that is hidden or not carried openly

The mental health system in this country has obviously failed, and if we don't pump more money into getting these people before they commit such horrible acts, we're not going to solve this problem.

There are some things we could do better: we could close the so-called "gun show loophole", which allows gun purchases without a background check, but that's not where criminals obtain their guns. ₄₅

Because we're dealing with mentally deranged individuals, I would focus on our mental health system. We can't take people off the streets until they actually do something that's dangerous. But it's too late if they've already committed murder or killed themselves. Our current mental health laws prevent us from helping them beforehand. I wouldn't do anything to change the gun laws. ₅₀

Belinda Walters, mother of a shooting victim

I'm a strong believer in our constitutional rights so I don't think that Americans should give up firearms. There might be some modifications made to our gun laws now, but I don't think there should be a ban on all guns. Maybe there should be a partial ban on certain kinds of handguns, like combat-style weapons. ₅₅

It's a pretty grim state of affairs when anybody can walk onto a school or university campus and there is no protection for the people in the school themselves. I think we should train people in schools – principals and administrative people – who want to carry guns for protection. ₆₀

I think it's OK if teachers want to have a concealed weapon, in case somebody came into their school carrying a gun. Teachers would have a way to defend their students and themselves.   (777 words)

WORKING WITH THE TEXT

2 a Copy this table and match the statements below to the speakers from the text. Put the statements in the correct column, according to whether the statement is more in favour of, or against, gun control.

	For	Against
Keith Garman	...	...
Linda dos Santos	...	...
Gus Berggruen	...	...
Belinda Walters	...	...

a Background checks only apply if you buy a gun from a registered gun dealer.
b Gun control is unconstitutional.
c No legislation can stop a determined killer carrying out a planned mass killing.
d Only a small minority of mentally-deranged people abuse firearms.
e Politicians should worry less about terrorism and more about preventing mass killings.
f School staff should be allowed to carry (concealed) weapons to protect their students.
g Society is characterised by too many guns, too much violence in the media and a mental-health crisis.
h Some types of weapons should be banned for private use.

b Compare your answers with a partner.

- Are there any statements you find surprising? Are there any opinions which you would not expect the speaker to hold?
- Which statements do you agree or disagree with?

Report your findings to the class

WORKING WITH WORDS

3 a Complete the following paragraph with suitable words or phrases from the text.

background checks | combat-style | commit | concealed | dealers | firearm freedoms | gun | gun-owning | killing | laws | mass shooting | mental | mentally | misuse | shows

With depressing regularity we read or hear about a gunman carrying out a …[1], either at a school, on a university campus, in a cinema or in some other public place. Most of the criminals are young men and are …[2] deranged individuals in some way. The outcome is mostly that they …[3] suicide, or allow themselves to be shot by the police. The …[4] lobbyists argue that only a tiny minority of people …[5] firearms in this way and that it is the country's …[6] health system that is to blame. They would like to see more people carrying …[7] weapons, even in schools, to protect themselves in the case of another mass …[8]. While the …[9] community refuses to give up its …[10], there are many other Americans who are calling for stricter gun …[11]. They would like to stop the proliferation of …[12] weapons and ban certain types of handgun. Above all, they are calling for federal …[13] for all weapon purchases, not just those from gun …[14], but also at gun …[15] or from friends and aquaintances.

Gun dealer in his shop

b Collect the highlighted collocations about firearms and gun control in a mind map or in your own word list. Add any other phrases that you know.

LOOKING AT LANGUAGE

4 Complete the sentences with a suitable modal verb, or substitute, as in the example.

G ▸ Modal auxiliary verbs, p. 271

1 You *can* (*Fähigkeit*) avoid a background check if you buy a gun from a friend or relative.
2 We … (*Möglichkeit*) improve our mental health system if we really want to reduce gun-related deaths.
3 Be careful when arguing with strangers. They … (*Möglichkeit*) be armed.
4 … (*Bitte*) I ask you a personal question? Have you ever been in a dangerous situation?
5 … (*Bitte*) I see your firearms permit, please?
6 You … (*Erlaubnis*) test the gun on the firing range downstairs.
7 You … (*Erlaubnis*) enter the building now. We've finished the search.
8 They … (*kein Erlaubnis*) enter the school building until the police had searched it for weapons.
9 Students … (*Verbot*) bring any form of weapons onto the university campus.
10 You … (*Pflicht*) have a licence if you carry a weapon.
11 Buyers … (*Wahl*) go through a background check if they buy guns at a trade fair.
12 The government … (*Empfehlung*) do more to stop the spread of firearms in the USA.

5 a The gun control debate is an emotional issue on both sides of the argument. Look at these car bumper stickers and say which arguments they are using to make their point.

b Which slogans do you find the most effective? Explain why?

c Think of your own slogan for a car sticker. Collect the slogans and vote on the most effective one.

→ EXAM PREPARATION
Textproduktion (p. 223)

S ▸ Writing an essay, p. 259

6 There has recently been another shooting at a high school. While you are surfing the Internet to find out more about it, you come across the following blog entry:

"Hey, what we really need are armed security guards in every high school, or teachers with concealed weapons trained how to use them. That's the only way we'll ever be safe from these crazy gunmen. We all know, it ain't the guns that kill, but the people with their finger on the trigger. Get yourself armed before it's too late!"

smokingcolt, May 27 20., 23.59PST

Write a comment on the blog entry, giving your opinion on why there is so much gun-related crime in the USA and the best way to deal with it.

TEXT 6   Surveillance or privacy?

 a Discuss these questions in small groups.

- Are your privacy settings on your social media accounts restrictive or can anybody read your posts?
- Have you read all the information about the privacy settings?
- Do you send messages to all your "friends" at the same time, or only to those people that the messages are intended for?
- Are you worried that other people might have access to your social media accounts?
- Would you give up your social media use if it was necessary to protect the country from a terrorist attack?

b Report your findings to the class.

NSA surveillance reforms

3.08

Barack Obama

The fall of the Soviet Union left America without a competing superpower, [and] emerging threats from terrorist groups, and the proliferation of weapons of mass destruction placed new – and, in
5 some ways more complicated – demands on our intelligence agencies. Globalization and the Internet made these threats more acute, as technology erased borders and empowered individuals to project great violence, as well as
10 great good. Moreover, these new threats raised new legal and new policy questions. For while few doubted the legitimacy of spying on hostile states, our framework of laws was not fully adapted to prevent terrorist attacks by individuals
15 acting on their own, or acting in small, ideologically driven groups on behalf of a foreign power.

The horror of September 11th brought all these issues to the fore. Across the political spectrum, Americans recognized that we had to adapt to a world in which a bomb could be built in a basement, and our electric grid could be shut down by
20 operators an ocean away. We were shaken by the signs we had missed leading up to the attacks – how the hijackers had made phone calls to known extremists, and travelled to suspicious places. So we demanded that our intelligence community improve its capabilities, and that law enforcement change practices to focus more on preventing attacks before they happen than prosecuting terrorists after an
25 attack. [...]

And yet, in our rush to respond to a very real and novel set of threats, the risks of government overreach – the possibility that we lose some of our core liberties in pursuit of security – also became more pronounced. We saw, in the immediate aftermath of 9/11, our government engaged in enhanced interrogation techniques

1 **surveillance** *Überwachung*
6 **intelligence agency** *Gemeindienst*
7 **threat** possibility of danger or disaster
7 **acute** very serious or severe
8 **erase sth** rub sth out
9 **project sth** plan sth
12 **legitimacy** *Rechtmäßigkeit, Gesetzmäßigkeit*
12 **hostile** acting as an enemy
16 **on behalf of sb** as a representative of sb
17 **bring an issue to the fore** make people very aware of a problem
19 **electric grid** *Stromnetz*
20 **be shaken by sth** be extremely worried by sth
23 **capability** the ability to do sth
23 **law enforcement** the police, FBI, etc
24 **prosecute sb** officially charge sb with a crime in court
26 **respond to sth** reply to sth
26 **novel** new
27 **overreach** the act of doing more than is allowed or necessary
28 **become pronounced** become more obvious or noticeable
29 **aftermath** the days/events immediately following a disaster
29 **enhanced** improved
29 **interrogation technique** *Verhörmethode*

30 contradict sb/sth disagree with or go against sb/sth

31 warrantless wiretaps listening secretly to other people's telephone conversations without legal authority

31 authorities (here:) agencies

31 institute sth set up or create sth

32 adequate enough in quality or quantity for a particular purpose

33 congressional oversight *Kontrolle durch den Kongress*

34 excess extreme behaviour that is unacceptable or illegal

35 curb sth control or limit sth that is bad or illegal

37 uphold our civil liberties keep individual freedoms safe

38 technological advances improvements in technology

38 pinpoint sth locate sth exactly

40 routine *normal*

41 prospect *Vorstellung*

42 disquieting worrying

44 sift through sth examine sth very carefully

45 pursue a lead *einem Hinweis nachgehen*

46 thwart sb/sth stop sb from doing what they want to do

46 impending *bevorstehend*

47 abuse use of sth in a way that is wrong or harmful

48 safeguard sth that is designed to protect people from harm or danger

49 warrant legal document signed by a judge that gives the police authority to do sth

50 constrain sb/sth *jdn/etw einschränken*

53 constraint *Einschränkung*

56 secrecy *Geheimhaltung, Verschwiegenheit*

57 inevitable unable to be avoided or stopped

57 bias ['baɪəs] *Voreingenommenheit, Befangenheit*

60 in the absence of sth *in Ermangelung einer Sache*

60 institutional requirement *gesetzliche Vorschrift*

61 overreach *Überreichweite*

63 reliance on sth the state of needing sth in order to survive, be successful, etc.

67 assume sth think that sth is true without having proof of it

71 at the forefront in a leading position

that contradicted our values. As a senator, I was critical of several practices, such as warrantless wiretaps. And all too often new authorities were instituted without adequate public debate.

Through a combination of action by the courts, increased congressional oversight, and adjustments by the previous Administration, some of the worst excesses that emerged after 9/11 were curbed by the time I took office. But a variety of factors have continued to complicate America's efforts to both defend our nation and uphold our civil liberties.

First, the same technological advances that allow U.S. intelligence agencies to pin-point an al Qaeda cell in Yemen or an email between two terrorists in the Sahel, also mean that many routine communications around the world are within our reach. At a time when more and more of our lives are digital, that prospect is disquieting for all of us.

Second, the combination of increased digital information and powerful super-computers offers intelligence agencies the possibility of sifting through massive amounts of bulk data to identify patterns or pursue leads that may thwart impending threats. It's a powerful tool. But the government collection and storage of such bulk data also creates a potential for abuse.

Third, the legal safeguards that restrict surveillance against U.S. persons without a warrant do not apply to foreign persons overseas. This is not unique to America; few, if any, spy agencies around the world constrain their activities beyond their own borders. And the whole point of intelligence is to obtain information that is not publicly available. But America's capabilities are unique. And the power of new technologies means that there are fewer and fewer technical constraints on what we can do. That places a special obligation on us to ask tough questions about what we should do.

And finally, intelligence agencies cannot function without secrecy, which makes their work less subject to public debate. Yet there is an inevitable bias not only within the intelligence community, but among all of us who are responsible for national security, to collect more information about the world, not less. So in the absence of institutional requirements for regular debate – and oversight that is public, as well as private or classified – the danger of government overreach becomes more acute. This is particularly true when surveillance technology and our reliance on digital information is evolving much faster than our laws. […]

One thing I'm certain of: this debate will make us stronger. And I also know that in this time of change, the United States of America will have to lead. It may seem sometimes that America is being held to a different standard, and I'll admit the readiness of some to assume the worst motives by our government can be frustrating. No one expects China to have an open debate about their surveillance programs, or Russia to take privacy concerns of citizens in other places into account. But let us remember that we are held to a different standard precisely because we have been at the forefront of defending personal privacy and human dignity.

(773 words)

From: speech held on 17 January 2014

WORKING WITH THE TEXT

2 Entscheiden Sie, ob die Aussagen zum Text richtig oder falsch sind. Begründen Sie Ihre Entscheidung auf Deutsch.

→ **EXAM PREPARATION**
Leseverstehen (p. 222)

S ▶ Doing comprehension tasks, p. 258

1 The Internet has increased the threat of terrorism to the United States from small, independent terrorist groups rather than from countries that are enemies of the USA.
2 After the 11 September terrorist attack, the main priority for intelligence agencies was to capture and imprison suspected terrorists.
3 Before becoming president, Barack Obama wholeheartedly supported the actions of the NSA.
4 There is no need for the USA to take over a leading role in the surveillance debate, as other major countries like China are having the same debate.
5 According to Barack Obama, America has to have the highest standards of control for its intelligence agencies because it has a long tradition of supporting civil liberties.

MEDIATING

3 In this speech Barack Obama lists five reasons why the USA's efforts to both defend itself and uphold its civil liberties come into conflict. Make a list of these reasons in German.

WORKING WITH WORDS

4 Barack Obama's speech uses formal language. Replace the verbs in the following phrases with a suitable verb from the box to create collocations.

gather | intercept | monitor | obtain | penetrate | pinpoint |
prevent | prosecute | pursue | uphold

1 <u>catch</u> secret communications
2 <u>charge</u> a suspected terrorist
3 <u>collect</u> vital intelligence
4 <u>get into</u> a secret network
5 <u>find</u> a hidden terrorist cell/group
6 <u>follow</u> a promising lead
7 <u>get</u> important information
8 <u>save</u> civil liberties
9 <u>stop</u> a terrorist attack
10 <u>watch</u> a hostile country

5 Explain the meaning of the <u>underlined</u> phrases in your own words.

1 … the <u>proliferation of weapons of mass destruction</u> … (ll. 3–4)
2 The horror of September 11th <u>brought these issues to the fore</u>. (l. 17)
3 <u>Across the political spectrum</u>, Americans recognized that … (ll. 17–18)
4 … that <u>prospect is disquieting</u> for all of us. (ll. 41–42)
5 … America <u>is being held to a different standard</u>, … (l. 66)
6 … to <u>take the privacy concerns</u> of citizens <u>into account</u>. (ll. 69–70)

LOOKING AT LANGUAGE

G ▶ tenses, pp. 267–271

6 Complete the sentences using the most suitable form of the verb in brackets. Sometimes more than one form is possible.

1 Throughout the history of the USA, its intelligence agencies … (help) to secure freedom by spying on enemies.
2 The international terrorist threat after 9/11 … (increase) the need for digital surveillance techniques.
3 The security services … (intercept) phone calls of world leaders for many years now.
4 The President … (just/meet) with the British Prime Minister when the news … (break) on TV.
5 According to newspaper reports, the Prime Minister … (knew) about the scandal for several weeks before he … (tell) Parliament.
6 The President … (currently/look) at ways of co-operating better with friendly states.
7 He … (make) a statement on the surveillance scandal tomorrow morning.
8 The press conference … (begin) at 9 am tomorrow local time.
9 The President … (hold) talks with several world leaders since the scandal … (become) public.
10 By the time the President … (arrive) in Europe, he … (talk) to all the G7 leaders on the phone.

DOING RESEARCH / SPEAKING

7 Barack Obama's speech presents the arguments for surveillance to increase national security <u>and</u> for the need to keep a check on the activities of intelligence agencies.

a In groups, research recent news items that support either of these arguments. Which argument seems to be winning?

b Discuss in your group which is more important: protecting citizens against terrorist attacks or protecting citizens' individual rights? Report your ideas to the class.

DOING A ROLE PLAY

8 Work in groups of four.

You are the board members of a large social media company; the US government has just demanded that your company releases the personal details of your account holders to help combat terrorism.

Each choose one of the roles from the role cards [at the back of the book].
Use the information on your role card to argue for your point of view with the other group members.

Partner A: Finance director: go to File 12, p. 221.
Partner B: Customer services director: go to File 13, p. 221.
Partner C: Marketing director: go to File 14, p. 221.
Partner D: Software development director: go to File 15, p. 221.

SPEAKING

9 Work with a partner and do the following tasks. (Partner A looks here; partner B looks at File 16 on p. 221.)

EXAM PRACTICE
Kommunikationsprüfung (p. 224)

S ▶ Interpreting pictures and cartoons, p. 262

a Look at your cartoon carefully and make notes. Describe and analyse your cartoon to your partner.

b With your partner, compare the two cartoons and discuss the consequences of unlimited digital surveillance for normal citizens.

WRITING

10 Choose one of the following tasks.

a Explain the following quote in relation to the text and describe how digital communications technology has changed the nature of anti-terrorist surveillance in the 21st century.

"We demanded that our intelligence community improve its capabilities, and that law enforcement change practices to focus more on preventing attacks before they happen." (ll. 22–24)

b Comment on this statement, with reference to the use of mass surveillance techniques to win "the War on Terror".

"Study after study has shown that human behaviour changes when we know we are being watched. Under observation we act less free, which means we *are* less free."
Edward Snowden

EXAM PREPARATION
Textproduktion (p. 223)

S ▶ Writing an essay, p. 259

ENGLISH FOR WORK Intercultural competence

AN INTERCULTURAL QUIZ

1 Germans who travel to the USA say that Americans are very polite but that they sometimes say things in an indirect way. Americans, on the other hand, can find the direct German way of saying things impolite or even rude. This can lead to intercultural misunderstandings. Do the following quiz to test your knowledge of what Americans really mean.

1 An American says "Nice to see you" when you meet. Does this mean …?
  a "I'm really, really pleased to meet you."
  b "Hello."
  c "It's been far too long since we last met."

2 The correct reply when an American greets you with "Hey, how are you?" is …
  a "I'm fine. How are you?"
  b "OK, I guess."
  c "Terrible. I've got toothache and a hangover."

3 When an American says "Let's have lunch sometime", does this mean …?
  a "It's been a pleasure meeting you. Shall we have lunch together tomorrow?"
  b "Please call my secretary to fix a lunch meeting."
  c "Nice meeting you. Bye."

4 During a meeting an American colleague asks: "Would you like to use the restroom?" What does this mean?
  a "Do you need to have a short break?"
  b "Do you need to use the toilet?"
  c "Are you hungry? Should we get something to eat now?"

5 You ask an American how she liked her trip to Germany and she answers: "It was different." Does she mean …?
  a "I couldn't wait to get back to the USA."
  b "The people were so interesting."
  c "I really enjoyed the different customs in Germany."

6 You're discussing a project with an American business partner. You explain your idea and she says: "I wonder if this really is the best solution to the problem?" How do you reply?
  a "Don't worry. It know it will work."
  b "Oh, OK. Maybe we should think about that again."
  c "I don't agree with you."

7 When an American asks: "How are you enjoying your stay in America?", what is the most suitable reply?
  a "It's hard to know what people really mean sometimes."
  b "It's OK, but I don't like junk food."
  c "Oh, it's great. The people are so friendly."

8 An American business partner gives you a small present before you leave. What do you reply?
  a "Thank you."
  b "That's nice, but it won't fit in my suitcase."
  c "Thank you so much. That's really kind of you."

LISTENING

3.09

2 a   Listen to four Americans talking about their experiences working in other cultures. Copy and complete the table. Fill in the country each speaker worked in, what happened and where the incident occured, e.g. "at the airport" *(am Flughafen)*.

	Country	What happened	Where the incident occured
Person 1			

     b   Listen again and make notes about the specific details of the stories.

     c   By talking about other cultures, people often reveal important things about their own culture. Listen again to the Americans. What does each of them unknowingly reveal about their own culture?

3 Read this email an American sends to her friend about the visit of an German business colleague to her family home. Talk about it with your partner.

- How many etiquette mistakes can you find?
- What are they and who made them?
- Why do you think they happened?

From: Linda Hathaway   To: Mary-Jo Weibrecht

Hi there Mary-Jo

How ya doin? You won't believe this, but we had a really weird visit from a young man from Stuttgart at the weekend.
He was over here from Europe on business and Al invited him for a barbecue on Sunday afternoon as he was all on his own.

First of all, he turned up at our door at 12 o'clock. I hadn't even finished making the salad and he was there already. And he was wearing a suit and tie … for a barbecue!

Al said his name was Michael, but he said something like "Doctor Green" when we were introduced. He kept calling Al "Mr Vice-President" and me "Mrs Hassavay" even though we called him Mikey all the time.

I tried to talk to him a bit and find out if he was married or had a girlfriend, but he wouldn't give me a straight answer. I said, I bet he earned a lot of money living over there in Europe, but he looked a bit embarrassed. There's nothing wrong with earning a good salary, is there? He looked a bit confused when I said I adored Mozart and really wanted to visit Vienna one day.

Anyway, as soon as he could, he started asking Al questions about their business deal, so that was me out of the conversation for the rest of the afternoon. He didn't go home until 8 in the evening!

He thanked us for an enjoyable visit, but I thought he was a bit strange.

All the best, Linda

DOING RESEARCH

4 a   Look at the topics in the list below. Research "business etiquette in the USA" on the internet and finds tips that are relevant for the topics.

small talk | greeting | using first names | punctuality | dress code at work | socializing with colleagues outside work | criticising colleagues in a meeting | negotiating

     b   Make a brochure based on your findings for Germans wanting to do business in the USA.

PARTNER FILES

FILE 1 ....

Topic 1, Text 7, p. 44

Partner B

a Listen to your partner talk about his or her cartoon and make notes.
b Describe your cartoon to your partner and explain what it says about globalization.
c Together decide which one you both prefer, and why.

FILE 2 ....

Topic 2, Text 4, p. 68

Partner B

a Listen to your partner talk about his or her cartoon. Make notes on what he or she says.
b Produce a five-minute uninterrupted discourse (monologue) based on your cartoon about the problems confronting a society dependent on fossil fuels. Then turn back to task 10 c on p. 68.

Topic 3, Text 3, p. 95

FILE 3 ....

Partner B

You are worried about GM foods. Use these arguments:
- Nobody can be sure what the consequences of eating GM foods will be to our health in the long term. Side effects might emerge in 20 years.
- It will be impossible to prevent GM foods from escaping into nature and cross-fertilizing other plants. Again, the consequences cannot be known, and laboratory experiments cannot tell us.
- Most GM foods are produced by private companies whose main motive is profit, not health.
- GM foods don't seem to reduce the need for pesticides.

FILE 4 ....

Partner C

You're not an expert on GM foods. You want to listen to the arguments of your partners. You do have ideas you want to introduce into the debate. Use these points:
- We rely on science in many areas (e.g. medicine, space exploration, water purification), so there must be benefits from using science in food production.
- Nothing is 100 % risk free in life, and progress is only possible by taking calculated risks.
- GM foods might add to the other health problems we have with food (e.g. processed food, added sugar, additives, flavourings).
- The need for meat has led to environmental pollution. Perhaps we need to reduce our food intake, and eat more vegetables.

Topic 3, Text 4, p. 100

FILE 5 ....

Explorer

Your views are the following:
- There are huge areas of the world that haven't been explored, e.g. the oceans. This should be a priority, not space exploration.
- We learn more about our world from our world, not from space.
- As we discover more about the natural world, we find more plants that can be used for medical drugs and as food sources.
- The priority is to protect the world we live in, not to escape from it.
- Exploring brings out the best in people: planning, determination, courage, cooperation and the desire to learn.

FILE 6 ....

Political activist

Your views are the following:
- The real problems we face include poverty, war and corruption.
- The money spent by NASA, etc. could be used to fight poverty and improve health and education.
- Exploration is just for the wealthy few. It divides society between the haves and have-nots.
- Governments use exploration in order to stop us thinking about the real problems in society.
- There is a long history of the misapplication of scientific knowledge, e.g. the atom bomb. It is time science discovered morality!

FILE 7 . . . .

Topic 4, Text 2, p. 129

Partner B

1 Look at your bar chart carefully and make notes. Prepare to present your findings to your partner.
2 Describe and analyse your bar chart to your partner.
3 With your partner, compare the two charts and discuss how they relate to the debate about the integration of ethnic minorities.

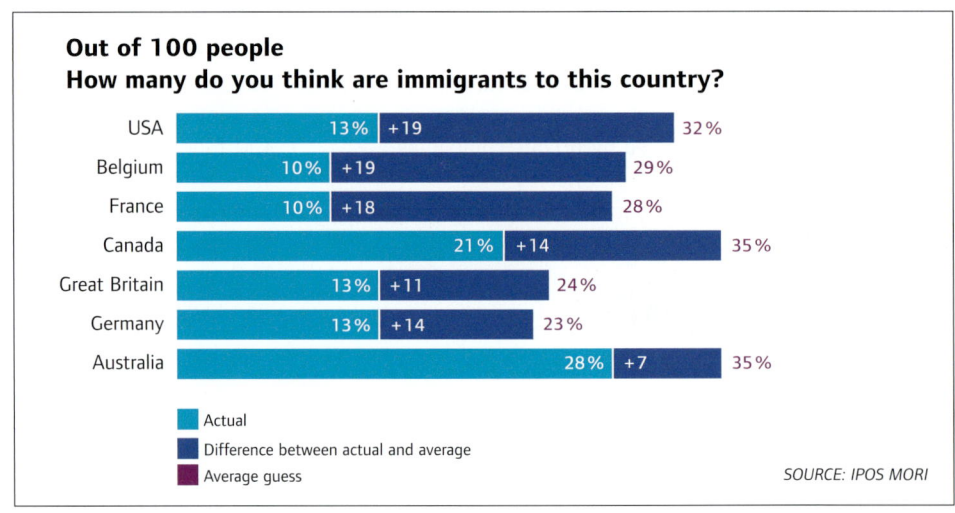

Out of 100 people
How many do you think are immigrants to this country?

USA	13% +19 32%
Belgium	10% +19 29%
France	10% +18 28%
Canada	21% +14 35%
Great Britain	13% +11 24%
Germany	13% +14 23%
Australia	28% +7 35%

▇ Actual
▇ Difference between actual and average
▇ Average guess

SOURCE: IPOS MORI

FILE 8 . . . .

Topic 4, Text 5, p. 142

Partner B

a Listen to your partner describe and analyse his or her cartoon.
b Produce a five-minute uninterrupted discourse based on the cartoon about the problems facing women in the workplace.
c Discuss whether you think the cartoons are relevant to today's society and what changes might be made to improve the situation of women.

"I don't mind working for a woman. I do, however, hate being paid like one."

FILE 9 ....

Topic 5, Text 1, p. 156

Partner B

Prepare a presentation on your visual.

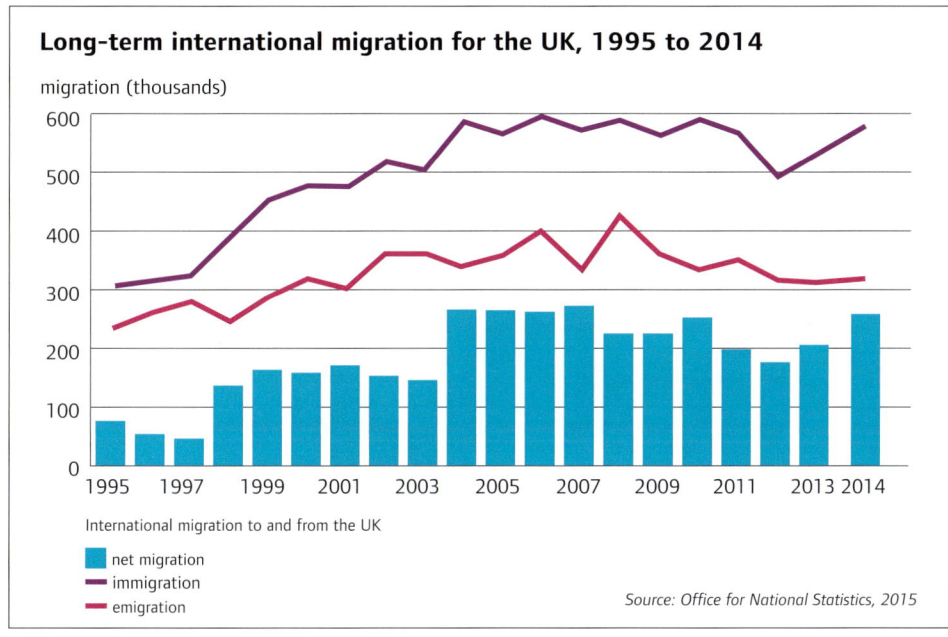

Long-term international migration for the UK, 1995 to 2014

migration (thousands)

International migration to and from the UK

- net migration
- immigration
- emigration

Source: Office for National Statistics, 2015

FILE 10 ....

Topic 5, Text 4, p. 171

Partner B

a Listen to you partner describe and analyse his or her cartoon.
b Produce a five-minute uninterrupted discourse based on the cartoon about Britain and its role in the world.
c Discuss how you see the future role of Britain in the world.

"A Japanese company will deliver these signs to us for £6.75 a thousand."

FILE 11

Topic 6, Text 3, p. 198

Partner B

a Describe the cartoon to your partner and analyse the point the cartoonist is trying to make.

b Compare the two cartoons and discuss their message with regard to the history of Native Americans in the USA.

c Present your findings to the class.

FILE 12

Topic 6, Text 4, p. 203

Partner B

a Look at your bar chart carefully and make notes. Describe and analyse your bar chart to your partner.

b Compare your two bar charts and discuss the consequences of further immigration to the USA.

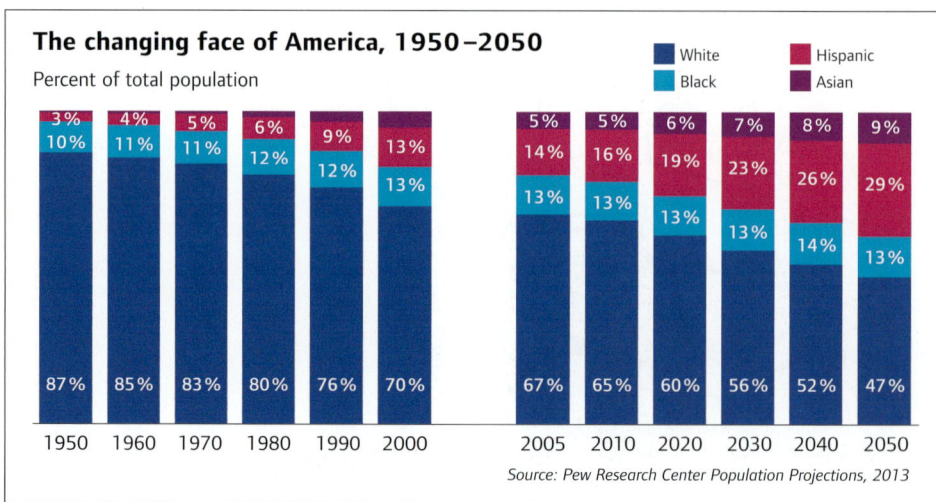

The changing face of America, 1950–2050

Percent of total population

Source: Pew Research Center Population Projections, 2013

Topic 6, Text 6, p. 212

FILE 12 ....

Partner A: Finance director

You are convinced that everything must be done to keep the country safe from terrorist attacks. This involves collecting data from internet service providers, monitoring phone calls and analysing mass data to pinpoint terrorist cells. Give an example of a recent terrorist plot that was averted using surveillance techniques. You do not want the costs of a legal dispute with the government security agencies.

FILE 13 ....

Partner B: Customer services director

You think that surveillance has got out of hand and that personal privacy is more important than the war against terrorism. You don't believe that terrorist plots can be avoided using mass surveillance and you think it is just an excuse to keep an eye on people with unwelcome political opinions. You would not allow any surveillance or data collection of private individuals under any circumstances.

FILE 14 ....

Partner C: Marketing director

Your company is in a difficult situation: On the one hand, it has millions of customers who want to keep their data private; on the other hand, the company does not want to be held responsible if a terrorist plot is carried out by someone who posts messages or videos on your website. Decide where public opinion is most strongly felt at the moment and argue in favour of that position.

FILE 15 ....

Partner D: Software development director

You think that most of your customers are not interested in politics or privacy; they are only interested in making the most of your service and adding to their "friends". You think you could change the privacy settings so that people have to click on a small box if they don't want their personal details to be released for security reasons. If they don't click the box, you are free to release their details.

FILE 16 ....

Topic 6, Text 6, p. 213

Partner B

a Look at your cartoon carefully and make notes. Describe and analyse your cartoon to your partner.
b With your partner, compare the two cartoons and discuss the consequences of unlimited digital surveillance for normal citizens.

"HONEY, IT'S ME... AND WHOEVER ELSE IS LISTENING AT THE NSA..."

EXAM PREPARATION AND PRACTICE

EXAM PREPARATION

EXAM PRACTICE

There is a lot you can do to prepare for your final exam in your last two years at school (Jahrgangsstufe 1 and 2). Try to become familiar with the structure of the exam and the skills and knowledge required by the different parts of the exam.

The final exam consists of the following parts:
- *Schriftliche Prüfung*
- *Kommunikationsprüfung*
- *Zentrale Klassenarbeit Hörverstehen*: This is obligatory but doesn't count to the final mark.
- *Präsentationsprüfung*: 5th exam subject for students who do not take the written exam in English.

Read on to find out about how to prepare for a successful final exam.

SCHRIFTLICHE PRÜFUNG

Leserverstehen

1. True/False statements

The first task in the *Leserverstehen* part of the exam is a true/false task. You are required to read a fairly long English text (700–800 words) to decide whether the statements given are true or false, and to give reasons for your choices in German.

▶ Skimming, p. 254

Step 1: Read the text quickly in order to gain a rough overview of the topic and the content. When you read the text for the first time, it is more important that you understand the gist rather than every single word.

▶ Scanning, p. 254

Step 2: Now read the statements carefully. Then read the text again, but in more detail. Watch out for clues and key words which may be relevant to the statements, and mark the relevant passages in the text.

Step 3: Write down your answers in German. Begin by saying whether the statement is true or false, and then underline your choice by writing down the reasons. You will need to mediate parts of the text from English into German to do this.

2. Finding information in a text

In the second task you will be asked to list between three and five key points (e.g. reasons, arguments, examples) about a certain aspect of the text in German. It is important to write full sentences. Watch out for key words in order to spot the relevant information quickly. The key points are all to be found in just one paragraph.

► Reading difficult texts, p. 254

► Dealing with unknown words, p. 255

Step 1: Read the question and make sure you understand the task.

Step 2: Now read the text again and mark the key points in the text. Do not waste time looking up every single word you do not know. Very often you can work out the meaning of a difficult word or phrase from the general context.

Step 3: Note down the key points, then write full sentences in German. To do this you will have to mediate parts of the text from English into German.

► Mediating, p. 266

Textproduktion

In the second part of the written exam you are asked to write two essays. A good essay should be clearly structured and make varied and differentiated use of language. The arguments should be logical and comprehensible. Simply listing arguments or statements is not sufficient. Rather, you should work as many detailed arguments as possible into your text. This requires a large vocabulary, a good grasp of language skills (grammar, sentence structure, etc.) and a sound knowledge of the topics that you have been dealing with in the classroom.

► Writing an essay, p. 259
► Improving your writing skills, p. 260

When practicing writing in class or at home, make sure you have the useful phrases listed on the inside back cover of the book ("Language for Writing") in front of you.

1. Text-based composition

The first essay is usually related to the topic of the reading text in Part I of the written exam. It requires a sound knowledge of the topics from the curriculum. You may refer to the text, but your arguments should go beyond the reading text – you should use information which you have learned over the course of your studies.

2. Composition

In the second essay you can choose between two topics which are not directly related to the reading text in Part I. As a rule, however, these two topics are closely related to the topics from the curriculum in *Kursstufe* 1 and 2. When deciding which essay to write, choose the topic you know most about. Do not start with one topic and then change your mind and start with the second, as this will cost you precious time.

The two essays carry the most points in the written exam, so it is very important that you are well prepared for the writing tasks. There are two forms of preparation:

1 Improve your vocabulary. You should be continually building up your topic-based vocabulary as you deal with the different topics in *Crossover*. The more words and phrases you know about a topic, the more confident you will feel while writing an essay.

2 Know your topics. While studying, you are going to come across a lot of information about the topics. Keep notes and diagrams of the information so that you will be able to recall easily the information you have learned.

When writing your essay, follow these steps.

Step 1: Brainstorm and structure your key words before you actually start writing. This could be in the form of a list, a table or a mind map.

Step 2: In the introduction to your essay, give a short description of the topic.

Step 3: Then write down your arguments (up to ten) carefully. Use phrases like *first*, *second*, *third*, and *finally* to structure your text. Make sure you stick to the topic.

Step 4: To end your essay, summarize your main points very briefly and write an overall conclusion.

KOMMUNIKATIONSPRÜFUNG

► Interpreting pictures and cartoons, p. 262

The *Kommunikationsprüfung* can either be done individually (*Einzelprüfung*) or together with another student (*Tandemprüfung*). It always starts with an uninterrupted 5-minute talk based on input material provided by your examiners, which could be a photo, a cartoon, graphs, statistics or a very short text. You will have 15 minutes preparation time, which you should use to jot down an outline of your talk.

After you have spoken for five minutes, you will be required to have a conversation with your examiner (*Einzelprüfung*) or with another student (*Tandemprüfung*), about the materials and other related questions. The examiner can introduce more material if he or she wishes. It is important that you have a broad vocabulary and good background knowledge of all curriculum topics.

When practicing speaking in class, make sure you have the useful phrases listed on the inside back cover of the book ("Language for Discussion") near at hand. Practise them as much as possible, so that you can use them easily in the oral exam.

Step 1: Prepare your 5-minute talk by analysing the input material. Think about what you know about the topic and make notes.

Step 2: Structure your talk carefully. You should think of good phrases to begin and conclude your talk. Try and work out how you will fill the 5 minutes: a time schedule in which you list the various aspects and when you should address them will ensure that you don't run out of things to say before the 5 minutes are over.

Step 3: In the discussion that follows be responsive and make eye contact. You should take the more active part. In an exam situation it is a good idea to have a variety of phrases ready for the discussion.

ZENTRALE KLASSENARBEIT HÖRVERSTEHEN

► Practising listening skills, p. 256

There is a separate listening comprehension exam in your last year of school in the form of a compulsory test that takes place some time before the written final exam. It is not part of the final exam and is marked like an ordinary written test. The listening comprehension text is in English, while the tasks are in German. The text is played twice.

You can improve your listening skills by doing the following:
- Listen to English or American speakers. You can find plenty of audio material on the internet (e.g. bbc.co.uk or npr.org).
- Watch English DVDs, first with subtitles, later without.
- Watch English or American TV programmes, e.g. CNN or BBC World. This is also a good way to increase your knowledge about current affairs.

Three different types of tasks make up the listening comprehension exam:

1 **Completing sentences:** You are given the beginning of a German sentence and asked to complete it using content from the listening text.

2 **Comprehension questions:** There are a number of questions in German that you should also answer in German.

3 **Filling in grids:** You must fill in grids in German using information from the listening text.

You should note that all these tasks involve mediation, as the English text must be mediated into German.

Step 1: Before you start, read the task carefully.

Step 2: Make notes while you are listening. Listen for key words that are relevant for the task.

Step 3: Complete the tasks in German. Write full sentences.

▶ Giving a presentation, p. 264

PRÄSENTATIONSPRÜFUNG

Those students who do not take the written exam in English might have to do a presentation. This exam takes place in the same time period as the final exam. You must choose five different topics beforehand and hand those in. You will be told which topic has been chosen one week before the presentation. You will have one week to prepare your presentation. Before you start, you will have to submit a written summary outlining the structure and containing your bibliography in addition to a written declaration that this is entirely your own work. Your presentation lasts 10 minutes and is followed by a 10-minute question-and-answer session about the contents of your presentation.

It is not just the content of a presentation that is important but also how clearly you present the content. This means structuring your talk so that it is easy to understand, making your presentation as varied and interesting as possible, and illustrating your points in a lively way.

In detail this means:
· Be confident. You can use prompt cards to aid you, but you must not read directly from your notes.
· Speak loudly and clearly so that everyone can hear you.
· Do not speak too fast.
· Be aware of your body language and maintain eye contact with the audience.
· Be proactive and flexible in your approach (ready to answer questions, etc.)

Prepare your topic well. The more you know, the more confident you will be. Use a good variety of material (note the sources!) and make sure you have a broad vocabulary on the topic. It is very important that you use adequate media equipment to add visual impact. You could make use of posters, computers, flipcharts or OHPs. You should have some handy phrases at hand to begin and end your presentation.

SCHRIFTLICHE PRÜFUNG Topic 1

Under the influence *Mindi Chahal*

Supermarkets sell food, broadcasters provide television shows and mobile phone companies give us the means to talk to and text each other. This may not seem out of the ordinary but a raft of brands are now trying to influence consumers beyond their original purpose by bringing hobbies, ideas and sport to the mass market and affect popular culture. 5

Sky has been contributing to the UK's cycling habits via its sponsorship of Team Sky, which has helped to increase the overall number of cyclists to 15.2 million, a rise of 17 per cent since 2010. Meanwhile, smartphone manufacturer Nokia is providing suggestions on the music customers might like by using its global team of musicologists to keep an eye on trends. 10

The success of Team Sky and the interest around the riders including Chris Froome and Bradley Wiggins, winner of the Tour of Britain, has raised the profile of cycling in the UK, but it could not have been achieved without Sky's backing. The aim of the partnership between Sky and British Cycling, which is now in its fifth year, was to make cycling a growing trend in UK sport and it has done that successfully. 15

"There has been huge growth and interest in cycling, which we feel quite confident has been a result of our investment in the sport," says Tricia Thompson, director of cycling at BSkyB. "The number of people going to watch the Tour of Britain, the enthusiasm of youngsters, the media profiles of the riders, the fact that cycling regularly features on news programmes such as the Today Programme, all this would 20 never have happened a few years ago."

Team Sky's key focus and strategy has always been about 'inspiration to drive participation'. But it has also influenced the public, by getting a million more people on their bikes since the partnership began in 2008.

Sky Ride initiatives have also been introduced by the brand where cyclists of all 25 abilities ride in a traffic-free environment. Thompson says: We bring the stars to the Sky Ride events as it's an opportunity for cyclists to meet them and for them to sprinkle their fairy dust. We were trying to create that behavioural change and get people to think about cycling as a part of their life." The Sky investment also created a shift in sentiment towards the brand. Independent research by GfK shows a 31 per 30 cent increase in favourable attitudes towards Sky because of its cycling initiatives and a third of the population associates the brand with cycling.

Technology is another area where influence is growing in terms of making recommendations and introducing consumers to new ideas. Digital artists were commissioned by department store John Lewis to showcase their art on super high- 35 definition televisions at a gallery in the W London hotel, as a way to promote how televisions can be used for more than just watching programmes. This prompted some consumers to ask the retailer if they could buy the art as well as the TVs in their stores.

Meanwhile, Nokia aims to bring the latest in music trends to its customers through 40 an app, available on its Lumia Windows Phones, which offers both a store of current music and Mix Radio, where the brand creates playlists for users. Nokia sees its influence on popular culture as a mutual relationship. The phone company uses trend spotters in 28 countries to pick up on the latest crazes and then aims to affect popular culture by influencing more consumers to follow what's becoming popular. 45

Richard Howard, publisher of *Heat* magazine at Bauer Media, says: "With the rise in

---

³ raft large number
⁷ overall total
¹⁰ **keep an eye on sb/sth** watch sb/sth carefully
¹³ **backing** support
¹⁹ media profile *mediale Präsenz*
²⁰ **feature** appear
²⁵ initiative new plan
²⁸ sprinkle fairy dust spread luck and magic
²⁸ behavioural change change in the way people live and behave
³⁵ commission sb pay sb to create sth
³⁵ **department store** *Kaufhaus*
³⁵ showcase sth display sth
³⁵ high definition *hochauflösend*
⁴² playlist list of favourite songs
⁴³ mutual for both people
⁴⁴ craze fashion

50 social media and platforms, *Heat* now focuses efforts on maximising our dialogues on the platforms that we operate on." He claims that *Heat* has influenced popular culture by inventing acronyms such as LOL (laughing out loud) and OMG (oh my god), contributing to a "fun" personality that advertisers want to engage with.

The explosion of interest around food is another prime example of influencing consumers. Brands such as Marks & Spencer have encouraged trends in the consumption of high quality food with initiatives including connections with
55 celebrity chefs. M&S Food has set trends in British culture by inventing pre-packed sandwiches and prepared meals which can be heated up at home.

Most consumers would recognise an M&S advertisement, which might state 'these aren't just potatoes, they are M&S potatoes', a technique that has been mimicked by other brands and consumers. "We know the brand occupies a special place in the hearts and minds of the British public – they notice even the smallest things we do
60 and say – and everyone has an opinion."   (787 words)

From: Marketing Week, 2 October 2013

[49] acronym word made from the first letters of other words
[51] prime example great example
[57] mimick sb/sth imitate sb/sth

TEIL I: AUFGABENFOKUS LESEVERSTEHEN ....

Aufgabe 1   6 VP

Entscheiden Sie, ob die Aussagen zum Text *Under the influence* richtig oder falsch sind. Begründen Sie Ihre Entscheidung auf Deutsch.

Aussagen zum Text:

1 Some companies have changed the products they advertise as a result of the influence of popular culture.
2 Sponsorship has resulted in increased participation in cycling in the UK.
3 Sky Ride was motivated by the intention to promote a different lifestyle.
4 Sky has been always been a sponsor of cycling in Britain.
5 Cycling stories appear in the news more often now than previously.
6 The majority of the British public associate cycling with advertising.

Aufgabe 2   4 VP

Im Text werden vier Beispiele genannt, an denen man merkt, dass sich das Interesse am Radfahren in den letzten Jahren gewandelt hat.
Erstellen Sie eine Liste dieser Beispiele. Formulieren Sie vollständige Sätze auf Deutsch.

TEIL II: AUFGABENFOKUS TEXTPRODUKTION ....

Bearbeiten Sie Aufgabe 1 und Aufgabe 2.

Aufgabe 1 *Text-based composition*   I: 10 VP / Spr: 15 VP

"Technology is another area where influence is growing in terms of making recommendations and introducing customers to new ideas." (ll. 33–34)
Explain the quotation in relation to the text and give further examples of how technology can be used by companies to advertise their products and services.

Aufgabe 2 *Composition*   I: 10 VP / Spr: 15 VP

Wählen Sie <u>eine</u> der beiden Alternativen aus:

2a Explain what companies can do to help their brand occupy "a special place in the hearts and minds" of the public.
2b Although we are bombarded by advertising every day, we rarely buy products just because we see adverts for them. Discuss.

SCHRIFTLICHE PRÜFUNG Topic 2

Where's the water coming from?

Lester Brown

We drink on average four litres of water per day, in one form or another, but the food we eat each day requires 2,000 litres of water to produce, or 500 times as much. Getting enough water to drink is relatively easy, but finding enough to produce the ever-growing quantities of grain the world consumes is another matter.

Grain consumed directly supplies nearly half of our calories. That consumed indirectly as meat, milk, and eggs supplies a large part of the remainder. Today roughly 40 % of the world grain harvest comes from irrigated land. It thus comes as no surprise that irrigation expansion has played a central role in tripling the world grain harvest over the last six decades.

During the last half of the twentieth century, the world's irrigated area expanded from close to 250m acres (100m hectares) in 1950 to roughly 700m in 2000. This near tripling of world irrigation within 50 years was historically unique. But since then the growth in irrigation has come to a near standstill, expanding only 10 % between 2000 and 2010. […]

Today some 18 countries, containing half the world's people, are overpumping their aquifers. Among these are the big three grain producers – China, India and the US – and several other populous countries, including Iran, Pakistan and Mexico. […]

Among the big three, dependence on irrigation varies widely. Some four-fifths of China's grain harvest comes from irrigated land, most of it drawing on surface water, principally the Yellow and Yangtze rivers. For India, three-fifths of its grain is irrigated, mostly with groundwater. For the US, only one-fifth of the harvest is from irrigated land. The bulk of the grain crop is rain-fed, produced in the highly productive Midwestern Corn Belt where there is little or no irrigation. […]

In large areas of the US, such as the southern Great Plains and the Southwest, virtually all water is now spoken for. The growing water needs of major cities and thousands of small towns often can be satisfied only by taking water from agriculture. As the value of water rises, more farmers are selling their irrigation rights to cities, letting their land dry up. Hardly a day goes by without the announcement of a new sale. Half or more of all sales are by individual farmers or their irrigation districts to cities and municipalities.

In the largest farm-to-city water transfer in U.S. history, farmers in California's highly productive Imperial Valley agreed in 2003 to send San Diego County enough water to meet the household needs of close to one million people each year. The agreement spans 45 years. This could reduce food production in the Imperial Valley, a huge vegetable garden not only for California, but for countless other markets as well. Writing from the area in the *New York Times*, Felicity Barringer notes that many fear that "a century after Colorado River water allowed this land to be a cornucopia, unfettered urban water transfers could turn it back into a desert."

[…] Farmers in rural India are also losing their irrigation water to cities. This is strikingly evident in Chennai (formerly Madras), a city of 9 million on the east coast. As a result of the city government's inability to supply water to many of its people, a thriving tank-truck industry has emerged that buys water from nearby farmers and hauls it to the city's thirsty residents.

For farmers near cities, the market price of water typically far exceeds the value of the crops they can produce with it. Unfortunately the 13,000 privately owned tank

5

10

15

20

25

30

35

40

45

6 **remainder** what is left over after sth has been taken away or used

7 **irrigate sth** *etw bewässern*

8 **expansion** growth in size or area

13 **standstill** *Stillstand*

15 **overpump sth** *etw überbeanspruchen/überstrapazieren*

16 **aquifer** a layer of water stored under the earth's surface

22 **bulk** largest part, majority

25 **spoken for** reserved, promised for a special purpose

30 **municipality** city (government)

34 **span sth** cover sth, stretch over sth

37 **cornucopia** something that is or contains a large supply of good things

38 **unfettered** not controlled or restricted in any way

trucks hauling water to Chennai are mining the region's underground water resources. As water tables fall, eventually even the deeper wells will go dry, depriving rural communities of both their food supply and their livelihood. […]

50 The bottom line is that water constraints – augmented by soil erosion, the loss of cropland to nonfarm uses, a plateauing of yields in major producing areas, and climate change – are making it more difficult to expand world food production. The question raised is this: Is it conceivable that the negative influences on future food production could one day offset the positive ones, leading to a cessation in the world grain harvest? (698 words)

From: The Observer, 6 July 2013

[47] **water table** the level at and below which water is found in the ground
[49] constraint restriction
[49] augment sth increase the amount or size of sth
[49] **soil erosion** *Bodenerosion*
[50] plateauing levelling off
[50] yield harvest
[52] **conceivable** that you can imagine or believe
[53] offset sth *etw ausgleichen*
[53] cessation the end (of a situation/process)

TEIL I: AUFGABENFOKUS LESEVERSTEHEN ....

Aufgabe 1   6 VP
Entscheiden Sie, ob die Aussagen zum Text *Where's the water coming from?* richtig oder falsch sind. Begründen Sie Ihre Entscheidung auf Deutsch.

Aussagen zum Text:
1 Over half of the grain grown worldwide relies on irrigation.
2 The amount of irrigated land in the world nearly tripled in the second half of the 20th century.
3 Most grain crops in the USA are irrigated from underwater aquifers.
4 Cities in the Southwest of the USA buy their water rights from surrounding farms.
5 The water transfer agreement between local farmers and San Diego has turned the Imperial Valley back into a desert.
6 Water for the residents of Chennai in India is now provided by private suppliers.

Aufgabe 2   4 VP
In dem vorliegenden Text werden neben Wassermangel vier weitere Faktoren genannt, die eine Steigerung der weltweiten Nahrungsproduktion schwieriger machen. Erstellen Sie eine Liste dieser Faktoren. Formulieren Sie vollständige deutsche Sätze.

TEIL II: AUFGABENFOKUS TEXTPRODUKTION ....

Bearbeiten Sie Aufgabe 1 und Aufgabe 2.

Aufgabe 1 *Text-based composition*   I: 10 VP / Spr: 15 VP
"The market price of water typically far exceeds the value of the crops" (ll. 44–45). Explain the quotation in relation to the text and outline why the global water supply is so vital for human survival.

Aufgabe 2: *Composition*   I: 10 VP / Spr: 15 VP
Wählen Sie <u>eine</u> der beiden Alternativen aus:

2a Explain how man-made factors are putting the global water supply under such extreme pressure.
2b Discuss the advantages and disadvantages of renewable sources of energy.

SCHRIFTLICHE PRÜFUNG Topic 3

How robots are changing employment patterns

Gavin Kelly

Whether it's our reliance on supermarket self-service tills, our iPhones, the emergence of the drone as a weapon of choice or the impending arrival of the driverless car, intelligent machines are woven into our lives as never before. It's increasingly common for us to read about the inexorable rise of the robot as the fundamental shift in advanced economies that will transform the nature of work and opportunity within society. The robot is supposedly threatening the economic security not just of the working poor but also the middle class. "Be afraid" is the message: the march of the machine is eating into our jobs, pay rises and children's prospects. [...]

This is because the power of intelligent machines is growing as their cost collapses. They are doing things reliably now that would have sounded implausible only a few years ago. By the end of the decade, Nissan pledges the driverless car, Amazon promises that electric drones will deliver us packages, Rolls-Royce says that unmanned robo-ships will sail our seas. [...]

As economically significant, perhaps, as the rise of super-gadgetry is the growing power of software to accurately process and respond to data patterns. This raises the prospect of machines reaching deep into previously protected areas of professional work like translation, medical diagnostics, the law, accountancy, even surgery.

As yet, this techno-hype isn't matched by much hard evidence. According to the International Federation for Robotics, the use of robotics in leading advanced economies has doubled in the last decade – significant, but less than you might expect. [...]

The key question is whether the upward trend is about to take off, giving rise to sweeping changes in production that dislocate large tranches of the workforce.

Brynjolfsson and McAfee [...] argue that the digital revolution is about to crash into our jobs market. It's taken a while – Time magazine awarded the personal computer machine of the year in 1982 – but, they contend, the technology has now matured to a point where it will have the same scale of impact on production as the steam engine once did. Similarly, Cowen speculates that the future belongs to a gilded 10%–15% of workers whose skills will augment intelligent machines – the rest can look forward to long-term stagnation or worse. The harsh labour market experience of the young over recent years is a mere taster of what's in store. Growing numbers of low-skilled workers risk being unemployable: there won't be a wage at which it will be worth employing them. Huge numbers of the working poor will make ends meet only by migrating to areas offering very cheap housing, crumbling infrastructure and low taxes. [...]

As with all prophecies of doom, or indeed those of an impending economic boom, we should treat such visions with caution. Predictions about the uniquely transformational yet job-killing impact of technological change are as old as capitalism itself. There's never been an era without plausible experts warning the population that they are on the cusp of a new, usually scary, world resulting from technological breakthrough. Occasionally they're not wrong; mostly they are. Which isn't to downplay technology as the motor of economic change. Time and again – from spinning wheel to steam engine – it has had disruptive implications for the workforce. But labour displaced from field or factory eventually found new, more productive roles, demand expanded, living standards rose.

---

1 reliance *Vertrauen*
1 till *(Laden)Kasse*
2 of choice that most people choose
3 weave sth (past: woven) *etw weben*
4 inexorable [ɪnˈeksərəbl] that cannot be stopped
6 supposedly *angeblich, vermutlich*
7 march of the machine *wachsender technologischer Fortschritt*
8 eat into sth *sich in etw hineinfressen*
10 implausible not likely to be true
11 pledge sth promise sth
14 super-gadgetry *hochentwickelte Technologie*
16 prospect future possibility
18 techno-hype *Begeisterung für Technologie*
22 upward trend increase
22 give rise to sth cause, create sth
23 sweeping radical
23 dislocate sth *etw verlagern*
23 tranche part, section
24 Brynjolfsson and McAfee US academics
26 contend give an opinion
26 mature *reifen*
28 Cowen US economist
29 augment sth increase, add to sth
31 a mere taster just a small example of sth that will happen
33 make ends meet have enough money to survive
36 impending that is about to happen
39 on the cusp of sth the moment before sth happens
41 downplay sth say that sth is not that important
42 spinning wheel *Spinnrad*
43 disruptive *störend*

The lag, however, can be a long one. Not long before his death in 1873, John Stuart Mill remarked that the industrial revolution had not yet had much impact. This seemed an extraordinary observation, but it captured at least a partial truth. As the economic historian Brad DeLong has shown, from 1800 to 1870 real working-class
50 wages grew at just 0.4% a year before tripling to 1.2% from 1870 to 1950 (reaching almost 2% in the golden postwar decades). Similarly, we are yet to experience the true gain, whatever it turns out to be, as well as the pain, of the robot era.

(688 words)

From: The Guardian, 4 January 2014

46 John Stuart Mill English philosopher and economist

TEIL I: AUFGABENFOKUS LESEVERSTEHEN

Aufgabe 1   6 VP
Entscheiden Sie, ob die Aussagen zum Text *How robots are changing employment patterns* richtig oder falsch sind. Begründen Sie Ihre Entscheidung auf Deutsch.

Aussagen zum Text:
1 Intelligent machines have become more powerful as they have become more expensive to design.
2 The use of robotics in developed countries has increased by three times in the last decade.
3 Only a minority of workers will benefit from the next digital revolution.
4 New areas will be created for those workers without digital skills.
5 Most predictions about how technology will transform the world of work have not come true.
6 The benefits of technological change are normally felt quite quickly.

Aufgabe 2   4 VP
In dem vorliegenden Text werden vier Beispiele genannt, die zeigen, wie sehr intelligente Maschinen Teil unseres Lebens sind.
Erstellen Sie eine Liste dieser Beispiele. Formulieren Sie vollständige deutsche Sätze.

TEIL II: AUFGABENFOKUS TEXTPRODUKTION

Bearbeiten Sie Aufgabe 1 und Aufgabe 2.

Aufgabe 1 *Text-based composition*   I: 10 VP / Spr: 15 VP
"We are yet to experience the true gain […] of the robot era" (ll. 51–52).
Explain the quotation in relation to the text and outline possible advantages of future developments in robotics.

Aufgabe 2 *Composition*   I: 10 VP / Spr: 15 VP
Wählen Sie <u>eine</u> der beiden Alternativen aus:

2 a Discuss whether technology might ultimately lead to humanity's downfall.
2 b "Circumstances are now right for the digital revolution to have a huge impact on our lives." Discuss.

SCHRIFTLICHE PRÜFUNG Topic 4

Canada prepares for an Asian future

Ayesha Bhatty

For centuries, Chinese immigrants have come to Canada and particularly Vancouver for economic opportunities. It began with the gold rush in northern and central BC in 1858. In the 1880s, some 6,500 Chinese migrants were directly employed by the Canadian Pacific Railway (CPR), settling in towns along the railway route, all the way to the terminus in Vancouver, where the fledgling Chinatown took root […]. ⁵

But resentment grew among the white working classes, who saw the migrants as cheap labour, the so-called "yellow peril" stealing jobs and sullying society. In 1885, the federal government enacted the first anti-Chinese legislation, imposing a "head tax" of CAN$50 on every migrant worker. Under the Chinese Exclusion Act of 1923, immigration ground to a halt. The ban was lifted in 1947 […] but Mao's red revolution ¹⁰ closed the door at the other end.

The next significant wave of migrants came in the 1980s and 90s. But they weren't about to do manual labour or settle in Chinatown […]. This was a largely wealthy class of Hong Kong Chinese who snapped up homes in the priciest neighbourhoods, sent their children to the best schools, and kicked off a construction boom which ¹⁵ transformed downtown Vancouver into a Hong Kong-style city of skyscrapers.

Their sudden impact brought a sharp backlash. Polite Vancouver society was aghast at the "monster houses" being built in the old-monied communities […]. Some politicians warned of an "Asian invasion" while the bitter elite coined the phrase "Hongcouver" to express their dismay at the perceived Asian-isation of their city. ²⁰

"The wealth of the newcomers was an irritation to some in the local community," says historian John Douglas Belshaw, a professor at the University of Victoria. But attitudes soon began to change, he says. "The elite says, 'Our bread's buttered on this side. We can sell a ton of real estate to this community and they're kind of like us. These people like their whiskey straight'." ²⁵

The Hong Kong wave subsided after the British handover to China in 1997. Since then, immigrants from Mainland China, and to a lesser extent, Taiwan are leading the westward charge. Mandarin is edging out Cantonese on the streets of the city. Overall, nearly one-in-five Vancouverites is now of Chinese origin – the biggest migrant community by far, with some 12,400 new arrivals each year. ³⁰

Privately, there have been grumblings. In the safety of living rooms or the anonymity of online forums, old-time Vancouverites blame the Chinese for the city's sky-high property prices […]. Language is another flashpoint, especially when it comes to older migrants. "There used to be a time when immigrants to this country were required to know the language," whispers a woman in a doctor's clinic, as the ³⁵ receptionist struggles to ask an elderly Chinese man when he last took his heart medication. […] There's concern too that foreign students are taking up places at university, bringing much-needed cash in foreign student fees. A similar problem is playing out in schools, some say. "My son wants out of private school," says one parent who asked not to be named. His teenager has become one of the few white ⁴⁰ students at an exclusive Christian academy in a Vancouver suburb. "All these Asian kids are playing the piano and violin in the evenings. My kid plays hockey," he says. It's not uncommon to find only one or two white students in Vancouver classrooms, says Thomas Tam, a Chinese CEO, especially in courses like finance or engineering.

---

² BC (= British Columbia) *kanadischer Bundesstaat*

⁵ terminus the station at the end of a railway line

⁵ fledgling (like) a young bird

⁶ **resentment** feeling of anger or unhappiness about sth. that you think is unfair

⁷ "yellow peril" *„die gelbe Gefahr"*

⁷ sully sth. make sth. dirty

¹⁰ grind to a halt (past: ground) stop suddenly

¹² **significant** important

¹⁴ snap sth. up buy sth. quickly

¹⁵ construction building work

¹⁷ sharp backlash heavy criticism

¹⁷ aghast horrified

¹⁹ coin a phrase *einen neuen Begriff erfinden*

²⁰ dismay worried, sad feeling after you have received an unpleasant surprise

²⁴ real estate buildings, or land you can build on

²⁵ straight *(here:)* without any water

²⁶ subside decrease, become less

²⁸ charge *Angriff, Massenbewegung*

²⁸ edge sth. out slowly become larger, bigger, etc. than sth.

³¹ grumblings quiet protests

³³ flashpoint situation or place in which violence or anger starts

³⁷ medication medicines and pills

45 He says he gives the same advice to all young people – Asian and non-Asian –
struggling to find their place: "Take this as an opportunity rather than a challenge.
The future is in Asia and Vancouver has a very good advantage, which is that of all
the Canadian cities, we are the closest to the Asia Pacific Rim." […]
"Our government is focused on making sure British Columbians are first in line to do
50 business with Asia to create jobs here at home," says Premier Christy Clark.
"Vancouver and British Columbia are a natural place for many Asian families because
of our diversity. There are countless personal and cultural connections here and our
economy and province are richer, more vibrant and attractive for newcomers as a
result," her office said in a statement.
55 For now, BC continues to prosper from its ties to Asia and its booming economy.

(878 words)

From: the website of the BBC, 25 May 2012

48 Asia Pacific Rim *die Region Asien-Pazifik*
53 province *Bundesstaat*
53 vibrant ['vaɪbrənt] full of colour, life and noise
55 prosper succeed economically

TEIL I: AUFGABENFOKUS LESEVERSTEHEN

Aufgabe 1   6 VP

Entscheiden Sie, ob die Aussagen zum Text *Canada prepares for an Asian future*
richtig oder falsch sind. Begründen Sie Ihre Entscheidung auf Deutsch.

Aussagen zum Text:
1 Chinese immigrants to Canada were attracted by work on the railways.
2 Before the Second World War, the Canadian government made attempts to restrict
   Chinese immigration to Canada.
3 The immigrants who later came to Canada from Hong Kong were mostly manual
   labourers who settled in Chinatown.
4 The Vancouver elite has now accepted the Chinese immigrants as valuable
   economic partners.
5 Most people living in Vancouver today have a Chinese immigrant background.
6 Asian kids now prefer to play hockey rather than study music after school.

Aufgabe 2   4 VP

Im Text werden vier Bereiche erwähnt, in denen die alteingesessene Bevölkerung von
Vancouver Probleme mit den Einwanderern aus Asien hat. Erstellen Sie eine Liste
dieser Bereiche. Formulieren Sie vollständige deutsche Sätze.

TEIL II: AUFGABENFOKUS TEXTPRODUKTION

Bearbeiten Sie Aufgabe 1 und Aufgabe 2.

Aufgabe 1 *Text-based composition*   I: 10 VP / Spr: 15 VP

"Vancouver and British Columbia are a natural place for many Asian families […] and
our economy and province are richer, more vibrant and attractive for newcomers as a
result." (ll. 51–54)
Explain the quotation in relation to the text and outline the positive and negative
aspects of immigration for western societies.

Aufgabe 2 *Composition*   I: 10 VP / Spr: 15 VP

Wählen Sie <u>eine</u> der beiden Alternativen aus:

2a Evaluate the importance of language learning and education for immigrants.
2b "Immigration is vital for western industrialized nations to survive and prosper."
   Comment on this statement in the light of ageing populations in Europe.

SCHRIFTLICHE PRÜFUNG Topic 5

The odd couple: Britain and India

When David Cameron became prime minister, one of his priorities was to deepen economic ties with India, which had been neglected for years. India's trade has shifted to the east. China is now India's biggest trading partner. Indians sell it raw materials and buy everything from toys to turbines. Yet in some ways the tilt east is overstated. Investment and financial links between the two Asian giants are feeble. There are no direct flights between the business hubs of Shanghai and Mumbai. And even as their sea lanes teem with trade, tension crackles over their Himalayan border, and high-level political meetings are rare.

Far from being a failure, Britain's economic relationship with India is a mirror image of the Chinese one. Planeloads of bankers and Bollywood stars jet between London and Mumbai on 84 flights a week. Britain's banks lend more to India than any other country's, accounting for 28% of the world's exposure to India. Britain is the favourite destination for foreign direct investment (FDI) by Indian firms with about $30 billion invested, or about a quarter of Indian FDI.

In the other direction, British firms have at stake perhaps $85 billion in India, more than any other country and about 30% of all FDI into India. Some are golden-oldie investors such as Unilever; two big banks, HSBC and Standard Chartered; and British American Tobacco, which owns a third of ITC, a smokes-to-biscuits conglomerate based in Kolkata. Newcomers include Vodafone, BP and Diageo, which have used big acquisitions to boost their exposure to India, with mixed results.

The disappointment is trade in goods. Germany has created lots of jobs at home by exporting to fast-growing emerging markets. Britain has done less well. At the turn of the 21st century it was in the top five countries with which India traded. Now it is India's eighth-biggest export market and 23rd-biggest source of imports. India ranks 18th on the list of Britain's export destinations and 17th as a supplier of imports. China trades more goods in a week with India than Britain does in a month. Trade is low because both countries are mediocre at manufacturing. Britain no longer makes things emerging economies want, and India is not yet a base for the kind of cheap, labour-intensive production, whether of trainers or iPads, that ends up on British high streets.

Economic reality is hard to change but India is in the front-line of Britain's push to make its diplomacy more commercial. British firms typically work alone and sell services such as feasibility studies and advice on regulation. Japanese and Korean companies get their hands dirty and are increasingly acting in concert to offer giant integrated packages to finance and build big projects, often with bilateral government agreements. "Britain is missing the bus," says an industry chief.

Getting more small British firms on the ground in India is another priority. They generate jobs and trade. The city of Pune, a carmaking hub, hosts 300 – 400 German companies. The southern state of Tamil Nadu has a cluster of over 70 South Korean firms. No such British hub exists.

Over time India may open up more industries that Britain is good at. Much attention has been focused on supermarkets, with Tesco and others knocking on India's door. But imagine what giant London-listed mining firms such as Rio Tinto and Anglo American could do to boost the flagging output of India's mines, helping its balance of payments in the process.

5
10
15
20
25
30
35
40
45

2 ties connections

2 neglect sb/sth ignore sb/sth

4 tilt movement towards sth

5 overstate sth exaggerate sth

6 business hub important centre for businesses

7 sea lane *Seestraße*

7 teem with sth be full of sth

7 crackle *knistern*

9 mirror image complete contrast

10 planeload a plane full of

12 exposure *Kreditinanspruchnahme*

15 at stake at risk

16 golden-oldie popular thing from the past

18 smokes-to-biscuits everything from cigarettes to biscuits (i.e. a large range)

18 conglomerate *Mischkonzern*

19 newcomer recent arrival

20 acquisition act of buying sth

20 boost sth increase sth dramatically

22 emerging market new market that is becoming important

22 at the turn when one century ends and another begins

27 mediocre not very good, average

29 trainers sports shoes (worn for fashion)

31 in the front line the main priority area

31 push effort

33 feasibility study research to see if something is possible and worth doing

33 advice on regulation advice about rules and laws

34 get their hands dirty get involved directly

35 integrated package a complete collection

37 on the ground situated there

38 host sth be home to sth

39 cluster a group

44 flag slow down

44 output production

44 balance of payments *Zahlungsbilanz*

Although trade in services between the two nations has grown fast, it is just $7 billion a year, a fraction of overall trade. Britain sells more services to Luxembourg than to India. By easing visa rules Britain could persuade more Indian firms to set up global bases in London and use the city's finance and business skills.

50 Today everyone wants to be best pals with India. France says its relationship is "special"; Russia believes its position is "special and privileged"; America says its ties are "indispensable"; Japan reckons its bond with India is "intimate"; and Germany counts itself as a "very close friend". Even China hails "two ancient civilisations, connected by mountains, rivers and cultures". Mr Cameron's claim that Britain can be

55 India's "partner of choice" is overblown. But he is right that the economic relationship is closer than many realise and that, though lopsided, it can be built on.

(718 words)

From: The Economist, 26 September 2013

[48] ease sth. make sth. easier
[50] best pal best friend
[52] indispensable absolutely necessary
[52] bond positive connection
[53] hail sth. describe sth. as very good
[55] overblown exaggerated
[56] lopsided unbalanced

TEIL I: AUFGABENFOKUS LESEVERSTEHEN

Aufgabe 1   6 VP

Entscheiden Sie, ob die Aussagen zum Text *The odd couple: Britain and India* richtig oder falsch sind. Begründen Sie Ihre Entscheidung auf Deutsch.

Aussagen zum Text:

1 China imports raw materials from India, and India imports manufactured goods from China.
2 Indian companies invest more in the UK than in any other country.
3 Trade between Britain and India has suffered because the quality of goods produced in India is lower than the British market can accept.
4 The article recommends that British businesses cooperate with Korean and Japanese companies in order to be part of large investment projects.
5 A change in visa restrictions might encourage Indian companies to choose London as a base for international operations.
6 Britain is just one of many countries that recognise the value of business partnerships with India.

Aufgabe 2   4 VP

Im vorliegenden Text werden vier Aspekte genannt, die zeigen, dass die Beziehungen zwischen Indien und China nicht optimal sind.
Erstellen Sie eine Liste dieser Aspekte. Formulieren Sie vollständige deutsche Sätze.

TEIL II: AUFGABENFOKUS TEXTPRODUKTION

Bearbeiten Sie Aufgabe 1 und Aufgabe 2.

Aufgabe 1 *Text-based composition*   I: 10 VP / Spr: 15 VP

Prime Minister Cameron believes that Britain can be India's "partner of choice" (l. 55)
Explain the quotation in relation to the text and outline why India and Britain could be good partners on the global stage.

Aufgabe 2 *Composition*   I: 10 VP / Spr: 15 VP

Wählen Sie <u>eine</u> der beiden Alternativen aus:

2 a Evaluate Britain's position on the world stage.
2 b Discuss the pros and cons that the British Empire brought to the countries it colonized.

SCHRIFTLICHE PRÜFUNG Topic 6

TEXT

Fading superpower?

David Rieff

In Washington these days, people talk a lot about the collapse of the bipartisan foreign policy consensus that existed during the Cold War. But however bitter today's disputes are about Iraq or the prosecution of the so-called global war on terrorism, there is one bedrock assumption about foreign policy that remains truly bipartisan: The United States will remain the sole superpower, and be the guarantor of international security and global trade, for the foreseeable future. In other words, whatever else may change in the decades to come, the 21st century will be every bit as much of an American century as the 20th. [...] 5

But what if the Americans who hold these beliefs are not, in fact, clear-eyed observers of the world scene stripped of its anti-imperial mystifications? Instead, what if they are people who have fallen for the same self-delusion that the British ruling class entertained before World War I, which was that their empire was so essential to world stability and, at least when compared with the alternatives and with empires past, so just that its hegemony could and would weather all challenges? 10

It is hardly farfetched to scan the historical record and conclude that self-love and imperialism go together, whether it was the British imperialist Cecil Rhodes insisting that British colonialism in Africa had been "philanthropy plus 5%" or President Bush insisting that it was America's special mission to spread democracy throughout the world. But what the historical record also shows is that imperial moments are, in fact, fleeting, and that hegemony has a shorter and shorter shelf life. The Roman Empire based around the Mediterranean lasted more than 700 years, while the Ottoman Empire threatened Europe but ultimately vanished into history; the Spanish Empire shaped the Western hemisphere for four centuries, while the British Empire lasted a little more than 300 years in India and less than a century in much of Africa. The economic challenges facing the U.S. at least suggest that America's time as sole superpower could be shorter still. 15 20 25

Americans, who grow up believing in their country's exceptionalism (which in foreign policy terms often seems to mean not believing that the historical constraints that apply to other nations apply to the U.S.), are not predisposed to believe that American predominance could possibly be coming to an end. And yet it seems more like wishful thinking than rational analysis to believe that the United States – which in the coming decades will certainly have to adapt to a multipolar world in geo-economic terms, as China and India reoccupy the central place in the global economy that they had 500 years ago – can continue indefinitely to play a hegemonic role. 30

The truth is that [...] economic strength and political strength have always gone together. Because no one denies that the U.S. will decline in comparative terms economically [...], the only way one can believe that geopolitics will not also become multipolar is to believe that the U.S. is somehow exempt from what seems one of history's few ironclad laws. [...] This is not to say that the U.S. will not continue to be one of the most important powers – only that its days of first dictating and then guaranteeing the rules are numbered in an era in which it has become a debtor nation. In any case, the post-World War II structures of international governance are crumbling [...] and need to be revised. 35 40

For the moment, the U.S. is the sole superpower. But instead of deluding ourselves that we will go on that way into the indeterminate future, an intelligently self-interested 45

---

1 bipartisan consensus agreement on an issue between two main political parties

4 bedrock assumption fundamental belief

10 strip sb/sth of sth remove sth completely from sb/sth

10 mystification a feeling of confusion because you do not understand something

11 self-delusion *Selbsttäuschung*

14 hegemony domination

14 weather sth survive sth, such as a storm, difficulties, etc.

15 farfetched *weit hergeholt*

17 philanthropy *Wohltätigkeit*

20 fleeting short-lived

20 shelf life *Haltbarkeit*

27 exceptionalism *Einzigartigkeit*

28 constraint *Einschränkung*

29 be predisposed be likely to behave or think in a certain way

30 predominance *Vorherrschaft, Überlegenheit*

30 wishful thinking *Wunschdenken*

32 multipolar having several different important centres

32 geo-economic *die Weltwirtschaft betreffend*

38 exempt from sth not affected by sth

39 ironclad so strong that it cannot be challenged or changed

41 debtor nation *Schuldnerstaat*

42 governance the activity of governing a country or organization

43 crumble fall apart slowly

44 delude oneself *sich selbst täuschen*

45 indeterminate *unbestimmt, unklar*

45 self-interested considering only your own interests and not caring about other people

foreign policy would have us do everything in our power to shape [...] the international rules that will govern relations between states after the American moment has passed – as it inevitably will.

50 The alternative is to go the route of the British before 1914 and imagine that because a certain set of political arrangements seems best to us, they must also be best for the world – and destined to endure indefinitely. The real choice that confronts us is not between a second American century and anarchy but between a multipolar world in which we will play an important role and an anti-American century.   (731 words)

From: The LA Times, 9 September 2007

51 be destined to do sth *für etw bestimmt sein*
51 endure last for a long time

TEIL I: AUFGABENFOKUS LESEVERSTEHEN

Aufgabe 1   6 VP

Entscheiden Sie, ob die Aussagen zum Text *Fading superpower?* richtig oder falsch sind. Begründen Sie Ihre Entscheidung auf Deutsch.

Aussagen zum Text:

1 American politicians are divided in their opinion as to whether the USA will remain the world's only superpower for the next few decades.
2 Before the First World War, British politicians could not imagine that there was any alternative to the British Empire.
3 Empires seem to maintain a position of world dominance for shorter and shorter periods as history progresses.
4 It is possible for a country to lose economic power compared to other nations, but for it still to remain a major political influence on the world stage.
5 The USA will be able to rely on international institutions to look after its interests should it lose its dominance over world affairs.
6 The USA must come to terms with the fact that there will be more than one centre of power in the world in the future.

Aufgabe 2   4 VP

Im vorliegenden Text werden vier Weltreiche genannt, die als Beispiele dafür dienen, dass Weltreiche nur für begrenzte Zeit existieren.
Erstellen Sie eine Liste dieser Weltreiche. Formulieren Sie vollständige deutsche Sätze.

TEIL II: AUFGABENFOKUS TEXTPRODUKTION

Bearbeiten Sie Aufgabe 1 und Aufgabe 2.

Aufgabe 1 *Text-based composition*   I: 10 VP / Spr: 15 VP

"The United States will remain the sole superpower, and be the guarantor of international security and global trade, for the foreseeable future." (ll. 5 – 6)
Explain the quote in relation to the text and comment on the possible strengths and weaknesses of the USA as a superpower in the coming decades.

Aufgabe 2 *Composition*   I: 10 VP / Spr: 15 VP

Wählen Sie <u>eine</u> der beiden Alternativen aus:

2 a Comment on how relevant the American Dream is for most Americans today.
2 b "I have a very strict gun control policy: if there's a gun around, I want to be in control of it." Clint Eastwood
Discuss the arguments for and against gun control in the USA.

237

KOMMUNIKATIONSPRÜFUNG Topic 1

EINZELPRÜFUNG

1. Sequenz: Monologisches Sprechen

Produce an uninterrupted 5-minute discourse based on the cartoons and quotation below, explaining how advertising works in today's world.

"As you can see, I've been targeted by advertisers."

> "Instead of one-way interruption, Web marketing is about delivering useful content at just the precise moment that a buyer needs it."
> David Meerman Scott
> *(American online marketing strategist)*

2. Sequenz: Dialogisches Sprechen

Discuss in depth the changes that are taking place in the world of advertising.

KOMMUNIKATIONSPRÜFUNG Topic 1

....

1. Sequenz: Monologisches Sprechen

Student A

Deliver an uninterrupted 5-minute monologue about the following cartoon and quote, relating them to the role of consumerism in modern-day society.

"Something is missing."

> "What consumerism really is, at its worst is getting people to buy things that don't actually improve their lives."
> Jeff Bezos
> *(founder of amazon.com)*

Student B

Deliver an uninterrupted 5-minute monologue about the following cartoon and quote, relating them to the role of consumerism in modern-day society.

"Today's consumer has new priorities, and it's our job to tell them what those priorities are…"

> "We live in an era of consumerism and it's all about desire-based consumerism and it has nothing to do with things we actually need."
> Aloe Blacc
> *(American hip-hop artist)*

2. Sequenz: Dialogisches Sprechen

Discuss in depth the topic of advertising and consumerism in the modern world.

KOMMUNIKATIONSPRÜFUNG Topic 2

EINZELPRÜFUNG

1. Sequenz: Monologisches Sprechen

Produce an uninterrupted 5-minute discourse based on the map, the photo and the quotation, explaining their relevance to climate change.

Europe if all the ice melts

Stockholm · St Petersburg · Copenhagen · Hamburg · London · Amsterdam · Venice

House on the English coast

> Deserts in Spain, snowless ski resorts in Italy, deforestation in Germany – and seas that keep on rising. A future Europe will look very different from today's Europe.

2. Sequenz: Dialogisches Sprechen

Discuss in depth the problems facing the world as a result of climate change.

KOMMUNIKATIONSPRÜFUNG Topic 2

TANDEMPRÜFUNG

1. Sequenz: Monologisches Sprechen

Student A

Deliver an uninterrupted 5-minute monologue about the following cartoon and quote, relating them to the role of consumerism in modern-day society.

Wind farm where a forest once stood.

Human nature involves destroying things, then thinking up ways to undo the damage – but there might be no solution to climate change.

Student B

Deliver an uninterrupted 5-minute monologue about the following chart and quote, relating them to the role of energy in the world today.

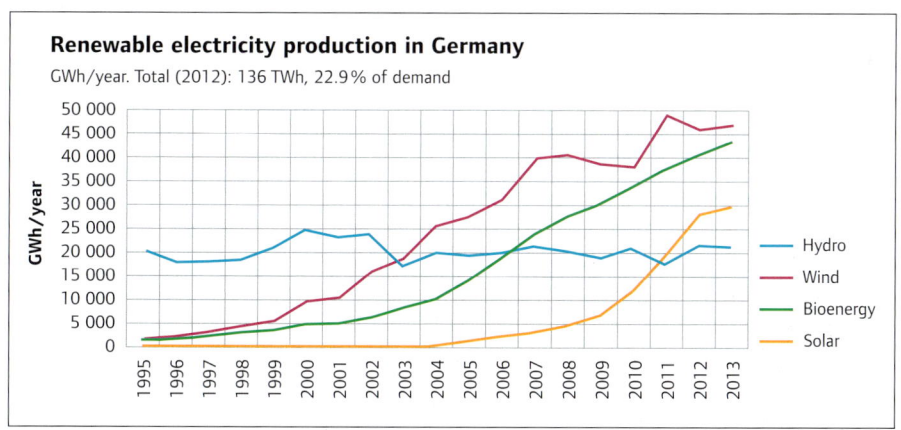

While a quarter of Germany's energy comes from renewable sources, the country will still be dependent on fossil fuels like oil, coal and natural gas for many years to come. Intermittent power from renewable sources can't replace the reliability of fossil-fuel plants.

2. Sequenz: Dialogisches Sprechen

Discuss in depth the topic of climate change and how we might deal with it.

KOMMUNIKATIONSPRÜFUNG Topic 3

EINZELPRÜFUNG

1. Sequenz: Monologisches Sprechen

Produce an uninterrupted 5-minute discourse based on the cartoon and quotation below, explaining what risks and opportunities progress in science offers society.

"Technology gives us power, but it does not and cannot tell us how to use that power. Thanks to technology, we can instantly communicate across the world, but it still doesn't help us know what to say."
Jonathan Sacks
(British rabbi and philosopher)

2. Sequenz: Dialogisches Sprechen

Discuss in depth the risks and opportunities that science and technology offer society.

KOMMUNIKATIONSPRÜFUNG Topic 3

TANDEMPRÜFUNG

1. Sequenz: Monologisches Sprechen

Student A

Deliver an uninterrupted 5-minute monologue about the following cartoon and quote, relating them to GM food.

"Now that is scary"

"Myths about the dire effects of genetically modified foods on health and the environment abound, but they have not held up to scientific scrutiny. And, although many concerns have been expressed about the potential for unexpected consequences, the unexpected effects that have been observed so far have been benign."
Nina Fedoroff
(US molecular biologist)

Student B

Deliver an uninterrupted 5-minute monologue about the following cartoon and quote, relating them to GM food.

"If food is labeled, some people might choose to eat stuff that's genetically modified. They might decide they love it. But give us a choice."
Ziggy Marley
(Jamaican musician)

2. Sequenz: Dialogisches Sprechen

Discuss in depth the topic of science and technology in the modern world.

KOMMUNIKATIONSPRÜFUNG Topic 4

EINZELPRÜFUNG

1. Sequenz: Monologisches Sprechen

Produce an uninterrupted 5-minute discourse based on the cartoon and quotations below about gender equality/inequality.

"No, this is not Mel's secretary. This is Mel."

A gender-equal society would be one where the word "gender" does not exist: where everyone can be themselves.
Gloria Steinem
(US feminist)

True equality means holding everyone accountable in the same way, regardless of race, gender, faith, ethnicity – or political ideology.
Monica Crowley
(US conservative political commentator)

2. Sequenz: Dialogisches Sprechen

Discuss in depth the topic of equality in society.

KOMMUNIKATIONSPRÜFUNG Topic 4

TANDEMPRÜFUNG

1. Sequenz: Monologisches Sprechen

Student A

Deliver an uninterrupted 5-minute monologue about the following cartoon and quote, relating them to discrimination in the USA.

> Views about the police remain splintered by race. Nearly three-quarters of blacks said police in most communities are more likely to use deadly force against a black person. Four-in-ten blacks said they had been stopped by the police just because of their race; only 5% of whites gave that response. The differences in blacks' and whites' perceptions of opportunity today are striking. Only 35% of blacks compared to 55% of whites said that white and black people have about an equal chance of getting ahead in today's society.
> Karilyn Bowman
> *(US journalist)*

Student B

Deliver an uninterrupted 5-minute monologue about the following cartoon and quote, relating them to discrimination in the USA.

> In 2015, the famous think tank, the Brookings Institution reported the following facts about African-Americans:
> 1. Half of African-Americans born poor stay poor.
> 2. Black middle-class kids are downwardly mobile.
> 3. Black wealth barely exists.
> 4. Black students attend worse schools.

2. Sequenz: Dialogisches Sprechen

Discuss your cartoons and texts, and what light they throw on the topic of race relations and equal opportunity in the USA.

KOMMUNIKATIONSPRÜFUNG Topic 5

EINZELPRÜFUNG

1. Sequenz: Monologisches Sprechen

Produce an uninterrupted 5-minute discourse based on the map and the quotations, explaining how the British Empire still can be felt today.

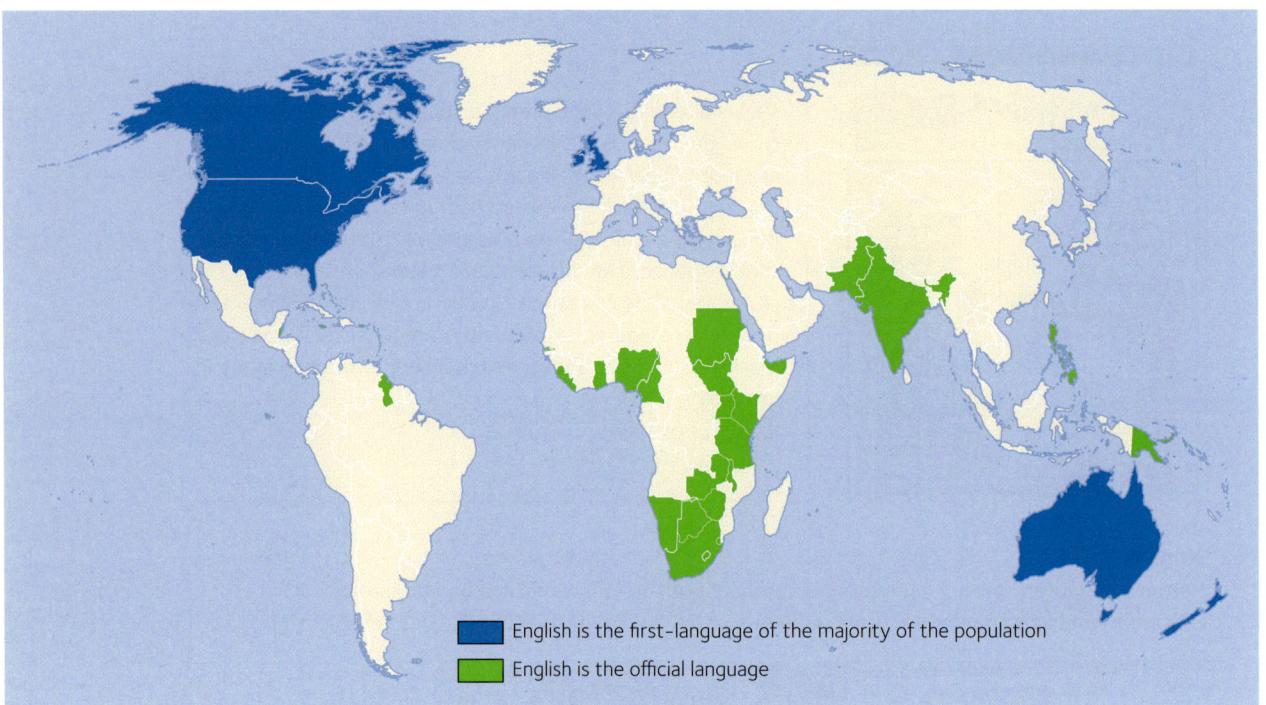

English is the first-language of the majority of the population

English is the official language

English through out the world

> By the time the British left India in 1947 they had given the subcontinent a number of priceless assets, including the English language, but also a structure of good government, local organization and logistical infrastructure that still holds good today. Far from damaging India, British imperial rule gave it a head start.
>
> The British Empire left a negative legacy in much of the world: it reinforced racial differences, downplayed local cultures, destroyed local traditions, and changed the economies of the world so that they served European interests.

2. Sequenz: Dialogisches Sprechen

Discuss in depth the role of Britain in a globalized world.

KOMMUNIKATIONSPRÜFUNG Topic 5

TANDEMPRÜFUNG

1. Sequenz: Monologisches Sprechen

Student A

Deliver an uninterrupted 5-minute monologue about the following cartoon and quote, explaining what they reveal about the US-British relationship.

The truth is that Britain is culturally, economically and intellectually a bit more American than the rest of Europe, while being geographically, historically and strategically Europe, not America. The unique characteristics that arise from that position give a British prime minister certain diplomatic privileges in Washington, but they also give him special status in Brussels should he choose to take advantage of it.
Rafael Behr
(political journalist)

Student B

Deliver an uninterrupted 5-minute monologue about the following cartoon and quote, relating them to the state of Britain.

What does it mean to be British? Ironically, those who most feel British belong to ethnic minorities. Large numbers of English, Scottish and Welsh people no longer identify mostly as British. If Britain has a long-term future, it will need to find a "British" identity that works for the future and involves the four countries and their peoples who are linked by kinship, history and culture.

2. Sequenz: Dialogisches Sprechen

Discuss your cartoons and texts, and what light they throw on Britain and its identity today.

KOMMUNIKATIONSPRÜFUNG Topic 6

EINZELPRÜFUNG

1. Sequenz: Monologisches Sprechen

Produce an uninterrupted 5-minute discourse based on the photo and the quotation from Emma Lazarus's poem "The New Colossus", explaining the role of immigration in the history of the USA.

The US–Mexican border

Give me your tired, your poor,
Your huddled masses yearning to breathe free,
The wretched refuse of your teeming shore.

2. Sequenz: Dialogisches Sprechen

Discuss in depth the challenges and opportunities that immigration offers a country like the USA.

KOMMUNIKATIONSPRÜFUNG Topic 6

TANDEMPRÜFUNG

1. Sequenz: Monologisches Sprechen

Student A
Deliver an uninterrupted 5-minute monologue about the following cartoon and quote, relating them to modern-day immigration to the USA.

For all the noise and anger that too often surrounds the immigration debate, America has nothing to fear from today's immigrants. They have come here for the same reason that families have always come here – for the hope that in America, they could build a better life for themselves and their families. Like the waves of immigrants that came before them and the Hispanic Americans whose families have been here for generations, the recent arrival of Latino immigrants will only enrich our country.
President Barack Obama

Student B
Deliver an uninterrupted 5-minute monologue about the following cartoon and quote, relating them to modern-day immigration to the USA.

Stopping illegal immigration would mean that wages would have to rise to a level where Americans would want the jobs currently taken by illegal aliens.
Thomas Sowell
(US economist)

2. Sequenz: Dialogisches Sprechen

Discuss your cartoons and texts, and what light they throw on the USA, traditionally considered to be a land of immigrants.

ZENTRALE KLASSENARBEIT
HÖRVERSTEHEN Topics 1–3

Die Arbeit umfasst drei Aufgabenteile:

1 Die unterschiedlichen Arten von Käufern (Topic 1)
2 Die Zukunft von Gas (Topic 2)
3 Wissenschaftsprojekte (Topic 3)

Arbeitszeit inklusive Abspielen der Audios: 45 min

Alle Aufgabenteile müssen bearbeitet werden.
Sie hören jeden Text <u>zwei</u> Mal.
Vor dem ersten Hören lesen Sie sich bitte die jeweilige Aufgabenstellung durch.
Während des Hörens dürfen Sie sich Notizen machen.

3.10

Aufgabe 1: Die unterschiedlichen Arten von Käufern   10 VP

Sie hören einen Bericht des Radiosenders BTC2, in dem der Konsumexperte
Dr. Phillip Lewis die unterschiedlichen Arten von Käufern erklärt.
Erläutern Sie, gegebenenfalls mit Beschreibung der jeweils unterschiedlichen
Eigenschaften, die sieben Arten von Käufern.
Kopieren Sie und vervollständigen Sie die Tabelle auf Deutsch mit Informationen aus
der Radiosendung.

Arten von Käufern	Eigenschaften

Aufgabe 2: Biodiversität und Artensterben   10 VP
3.11

Sie hören ein Radiointerview mit Louise Cameron, einer Dozentin
an der Universität London, über Biodiversität.
Beantworten Sie die Fragen auf Deutsch in Stichworten.

1	Was genau bedeutet Biodiversität?	1 VP
2	Wieso ist Biodiversität ein aktuelles und dringendes Thema geworden?	2 VP
3	Was scheint die primäre Ursache des jetzigen Artensterbens zu sein?	1 VP
4	Wieso sterben die großen Säugetiere aus?	1 VP
5	Warum können bestimmte Pflanzen-, Insekten- und Pilzarten der Menschheit von Nutzen sein?	1 VP
6	Erklären Sie, warum die zwei von Louise Cameron erwähnten gefährdeten Arten wichtig für die Nahrungskette sind.	2 VP
7	Erklären Sie, welche Hoffnung Louise Cameron für die Zukunft hat.	2 VP

Aufgabe 3: Wissenschaftsprojekte   10 VP
3.12

Sie hören eine Unterhaltung zwischen drei Schülern – Amy, Mark und Keiko –
über ihre verschiedenen Wissenschaftsprojekte.
Kopieren Sie und vervollständigen Sie die unten stehenden Sätze auf Deutsch.

1 Amys Projekt thematisiert gentechnisch veränderte Lebensmittel, da sie bei diesem
Thema zwei Bedenken hat: Erstens, …
(2 Nennungen)

2 Nick meint, dass Menschen seit eh und je Wissenschaft in der
Lebensmittelproduktion angewandt haben, und nennt folgende Beispiele: …
(3 Nennungen)

3 Keiko hat das Thema Übergewicht ausgewählt, da …
(3 Nennungen)

4 Nick möchte in seinem Projekt über Hungersnot zwei Sachen herausfinden: …
(2 Nennungen)

ZENTRALE KLASSENARBEIT
HÖRVERSTEHEN Topics 4–6

Die Arbeit umfasst drei Aufgabenteile:

1 Muslime in Großbritannien (Topic 4)
2 Was die Briten über ihr Imperium denken (Topic 5)
3 Waffenkontrolle in den USA (Topic 6)

Arbeitszeit inklusive Abspielen der Audios: 45 min
Alle Aufgabenteile müssen bearbeitet werden.
Sie hören jeden Text <u>zwei</u> Mal.
Vor dem ersten Hören lesen Sie sich bitte die jeweilige Aufgabenstellung durch.
Während des Hörens dürfen Sie sich Notizen machen.

3.13

Aufgabe 1: Muslime in Großbritannien   10 VP

Sie hören ein Radiointerview, in dem Dr Athar Patel, Mitglied des British Muslim Council, über die Ergebnisse der letzten Volkszählung in Hinblick auf die muslimische Minderheit berichtet.

Erläutern Sie, gegebenenfalls mit Zahlen, welche Vorurteile gegenüber der muslimischen Bevölkerung in Großbritannien gängig sind, und zu welchen Ergebnissen die Volkszählung gekommen ist.

Kopieren Sie und vervollständigen Sie auf Deutsch die Tabelle mit Informationen aus der Radiosendung.

Vorurteile	Ergebnisse der Volkszählung

3.14

Aufgabe 2: Was die Briten über ihr Imperium denken   10 VP

Sie hören eine Radioreportage über das britische Imperium.
Kopieren Sie und vervollständigen Sie die unten stehenden Sätze auf Deutsch.

1	Nach einer neueren Umfrage glaubt die Mehrheit der Briten …	1 VP
2	Großbritannien hat seinen Kolonien einige positive Dinge hinterlassen, zum Beispiel …	3 VP
3	Als Teil des Nordatlantischen Sklavenhandels wurden …	2 VP
4	Im 19. Jahrhundert arbeiteten viele Briten im Kolonialdienst, da …	2 VP
5	Um beruflich voranzukommen mussten junge Leute in den Kolonien …	2 VP

Aufgabe 3: Waffenkontrolle in den USA   10 VP
3.15

Sie hören ein Interview mit Professorin Jean Daly, in dem sie über
Waffenkontrolle redet.
Hören Sie zu und beantworten Sie die Fragen auf Deutsch in Stichwörtern.

1	Welches Argument wird am häufigsten verwendet, um den privaten Kauf und Besitz von Feuerwaffen zu rechtfertigen?	1 VP
2	Wie interpretieren die Befürwörter der Waffenkontrolle die "Second Amendment" zur Verfassung der Vereinigten Staaten?	1 VP
3	Mit welcher Zahl kann man die jährlichen Todesfälle durch Waffengewalt in den USA vergleichen?	1 VP
4	Wo liegt die USA im Vergleich zu anderen Ländern, was den Besitz von privaten Feuerwaffen betrifft?	2 VP
5	Welche Argumente werden verwendet, um gegen Beschränkungen im Waffenbesitz zu argumentieren?	2 VP
6	Welches Schlupfloch kann ein potentieller Waffenkäufer ausnutzen, um einem Hintergrundcheck zu entgehen?	1 VP
7	Wie gehen normale Amerikaner mit ihren Waffen um?	1 VP
8	Warum sind die Chancen gering, dass sich etwas an der Waffenfreiheit in naher Zukunft ändern wird?	1 VP

STUDY SKILLS

RECEPTION: READING AND LISTENING

PRODUCTION: WRITING AND SPEAKING

INTERACTION

MEDIATION

RECEPTION: READING AND LISTENING

Reading difficult texts

Texts are read for different reasons. Sometimes you only need to know what the text is about, so it is usually enough just to **skim** the text carefully. When specific information has to be found, the important thing is to pick out key words by **scanning**. If you need to examine a text in order to answer questions or write an essay on it, then you have to read it thoroughly, possibly twice.

Skimming: gaining a quick overview of a text

Step 1: Look for clues which give you information about the content of the text: the title and sub-headings, words in bold, pictures and their captions.

Step 2: If you are still not sure what the text is about, read the first and last sentences of each paragraph. Don't worry about individual words, difficult quotations, etc. which you do not understand.

Scanning: finding details in a text

Many questions which test your understanding of a text, or exercises like **true or false**, require you to find pieces of information quickly, rather than reading the whole text. Search the text for key words that will help you find the required information. If you're looking for the author's opinion on a particular subject, look out for words like *think*, *believe*, *opinion*, etc. If you're looking for information on a topic, try to think of a few key expressions that you could look out for.

Close reading: understanding a text in detail

Do not just start reading. A few simple steps will help you to understand the text better, without getting lost in the details.

Step 1: Your first step should be to gain a basic understanding of what the text is about (see "Skimming" above). It will be easier to understand difficult words or phrases when you understand the general context. Note down the most important points.

Step 2: Be aware of the structure of the text. Find out which part contains the main information and how is it set out (sub-headings, paragraphs, etc.). Pay attention to expressions like *only, but, while, that's why, while, however*, etc., which the author uses to organize his or her arguments.

Step 3: Now read the text more intensively and note down more points. When reading a text for the first time, only look a word up in a dictionary if the meaning of the whole sentence is dependent on it. The essential meaning can often be worked out from the context.

Step 4: Make notes on the content of the text in a structured form, e.g. as a mind map or a list (of themes or of advantages/disadvantages). Add phrases that will be helpful later when you write about the content of the text in your own words. Now look up the most important vocabulary.

Dealing with unknown words

When you come across a word you don't know, ask yourself whether it is really necessary to understand that word in order to understand the overall message of the text. Looking up words takes time and often doesn't help you to understand the most important points.

Working out the meaning from similar words

A word that you don't know could be related to another word that you already know (e.g. derivations like *aggressor/aggressive*). Or the word may be made up of a word stem that you know and a word part that will help you to work out the meaning of the word (*formal/informal, clockwise/anticlockwise, change/changeable, stupid/stupidity*). Some words are also similar to German words, especially those of foreign origin (compare *initial* and "Initialen" or *potential* and "potenziell"). However, watch out for "false friends": *actual* does not mean "aktuell" (= *current, present*) but "tatsächlich" or "eigentlich".

Working out the meaning from the context

If you are still not sure, looking at the word in the context of the sentence can give you more information. First think about what part of speech you are dealing with. Are you looking for a noun? What does the noun you are looking for represent – a building? A person? If you're looking for an adjective, is it one which describes an exact situation or someone's character? Look at the following sentences and try to work out the meanings of the words in bold from the context:
Business is very bad at the moment and we don't expect it to **rally** *for at least a year. All the signals are very* **inauspicious**, *I'm afraid.*

Using a monolingual dictionary

Get to know your dictionary so that you understand the symbols, abbreviations and phonetic transcriptions and can use the reference sections, which are usually found at the front and back of the dictionary or on additional pages. Look at the following example of a typical entry in a dictionary.

ab·sorb /əb'sɔːb; *NAmE* -'sɔːrb -'zɔːrb/ *verb*
▶ LIQUID/GAS **1** to take in liquid, gas or other substance from the surface or space around: **~ sth** *Plants absorb oxygen.* ◊ **~ sth into sth** *The cream is easily absorbed into the skin.*
▶ MAKE PART OF STH LARGER **2** [often passive] to make sth smaller become part of sth larger: **~ sth** *The country simply cannot absorb this influx of refugees.* ◊ **~ sth into sth** *The surrounding small towns have been absorbed into the city.*
▶ INFORMATION **3** **~ sth** to take sth into the mind and learn and understand it **SYN take in:** *It's a lot of information to absorb all at once.*
▶ INTEREST SB **4** **~ sb** to interest sb very much so that they pay no attention to anything else **SYN engross:** *This work had absorbed him for several years.*
▶ HEAT/LIGHT/ENERGY **5** **~ sth** to take in and keep heat, light, energy, etc. instead of reflecting it: *Black walls absorb a lot of heat during the day.*

Labels pointing to the entry:
- pronunciation
- part of speech
- regional variant (North American English)
- first meaning
- second meaning
- synonym
- sample sentence
- context/general meaning

- Don't read the whole dictionary entry, just look for the particular part of speech you need. For example, if you want to know what *absorb energy from the sun* means go for the 5th meaning (HEAT/LIGHT/ENERGY). You can ignore the first part of the entry.
- Make sure you read the relevant section and the example sentences carefully, as they will help you to tell which meaning applies in which context.
- Note down the right meaning so that you don't forget it again.

Learning new vocabulary

pay (noun)	– Bezahlung, Gehalt, Lohn
payslip	– Gehaltsabrechnung
pay day	– Zahltag
pay-off	– Abfindung
pay (verb)	– zahlen
pay for sth	– etw bezahlen
pay off	– auszahlen
pay as you go (mobile phone)	– Prepaid(-Handy)

There are various ways of learning new words. Find out which method is best for you. But whichever method you use, don't forget: words are easier to remember if you don't just write down the key word, but also expressions, synonyms, opposites, related words, examples and possibly even notes on pronunciation. Compound expressions are particularly important. These include phrasal verbs, such as *set about* and *put off*. Your notes for the word *pay*, for example, might look like the note on the left.

Index cards: Write the English word and any related comments on one side of the card and the meaning in German on the other side. When you think you know a word, move it from the first section to the second section. Look at the cards in the second section at intervals. Put the ones you know in the third section and look at these cards less often. If you don't know a word, put it back in the first section and look at these words as often as possible.

Word families: Make lists of word families – that way you not only learn the new word, but also its derivations (*approve – approval – approving – disapprove – disapproval*).

Word fields: A good way to learn word families (groups of words related to a particular topic) is to draw mind maps (networks of words). This method is very good for learning words on a specific topic for a class test. Write the key word in the centre and the general terms for the most important aspects of the topic around it. Then write related words around each general term.

Doing exercises: *The Vocabulary Practice Book* that is available for *Crossover 2* offers the key topic vocabulary from the student's book plus a variety of exercises. If you like learning on the computer, then the Crossover vocabulary trainer is the best solution. Go to www.phase-6.de, select Cornelsen and then Crossover 2.

Practising listening skills

In order to understand spoken English, you should prepare yourself well for the particular situation, for example discussions, telephone conversations, etc. Often the accents, background noises and other disturbances will make it hard to understand what is being said, so you have to concentrate on what is most important. Use the methods described below when you do the listening exercises in *Crossover 2*.

Before you listen

- Read carefully to find out exactly what you are expected to do. Make use of anything that is there to help you – pictures, headings, etc.
- If possible, write down key words connected to the topic. You might find it helpful translating the German words in the tasks into English and then listening out for them.

While you are listening

- Firstly, listen to the entire listening text to understand what it's about. You should write down key words during this first listening.
- Listen again, and only listen for the information which is important for the exercise. Don't concentrate on individual words and expressions which you don't understand.
- Pay attention to expressions which make the logical train of thought clearer, such as

however, *in my view*, *in conclusion* and so on. They will help you to follow the central theme of the text.

- Write the information down in note form, never in full sentences. A table or framework can help you to organize your notes. Here is an example framework for notes on a text about alternative energy sources:

	advantages	disadvantages	amount used per person
wave energy			
solar energy			
wind energy			

- Use symbols, abbreviations and short forms of words to save time when making notes:

symbols		abbreviations		short forms	
=	*the same as*	e.g.	*for example*	adv	*advantage*
≠	*not the same as*	km	*kilometres*	govt	*government*
+	*and*	w., w/o	*with, without*	impt!	*important*

After you listen
- Write out the main points as quickly as possible using your notes – you might not be able to read all your symbols or understand your abbreviations later on.
- If there are some details you haven't understood when writing your answers, then make a guess based on what you have understood.

There are plenty of useful websites where you can listen to radio broadcasts to practise your listening skills. The best place to find British English is www.bbc.co.uk where you can choose programmes from a huge radio archive. The British Council offers transcripts to their listening material: www.britishcouncil.org. If you prefer to listen to American programmes, go to www.npr.org, the National Public Radio website.

PRODUCTION: WRITING AND SPEAKING

Making notes

It is a good idea to make notes when you are reading or listening to a text. This makes it easier to remember the information later on. At first glance it seems fairly easy to make notes when you read a text. However, many people find it difficult to make short, meaningful notes. Here are some useful tips to help you:
- Try not to copy out whole sentences from the original text. This wastes time and also makes it harder to write about the text using your own words later on.
- Give your notes a heading that makes the topic clear, e.g. "Effects of genetic engineering on the environment".
- Go through the text and look for the most important aspects of the topic, which you can use as sub-headings. Remember to leave enough space under each heading for your notes.
- Look out for signals such as emphasis and repetition, as well as expressive adjectives like *huge, incredible, devastating*, etc. These show what the author considers important.
- Only write short notes, not full sentences.
- Make the logical development of the information clear, e.g. by writing certain points in a list or underlining the most important terms.
- Check that you have included all the necessary information. Don't forget that the important points are often scattered throughout the whole text.

Doing comprehension tasks

Always read the exercise instructions carefully to understand exactly what sort of answer is required – a common mistake is to write something that does not answer the task properly. Also be careful not to use information in one answer which could be necessary for answering a different task.

- Make notes in the form of short points and lists, instead of writing out whole sentences from the text. In class tests and exams you should mark the most important parts of the text. It is best to mark everything that is important for one question with one colour, and then use a different colour for the next question.
- Use the same verb tense in your answer as was used in the question.
- Replace terms from the text with synonyms and rewrite sentences as much as possible, e.g. *recently → in recent years; violent crime → crime involving violence; think → believe; to a great extent → greatly; when she was a child → in her childhood* and so on.
- Look for signals in the text such as emphasis and repetition, as well as meaningful adjectives or adverbs like *absolutely, unbelievably, amazing*. These show what the author considers important.
- Do not bring your own opinion into your answer.

Dealing with instructions (*Operatoren*)

You will often be asked questions about the text. Sometimes, however, you will be given specific instructions that tell you what to do. These instructions are called *Operatoren*. There are many different instructions, so it is important to know what type of task they demand.

Instruction	German	What you have to do	Tips
Analyse	analysieren	Describe and explain certain aspects in detail.	• **Before you write:** List the aspects in question and explain how they came to be. • **Language to know:** *This suggests … / This seems to suggest … / This implies …*
Comment on	Stellung nehmen zu	State clearly your opinions on the topic in question and support your views with evidence.	• **When you write:** Argue your case but always mention the counter-argument to show you understand it. • **Language to know:** phrases to express your opinion, e.g. *it seems to me that …; considering these arguments; I agree that …*
Compare	vergleichen	Point out the similarities and differences between two things/concepts/ systems, etc.	• **Before you write:** Make a table in two columns, comparing individual aspects. • **Language to know:** *On the one hand, … On the other hand, …;*
Contrast	gegenüber-stellen	Point out the differences between two things/concepts/ systems, etc.	
Describe	beschreiben	Say what something is like by giving details about a person, situation or object.	• **Before you write:** Collect all the aspects you want to mention. • **Language to know:** *In the following, I shall describe …*

Discuss	erörtern	Weigh up both sides of an issue, giving reasons for and against.	• **Before you write:** Remember that "discuss" means you have to consider both sides of an issue. It is useful to structure your ideas first, e.g. in a mind map or an outline. • **Language to know:** *On the one hand, ... on the other hand, ...; While it is true that ..., one can also say that ...*
Examine	untersuchen	Describe and explain certain aspects in detail.	• **Before you write:** Make sure you know not just *what* happened but *why* it happened. Make a list.
Explain	erklären	Describe and define in detail.	• **Before you write:** Make sure you know not just *what* happened but *why* it happened.
Outline	darstellen	Give a description of the main facts. You can divide the outline into main points and subordinate points.	• **Before you write:** Collect your ideas in a flowchart (if the question is about a development or process) or a mind map (if the text is an argumentative one).
Point out	aufzeigen, benennen	Find and explain certain aspects of something as they are presented in the text.	• **Before you write:** Make a list of the different points. • **Language to know:** *The first point the author makes about ... is that ... However, the text goes on to say that ...*
State why ... / the reasons for ...	angeben .../ sagen warum ... die Gründe angeben für ...	Say why someone did something or why something happened.	• **Before you write:** List all the reasons on a piece of paper. • **Language to know:** *To state the reasons for ..., one has to look at ...; The text gives a number of reasons why ...; because / as a result / therefore / consequently / for this reason*

Writing an essay

When you write an essay, make sure you know what you need to write.
If you are asked to **comment on** an issue, you are expected to give your opinion on a particular topic in a way that you convince the reader that your opinion is the right one. It is important that you justify your opinion and use examples to illustrate it.
If you are asked to **discuss** an issue, you are expected to present both sides of an argument, and come to a conclusion based on the arguments that you have presented.
When writing, follow these steps:

Step 1: Make sure you know exactly what you have to write about. Read through the exercise instructions several times.

Step 2: Make notes. Organize your points clearly, for example in a mind map, list or table.

Step 3: Make sure you have a clear structure: an introduction, the main part and the conclusion. Writing an outline will help you.

Step 4: Write an introduction that refers to the question.

Step 5: Deal with each argument/issue in one paragraph. Make your line of argument clear by using structural words; look at the list on the cover flap at the back of this book ("Language for Writing").

Step 6: Emphasize the point of your argument with a concise conclusion (in a comment) or sum up the ideas you presented in a way that some resolution is offered (in a discussion).

Introducing an essay
– *In the following, I shall deal with the problem/subject/issue of …*
– *I would like to discuss …*
– *I intend to present arguments in favour of … and against …*

Concluding a comment
– *All in all, I think it can be said that …*
– *In conclusion, I would like to say that …*
– *I would like to conclude by saying that …*

Step 7: Check your draft for the following:
- Spelling mistakes (e.g. words that sound the same, like *there/their*, *meet/meat*).
- Grammatical mistakes (for example, make sure all the verbs are in the right tense; check that regular adverbs end in *-ly*).
- Choice of words (for example, check that there aren't repetitions; check for false friends like "aktuell" ≠ *actual* [but = *current, present*], "eventuell" ≠ *eventual* [but = *possible*], "spenden" ≠ *spend* [but = *donate*]).
- Sentence structure (for example, check that there are no incomplete answers beginning with *Because;* check the correct order of adverbs, e.g. place before time).
- Logical line of argument (for example, make sure the expressions you have used are clear; make sure you have included structural expressions such as *however, on the one hand, on the other hand, in addition, as a result*, etc.)

Improving your writing skills

Here are some ideas for improving your writing skills.

1 Connecting sentences

It is easy to write a simple English sentence and you are less likely to make mistakes. To improve your style, however, it is necessary to combine simple sentences to make more complex sentences. This can be done by using subordinate sentences.

Examples:
a Nuclear energy does not harm the environment. It is cheap to produce.
→ *Nuclear energy, which is cheap to produce, does not harm the environment.*

b He is overweight. He feels unhappy about his appearance.
→ *He is unhappy about his appearance because he is overweight.*

c He was feeling ill. But he went to school.
→ *Although he was feeling ill, he went to school.*

d In the foreground we see a man. He is spraying a cornfield with chemical fertilizer.
→ *In the foreground we see a man spraying a cornfield with chemical fertilizer.*

2 Connecting arguments and making transitions

When you outline a new argument, start a new paragraph or conclude your composition, it is good style to use connectors.

Examples (See also "Language for Writing" on the back cover flap of the book.):

Listing	besides, equally important, first (second, etc.), further, furthermore, in addition, in the first place, moreover
Giving examples	for example, for instance, in fact, to illustrate
Comparing	likewise, similarly
Contrasting	although, and yet, despite, even though, however, in on the other hand
Summarizing or concluding	all in all, in conclusion, in other words, in short, in summary, on the whole, therefore, to sum up
Showing your argument is logical	accordingly, as a result, because, consequently, for this reason, hence, if, otherwise, since, so, then, therefore, thus

3 Varying your vocabulary

With a large vocabulary you will be able to express yourself in a more interesting way. Read the section "Learning new vocabulary" (p. 256) for tips on how to learn new words. Here are some ideas on how to vary the vocabulary you use when you write.

a Try to use more interesting and specific verbs instead of the usual ones:

say	mention, remark, state, argue, express, claim
get	come into possession of, obtain, receive
use	employ, make use of
do	carry out, perform
feel	realize, consider, experience
make	build, assemble, put together, manufacture, produce
think	believe, be of the opinion, imagine, suppose
have	possess, comprise, consist of, contain, include, be made up of
see	notice, observe, recognize, regard, understand, realize
like	be fond of (+ gerund), be keen on (+ gerund), cherish, enjoy
show	demonstrate, indicate, reveal, prove
be about	deal with, concern, have to do with, discuss, explore

b When describing things use a greater variety of adjectives:

nice	agreeable, charming, delightful, enjoyable, pleasant
beautiful	attractive, good-looking, gorgeous, lovely, stunning
not good	awful, disgusting, dreadful, horrible, terrible, unpleasant
very good	great, magnificent, outstanding, superb, wonderful
important	significant, major, essential, notable
interesting	absorbing, fascinating, gripping, engaging, thought-provoking
main	principal, major, foremost
clear	plain, explicit, evident
unclear	ambiguous, uncertain, in doubt

c Other important words that tend to be used too frequently:

part (of a text)	passage, paragraph, section
mainly	mostly, on the whole, to a large extent, predominantly
very	extremely, highly, remarkably, really
theme	topic, subject
about	approximately, around, roughly

4 Using typical English grammar

a The gerund

Try to use the gerund as often as possible. Here are some examples of words and expressions that are followed by the gerund and automatically sound good in compositions.

begin	He began working.
love	I love watching fantasy films.
hate	She hates learning vocabulary.
prefer	I prefer watching love stories.
be fun	It's fun working in the disco.
be worth	The film is worth seeing.
by	He improved his English by learning ten new words every day.
without	He passed his exam without working very hard.

b Participle constructions

English, especially written English, is full of sentences shortened by a participle. This automatically sounds more elegant. For foreign students, using the participle to shorten sentences is not always easy, but shortening relative sentences is one of the easier structures. Using the *–ing* form after *before* and *after* also improves style.

Examples:

After he saw the ad on TV, she ...	*After seeing the ad on TV, she ...*
Before she went to school, she ...	*Before going to school, she ...*
The goods which were advertized were ...	*The goods advertized were ...*
One ad which showed toys was ...	*One ad showing toys was ...*

Interpreting pictures and cartoons

It is a good idea to learn some phrases for describing and interpreting pictures and cartoons. Make sure you concentrate on the essential message of the picture rather than getting lost in the details. Keep to the following steps in order to structure your answer in a sensible way.

"Nobody's perfect, but we're working on it."

Step 1: Describe the picture. Look at all aspects of the picture but only describe the elements which are important for the picture's message. Use the present progressive when you describe the content of the picture – unless you are using a verb that does not usually appear in this tense. For example, if you were writing about the cartoon on the right you could write:
*The cartoon shows two men in a lab. They look like scientists, as they **are** both **wearing** white coats. In front of them is a large test tube with a man inside it. It seems as if they **are creating** a new person. One of the scientists **is saying** …*
(Note "look" is in the present simple, as it is rarely used in the present progressive.)
But be careful: the present progressive is only used for the situations and actions shown in the cartoon and not for verbs which you use to describe and interpret the picture (*The cartoon **shows** … It **seems** as if they …*).

Step 2: Interpret the picture. If you don't think the picture says much, then you can mention this in your interpretation by referring to it as ambiguous or unclear.

Step 3: Comment on the picture. Sum up the central message of the picture and/or make a comment on it, for example by saying how much of an effect you think the picture has.

Step 4: Compare the picture/cartoon with a short text (when the task requires this). State whether you think the picture/cartoon supports the message of the text or contradicts it.

1. Describing the picture

– *The cartoon shows / appears to show ...*
– *The scene depicts / shows ...*
– *In the foreground / background / centre there is ...*
– *The speech bubble / thought bubble / caption / label says that ...*
– *On the left / right you can see ...*
– *The ... looks as if ...*
– *The person on the left appears to ... / It seems as if the person ...*
– *He / She is wearing / holding ...*

2. Interpreting the picture

– *The picture / cartoon deals with the recent discussion of ...*
– *I think the cartoonist's / artist's / photographer's use of irony / exaggeration is intended to create ... / is aimed at making ... / conveys ...*
– *The person in the centre represents / symbolizes / shows ...*
– *This indicates / shows / reveals that ...*
– *The ... represents / is in fact / stands for ...*
– *The cartoonist / artist / photographer criticizes / wants to say / express the idea that ...*
– *Because the foreground / background is ..., the impression is given that ...*
– *From the way the people are depicted, it is obvious that ...*
– *The point of the cartoon seems to be that ...*

3. Commenting on the picture

– *I think the cartoon is quite right / makes a fair point.*
– *I agree / disagree with the cartoonist / artist, but ...*
– *In my opinion, the cartoonist is partly right / exaggerates a little / a lot.*
– *Because of ..., the picture touches me / leaves me cold.*
– *The ... helps to create a ... atmosphere, which forces you to / has the effect of ...*

4. Comparing the picture with the text

– *While the text says that ..., the cartoon / picture shows / makes the point that ...*
– *In the text we found out that ...*
– *The cartoon / picture illustrates the facts / information in the text in the following way.*
– *The cartoon / picture gives a completely different opinion about the information in the text.*

Interpreting charts and graphs

As when describing cartoons, it is also useful to learn a number of set phrases for describing and interpreting diagrams. Follow these steps to structure your answers well.

Step 1: Describe the diagram. This does not mean listing all the details but describing what the diagram shows and what sort of information is represented.

Step 2: Summarize the trends, developments or levels shown. What conclusions can be drawn from the data? Is it possible to summarize the results?

Step 3: Compare the diagram with a text (when the task requires this). Go back to the text and look for sections which are significant in relation to the diagram. State whether you think the diagram supports the message of the text or contradicts it.

Types of diagrams

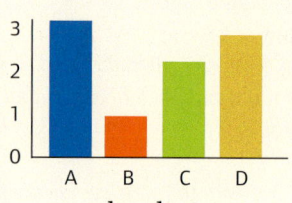

graph, line graph

bar chart

pie chart

Talking about values and amounts

– *more / less than ...*
– *no less than ...*

– *85 % (said that ...)*
– *On the other hand, almost ...*

Talking about proportions, shares and percentages

– *(over) half of ...*
– *more/less than one third/quarter of ...*
– *the (vast) majority of ..*

– *a mere third of ...*
– *to make up / comprise half of ...*

Talking about developments and trends

– *a huge/sharp increase/decrease*
– *a small / slight rise*
– *levels out, remains constant*
– *drastically, gradually, sharply, steadily*

– *rises/increases, hits a maximum*
– *drops/decreases/falls/plunges*
– *over a period of ...*
– *between 2000 and 2010*

Comparing the information in a diagram with a text

– *While the text says that ..., the diagram shows that ...*
– *The graph illustrates the facts/information in the text in the following way.*
– *The diagram shows something completely different to the information in the text.*

Giving a presentation

The ability to give a presentation effectively is important in the world of work and also, increasingly, at school. It is not just the content of a presentation that is important but also how clearly you present that content. Structure your talk so that it is easy to understand, and illustrate your points in a lively way to make it varied and interesting.

As most people in your audience need some visual stimulation, you should show some key words and figures on the board or the screen. If possible, show photos, pictures, graphs, etc., related to your topic as this is sure to make an impact on your audience.

Before the presentation

Step 1: Prepare your topic thoroughly and make notes in English. Check that your notes are correct in terms of language and that you can pronounce all the words correctly. Write all your notes onto prompt cards that you will use to guide you through your presentation.

Step 2: Think about whether you could make your presentation livelier and more interesting by adding anecdotes, visual materials, audio materials, etc.

Step 3: Organize and check all the materials you need (laptop, OHP, flipchart, etc.).

Step 4: Practise giving the presentation, ideally in front of a small audience.

During the presentation

Step 1: Begin by giving a short overview of your presentation, saying what you are going to present.

Step 2: Make it easy for your audience to follow the presentation by expressing yourself clearly, using short sentences and speaking slowly and clearly.

Step 3: The audience is more likely to stay interested if you make your presentation as varied as possible. Use visual material from time to time (OHP, flip chart, etc.) and prepare handouts.

Step 4: Do not read your presentation. Use prompt cards to help you do your presentation.

Step 5: Think about your body language: face the audience, make eye contact with them, and use gestures to make what you are saying clearer.

Step 6: Sum up the most important points at the end of your presentation. Thank the audience for their attention and encourage them to ask questions.

Starting your presentation
Good morning/afternoon, my name is …
Today I am going to talk about …
The subject of my talk is …
If I am not speaking clearly enough, please say so.
Can you see the screen/overhead projector/chart/…?

Introducing the main points
I'd like to begin by saying/showing … I want to start by explaining … / saying something about …
As shown in the cartoon/picture/graph, …
The graph/cartoon, etc. demonstrates …
I would like to give an example …

Finishing your presentation
In conclusion, I would like to … / I would like to finish by saying …
Finally, … / Thank you very much for your attention.
If you have any questions, I would be pleased to answer them.

INTERACTION

Discussing in groups

Whether you are taking part in a group discussion, a debate or a role-play, get the most out of it by following the points below.

· Learn the phrases on the cover flap at the back of the book ("Language for Discussion") and try to use them in your lessons.
· Think about what you are going to say by preparing some bullet points related to individual aspects of the topic and noting down key terms in English.
· If there is time, prepare a few questions/answers on the topic.
· Always stay calm and think before you speak, and keep to the topic.
· Join in! Group work is a great opportunity to speak freely.

Expressing understanding, surprise, etc.

Ach so. / Ah ja.	*I see. / Right. / Oh, right.*
Oh je!	*Oh dear!*
Echt?	*Really?*
Gut. / Okay.	*Fine.*
Alles klar.	*OK then.*
Das ist doch wohl nicht dein Ernst!	*You're kidding!*

....

Mediating

Mediation means conveying the general sense of a text in another language for someone who does not understand the original. When answering the comprehension questions and tasks on an exam text or doing listening comprehension tasks, you will make use of mediating. Cconcentrate on the essential information, rather than translating word for word. Specific details and stylistic subtleties are only of secondary importance.

Step 1: Know exactly what information the task requires.

Step 2: Read the whole text through without concentrating on individual words. Where possible, ignore vocabulary which you don't understand – often it is not essential for understanding the meaning of the text as a whole.

Step 3: Read the instructions again to find out exactly what you are supposed to do and in what form your answer should be written. If there are several questions, use different colours to mark sections of the text that are relevant to each question.

Step 4: Summarize the main points of the part of the text you need to mediate. Express yourself clearly, and simplify the language of the original text by concentrating on what is said, not how it is said.

Step 5: Read your answer through again and make sure that you have expressed the content of the original in a way that is appropriate and easy to understand.

GRAMMAR SUMMARY

The simple present

1 We **recycle** our glass bottles once a week.
2 The Arctic **consists** mostly of ice.
3 Biofuels from seaweed **don't cause** extra CO_2 emissions.
4 **Does** he **care** about the environment?

· Man gebraucht das *simple present* für regelmäßige, sich wiederholende Ereignisse oder Handlungen (1, 3) und für Dauerzustände (2–4).
· Mit Ausnahme der 3. Person Singular (*he, she, it*) hat das *simple present* dieselbe Form wie der Infinitiv (1).
   ⚠ Die 3. Person Singular endet auf *-(e)s* (2).
· Ist kein Hilfsverb im Satz vorhanden, werden Verneinung und Fragen mit der entsprechenden Form von *do* gebildet (3, 4).

Das *simple present* wird häufig mit den folgenden Zeitangaben benutzt:

– *always, never, often, rarely, seldom, sometimes*
– *generally, mostly, normally, regularly, usually*
– *every day/week/month/..., every morning/afternoon/...*
– *on Mondays/Tuesdays/..., on weekdays*
– *in (the) summer/winter/...*
– *at Christmas/Easter, at weekends*

The present progressive

1 Scientists **are looking** for ways to reduce CO_2 emissions.
2 The workers **are harvesting** the seaweed today.
3 The vertical farm **isn't working** at the moment.
4 **Are** biofuels **damaging** the environment?

Verwendung:
· Man benutzt das *present progressive* für Vorgänge oder Handlungen, die im Moment des Sprechens oder Schreibens passieren und noch nicht abgeschlossen sind (1, 4).
· Es wird auch für vorübergehende Situationen gebraucht (2, 3).

Bildung:
· Das *present progressive* wird mit dem Präsens von *be* und der *-ing*-Form des Vollverbs gebildet.

- Da beim *present progressive* immer ein Hilfsverb vorhanden ist, wird die Verneinung mit *not/-n't* gebildet (3).
- Fragen werden durch Umstellung gebildet (4).

Das *present progressive* wird oft mit den folgenden Zeitangaben benutzt:

at the moment, at present, now, this week/month

⚠ Diese Verben bilden normalerweise keine *progressive*-Form:

be, believe, doubt, feel (meinen), *hate, hear, imagine, know, like/dislike, love, mean, notice, prefer, realize, recognize, remember, see* (begreifen), *seem, suppose, think* (meinen), *understand, want, wish*

The simple past

1 Los Angeles **opened** its first aqueduct in 1913.
2 She **went** with her friends to the public swimming pool.
3 They **didn't use** their pool during the drought last summer.
4 How much water **did** you **save** last year?

Verwendung:
- Man benutzt das *simple past*, um über Vergangenes zu berichten.
- Das *simple past* wird auch gebraucht, wenn man sagen will, wann etwas geschehen ist (1, 3, 4).

Bildung:
- Bei regelmäßigen Verben wird das *simple past* durch das Anhängen von *-ed* an den Infinitiv gebildet (1).
  ⚠ Die unregelmäßigen Verben haben eine Sonderform (2), die man sich merken (= auswendig lernen) muss.
- Ist kein Hilfsverb im Satz vorhanden, bildet man die Verneinung und Fragen mit *did/ didn't* (3, 4).

Das *simple past* wird häufig mit den folgenden Zeitangaben benutzt:

- *yesterday, the day before yesterday, the week/month/... before last*
- *last night/week/month/summer/December/Easter/...*
- *two/three/... hours/days/years/... ago*
- *in 2005 / in the 20th century ...*
- *at that time, in those days*

The past progressive

1 It was difficult to sleep because the storm **was making** such a noise.
2 The tourists **were taking** photos when a wave crashed over the sea wall.
3 Luckily I **wasn't driving** across the bridge when the flood destroyed it.
4 **Were** you **driving** to work when the flood started?

Verwendung:
- Wenn man ausdrücken möchte, dass eine Handlung zu einem bestimmten Zeitpunkt oder während eines bestimmten Zeitraumes in der Vergangenheit im Gange war, benutzt man das *past progressive* (1).
- Das *past progressive* wird auch benutzt, um zu verdeutlichen, dass eine Handlung im Gange war, als ein neues Ereignis (plötzlich) eintrat (2, 3, 4).

Bildung:
- Man bildet das *past progressive* mit *was/were* und der *-ing*-Form des Vollverbs (1).
- Die Verneinung wird mit *was not / wasn't* bzw. *were not / weren't* gebildet (3).
- Fragen bildet man durch Umstellung (4).
  ⚠ Einige Verben haben keine *progressive*-Form (siehe die Liste unter *present progressive*).

The present perfect

1 Two scientists **have published** an atlas of the city's swimming pools.
2 The city **hasn't started** rationing water yet.
3 How long **have** you **known** about the water shortage?
4 Southern California **has had** a drought for over two years.
5 The reservoir **has lost** 10,000 gallons of water since last year.

Verwendung:
- Wenn man ausdrücken will, dass etwas geschehen ist, ohne dass der genaue Zeitpunkt des Ereignisses wichtig ist, wird das *present perfect* benutzt (1, 2).
- Man gebraucht das *present perfect* auch, um zu sagen, seit wann oder wie lange ein Zustand oder eine Handlung schon andauert (3–5). Dafür wird sehr oft *for* bzw. *since* verwendet. (Im Deutschen steht dafür „seit" plus Gegenwart.)

Bildung:
- Das *present perfect* wird mit *have/has* und der 3. Form des Vollverbs gebildet (1–5).
- Die Verneinung wird durch das Einfügen von *not/-n't* unmittelbar nach *have/has* gebildet (2).
  ⚠ Die unregelmäßigen Verben haben eine Sonderform (3–5), die man auswendig lernen muss.
- Fragen bildet man durch Umstellung (3).

Das *present perfect* wird oft mit den folgenden Zeitangaben benutzt:

- *already, still (not), (not) yet*
- *(not) ever, just, lately, never, recently*
- *so far this week/month/…, till/until now*

The present perfect progressive

1 We**'ve been recycling** organic waste since the 1990s.
2 They **haven't been using** their hosepipe to water the garden recently.
3 **Has** he **been driving** an electric car for long?

Verwendung:
- Das *present perfect progressive* benutzt man für Handlungen und Vorgänge, die in der Vergangenheit begonnen haben und zum Zeitpunkt des Sprechens bzw. Schreibens noch nicht beendet sind.

Bildung:
- Das *present perfect progressive* wird mit *have/has been* und der *-ing*-Form des Vollverbs gebildet (1).
- Die Verneinung bildet man durch das Einfügen von *not/-n't* unmittelbar nach *have/has* (2).
- Fragen werden durch Umstellung gebildet (3).
  ⚠ Einige Verben haben normalerweise keine *progressive*-Form (siehe die Liste unter *present progressive*).

The past perfect

1 After the Civil War many African-Americans still lived in poverty although the government **had abolished** slavery.
2 The government **hadn't** yet **abolished** slavery when the Civil War began.
3 When the Civil War was finally over, the fighting **had lasted** for more than four years.

Verwendung:
- Mit Hilfe des *past perfect* drückt man aus, dass zwei Handlungen oder Vorgänge in der Vergangenheit aufeinander folgten (1, 2). Die Handlung, die zeitlich voranging, steht im *past perfect*.
- Das *past perfect* wird auch verwendet, um auszudrücken, dass ein Zustand vor einem Zeitpunkt der Vergangenheit begann und zu diesem Zeitpunkt noch andauerte (3).
  ⚠ Wenn zwei oder mehrere kurze Handlungen in der Vergangenheit direkt aufeinander folgen, wird für alle Handlungen das simple past verwendet: *The soldiers **started** to shoot when they **saw** the enemy.*

Bildung:
- Das *past perfect* wird mit *had* und der 3. Form des Vollverbs gebildet (1, 3).
- Die Verneinung wird durch das Einfügen von *not/-n't* unmittelbar nach *had* gebildet (2).

The past perfect progressive

1 When I saw the protesters, I could see that some of them **had been crying**.

- Das *past perfect progressive* wird verwendet, wenn man ausdrücken will, dass eine Handlung oder ein Vorgang vor einem Zeitpunkt in der Vergangenheit begonnen hatte und bis (oder fast bis) zu diesem Zeitpunkt andauerte.

The future

A will

1 In the future, young Native Americans **will find** jobs outside the reservation.
2 We can only hope that the job situation on the reservation **will improve** soon.
3 You can't find fruit at the local shop? Don't worry! I**'ll drive** you to the market.
4 People **will not stop** buying junk food just because they put a tax on it.
5 I **won't stop** buying it either.
6 **Will** the tax **raise** money for the people on the reservation?

Verwendung:
- Das *will-future* benutzt man, um Vorhersagen zu machen (1) oder Vermutungen über die Zukunft zu äußern (2).
- Man benutzt es auch, wenn man sich spontan zu etwas entschließt, Angebote oder Versprechen macht (3).

Bildung:
- Das *will-future* wird mit *will* + Infinitiv des Vollverbs gebildet. Es hat für alle Personen die gleiche Form (1–3).
- Die Verneinung bildet man durch das Einfügen von *not* unmittelbar nach *will* (4). Im gesprochenen Englisch sagt man häufig *won't* (5).
- Fragen werden durch Umstellung gebildet (6).

Das *will-future* kommt häufig mit den folgenden einleitenden Verben und Ausdrücken vor:

- *believe, expect, forecast, hope, imagine, suppose, think*
- *It's clear/obvious that ..., There's no doubt that ...*

B going to

1 Look at those storm clouds. It**'s going to** rain soon.
2 The tribal chief's son **is going to** study Physiotherapy when he finishes high school.
3 PJ Simmons **isn't going to** play for his high school team any more.
4 When **is** Ranger **going to** take his driving test?

Verwendung:
- Das *going to-future* benutzt man für Ereignisse und Situationen, die nach Meinung des Sprechers bald eintreten werden (weil es bereits Anzeichen dafür gibt) (1).
- Es wird auch für Pläne und Absichten gebraucht (2).

Bildung:
- Das *going to-future* wird mit *am/is/are* + *going to* + Infinitiv gebildet (1, 2).
- Die Verneinung bildet man durch das Einfügen von *not/-n't* unmittelbar nach *am/is/are* (3).
- Fragen werden durch Umstellung gebildet (4).
  ⚠ Der Gebrauch des Futurs hängt in gewissem Maße von der Absicht oder Sichtweise des Sprechers ab. Dies gilt insbesondere für das *going to-future* und für zukünftige Ereignisse. Daher ist es im Zweifelsfall ratsam, das neutralere *will-future* zu benutzen.

C The present progressive / the simple present

1 We**'re leaving** home at 10.30.
2 The bus **goes** at 11 o'clock.

- Man kann *das present progressive* auch mit einer Zeitbestimmung der Zukunft (*at 10.30, this afternoon, on Sunday*) für bereits feststehende Pläne und Verabredungen verwenden (1).
- Genau wie im Deutschen wird auch im Englischen das *simple present* mit einer Zeitangabe benutzt, um fest terminierte Vorgänge (Fahrpläne, Stundenpläne, Programme usw.) anzugeben (2).

The future perfect

1 The last train **will have left** when we get to the station
2 Mike hasn't arrived yet. I expect he'll **have missed** the train.

Verwendung:
- Das *future perfect* verwendet man für Handlungen oder Vorgänge, die zu einem bestimmten Zeitpunkt in der Zukunft abgeschlossen sein werden. (1).
- Mit dem *future perfect* kann man auch eine Vermutung über ein Geschehen in der Vergangenheit ausdrücken (2).

Bildung:
- Das *future perfect* wird mit *will have* + Partizip Perfekt gebildet (1). Meist werden die Kurzformen *'ll* und *won't* verwendet (2).

Modal auxiliary verbs

1 Adverts **can** make a product more memorable.
2 Adverts **don't need** to be long or expensive to be effective.
3 All adverts **must** be honest.
4 The advert couldn't persuade people to buy the product.
5 **May** I explain why I think you **should** change your marketing?

Verwendung:
- Um zu sagen, was geschehen kann, muss, darf, soll usw., benutzt man ein modales Hilfsverb in Verbindung mit einem Vollverb (1–4).

⚠ Im Englischen steht ein Hilfsverb – anders als im Deutschen – nie ohne Vollverb:
– Lena kann Spanisch ⇒ Lena **can speak** Spanish. NICHT: ~~can Spanish~~

Bildung:
- Modale Hilfsverben – nicht jedoch die Ersatzverben (siehe unten) – haben bei allen Personen immer die gleiche Form, einschließlich der 3. Person Singular (keine –s-Endung) (1, 3–5).
- Die Verneinung wird durch das Einfügen von *not/–n't* unmittelbar nach dem Hilfsverb gebildet (4), außer bei *need*, wo das Hilfsverb *do* verwendet werden kann. (2)
- Fragen bildet man durch Umstellung (4).
- Abgesehen von *could* (wenn es für eine Fähigkeit gebraucht wird) kann man modale Hilfsverben nur im Präsens und – mit einer geeigneten Zeitangabe – mit zukünftiger Bedeutung benutzen, zum Beispiel:
  – You **can go** home now. *(Präsens)*
  – You **can go** home an hour early tomorrow. *(Futur)*
  – I **must write** these letters now. *(Präsens)*
  – I **must write** a long report next week. *(Futur)*

⚠ Um andere Zeitformen bei modalen Hilfsverben zu bilden, z.B. die Vergangenheit, muss ein geeignetes Ersatzverb gebraucht werden:

must	The provider **had to** block access to the Internet last December.
can	I **couldn't** get online yesterday. *(Fähigkeit)*
	We **weren't allowed to** use our mobiles during the class yesterday. *(Erlaubnis)*

Übersicht der modalen Hilfsverben nach Funktion

Funktion	Modale(s) Hilfsverb(en)	
Fähigkeit	He **can** speak several languages.	
	The first satellites **could** only transmit sound.	
Möglichkeit	With your qualifications you **could** work abroad.	
	The situation **may** change at any moment.	
	It **might** become much more serious.	
Bitte	**Can** I speak to Ms Sims, please?	(neutral)
	Could I speak to Ms Sims, please?	(höflich)
	May I speak to Ms Sims, please?	(betont höflich)
	Might I speak to Ms Sims, please?	(äußerst höflich)
Erlaubnis	The boss is free. You **can** go in now.	(neutral)
	The boss is free. You **may** go in now.	(gefällig)
Verbot	We **mustn't** be late for work tomorrow.	
Pflicht	You **must** wear a hard hat in the factory.	
Wahl	Most shop workers **needn't** work on Sundays.	
Empfehlung	You **should** get better advertising.	(neutral)
	You **ought to** get better advertising.	(betont)
	You **must** get better advertising.	(streng)

Reported speech

A Aussagesätze

1 Some people **claim** that "servant" robots **are putting** people out of work.
2 The speaker **reminded** his audience that there **were** some jobs robots **couldn't do**.

- Wenn man einem Dritten berichten möchte, was während eines Gespräches gesagt wurde, benutzt man die indirekte Rede.
- Bei Verwendung der indirekten Rede benutzt man ein einleitendes Verb wie *claim, say, remind, answer, think, mention* usw., um zu verdeutlichen, dass eine Äußerung wiedergegeben wird.
- Steht das einleitende Verb in der Vergangenheit – also *said, answered, mentioned* usw. –, dann verschieben sich die Zeiten wie folgt:

direkte Rede		indirekte Rede
simple present *she works hard*	⇒	simple past *she worked hard*
present progressive *she is working hard*	⇒	past progressive *she was working hard*
simple past *she worked hard*	⇒	past perfect *she had worked hard*
past progressive *she was working hard*	⇒	past perfect progressive *she had been working hard*
present perfect *she has worked hard*	⇒	past perfect *she had worked hard*
present perfect progressive *she has been working hard*	⇒	past perfect progressive *she had been working hard*
past perfect *she had worked hard*	⇒	(keine Verschiebung) –
past perfect progressive *she had been working hard*	⇒	(keine Verschiebung) –
will *she will work hard*	⇒	would *she would work hard*
am/is/are going to *she is going to work hard*	⇒	was/were going to *she was going to work hard*
would/might, etc. *she would work hard*	⇒	(keine Verschiebung) –
would have/might have, etc. *she had been working hard*	⇒	(keine Verschiebung) –

⚠ Die modalen Hilfsverben werden folgendermaßen verschoben:

Modalverb	Bedeutung	indirekte Rede
can	Fähigkeit	*could, was/were able to*
can	Erlaubnis	*was/were allowed to*
may	Möglichkeit	*might*
may	Erlaubnis	*was/were allowed to*
must	Pflicht	*had to*
mustn't	Verbot	*was/were not allowed to*
needn't	freie Wahl	*did not/didn't have to*

- Außer wenn man über ein Gespräch berichtet, das am selben Tage stattgefunden hat, müssen fast alle Zeit- und einige Ortsangaben entsprechend der folgenden Tabelle geändert werden. (Angaben, die nicht aufgeführt sind, bleiben unverändert.)

direkte Rede	indirekte Rede
today	*on that day*
tomorrow	*the next day*
yesterday	*the day before*
the day after tomorrow	*two days later*
the day before yesterday	*two days before*
next day/Friday/week/Christmas/...	*the following day/Friday/week/Christmas/...*
last Friday/week/summer/...	*the Friday/week/summer/... before*
two years/months/weeks/... ago	*two years/months/weeks/... before*
now, at present	*then*
at the moment	*at that moment*
at this time	*at that time*
here	*there*
in this place	*at that place*
this/these	*that/ those*
come	*go*
bring	*take*

B Fragesätze

1 A member of the audience **asked what had led** to the widespread use of robots in factories.
2 She **wanted to know if/whether** the company **was planning** to introduce more robots.

- Bei indirekten Fragen unterscheidet man zwischen Fragen mit Fragewort (1) und Fragen ohne Fragewort (2).
- Bei Fragen mit Fragewort wird das Fragewort übernommen (1).
- Bei Fragen ohne Fragewort benutzt man *if* bzw. *whether* (= ob), um zu verdeut lichen, dass es sich um eine Frage handelt (2).
- Alle anderen Änderungen erfolgen wie bei den Aussagesätzen (siehe Aussage sätze oben).

C Bitten, Aufforderungen und Befehle

1 Lucy **asked the engineer to show** her the robot.
2 He **told her not to go** too close to it.

- Bitten werden meist durch *asked* (= bitten) (1), Aufforderungen und Befehle durch *told* (= sagen) (2) eingeleitet.
- Bei positiven Sätzen erscheint das Verb als *to* + Infinitiv (1).
- Bei negativen Sätzen setzen wir *not* unmittelbar vor *to* (2).

⚠ Die beiden Verben *tell* und *ask* stehen immer mit einem Objekt, das die angesprochene Person erwähnt (1, 2). Ist dies vom Kontext her nicht erkennbar, wird einfach ein passender Begriff eingesetzt:
– Jack said, 'Ann, can you tell Carol to give me a ring, please?'
– Jack **asked Ann** to tell Carol to give him a ring.
– Ben said, 'Don't enter the studio when the red light is on.'
– Ben **told everybody** not to enter the studio when the red light was on.

The passive

1 Measures **are being introduced** to reduce traffic pollution.
2 Pollution **is caused by** most companies that produce goods.

- Ist der Verursacher einer Handlung unbekannt oder zweitrangig, benutzt man das Passiv. Im Vordergrund steht also das Ergebnis des Vorgangs (1).
- Möchte man den Verursacher doch angeben, benutzt man einen by agent (2).
  ⚠ Der Verursacher wird mit *by* – auf keinen mit Fall *from*! – eingeleitet.
- Das Passiv wird mit einer Zeitform von *be* und der 3. Form des Vollverbs gebildet:

Zeit	Zeitform von *be*	3. Form
simple present	*am/is/are*	*caused*
present progressive	*am/is/are being*	*introduced*
simple past	*was/were*	*buried*
past progressive	*was/were being*	*built*
present perfect	*has/have been*	*installed*
will-future	*will be*	*blocked*
going to-future	*am/is/are going to be*	*sacked*

- Beim Gebrauch von modalen Hilfsverben wird nach folgendem Muster verfahren:

bei Aussagen	Hilfsverb + *be* + 3. Form	*must be displayed*
bei Fragen	Hilfsverb + Subjekt + *be* + 3. Form	*Can ... be persuaded?*

⚠ Das Verb *be* bleibt im Infinitiv immer unverändert.

The impersonal passive

1 **It is sometimes said that** GM foods should be illegal.
2 He **is thought to have been** responsible for organizing the protests.

- Das *impersonal passive* wird vor allem dann benutzt, wenn man sich objektiv bzw. unbeteiligt ausdrücken möchte. Daher kommt diese Struktur oft in Polizeiberichten, seriösen Zeitungsartikeln usw. vor.
- Bei Verben des Berichtens, Denkens usw. benutzt man häufig das Satzmuster:
  – *It is/was/...* + 3. Form des einleitenden Verbs + *that*-Satz (1).

  Hier sind weitere Beispiele dieses Musters:
  Aktiv Some **say that** companies which cause pollution should be heavily fined.
  Passiv **It is said that** companies which cause pollution should be heavily fined.
  Aktiv Experts **recommended that** more money be spent on public transport.
  Passiv **It was recommended that** more money be spent on public transport.

- Um das Subjekt des *that*-Satzes zu betonen, kann man folgendes Muster benutzen:
  – Subjekt + *is/was/...* + 3. Form + *be* + andere Satzteile (2):
  Aktiv Many **believe** that the minister is thinking of raising fuel taxes.
  Passiv The minister **is believed to be** thinking of raising fuel taxes.

  ⚠ Der *by*-agent wird in solchen Passivsätzen folgendermaßen verwendet:
  Aktiv The government minister felt that the idea was too radical.
  Passiv The idea was felt to be too radical **by** the government minister.

Conditionals

1 If you travel in space, you take great risks.
2 If we **invest** in new technology, we **will/can/might** improve our production.
3 If more people **took part** in re-training schemes, they **wouldn't have to** worry about finding new employment.
4 We **won't learn** more about Pluto if we **don't continue** our space programme.
5 How **will** we **know** if life is possible in space if we **don't continue** our space programme?
6 If this technology **had existed** 20 years ago, life **could/would have been** very different.

- Wenn man ausdrücken will, dass unter gleichen Bedingungen immer wieder die gleiche Wirkung auftritt, steht im *if*-Satz und im Hauptsatz das *simple present* (1).
- Bei Konditionalsätzen kommen folgende Zeitmuster am häufigsten vor:

Typ I	If + simple present	+	will/can/may/might + future (2, 4, 5)
Typ II	If + simple past	+	would/could/might + Infinitiv (3)
Typ III	If + past perfect	+	would /could/might have + 3. Form des Verbs (6)

- Ein Konditionalsatz besteht aus zwei Teilen: dem *if*-Teil und dem Hauptteil. Der *if*-Teil drückt eine Bedingung aus, der Hauptteil eine Folge.
- Je nach Sinn kann der *if*-Teil, der Hauptteil oder beide Teile des Satzes verneint werden (3, 4).
- Bei Fragen kann nur der Hauptteil zu einer Frage geformt werden. Dann steht dieser Teil an erster Stelle (5).
- *if*-Sätze werden gemäß der Wahrscheinlichkeit der zu erwartenden Folge eingesetzt:

Typ I: Folge (fast) sicher.
If we **invest** in new technology, we **will improve** our production.
D. h., wir werden (vermutlich) unsere Produktion verbessern, da wir (sehr wahrscheinlich) in die neue Technologie investieren werden.

Typ II: Folge theoretisch möglich, aber kaum wahrscheinlich.
If we **invested** in new technology, our production **would improve**.
D. h., es ist kaum zu erwarten, dass unsere Produktion sich verbessern wird, da wir (wahrscheinlich) nicht in die neue Technologie investieren werden.

Typ III: Folge unmöglich, da die Bedingung nicht erfüllt wurde und bereits in der Vergangenheit liegt.
If we **had invested** in new technology, our production **would have improved**.
D. h., der Sprecher weiß schon, dass die Produktion sich nicht verbessert hat, da wir nicht in die neue Technologie investiert haben.

The gerund and infinitive

A Gerunds in the place of noun phrases

1 **Understanding** the effects of globalization is important.
2 Do you like **books** about globalization? ⇒ Do you like **reading** about globalisation?
3 You get a lot of information from **books**. ⇒ You get a lot of information from **reading**.
4 A person cannot live without **air**. ⇒ A person cannot live without **breathing**.

5 An inactive lifestyle causes you to   ⇒ **Not exercising** causes you to
   age faster.   age faster.
6 A person cannot live without eventually **paying taxes**.
7 **Not drinking** enough fluids causes you to dehydrate.

· Ein Verb in der –ing-Form kann als Gerundium die Rolle eines Substantivs übernehmen
  (1–7).
· Das Gerundium kann verwendet werden als Subjekt (1, 5, 7), als Objekt (2) oder nach
  Präpositionen (3, 4, 6).
· Gerundien können erweitert werden, und zwar durch eine adverbiale Bestimmung (1, 6)
  oder ein Objekt (6, 7).
· Durch die Verwendung eines Gerundiums anstelle eines Substantivs kann der
  entsprechende Satzteil länger und komplexer werden (6, 7). Gerundien helfen Ihnen also
  dabei, sich differenzierter auszudrücken.

B Gerund and infinitive

1 Max **enjoys learning** about new technologies.
2 Can you **afford to buy** that laptop?
3 The scientists **continued to discuss** the issue after the conference.
4 The scientists **continued discussing** the issue after the conference.
5 Alison **normally prefers working** alone to working in groups, but **today** she would
   prefer to work in a group.

· Nach einigen Verben folgt immer die –ing-Form *(gerund)* (1). Am wichtigsten sind:

  admit, avoid, consider, deny, enjoy, finish, imagine, mention, mind (etwas dagegen
  haben), *miss, practise, risk, suggest*

  ⚠ Nach einigen Verben folgt immer der Infinitiv *(infinitive)* (2). Die wichtigsten Verben
  dieser Gruppe sind:

  afford, choose, decide, expect, hope, mean, promise, refuse, want

· Nach einigen Verben können der Infinitiv oder die –ing-Form beliebig benutzt werden
  (3, 4). Am wichtigsten sind:

  begin, continue, intend, start

· Einige Verben werden je nach Bedeutung entweder mit dem Infinitiv oder mit der -ing-
  Form benutzt (5). Die wichtigsten Verben dieser Gruppe sind:

  like, dislike, love, hate, prefer

  Wenn von einer allgemeingültigen Situation die Rede ist, folgt auf diese Verben die
  -ing-Form. Handelt es sich aber um eine Ausnahmesituation, dann verwendet man den
  Infinitiv (5).

advise, allow, encourage, forbid, permit, recommend
· Handelt es sich um einen konkreten Einzelfall, wird mit diesen Verben ein Objekt +
  Infinitiv verwendet.
  I strongly **advise you to** keep a copy of all your work.

· Wenn es sich aber um eine allgemeine Situation handelt, dann steht das nachfolgende
  Verb in der -ing-Form.
  Most firms **don't allow smoking** in their offices.

forget/remember

- Die Struktur *forget/remember* + *–ing*-Form bezieht sich auf die Vergangenheit. Sie drückt etwa die Idee „Ich werde nie vergessen …" aus.

  ⚠ „Vergangenheit" bezieht sich hier nicht auf *forget/remember*, sondern auf das nachfolgende Verb.

  I still **remember getting** my first computer.

  I'll never **forget going** on the protest march against GM foods last year.

- Die Struktur *forget/remember* + Infinitiv dagegen bezieht sich auf die Zukunft. Sie drückt etwa die Idee aus „Ich darf nicht vergessen, etwas zu tun" bzw. „Ich habe noch etwas zu tun, weil ich es bis jetzt vergessen habe".

  Sam, please **remember / don't forget to** email me a copy of that article.

  Oh dear. I **forgot / didn't remember to** email Sam a copy of that article.

regret

- Die Struktur *regret* + *–ing*-Form drückt Bedauern über eine vergangene Situation bzw. einen vergangenen Vorfall aus. Häufig geht es dabei um verpasste Chancen.

  I really **regret leaving** school without any qualifications.

  I know they will **regret buying** such a big, expensive car.

- Die Struktur *regret* + Infinitiv – fast immer mit einem Verb des Mitteilens wie *inform, say, tell* kombiniert – drückt eine schlechte Nachricht aus.

  I **regret to say** that I can't attend the meeting tomorrow.

  We **regret to inform** you that your application for the job was not successful.

stop

- Bedeutet *stop* „aufhören, etwas zu tun", steht das nachfolgende Verb in der *–ing*-Form. Bedeutet aber *stop* „kurz anhalten, um etwas anderes zu tun", folgt ein Verb im Infinitiv.

  For heaven's sake **stop complaining**.

  I'm a little late because I **stopped to give** somebody a lift.

try

- Bedeutet *try* „etwas ausprobieren", steht das nachfolgende Verb in der *–ing*-Form. Bedeutet aber *try* „sich anstrengen, etwas zu tun", folgt ein Verb im Infinitiv.

  I **tried phoning** Ellie, but she wasn't at home.

  We'll **try to repair** your computer by the weekend.

Verb + object + to-infinitive

1 Mr Hill **asked** Kevin to be quiet.
2 He didn't **allow the class to use** a dictionary.
3 And he **warned us not to waste** time.
4 Ms Foster **expected her pupils to work** hard.
5 She **didn't want them to get** nervous
6 She said, "I **would like you all to get** good marks in the exam".

- Nach bestimmten Verben kann ein Objekt mit einem *to*-Infinitiv stehen (1–6). Im Deutschen folgt auf das entsprechende Verb meist ein Infinitiv mit „zu". Beispiele sind:

  advise, allow, ask, encourage, force, help, invite, remind, teach, warn

- Auch bei den folgenden Verben kann ein Objekt mit einem *to*-Infinitiv stehen. Im Gegensatz zu den oben aufgeführten Verben steht im Deutschen jedoch kein Infinitiv, sondern ein „dass"-Satz.

cause	verursachen, dass
expect	erwarten, dass
tell	sagen, dass ... soll
want	wollen, dass
would like/love	möchte(n) gern, dass

- Ist das Objekt ein Personalpronomen, steht dies in der Objektform (5).

Adjectives and adverbs

1 John has a **new** DVD player.
2 He always buys **expensive** equipment.
3 My computer has become **very slow**.
4 That CD sounds **terrible**.
5 We can make printouts **quickly** and **cheaply**.

- Um Personen oder Sachen näher zu beschreiben, benutzt man Adjektive (1– 4).
- Adjektive stehen unmittelbar vor Substantiven oder unmittelbar nach einer Form von *be* (bzw. *become* oder *seem*, die *be* ersetzen können) (3).
- Adjektive können mit Verben wie *feel*, *look* (aussehen), *sound, smell* und *taste* eine sinnliche Wahrnehmung ausdrücken (4).
- Um ein Tätigkeitsverb näher zu beschreiben, setzt man ein Adverb unmittelbar hinter das Verb bzw. Verb + Objekt (5).
  ⚠ Im Englischen können ein Verb und sein Objekt – anders als im Deutschen – nicht durch ein Adverb getrennt werden. Also NICHT: ~~We can make quickly printouts.~~
- Adverbien werden auch benutzt, um Adjektive, andere Adverbien und ganze Sätze näher zu bestimmen:
  MP3 players have become **surprisingly cheap**.   *(Adverb + Adjektiv)*
  My fax machine prints out **terribly slowly**.   *(Adverb + Adverb)*
  Luckily Gerd left a message on my mailbox.   *(Satzadverb)*
- Die meisten Adverbien werden durch Anhängen von *–ly* an das Adjektiv gebildet (5). Eine kleine Anzahl von Adverbien hat dieselbe Form wie Adjektive; die häufigsten sind:

  fast, hard, early, late, long, daily

Comparison of adjectives and adverbs

1 A hundred years ago life was **slower** and people may have been **happier**.
2 Which technological innovation is the **most/least important**?
3 Today you can copy data **more easily than** ever before.

- Einsilbige und zweisilbige Adjektive, die auf *–y* enden – zum Beispiel *easy, happy* und *lucky* –, werden mit *–(i)er/-(i)est* gesteigert (1).
- Mehrsilbige Adjektive und Adverbien, die auf *–ly* enden, werden mit *more/most* gesteigert (2, 3).
  ⚠ Die Adverbien, die dieselbe Form wie das entsprechende Adjektiv haben (*fast, hard, early* usw.), werden mit *–er/–est* gesteigert.
- Um Personen oder Sachen im Satz miteinander zu vergleichen, gibt es folgende Möglichkeiten:

– Kein Unterschied	**as** good **as**	genau so gut wie
– Unterschied	**not as** good **as**	nicht so gut wie
– Unterschied	better **than**	besser als

Word order – positions of adverbs of time, place and frequency

1 There are new cases of cyber crime **every day**.
2 Someone hacked into the computers **in our office**.
3 **Last year** we went to a conference on cyber crime.
4 The cyber crime conference was in **the USA last year**.
5 She **always** buys the best anti-virus software.
6 He **never** opens email attachments from people he doesn't know.
7 I work from home **now and then**.
8 This software programme acts **strangely on some computers when you install it**.

- Zeitangaben (Wann?) und Ortsangaben (Wo?, Wohin?) stehen in der Regel am Satzende (1, 2).
- Um die Zeit eines bestimmten Ereignisses hervorzuheben, kann man die Zeitangabe an die erste Stelle setzen (3).
- Stehen eine Zeitangabe und eine Ortsangabe zusammen am Satzende, dann gilt die Reihenfolge Ort vor Zeit (alphabetisch merken: O vor Z!) (4).
- Besteht eine Häufigkeitsangabe aus einem Wort, z. B. *always, often, sometimes*, steht sie unmittelbar vor dem Vollverb (5).
- Lautet das Vollverb *be*, steht das Adverb direkt dahinter (6).
- Besteht die Häufigkeitsangabe aus mehreren Wörtern, z. B. *every day, now and then*, steht sie wie eine Zeitangabe am Satzende (7).
- Adverbien der Art und Weise stehen in der Regel am Satzende. Kommen noch Zeit- oder Ortsadverbien hinzu, lautet die Reihenfolge: Art und Weise – Ort – Zeit (AOZ) (8).

Relative clauses and contact clauses

1 Immigration is a topic **which/that** can be very controversial.
2 Immigrants are people **who/that** start a new life in a different country.
3 Sanjay filled in an application form **(which/that)** he found on the government website.
4 Sanjay is a British citizen **whose** parents left India in the 1980s.
5 Muslims in Britain, many **of whom** come from Pakistan, often suffer discrimination.
6 Jasmine Khan has just been given British citizenship, **of which** she is very proud.

- Relativsätze werden benutzt, um den Hauptsatz durch zusätzliche Informationen genauer zu bestimmen.
- Für Sachen benutzt man das Relativpronomen *which* bzw. *that* (1) und für Personen *who* bzw. *that* (2).
- Steht das Relativpronomen für das Objekt des Hauptsatzes, dann kann man es weglassen (3). Solche Relativsätze heißen *contact clauses*.
- Um Besitz bzw. Zugehörigkeit anzuzeigen, gebraucht man *whose* unmittelbar vor dem Substantiv bei Personen und Sachen (4).
- Steht eine Präposition vor dem Relativpronomen, wird *whom* für Personen und *which* für Sachen benutzt (5, 6). In solchen Fällen ist der Gebrauch von *that* nicht möglich.

Defining and non-defining relative clauses

1 People **who** have the highest levels of income are part of the so-called "elite".
2 The upper class, **which** was wealthy, ruled the land.

- Im ersten Beispielsatz ist der Sinn des Hauptsatzes *People are part of the so-called „elite"* ohne den Relativsatz *who have the highest levels of income* offensichtlich falsch bzw. unvollständig. Relativsätze dieser Art – die wesentlich für das Verständnis des gesamten Satzes sind – nennt man *defining relative clauses* (notwendige oder bestimmende Relativsätze).

- Im zweiten Beispielsatz ist die Aussage des Hauptsatzes *The English upper class is a relatively small class group* ohne den Relativsatz völlig verständlich, weil der Relativsatz *which is characterized by wealth, good education and elitism* eine zusätzliche, also nebensächliche, Information enhält. Daher werden solche Relativsätze *non-defining relative clauses* (nicht notwendige oder nicht bestimmende Relativsätze) genannt.

⚠ Notwendige Relativsätze werden immer ohne trennende Kommas benutzt. Dies signalisiert, dass sie fester Bestandteil der Hauptaussage sind.

Participle constructions

1 Gender inequality is a problem **affecting** almost every country in the world.
2 Feminism is a term **defined** as "equal rights and opportunities for men and women".
3 **Questioning** gender-based assumptions, Emma Watson was confused when people called her "bossy".
4 **Appointed** as a UN ambassador in 2014, Emma Watson has championed women's rights since then.
5 **Having seen** male friends suffering from insecurity, she is campaigning for equal rights for men too.
6 **Despite facing** criticism from the press, she has launched a new campaign.
7 Men should feel free to be sensitive, **thereby making** it easier for women not to be submissive.
8 Health is now an issue, **with** many teens **worrying** about their body image.

Die englische Sprache ist geprägt durch häufige Verwendung von Partizipialkonstruktionen. Diese ermöglichen einen eleganteren Sprachfluss.

- Partizipialkonstruktionen verkürzen Relativsätze; dabei kann entweder das *present participle* (1) oder das *past participle* (2) verwendet werden.
- Sie werden auch verwendet, um adverbiale Nebensätze zu verkürzen; in diesen Fällen unterscheidet man zwischen Partizipial konstruktionen ohne Konjunktion (3–5) und solchen mit Konjunktion (6–8). In Sätzen ohne Konjunktion ist der Inhalt des Satzes auch ohne eine solche klar. Dagegen sind Konjunktionen nötig, um zu verhindern, dass der logische Zusammenhang des Satzes verloren geht. Zum Beispiel wird der Inhalt von Satz 6 unklar, wenn die Konjunktion *despite* ausgelassen wird.
- Wie bei der Verkürzung von Relativsätzen kommen auch bei der Verkürzung von adverbialen Nebensätzen das *present participle* (3, 6–8) und das *past participle* (4) zur Anwendung. Darüber hinaus wird hier auch noch das *perfect participle* verwendet (5), und zwar um die Vorzeitigkeit der Handlung im Nebensatz auszudrücken.
  (= Nachdem sie ihre Freunde leiden gesehen hatte, ...).

Countable and uncountable nouns

1 Visit the website for more **information** on equal opportunities.   NICHT ~~informations~~
2 Have you read the paper today? The political **news** is interesting.   NICHT ~~news are~~
3 Where can I get some **advice** on civil partnerships?   NICHT ~~an advice~~

- Einige wichtige Substantive sind zählbar im Deutschen, nicht jedoch im Englischen. Diese Substantive können also nicht ohne weiteres mit dem unbestimmten Artikel *a/an* oder mit einem Zahlwort benutzt werden.

Hier ist eine Liste solcher Wörter, die Sie auswendig lernen sollten:

advice, baggage, damage, data, equipment, evidence, furniture, garbage (Abfall), *information, knowledge, luck, luggage, machinery, news, progress, research, rubbish, work* (*housework, homework*)

- Um diese Substantive im Plural zu verwenden, muss *some, a bit of* bzw. *a piece of* hinzugefügt werden (3).

The definite article

1 **Sociologists** say that **violence** is increasing among young people.
2 Is **the current trend** partly caused by **the violent films** they watch?
3 **Most prison sentences** are not tough enough.
4 Nearly **half the prisoners** in **British prisons** are under 25.
5 **Spring** is my favourite season but **the spring** we're having this year is more like winter.
6 We had **breakfast** late this morning so we came to school **by car** instead of **by bus.**
7 They are thinking of legalizing soft drugs in **the Netherlands**.

- Hat ein Substantiv eine allgemeine, uneingeschränkte Bedeutung – also „alle ohne Ausnahme" – dann steht es ohne Artikel (1, 5).
- Ist die Bedeutung eines Substantives auf bestimmte Fälle eingeschränkt, benutzt man den Artikel (2, 5).
- Ferner wird der Artikel in den folgenden Fällen und Wendungen im Englischen – z. T. anders als im Deutschen – nicht gebraucht:
  - bei *most* in der Bedeutung „die meisten" (3),
  - bei öffentlichen Gebäuden im allgemeinen Sinn (4),
  - bei Mahlzeiten (6),
  - bei Verkehrsmitteln (6),
  - bei Straßennamen,
  - bei Tageszeiten, Wochentagen, Monaten und Jahreszeiten im allgemeinen Sinn (5).

- Der Artikel wird verwendet nach *all* und *half* (4) und mit den Pluralnamen von Staaten (7).

⚠ Der bestimmte Artikel steht im Englischen (viel) seltener als im Deutschen.
Daher: *When in doubt, leave it out!*

UNIT WORD LIST

Dieses Wörterverzeichnis enthält alle Wörter in der Reihenfolge ihres Erscheinens (Seitenzahlen sind angegeben). Nicht aufgeführt sind Wörter, die nicht unbedingt zum aktiven Wortschatz gehören. Daher eignet sich diese Liste hervorragend für die Vorbereitung auf die Abiturprüfung. Wörter aus den Hörverständnisübungen sind gelb markiert.

Abkürzungen:

AE = amerikanisches Englisch	jdm = jemandem	pl = plural
BE = britisches Englisch	jdn = jemanden	sb = somebody
etw = etwas	jds = jemandes	sth = something

TOPIC 1   The world of work and consumerism

BACKGROUND INFORMATION

consumer society [kən'sjuːmə səsaɪəti]	a society in which buying and selling is the most important activity	*Konsumgesellschaft*	page 8
Industrial Revolution [ɪn͵dʌstriəl revə'luːʃn]	the introduction of power-driven machinery in the 18th century	*industrielle Revolution*	
factory ['fæktəri]	a building or group of buildings where goods are made	*Fabrik, Werk*	
mass production [͵mæs prə'dʌkʃn]	production of large quantities of goods	*Massenproduktion*	
fundamental [͵fʌndə'mentl]	basic, radical	*grundlegend*	
pattern of consumption [͵pætn əf kən'sʌmpʃn]	the way things are bought, sold, used	*Konsumverhalten*	
leisure activity ['leʒər æktɪvəti]	sth you do in your free time	*Freizeitaktivitäten*	
wealthy elite [͵welθi ɪ'liːt]	the most powerful and rich people	*wohlhabende Elite*	
possession [pə'zeʃn]	sth that belongs to sb	*Besitztum*	
to earn [ɜːn]	to get money for your work	*verdienen*	
wages pl ['weɪdʒɪz]	money for work paid by the hour, day or week	*Löhne*	
essentials pl [ɪ'senʃlz]	most important things	*notwendige Güter*	
basic needs pl [͵beɪsɪk 'niːdz]	food, shelter, clothing	*Grundbedürfnisse*	
trade union [͵treɪd 'juːniən]	an organization that protects workers	*Gewerkschaft*	
to increase [ɪn'kriːs]	to become bigger or greater	*zunehmen, steigen, steigern*	
working conditions pl [͵wɜːkɪŋ kən'dɪʃnz]	the environment in which sb works	*Arbeitsbedingungen*	
urban poverty [͵ɜːbən 'pɒvəti]	poor living conditions in cities	*Stadtarmut*	
child labour ['tʃaɪld leɪbə]	using children to work	*Kinderarbeit*	
improvement [ɪm'pruːvmənt]	a change in sth that makes it better	*Verbesserung*	
healthcare ['helθkeə]	treatment and prevention of disease	*Gesundheitsfürsorge*	
day of rest [͵deɪ əv 'rest]	free day with no work	*Ruhetag*	
computer-related skills pl [kəm͵pjuːtə rɪleɪtɪd 'skɪlz]	the ability to use computers and technology	*Computerkenntnisse*	
job for life [͵dʒɒb fə 'laɪf]	a job you stay in for your whole working life	*lebenslange Beschäftigung*	
growing demand [͵grəʊɪŋ dɪ'mɑːnd]	increasing need for sth	*wachsende Nachfrage*	
transportation [͵trænspɔː'teɪʃn]	moving people or things from one place to another	*Transportwesen*	
enormous [ɪ'nɔːməs]	very big	*gewaltig, enorm*	
range [reɪndʒ]	a large number and variety	*Angebot, (Produkt-)Palette*	
on offer [ɒn 'ɒfə]	for sale	*im Angebot*	
buying habits pl ['baɪɪŋ hæbɪts]	the way people buy things	*Konsumgewohnheiten*	
available [ə'veɪləbl]	ready to be used	*verfügbar, erhältlich*	
non-essentials pl [͵nɒn ɪ'senʃlz]	things sb doesn't really need	*Unwesentliches*	
luxury item ['lʌkʃəri aɪtəm]	fine products with a high price	*Luxusgut, Luxusartikel*	
standard of living [͵stændəd əv 'lɪvɪŋ]	how well or poorly people live	*Lebensstandard*	
conspicuous consumption [kən͵spɪkjuəs kən'sʌmpʃn]	spending money on expensive things to impress other people	*beträchtlicher Konsum*	

	identity statement [aɪ'dentəti steɪtmənt]	what sth says about sb	*Produktidentität (seinen Sozialstatus durch teuren Konsum definieren)*
	shopaholic [ˌʃɒpə'hɒlɪk]	sb addicted to shopping	*Kaufsüchtige/r*
	access (to sth) ['ækses]	a way to get sth	*Zugang (zu etw), Zugriff (auf etw)*
	spending habits pl ['spendɪŋ hæbɪts]	the way sb spends money	*Konsumgewohnheiten*
	level ['levl]	amount	*Niveau, Stand, Höhe*
page 9	**personal debt** [ˌpɜːsənl 'det]	money sb owes (and must pay back)	*Privatverschuldung*
	to saturate sth ['sætʃəreɪt]	to be everywhere	*etw durchdringen*
	basic ['beɪsɪk]	simple, uncomplicated	*grundsätzlich, einfach, Grund-*
	strict controls pl [ˌstrɪkt kən'trəʊlz]	very strong rules	*strenge Kontrollen*
	brand [brænd]	a type of product manufactured by a particular company under a particular name	*Marke, Markenlogo*
	in the public eye [ɪn ðə ˌpʌblɪk 'aɪ]	often seen in the media	*im Bewusstsein der Öffentlichkeit*
	sponsorship ['spɒnsəʃɪp]	money provided by a company for an event	*Unterstützung, Förderung, Sponsoring*
	event [ɪ'vent]	a planned public or social occasion	*Veranstaltung, Ereignis*
	product placement ['prɒdʌkt pleɪsmənt]	advertising products by showing them in films, TV series, etc	*Schleichwerbung*
	middle class ['mɪdl klɑːs]	the people in society who are not rich and not poor	*Mittelschicht*
	status ['steɪtəs]	place in society	*Status, Stand, Stellung*
	to aspire to sth [ə'spaɪə]	to have a strong wish for sth	*nach etw streben*
	lifestyle ['laɪfstaɪl]	the way sb lives	*Lebensstil, -führung, -art*
	to look up to sb [ˌlʊk 'ʌp tə]	to admire and respect sb	*zu jdm aufsehen*
	development [dɪ'veləpmənt]	a new event or stage that is likely to affect what happens in a continuing situation	*Entwicklung*
	century ['sentʃəri]	one hundred years	*Jahrhundert*
	to constitute sth ['kɒnstɪtjuːt]	to make up, to form	*etw zahlenmäßig ausmachen*
	percentage [pə'sentɪdʒ]	the number of sth as if it is part of a total which is 100	*Prozentsatz, Anteil*
	to double ['dʌbl]	to become twice the amount	*(sich) verdoppeln*
	to be hard to ignore [bi ˌhɑːd tə ɪg'nɔː]	be difficult not to be noticed	*schwer zu übersehen sein*
	resources pl [rɪ'sɔːsɪz]	natural material used to produce things e.g wood, metal, minerals	*Rohstoffe, Mittel, Ressourcen*
	extent [ɪk'stent]	how large, important, etc. sth is	*Umfang, Maßstab*
	major ['meɪdʒə]	important	*groß, bedeutend*
	interdependent [ˌɪntədɪ'pendənt]	needing one another	*voneinander abhängig, verflochten*
	proponent [prə'pəʊnənt]	supporter, sb who thinks sth is a good idea	*Befürworter/in, Anhänger/in*
	business leader ['bɪznəs liːdə]	important businessperson	*Betriebsleiter/in, Führungskraft*
	multinational company [mʌltiˌnæʃnəl 'kʌmpəni]	a large business with branches in different countries	*multinationales Unternehmen, Konzern*
	to benefit (from sth) ['benɪfɪt]	to get sth good out of a situation	*(von etw) profitieren*
	local enterprise [ˌləʊkl 'entəpraɪz]	small local business	*lokales Unternehmen*
page 10	**to improve** [ɪm'pruːv]	to become better	*verbessern*
	to face sth [feɪs]	to confront sth	*mit etw konfrontiert werden, einer Sache gegenüberstehen*
	purpose ['pɜːpəs]	the reason to do sth	*Absicht, Ziel, Zweck*
	to encourage [ɪn'kʌrɪdʒ]	to give support to sb/sth	*ermuntern, auffordern, ermutigen*
	to achieve sth [ə'tʃiːv]	to do sth successfully	*etw erreichen, etw erzielen*
	goal [gəʊl]	sth you want to do or get	*Ziel*
	organization [ˌɔːgənaɪ'zeɪʃn]	company	*Unternehmen, Organisation*
	to afford sth [ə'fɔːd]	to have enough money for sth	*sich etw leisten*
	salary ['sæləri]	money you get for work, paid by the month	*Gehalt*
	nowadays ['naʊədeɪz]	today, at the moment	*heutzutage, heute*
	to rely on sth [rɪ'laɪ ɒn]	to need sth, to be dependent on sth	*auf etw angewiesen sein*
	to affect sth [ə'fekt]	to have an influence on sth	*etw beeinflussen, etw beeinträchtigen*
	disadvantage [ˌdɪsəd'vɑːntɪdʒ]	sth bad, sth negative	*Nachteil*

TEXT 1 Advertising and the effects of consumerism

worth [wɜːθ]	important, good or enjoyable enough to make sb feel satisfied, esp. when difficulty is involved	wert	page 11
convenient [kən'viːniənt]	easy to use	praktisch, bequem	
exposure [ɪk'spəʊʒə]	having contact with sth	Ausgesetztsein; Kontakt	
to **promote sth** [prə'məʊt]	to support sth, to make sth grow	etw fördern, etw vorantreiben, etw bewerben	
to **trap sb** [træp]	to catch sb with no escape	jdn fangen	
worldview ['wɜːldvjuː]	the way we think of the world	Weltanschauung	
aspiration [ˌæspə'reɪʃn]	hope and ambition	Ziel, Bestreben	
effect [ɪ'fekt]	impact	Auswirkung, Effekt	
to **slip into sth** ['slɪp ɪntə]	easily fall into sth	in etw hineinrutschen	
particular [pə'tɪkjələ]	used to emphasize one individual type of thing and not others	speziell, bestimmt	
constant ['kɒnstənt]	without stopping	ständig	page 12
dissatisfaction [ˌdɪsˌsætɪs'fækʃn]	unhappiness	Unzufriedenheit	
attitude ['ætɪtjuːd]	way of viewing sth	Einstellung, Haltung	
to **dominate sb/sth** ['dɒmɪneɪt]	to have control and power over sb/sth	jdn/etw beherrschen, jdn/etw dominieren	
potentially [pə'tenʃəli]	possibly	möglicherweise	
annoying [ə'nɔɪɪŋ]	irritating, getting on your nerves	lästig, nervig, ärgerlich	
to **spoil sth** [spɔɪl]	to ruin or damage	etw verderben, etw ruinieren	
needs pl [niːdz]	things we cannot live without	Bedürfnisse, Bedarf	
to **manipulate sb/sth** [mə'nɪpjuleɪt]	to control sb/sth in a negative way	jdn/etw manipulieren	
appropriate [ə'prəʊpriət]	right for a particular situation	angemessen, passend	
to **restrict sth** [rɪ'strɪkt]	to limit the amount of sth	etw einschränken	
significant influence [sɪgˌnɪfɪkənt 'ɪnfluəns]	a special power that controls the way sb thinks or acts	erheblicher Einfluss	
to **broaden your horizons** [ˌbrɔːdn jɔː hə'raɪznz]	to experience more of the world	den eigenen Horizont erweitern	
unlikely [ʌn'laɪkli]	not probable	unwahrscheinlich	
to **maintain sth** [meɪn'teɪn]	to continue sth without change	etw aufrechterhalten, etw (finanziell) unterhalten	
to **generate sth** ['dʒenəreɪt]	to produce sth, to create sth	etw erzeugen	
finite ['faɪnaɪt]	limited	endlich, begrenzt	
given sth ['gɪvn]	taking sth into account	angesichts von etw	page 13
consequence ['kɒnsɪkwəns]	the result of an action	Folge, Konsequenz	
urgent ['ɜːdʒənt]	needing to be dealt with or done immediately	dringend, dringlich	
to **reduce sth** [rɪ'djuːs]	to make sth smaller	verringern, senken	
investment [ɪn'vestmənt]	money put into a product or service for which you expect a profit	Investition	page 14
quantity ['kwɒntəti]	a large number	Menge	
success [sək'ses]	reaching a goal, achievement	Erfolg	
critic ['krɪtɪk]	sb who has a negative opinion of sth	Kritiker/in	
current ['kʌrənt]	at the moment, present	gegenwärtig, derzeitig, aktuell	
amount [ə'maʊnt]	how much you have or use	Menge, Betrag	
career [kə'rɪə]	a job or profession that sb does for a long time	berufliche Laufbahn, Karriere	
survey ['sɜːveɪ]	an investigation of the opinions of a group of people by asking questions	Umfrage	
item ['aɪtəm]	thing or article that is part of a larger set	Artikel, Ware	
to **illustrate sth** ['ɪləstreɪt]	to show sth	veranschaulichen, illustrieren	page 15
to **include sth** [ɪn'kluːd]	to have as part of sth	beinhalten, umfassen, einschließen	
to **analyse sth** ['ænəlaɪz]	to examine and explain sth carefully	analysieren	
to **depict sth** [dɪ'pɪkt]	to show sth	abbilden, darstellen	
connection [kə'nekʃn]	relationship, link	Verbindung	
impression [ɪm'preʃn]	effect, feeling from sth	Eindruck	
means [miːnz]	method, way of doing sth	Mittel	
stuff [stʌf]	things	Zeug, Sachen	

rubbish ['rʌbɪʃ]	things you throw away	Müll
knowledge ['nɒlɪdʒ]	what you know from education or experience	Wissen
to reflect [rɪ'flekt]	be a sign of the nature of sth or of sb.'s attitude or feeling	widerspiegeln, wiedergeben, darstellen
humorous ['hju:mərəs]	funny, making you laugh	witzig, humorvoll

TEXT 2 Our throwaway society

page 16	according to [ə'kɔːdɪŋ tə]	in relation to, as said by	(je) nach, gemäß, laut
	prediction [prɪ'dɪkʃn]	what will/might happen in the future	Voraussage, Vorhersage
	to mention sth ['menʃn]	to write about sth	etw erwähnen, etw nennen
	to repair sth [rɪ'peə]	to fix sth	etw reparieren
	to recycle sth [ˌriː'saɪkl]	to use sth again, make sth new from it	etw wiederverwerten, etw recyceln
	to deplete sth [dɪ'pliːt]	to use sth up	aufbrauchen, erschöpfen
	to run out [ˌrʌn 'aʊt]	to be used up, finished	zu Ende gehen, knapp werden
	everyday ['evrideɪ]	ordinary, general	alltäglich, Alltags-
	increasingly [ɪn'kriːsɪŋli]	more and more	zunehmend, immer + Komparativ
	gadget ['gædʒɪt]	mechanical or electronic device	Gerät, technische Spielerei
	indispensable [ˌɪndɪ'spensəbl]	absolutely necessary	unverzichtbar, unerlässlich
	to be addicted to sth [bi ə'dɪktɪd tə]	to be unable to live without sth	nach etw süchtig sein
	doubt [daʊt]	feeling of uncertainty	Zweifel
	rip [rɪp]	cut, slit, tear	Riss
	zipper ['zɪpə]	a device for fastening clothes	Reißverschluss
	memory card ['meməri kɑːd]	storage device for digital data	Speicherkarte
	ingenious [ɪn'dʒiːniəs]	clever, intelligent	einfallsreich, genial
	issue ['ɪʃuː]	problem, trouble	Problem
	dust [dʌst]	dry dirt	Staub
	to be designed to do sth [bi dɪ'zaɪnd tə]	to be made for a special reason or purpose	dazu gedacht sein, etw zu tun
page 17	device [dɪ'vaɪs]	a piece of mechanical or electronic equipment	Gerät
	to fail [feɪl]	to no longer function	versagen, ausfallen
	to purchase sth ['pɜːtʃəs]	to buy sth	etw kaufen, etw erwerben
	to replace sth [rɪ'pleɪs]	to get a new model of sth you already have	etw ersetzen
	existing [ɪg'zɪstɪŋ]	availble, present	vorhanden
	recent ['riːsnt]	new, current	aktuell, neu
	to convince sb of sth [kən'vɪns]	to make sb think differently about sth	jdn von etw überzeugen
	to last [lɑːst]	to continue to function	halten, andauern
	to exist [ɪg'zɪst]	to be available	(es) geben, vorhanden sein, bestehen, existieren
	deliberate(ly) [dɪ'lɪbərət]	designed, intentional(ly)	absichtlich, vorsätzlich
	sophisticated [sə'fɪstɪkeɪtɪd]	having a lot of experience and knowledge	raffiniert, ausgeklügelt
	to persuade sb [pə'sweɪd]	to make sb do sth	jdn überzeugen, jdn überreden
	share [ʃeə]	part, piece	Anteil
	durable ['djʊərəbl]	lasting a long time	langlebig, robust
	to release sth [rɪ'liːs]	to sell sth, make sth public	veröffentlichen, auf den Markt bringen
	glued-in [ˌgluːd 'ɪn]	fixed so it can't be removed	eingeklebt
	in circulation [ɪn ˌsɜːkjə'leɪʃn]	available	in/im Umlauf
	to issue sth ['ɪʃuː]	to provide sth	etw ausstellen, etw ausgeben
	guarantee [ˌgærən'tiː]	a written promise	Garantie
	damage ['dæmɪdʒ]	injury, harm	Schaden, Schäden
page 18	likely ['laɪkli]	probably	wahrscheinlich
	profit ['prɒfɪt]	the money made when sales are higher than costs	Gewinn
	meaning ['miːnɪŋ]	the thing or idea that a sound, word, sign, etc. represents	Bedeutung, Sinn
	short-term [ˌʃɔːt'tɜːm]	temporary	kurzfristig
	permanent ['pɜːmənənt]	long-lasting	dauerhaft
page 19	dramatic(ally) [drə'mætɪk]	sudden(ly), extreme(ly)	dramatisch

recently ['riːsntli]	not long ago in the past, relatively new	*in letzter/jüngster Zeit, neulich*	
result [rɪ'zʌlt]	outcome	*Ergebnis, Resultat*	
to **concentrate on sth** ['kɒnsntreɪt ɒn]	to look closely at sth	*sich auf etw konzentrieren*	
method ['meθəd]	the way of doing sth	*Verfahren, Methode*	
action ['ækʃn]	sth to do	*Handlung, Tat*	
impact ['ɪmpækt]	effect, influence	*Auswirkung(en), Einfluss*	
to **be involved in sth** [bi ɪn'vɒlvd ɪn]	to be part of sth	*zu etw dazugehören, an etw beteiligt sein*	
plain [pleɪn]	simple, easy	*einfach*	
stage [steɪdʒ]	phase, step	*Phase, Stadium, Etappe*	
to **dispose of sth** [dɪ'spəʊz əv]	to throw sth away	*etw entsorgen*	
to **irrigate sth** ['ɪrɪgeɪt]	to supply sth with water	*etw bewässern*	
sufficient [sə'fɪʃnt]	enough, having the right amount	*genügend, hinreichend*	
harmful ['hɑːmfl]	causing damage or injury to sb/sth	*schädlich*	
to **require sth** [rɪ'kwaɪə]	to need sth	*etw erfordern, etw benötigen*	
considerable [kən'sɪdərəbl]	significant, a lot of sth	*erheblich*	
to **protect sth** [prə'tekt]	to stop sth from being hurt or damaged	*etw schützen*	
crop [krɒp]	plants grown for food	*(Nutz-, Anbau-)Pflanze, Ernte*	
process ['prəʊses]	system, way of doing sth	*Verfahren*	
damaging ['dæmɪdʒɪŋ]	causing harm or injury	*schädlich*	
electricity [ɪˌlek'trɪsəti]	a form of energy	*Strom*	
to **structure sth** ['strʌktʃə]	to organize sth, to build sth	*etw strukturieren*	page 21
to **preserve sth** [prɪ'zɜːv]	to protect sth, to keep sth safe	*etw bewahren, etw schützen*	
fine [faɪn]	money paid as a punishment	*Geldstrafe, Bußgeld*	
tax [tæks]	money paid to the government	*Steuer*	
introduction [ˌɪntrə'dʌkʃn]	the first part of a book or speech that gives a general idea of what is to follow	*Einleitung*	page 22
conclusion [kən'kluːʒn]	the end of sth such as a speech or a piece of writing	*Schluss*	
paragraph ['pærəgrɑːf]	a section of a piece of writing, usually dealing with a single subject	*(Text:) Absatz*	
threat [θret]	danger	*Bedrohung*	
to **pass sth** [pɑːs]	to make sth (a law)	*etw (Gesetz) verabschieden, etw beschließen*	
stage [steɪdʒ]	an area for discussions, etc	*Bühne*	
to **state sth** [steɪt]	to say what sth is	*etw angeben, etw nennen*	

TEXT 3 The global division of labour

category ['kætəgəri]	a group of things that are similar	*Rubrik, Kategorie*	page 23
statement ['steɪtmənt]	declaration, opinion	*Aussage*	
economy [ɪ'kɒnəmi]	the movement of money	*Wirtschaft*	
to **value sb/sth** ['væljuː]	think that sb/sth is important	*jdn/etw (sehr) schätzen, jdn/etw zu schätzen wissen*	
to **invest** [ɪn'vest]	to put money into a project	*investieren*	
ambitious [æm'bɪʃəs]	wanting success or power	*ehrgeizig*	
dependent on sth [dɪ'pendənt ɒn]	needing sth to be able to live normally	*abhängig von*	
to **transform sth** [træns'fɔːm]	to make sth change completely	*verwandeln*	
numerous ['njuːmərəs]	many	*zahlreich*	
labour force ['leɪbə fɔːs]	the people working or available for work	*Arbeitskräfte*	
to **suggest sth** [sə'dʒest]	to introduce sth for consideration	*darauf hindeuten*	
prospects pl ['prɒspekts]	view, outlook	*Aussichten, Perspektiven*	
raw materials pl [ˌrɔː mə'tɪəriəlz]	basic substances that can be used to make sth else	*Rohstoffe, -materialien*	
agriculture ['ægrɪkʌltʃə]	growing food and raising animals for food production	*Landwirtschaft*	
manufacturing [ˌmænju'fæktʃərɪŋ]	processing raw materials into a finished product	*Herstellung, Produktion*	
retail ['riːteɪl]	selling goods to the general public	*Einzelhandel*	
advanced [əd'vɑːnst]	ahead in complexity, knowledge, skill, etc	*fortgeschritten, modern, weiterentwickelt*	

	substantial [səbˈstænʃl]	large, serious	*bedeutend, erheblich*
	shift [ʃɪft]	a move away from sth	*Verlagerung*
page 24	income [ˈɪnkʌm]	money from work, business, investments	*Einkommen*
	to exploit sth [ɪkˈsplɔɪt]	to use sth in a way that helps you	*etw ausnutzen*
	graduate [ˈɡrædʒuət]	student who finishes university with a qualification	*Hochschulabsolvent/in*
	contract [ˈkɒntrækt]	an agreement for work	*Vertrag*
	solar technology [ˌsəʊlə tekˈnɒlədʒi]	using the sun's energy to get electricity	*Solartechnik*
	to forecast [ˈfɔːkɑːst]	to say that sth will happen in the future	*vorhersagen*
	combination [ˌkɒmbɪˈneɪʃn]	mixing or joining several things together	*Verbindung, Verknüpfung, Kombination*
	growth [ɡrəʊθ]	development, increase	*Wachstum*
	aging [ˈeɪdʒɪŋ]	getting older	*alternd*
	contribution [ˌkɒntrɪˈbjuːʃn]	thing given to help sth	*Beitrag*
	to depend on sb/sth [dɪˈpend ɒn]	to need/require sb/sth for sth to happen	*von jdm/etw abhängen*
	sustained [səˈsteɪnd]	ongoing, continued	*kontinuierlich, anhaltend*
	infrastructure [ˈɪnfrəstrʌktʃə]	the physical structures needed to operate a society	*Infrastruktur*
	knowledge-based [ˈnɒlɪdʒ beɪst]	an economy dominated by intellectual services	*wissensbasiert*
	consultation [ˌkɒnslˈteɪʃn]	offering specialist advice	*Beratung*
	wealth creation [ˈwelθ krieɪʃn]	activities that help people make money	*Vermögensbildung, Schaffung von Wohlstand*
page 25	austerity measures pl [ɒˈsterɪti meʒəz]	actions taken by a government to spend less money	*Sparmaßnahmen*
	training [ˈtreɪnɪŋ]	learning to do a particular thing	*Schulung, Ausbildung*
	retired [rɪˈtaɪəd]	no longer working	*im Ruhestand*
	to struggle [ˈstrʌɡl]	try very hard to do sth when it is difficult	*kämpfen, sich abmühen*
page 26	to present sth [prɪˈzent]	to show sth	*etw vorstellen, etw präsentieren*
	to represent sth [ˌreprɪˈzent]	to amount to sth, describe sth in a particular way	*etw darstellen, etw repräsentieren*
	source [sɔːs]	origin, starting point	*Quelle*
	to identify sth [aɪˈdentɪfaɪ]	to state what sth is	*etw genau bestimmen*
	figure [ˈfɪɡə]	number	*Zahl*
	to publish sth [ˈpʌblɪʃ]	to print sth for the general public	*etw veröffentlichen*
page 27	suggestion [səˈdʒestʃən]	an idea or plan to think about	*Vorschlag*
	typically [ˈtɪpɪkli]	normally	*üblicherweise, normalerweise*
	steady [ˈstedi]	continuous, unchanging	*stetig, beständig*
	decline [dɪˈklaɪn]	to go down	*Rückgang, Abnahme*
	quotation [kwəʊˈteɪʃn]	a group of words or a short piece of writing taken from a book, play, speech, etc.	*Zitat*

TEXT 4 The effect of automation on work

page 28	speed [spiːd]	how fast sth goes	*Geschwindigkeit*
	to perform sth [pəˈfɔːm]	to do sth successfully	*etw ausführen*
	redundant [rɪˈdʌndənt]	not needed	*überflüssig*
	artificial intelligence [ɑːtɪˌfɪʃl ɪnˈtelɪdʒəns]	highly intelligent computers	*künstliche Intelligenz*
page 29	to disappear [ˌdɪsəˈpɪə]	no longer exist or be seen	*verschwinden*
	to predict sth [prɪˈdɪkt]	to say that sth will happen in the future	*etw voraussagen, etw vorhersagen*
	to evolve [ɪˈvɒlv]	develop	*entstehen, sich entwickeln*
	row [rəʊ]	line	*Reihe*
	tool [tuːl]	helpful instrument	*Werkzeug*
	to undertake sth [ˌʌndəˈteɪk]	to make sth happen	*etw übernehmen, etw durchführen*
	scale [skeɪl]	size, amount	*Umfang, Maßstab*
	unimaginable [ˌʌnɪˈmædʒɪnəbl]	impossible to think of or to believe exists	*unvorstellbar*

rewarding [rɪˈwɔːdɪŋ]	making you feel good from doing important work	*lohnend, bereichernd*	
to **destroy sth** [dɪˈstrɔɪ]	to break /ruin sth	*etw zerstören*	
to **occur** [əˈkɜː]	to happen, to start	*vorkommen, auftreten*	
freelancer [ˈfriːlɑːnsə]	sb who works for themselves, not a company	*Selbstständige/r*	
emergence [ɪˈmɜːdʒəns]	coming into the world	*Entstehung, Aufkommen*	
to **challenge sb** [ˈtʃælɪndʒ]	to test sb's ability	*jdn herausfordern, es mit jdm aufnehmen*	
major corporation [ˌmeɪdʒə kɔːpəˈreɪʃn]	big business	*Großunternehmen*	
decade [ˈdekeɪd]	period of ten years	*Jahrzehnt*	
to **displace sth** [dɪsˈpleɪs]	to move sth out of its usual place	*etw verdrängen, etw ersetzen*	
unemployed [ˌʌnɪmˈplɔɪd]	without a job	*arbeitslos, ohne Arbeit*	
shortage [ˈʃɔːtɪdʒ]	not having enough of sth	*Mangel*	
inefficient [ˌɪnɪˈfɪʃnt]	wasting time, energy and resources	*ineffizient, unwirtschaftlich*	page 30
advance [ədˈvɑːns]	move forward, development	*Fortschritt, (Weiter-)Entwicklung*	
lack [læk]	sth missing or needed	*Mangel*	
relevant [ˈreləvənt]	necessary or important for sth	*nötig (für etw), wichtig (für etw), relevant*	
accurate [ˈækjərət]	exact	*genau*	page 31
reliable [rɪˈlaɪəbl]	certain, dependable	*zuverlässig*	
considerable [kənˈsɪdərəbl]	large, important	*beträchtlich, erheblich*	
loss [lɒs]	the state of no longer having sth	*Verlust*	
victim [ˈvɪktɪm]	sb who has been hurt by sb/sth	*Opfer*	
crime [kraɪm]	sth against the law	*Kriminalität, Verbrechen*	

TEXT 5 Being a leader

CEO (Chief Executive Officer) [ˌtʃiːf ɪɡˈzekjətɪv ɒfɪsə]	the head of a business, company	*Geschäftsführer/in*	page 32
to **conduct sth** [kənˈdʌkt]	organize sth and carry it out	*etw durchführen, etw ausführen*	
trait [treɪt]	characteristic, quality	*Charakterzug*	
employee [ɪmˈplɔɪiː]	a person who works for a company	*Angestellte/r, Arbeitnehmer/in*	
leader [ˈliːdə]	a person who directs a group/business	*Führungskraft*	
to **project sth** [prəˈdʒekt]	to present sth in a particular way	*etw ausstrahlen*	
curious [ˈkjʊəriəs]	interested in many things	*neugierig*	
confidence [ˈkɒnfɪdəns]	belief that what you do and say is correct	*Selbstbewusstsein, Zuversicht*	
breezy [ˈbriːzi]	seeming relaxed and easy	*locker, unbeschwert*	
authority [ɔːˈθɒrəti]	the power to give orders to people	*Autorität, Kompetenz, Macht*	
to **spot sth** [spɒt]	to see/notice sth	*etw erkennen, etw entdecken*	
opportunity [ˌɒpəˈtjuːnəti]	chance, possibility	*Chance, Gelegenheit*	
relentless [rɪˈlentləs]	without stopping	*unermüdlich, unablässig*	
coincidence [kəʊˈɪnsɪdəns]	luck, chance	*Zufall*	
battle-hardened [ˈbætl hɑːdnd]	having survived difficult experiences	*kampferprobt*	
to **overcome sth** [ˌəʊvəˈkʌm]	to successfully solve or deal with sth	*etw überwinden*	
performance [pəˈfɔːməns]	effort, achievement	*Leistung(en), Abschneiden*	
failure [ˈfeɪljə]	being unsuccessful	*Versagen, Misserfolg*	
notion [ˈnəʊʃn]	opinion, concept	*Gedanke, Auffassung*	
to **wow sb** [waʊ]	to impress sb	*jdn beeindrucken*	
to **recruit sb** [rɪˈkruːt]	to hire sb	*(Personal) einstellen, anwerben*	page 33
concise [kənˈsaɪs]	offering only the information that is necessary and important	*prägnant, kurz (und bündig)*	
to **get to the point** [ˌget tə ðə ˈpɔɪnt]	to be direct	*(direkt) zur Sache kommen*	
to **deliver** [dɪˈlɪvə]	do what you promised to do	*liefern, bieten*	
to **assume sth** [əˈsjuːm]	think or accept that sth is true but without proof of it	*etw annehmen, etw vermuten*	
competitive advantage [kəmˌpetətɪv ədˈvɑːntɪdʒ]	a better position over other companies	*Wettbewerbsvorteil*	
waste of time [ˌweɪst əf ˈtaɪm]	time spent on sth useless	*Zeitverschwendung*	
consistently [kənˈsɪstəntli]	always acting or behaving in the same way	*durchweg, beständig, konsequent*	page 34

289

TEXT 6 Gender issues in the workplace

page 35	property ['prɒpəti]	things that belong to sb	*Eigentum, Besitz*
	to **own sth** [əʊn]	to have/possess sth	*etw besitzen*
	to **empower sb** [ɪm'paʊə]	give power to sb	*jdn stärken*
	noticeable ['nəʊtɪsəbl]	clear	*erkennbar, merklich, spürbar*
	discrimination [dɪˌskrɪmɪ'neɪʃn]	treating a group of people in a worse way than others	*Diskriminierung, Benachteiligung*
	member of parliament [ˌmembər əf 'pɑːləmənt]	sb elected to represent the people	*(Parlaments-)Abgeordnete/r*
	to **be well short of sth** [bi ˌwel 'ʃɔːt əv]	much less than sth	*weit unter etw liegen*
	Nordic ['nɔːdɪk]	from northern Europe	*nordeuropäisch*
	to **account for sth** [ə'kaʊnt fə]	to be a particular amount of sth	*etw ausmachen*
	legal ['liːgl]	regulated by the law	*gesetzlich, rechtlich*
	slowly and steadily [ˌsləʊli ən 'stedɪli]	gradually	*langsam und stetig*
	achievement [ə'tʃiːvmənt]	a good result from hard work	*Leistung, Erfolg*
	the humanities [ðə hjuː'mænətiz]	subjects such as literature, philosophy, history	*Geisteswissenschaften*
	gender gap ['dʒendə gæp]	the negative divide between men and women	*Kluft (zwischen den Geschlechtern), Ungleichbehandlung*
	obstacle ['ɒbstəkl]	sth that stops progress	*Hindernis*
	to **prove yourself** [pruːv]	to show that you are good at sth	*sich beweisen, sich bewähren*
	past accomplishments pl [ˌpɑːst ə'kʌmplɪʃmənts]	good things that sb has already done	*bisherige Leistungen/Erfolge*
page 36	**diversity** [daɪ'vɜːsəti]	range of differences	*Vielfalt*
	to **tap sth** [tæp]	to make use of sth	*anzapfen, nutzen*
	pool of human resources [ˌpuːl əv ˌhjuːmən rɪ'sɔːsɪz]	the total talent of everyone	*Gesamtvorrat an Humanvermögen*
	sustainable [sə'steɪnəbl]	able to stay at a certain level	*nachhaltig*
	crucially ['kruːʃli]	absolutely necessary	*vor allem, von entscheidender Bedeutung ist*
	fundamentally [ˌfʌndə'mentli]	basically	*grundsätzlich*
	sheer [ʃɪə]	simple	*schier, rein*
	degrading [dɪ'greɪdɪŋ]	without respect	*entwürdigend*
	virtually ['vɜːtʃuəli]	almost or very nearly	*praktisch, quasi*
	violence ['vaɪələns]	violent behaviour that is intended to hurt or kill	*Gewalt*
	to **sb's discredit** [tə sʌmbədiz dɪs'kredɪt]	causing damage to sb's reputation	*zu jds Schande*
	reflection [rɪ'flekʃn]	showing an image	*Abbild*
	to **oppress sb** [ə'pres]	to treat sb in a cruel, unfair way	*jdn unterdrücken*
page 37	to **waste sth** [weɪst]	to not use sth well	*etw verschwenden, etw vergeuden*
	pottery ['pɒtəri]	ceramic ware, usually made out of clay	*Töpferwaren, Keramik*
	to **unearth sth** [ʌn'ɜːθ]	to find/discover sth	*ausgraben, finden*
	to **engulf sth** [ɪn'gʌlf]	to surround sth completely	*einhüllen, umschließen*
	to **relocate** [riːləʊ'keɪt]	to move to a new location	*verlagern, verlegen, umsiedeln*
page 38	**contrast** ['kɒntrɑːst]	difference	*Gegensatz*
page 39	**struggle** ['strʌgl]	fight	*Kampf*
	to **campaign for sth** [kæm'peɪn fə]	to engage in activities towards achieving sth	*sich für etw engagieren, für etw auf die Straße gehen*
	publicity [pʌb'lɪsəti]	raising public awareness	*öffentliche Aufmerksamkeit, Bekanntheit(sgrad)*
	massive ['mæsɪv]	very big	*groß, gewaltig*
	to **refuse to do sth** [rɪ'fjuːz]	to say you will not do sth	*sich weigern, etw zu tun*
	secure [sɪ'kjʊə]	safe, sure	*sicher*
	to **suggest** [sə'dʒest]	to give sb an idea or possible plan	*vorschlagen*

TEXT 7 Globalization: its risks and opportunities

page 40	extract ['ekstrækt]	a short passage from a book, piece of music, etc.	*Auszug, Ausschnitt*

subsidiary [səb'sɪdɪəri]	a company that is owned or controlled by another company	*Niederlassung*	
to **decrease** [dɪ'kriːs]	to become smaller/less	*sinken, zurückgehen*	
accessible [ək'sesəbl]	a place that is easy to get to	*erreichbar, zugänglich*	
similarly ['sɪmələli]	in the same way	*ebenso, auf gleiche Weise*	
worldwide ['wɜːldwaɪd]	everywhere in the world	*weltweit*	
approach [ə'prəʊtʃ]	a way of doing or thinking about sth such as a problem or a task	*Herangehensweise, Ansatz*	
commodity [kə'mɒdɪti]	sth to buy or sell	*(Handels-)Ware*	
decisively [dɪ'saɪsɪvli]	very importantly	*entscheidend*	
to **shape sth** [ʃeɪp]	to form sth	*etw formen, etw gestalten*	
agreement [ə'griːmənt]	contract, understanding	*Vereinbarung, Einigung, Abkommen, Vertrag*	
cooperation [kəʊ,ɒpə'reɪʃn]	doing sth together or of working together towards a shared aim	*Zusammenarbeit*	**page 41**
scarce [skeəs]	not much/many of sth	*knapp*	
to **cooperate** [kəʊ'ɒpəreɪt]	to work together	*zusammenarbeiten, kooperieren*	
to **integrate** ['ɪntɪgreɪt]	to become part of sth	*integrieren, eingliedern*	
to **stroll** [strəʊl]	to walk casually	*schlendern, spazieren*	
outlet ['aʊtlet]	shop	*Laden, Geschäft*	
identical [aɪ'dentɪkl]	exactly the same as sth else	*identisch*	
to **fare** [feə]	survive	*ergehen (es ergeht jdm)*	
to **provide sth** [prə'vaɪd]	to give sth that is wanted or needed	*etw bieten, etw liefern, etw zur Verfügung stellen, für etw sorgen*	
prosperity [prɒ'sperəti]	wealth	*Wohlstand*	
rate [reɪt]	how fast sth goes	*Tempo, Geschwindigkeit*	
unification [,juːnɪfɪ'keɪʃn]	bringing things, people together	*Vereinigung, Vereinheitlichung*	
self-interested [,self 'ɪntrəstɪd]	motivated by your own personal concerns	*eigennützig*	
related to sth [rɪ'leɪtɪd tə]	connected to sth	*mit etw verbunden, im Zusammenhang mit etw*	
to **squabble over sth** ['skwɒbl əʊvə]	to argue about sth	*sich wegen etw zanken/streiten*	**page 42**
troubling ['trʌblɪŋ]	worrying	*beunruhigend*	
to **seek to do sth** [,siːk tə 'duː]	to try to do sth	*versuchen, etw zu tun*	
decline [dɪ'klaɪn]	fall	*Verfall, Niedergang*	
tendency ['tendənsi]	trend, lean	*Neigung, Tendenz*	
self-interest [,self 'ɪntrəst]	egoism, selfishness	*Egoismus, Eigennutz*	
backdrop ['bækdrɒp]	the area behind the main action	*Kulisse, Hintergrund*	
upheaval [ʌp'hiːvəl]	great change	*Umbruch*	
setback ['setbæk]	problem	*Rückschlag*	
species ['spiːʃiːz]	sort, type, kind	*Art, Gattung*	
to **approach** [ə'prəʊtʃ]	to come closer	*näher kommen, sich nähern*	**page 43**
workload ['wɜːkləʊd]	the amount of work sb has to do	*Arbeitspensum*	
to **benefit sb** ['benɪfɪt]	to be good to sb	*jdm nützen*	
pressure ['preʃə]	stress	*Druck*	
concern for sth [kən'sɜːn fə]	thinking about sth	*Rücksicht auf etw*	**page 45**
immense [ɪ'mens]	very big	*gewaltig, immens*	
petrol BE ['petrəl]	fuel for cars, planes, etc	*Benzin*	
to **compete** [kəm'piːt]	to try to win	*konkurrieren*	
to **explore sth** [ɪk'splɔː]	to find out sth	*etw erkunden, etw entdecken*	

ENGLISH FOR WORK

ambition [æm'bɪʃn]	sth you want to do or achieve very much	*Ziel, Ehrgeiz, Ambition*	**page 46**
to **prove sth** [pruːv]	to show that sth is correct	*etw beweisen, etw belegen*	**page 47**
suitable ['suːtəbl]	right, correct, appropriate	*geeignet*	
tight [taɪt]	difficult to manage because there is not enough time, money etc.	*eng*	

TOPIC 2   The future of Planet Earth

BACKGROUND INFORMATION

page 48	climate change ['klaɪmət tʃeɪndʒ]	rise of temperature and different weather patterns across the world caused by increased levels of carbon dioxide	Klimawandel
	global warming [ˌgləʊbl 'wɔːmɪŋ]	increase in the overall temperature of the earth's atmosphere	Erderwärmung
	man-made ['mænmeɪd]	created by humans	von Menschen verursacht
	cause [kɔːz]	the reason sth happens	Ursache
	greenhouse gas [ˌgriːnhaʊs 'gæs]	a gas that contributes to the greenhouse effect e.g. carbon dioxide and chlorofluorocarbons	Treibhausgas
	carbon dioxide (CO₂) [ˌkɑːbən daɪ'ɒksaɪd]	a gas made by burning and by respiration, which is absorbed by plants	Kohlendioxid
	to release sth [rɪ'liːs]	to allow sth to be free	etw abgeben
	atmosphere ['ætməsfɪə]	the gas surrounding the Earth	Atmosphäre
	emission [ɪ'mɪʃn]	the production and output of sth	Ausstoß
	natural disaster [ˌnætʃrəl dɪ'zɑːstə]	violent weather or other natural event that causes great damage	Naturkatastrophe
	flooding ['flʌdɪŋ]	water covering a large area of land that is usually dry	Hochwasser
	drought [draʊt]	a long period of time with low rainfall	Dürre
	heatwave ['hiːtweɪv]	abnormally hot weather	Hitzewelle
	to claim sth [kleɪm]	cause sth (e.g. sb.'s death)	etw fordern
	desertification [dɪˌzɜːtɪfɪ'keɪʃn]	when fertile land becomes a desert	Wüstenbildung
	water shortage ['wɔːtə ʃɔːtɪdʒ]	not having enough water	Wasserknappheit
	melting of glaciers [ˌmeltɪŋ əv 'glæsiəz]	when a slow-moving river of ice is turned into water	Gletscherschmelze
	rising sea levels pl [ˌraɪzɪŋ 'siː levlz]	the increase in level of the sea's surface	steigende Meeresspiegel
	climate-change refugee [ˌklaɪmət tʃeɪndʒ ˌrefju'dʒiː]	a person forced to leave their country to escape the effects of climate change	Klimaflüchtling
	water supply ['wɔːtə səplaɪ]	the amount of drinkable water available	Wasserversorgung
	urban population [ˌɜːbən pɒpju'leɪʃn]	the number of people living in cities	städtische Bevölkerung
	grain [greɪn]	seeds from cereal plants, e.g. wheat, corn	Getreide
	to overpump [ˌəʊvə'pʌmp]	to take too much water	abpumpen, trockenpumpen
	groundwater ['graʊndwɔːtə]	water held underground in the soil	Grundwasser
	drinking water ['drɪŋkɪŋ wɔːtə]	water that is pure and can be drunk	Trinkwasser
	sanitation [ˌsænɪ'teɪʃn]	system of pipes to take away waste water	sanitäre Anlagen
	water rationing ['wɔːtə ræʃnɪŋ]	the policy of allowing each person to have a fixed amount of water	Wasserrationierung
	awareness [ə'weənəs]	knowledge of a situation or fact	Bewusstsein, Bekanntheit
	finite natural resource [faɪnaɪt ˌnætʃrəl rɪ'sɔːs]	things from nature which can be used by humans that have a limited supply	begrenzte Naturressource
	pollution [pə'luːʃn]	things in the environment that are harmful or poisonous	(Umwelt-)Verschmutzung
	exhaust [ɪg'zɔːst]	waste gas from a machine	Abgas(e)
	acid rain [ˌæsɪd 'reɪn]	rainfall that is made poisonous from pollution	saurer Regen
	agribusiness ['ægrɪbɪznəs]	industrialized farming	Agrarindustrie, industrielle Landwirtschaft
	pollutant [pə'luːtənt]	sth that makes the air or water unclean	Schadstoff
	pesticide ['pestɪsaɪd]	a poison used to kill insects	Schädlingsbekämpfungsmittel, Pestizid
	herbicide ['hɜːbɪsaɪd]	a poison used to kill plants	Unkrautbekämpfungsmittel, Herbizid
	to contaminate the soil [kənˌtæmɪneɪt ðə 'sɔɪl]	making the upper layer of the earth polluted	den Erdboden verseuchen
	animal waste [ˌænɪml 'weɪst]	excrement and by-products of meat production from animals	tierische Abfallstoffe, Exkremente

sewage ['suːɪdʒ]	waste water	*Ab-/Schmutzwasser*	
toxic/poisonous ['tɒksɪk, 'pɔɪzənəs]	harmful, life-threatening	*giftig*	
marine life [mə'riːn laɪf]	plants and animals that live in the ocean	*Meereslebewesen*	
waste disposal ['weɪst dɪspəʊzl]	removing, destroying or storing used or unwanted products and substances	*Abfallentsorgung*	**page 49**
rubbish/trash ['rʌbɪʃ, træʃ]	things that are unwanted or without value	*Müll*	
reuse sth [ˌriː'juːz]	use sth more than once	*etw wiederverwenden*	
organic waste [ɔːˌgænɪk 'weɪst]	waste material that comes from a plant or animal	*Biomüll*	
biodegradable [ˌbaɪəʊdɪ'greɪdəbl]	able to break down or rot naturally	*biologisch abbaubar*	
to compost ['kɒmpɒst]	to make natural waste products into fertilizer	*kompostieren*	
landfill site ['lændfɪl saɪt]	an area of land where waste/rubbish is buried	*Mülldeponie*	
incineration [ɪnˌsɪnə'reɪʃn]	burning of waste material	*Abfallverbrennung*	
to pollute sth [pə'luːt]	to make sth, e.g. air, water, soil unclean	*etw verschmutzen*	
energy source ['enədʒi sɔːs]	material used to produce heat or power	*Energiequelle*	
climate crisis ['klaɪmət kraɪsɪs]	intense difficulty caused by climate change	*Klimakrise*	
dependence [dɪ'pendəns]	relying on or being controlled by sb/sth	*Abhängigkeit*	
oil [ɔɪl]	liquid from petroleum, used as fuel	*Erdöl*	
fossil fuel ['fɒsl fjuːəl]	coal, fuel oil or natural gas, made from the remains of dead plants and animals	*fossile Brennstoffe*	
environment [ɪn'vaɪrənmənt]	the surroundings in which people live	*Umwelt*	
nuclear energy [ˌnjuːkliə 'enədʒi]	energy released during nuclear fusion	*Atomenergie*	
radioactive fallout [reɪdiəʊˌæktɪv 'fɔːlaʊt]	radioactive particles that fall to earth as a result of a nuclear explosion	*radioaktiver Niederschlag*	
radiation [ˌreɪdi'eɪʃn]	energy made up of electro-magnetic waves	*Strahlung*	
to dispose of sth [dɪ'spəʊz əv]	to throw sth away	*etw entsorgen*	
nuclear waste [ˌnjuːkliə 'weɪst]	radioactive waste material	*Atommüll*	
to solve sth [sɒlv]	to find an answer or explanation to sth	*etw lösen*	
to conserve sth [kən'sɜːv]	to protect sth from harm or destruction	*etw sparen*	
alternative sources of energy [ɔːlˌtɜːnətɪv ˌsɔːsɪz əv 'enədʒi]	forms of energy that come from nature	*alternative Energiequellen*	
wind power ['wɪnd paʊə]	energy from the wind	*Windkraft*	
solar power [ˌsəʊlə 'paʊə]	energy from the sun	*Solarenergie*	
renewable energy [rɪˌnjuːəbl 'enədʒi]	energy from a source that does not become less when it is used	*erneuerbare Energie(quellen)*	
biofuel [ˌbaɪəʊ'fjuːəl]	a fuel made from living matter	*Biotreibstoff*	
corn [kɔːn]	a type of cereal plant	*Mais*	
palm oil ['pɑːm ɔɪl]	oil from the fruit of palms	*Palmöl*	
carbon ['kɑːbən]	a chemical element	*Kohlenstoff*	
to absorb sth [əb'sɔːb]	to take in or soak up sth	*etw aufnehmen, absorbieren*	
deforestation [diːˌfɒrɪ'steɪʃn]	clearing of large areas with trees	*Entwaldung*	
unsustainable [ˌʌnsə'steɪnəbl]	not able to be continued	*untragbar*	
tropical rainforest [ˌtrɒpɪkl 'reɪnfɒrɪst]	thick forest with heavy rainfall found in warm climates	*tropischer Regenwald*	
ecosystem ['iːkəʊsɪstəm]	a complex biological network	*Ökosystem*	
habitat ['hæbɪtæt]	the natural home of an animal or plant	*Lebensraum*	
extinction of species [ɪkˌstɪŋkʃn əf 'spiːʃiːz]	the end of a type of animal as it is unable to reproduce or is killed out	*Artensterben*	
vital ['vaɪtl]	absolutely necessary	*lebensnotwendig, unverzichtbar*	
widespread ['waɪdspred]	over a large area	*ausgedehnt, großflächig*	**page 50**
survival [sə'vaɪvl]	continuing to live or exist	*Überleben*	

TEXT 1 The human impact on the Earth

to emit sth [ɪ'mɪt]	to produce sth then give it out	*etw ausstoßen*	**page 51**
to release sth [rɪ'liːs]	to set sth free	*etw freisetzen*	
to ensure sth [ɪn'ʃʊə]	to make sure sth happens	*etw gewährleisten, für etw sorgen*	

	human-driven ['hju:mən drɪvn]	caused by humans	*von Menschen verursacht*
	fertiliser ['fɜːtəlaɪzə]	a chemical or natural product, added to land to increase the fertility	*Dünger*
page 52	to **become extinct** [bɪˌkʌm ɪk'stɪŋkt]	to no longer exist	*aussterben*
	to **shift** [ʃɪft]	change from one state, position, etc. to another	*(sich) verlagern, (sich) verschieben*
	evidence ['evɪdəns]	fact(s) that make you believe sth is true	*Beweis(e)*
	ice cap ['aɪs kæp]	the covering of ice over the north and south poles	*Polkappe*
	to **adapt** [ə'dæpt]	to become used to sth	*sich anpassen*
	belief [bɪ'liːf]	sth that you think is true	*Glaube, Überzeugung*
	critical ['krɪtɪkl]	very important, decisive	*entscheidend (für etw)*
page 53	to **contribute to sth** [kən'trɪbjuːt tə]	to be a cause of sth	*zu etw beitragen*
	to **sustain** [sə'steɪn]	to continue	*erhalten, aufrechterhalten*
	alarming [ə'lɑːmɪŋ]	worrying, disturbing	*beunruhigend, erschreckend*
	to **supply** [sə'plaɪ]	to provide sth that is needed or wanted	*liefern, beliefern, (mit etw) versorgen*
	stable ['steɪbl]	not likely to change or fail	*stabil*
	to **be heading towards sth** [bi 'hedɪŋ təwɔːdz]	to go in a particular direction	*zu etw unterwegs sein, auf dem Weg zu etw sein*
page 54	**excessive** [ɪk'sesɪv]	too much	*übermäßig, überhöht*
	to **attribute sth to sth** [ə'trɪbjuːt tə]	to say sth was caused by sth else	*etw einer Sache zuschreiben*
page 55	**inhospitable** [ˌɪnhɒ'spɪtəbl]	difficult to live in	*unwirtlich*

TEXT 2   Earth's precious resources

page 56	**direction** [də'rekʃn]	the general position that a person or thing moves towards	*Richtung*
	to **evaporate** [ɪ'væpəreɪt]	to turn a liquid into a gas	*verdunsten*
	drought-hit ['draʊt hɪt]	suffering from long periods without rain	*von Trockenheit/Dürre heimgesucht*
page 57	**concern** [kən'sɜːn]	anxiety, worry	*Sorge, Besorgnis*
	severe [sɪ'vɪə]	extremely bad or serious	*schwer, heftig, ernst*
	to **drain** [dreɪn]	to remove all water from sth	*entleeren*
	reservoir ['rezəvwɑː]	man-made lake where drinking water is stored	*Stausee*
	to **fine sb** [faɪn]	to make sb pay money as a punishment	*jdn zu einer Geldstrafe verurteilen*
	authority [ɔː'θɒrəti]	permission or power to do sth	*Vollmacht*
	to **be aware of sth** [bi ə'weər əv]	to know about sth	*sich einer Sache bewusst sein*
	democracy [dɪ'mɒkrəsi]	a system of government in which the whole population votes	*Demokratie*
page 58	to **criticize** ['krɪtɪsaɪz]	to point out the problems	*kritisieren*
	powerless ['paʊələs]	without the ability or possibility to do anything	*machtlos*
	to **save sth** [seɪv]	to keep and store sth for the future	*etw sparen, etw einsparen*
	to **blame sth on sb/sth** [bleɪm]	to say that sb/sth is responsible for sth bad that has happened	*jdm/einer Sache für etw die Schuld geben*
	to **collect sth** [kə'lekt]	to bring things together	*etw sammeln, etw zusammentragen*
page 59	to **symbolize sth** ['sɪmbəlaɪz]	to represent sth	*etw symbolisieren*
	campaign [kæm'peɪn]	a course of action to achieve a goal	*Kampagne*
	aim [eɪm]	direction, purpose	*Ziel, Zweck*
	confident ['kɒnfɪdənt]	showing certainty	*zuversichtlich*

TEXT 3   Polluting the environment

page 60	**litter** ['lɪtə]	rubbish left in a public space	*Abfall, Müll*
	eventually [ɪ'ventʃuəli]	in the end	*schließlich, am Ende, irgendwann*
	to **disintegrate** [dɪs'ɪntɪgreɪt]	break into small pieces	*zerfallen, sich auflösen*
	to **circulate** ['sɜːkjəleɪt]	move in a circular direction	*zirkulieren*
	current ['kʌrənt]	water moving in a partiucular direction	*Strömung*
	patch [pætʃ]	area (of land)	*Stück (Land), Fläche*
	microplastics pl ['maɪkrəʊplæstɪks]	very small pieces of plastic	*Mikroplastikteile*
	marine [mə'riːn]	connected with the sea and sealife	*Meeres-, See-*
	to **soak sth up** [ˌsəʊk 'ʌp]	absorb sth (esp. a liquid)	*etw aufnehmen, etw absorbieren*

food chain [ˈfuːd tʃeɪn]	the process by which food is produced then consumed	*Nahrungskette*	
ban (on sth) [bæn]	an official rule that says that sth is not allowed	*Verbot (von etw)*	page 62
unusual [ʌnˈjuːʒʊəl]	different, not normal	*ungewöhnlich*	page 63
to **save sb/sth** [seɪv]	to rescue sb/sth	*jdn/etw retten*	

TEXT 4 Meeting our energy needs

renewables pl [rɪˈnjuːəblz]	natural sources of energy that do not decrease from use	*erneuerbare Energiequellen*	page 64
rural [ˈrʊərəl]	from the countryside	*ländlich*	
shale gas [ˈʃeɪl gæs]	the gas extracted from shale rock by fracking	*Schiefergas*	
energy efficiency [ˌenədʒi ɪˈfɪʃnsi]	not wasting energy	*Energieeffizienz*	page 65
to **admit sth** [ədˈmɪt]	to say sth is true	*etw zugeben, etw eingestehen*	
leakage [ˈliːkɪdʒ]	an amount of liquid or gas escaping through a hole in sth	*Verlust durch Auslaufen*	
distribution network [ˌdɪstrɪˈbjuːʃn netwɜːk]	the system of pipes and pumping stations needed to deliver gas to consumers	*Leitungsnetz*	
methane [ˈmiːθeɪn]	a natural gas (CH₄)	*Methangas*	
to **claim sth** [kleɪm]	say that sth is true	*etw behaupten*	
to **deny sth** [dɪˈnaɪ]	to say that sth is not true	*etw leugnen, etw bestreiten*	page 66
to **insist** [ɪnˈsɪst]	to say sth positively and assertively	*darauf bestehen*	

TEXT 5 Climate change: running out of time

tide [taɪd]	the regular rise and fall in the level of the sea	*Gezeiten, Ebbe und Flut*	page 70
hurricane [ˈhʌrɪkən]	a violent storm with strong winds	*Orkan*	
to **flood** [flʌd]	to cover an area of land with water	*(über)strömen, (über)fluten*	
to **pour** [pɔː]	to flow quickly and strongly	*fließen, strömen*	
humanity [hjuːˈmænəti]	people, humans	*Menschheit*	
devastating [ˈdevəsteɪtɪŋ]	causing a lot of damage and destruction	*verheerend*	
construction [kənˈstrʌkʃn]	the process or method of building or making sth, especially roads, buildings, etc.	*Bau*	
former [ˈfɔːmə]	that used to have a particular position or status in the past	*ehemalig, früher*	
to **respond to sth** [rɪˈspɒnd tə]	do sth as a reaction to sth that sb has said or done	*auf etw reagieren*	
to **be in denial** [bi ɪn dɪˈnaɪəl]	to refuse to accept that sth unpleasant or painful is true	*etw nicht wahrhaben wollen, die Augen vor der Wahrheit verschließen*	
election [ɪˈlekʃn]	the process of choosing a person or a group of people for a position, esp. a political position, by voting	*Wahl*	page 71
sewage system [ˈsuːɪdʒ sɪstəm]	a system of pipes to take away waste water	*Abwassersystem*	
to **raise sth** [reɪz]	to increase the amount of sth	*etw (Geldmittel) aufbringen, beschaffen*	
to **fund sth** [fʌnd]	to give sth (esp. money) for a particular purpose	*finanzieren*	
to **tackle sth** [ˈtækl]	to try to deal with sth	*etw bekämpfen*	
mayhem [ˈmeɪhem]	confusion and fear, caused by a sudden shocking event	*(fürchterliches) Chaos*	
to **be vulnerable to sth** [bi ˈvʌlnərəbl tə]	to have a high possibility of being harmed or damaged by sth	*anfällig für etw sein, einer Sache schutzlos ausgesetzt sein*	page 72
feeling [ˈfiːlɪŋ]	attitude or opinion	*Ansicht, Meinung*	

TEXT 6 Unusual solutions

| **harvest** [ˈhɑːvɪst] | food collected for human consumption | *Ernte* | page 73 |
| to **consist of sth** [kənˈsɪst əv] | be formed from sth | *aus etw bestehen* | |

	to **enable** [ɪˈneɪbl]	to make it possible for sth to happen	*ermöglichen, möglich machen*
	in keeping with [ɪn ˈkiːpɪŋ wɪð]	in agreement with	*in Übereinstimmung mit*
	to **have sth in common** [həv ɪn ˈkɒmən]	to have the same features or characteristics	*etw gemeinsam haben*
	ancient [ˈeɪnʃənt]	very old	*alt, historisch*
page 74	to **convert sth into sth** [kənˈvɜːt ɪntə]	to change sth into sth else through a chemical process	*etw in etw umwandeln*
	cost-effective [ˌkɒstɪˈfektɪv]	giving the best possible profit for the money that is spent	*wirtschaftlich, rentabel, kostengünstig*
	to **extract sth** [ɪkˈstrækt]	to take sth out through a chemical process	*etw (aus etw) gewinnen, etw entziehen*
	entirely [ɪnˈtaɪəli]	completely, 100%	*vollständig, völlig*
	literally [ˈlɪtərəli]	exactly	*buchstäblich*
	landfill site [ˈlændfɪl saɪt]	an area of land where waste/rubbish is buried	*Mülldeponie*
	incineration plant [ɪnˌsɪnəˈreɪʃn plɑːnt]	place where household waste is burnt	*Müllverbrennungsanlage*
page 76	to **make sense** [meɪk ˈsens]	to be justifiable or praticable	*sinnvoll sein, vernünftig sein*
	to **emphasize sth** [ˈemfəsaɪz]	to give special importance to sth	*etw betonen*
	obligation [ˌɒblɪˈɡeɪʃn]	sth you must do because you have promised, because of the law, etc.	*Verpflichtung*

ENGLISH FOR WORK

page 78	to **advise sb** [ədˈvaɪz]	to give hints and direction to sb	*jdn beraten*
	to **handle sth** [ˈhændl]	to deal with sth, to manage sth	*etw bearbeiten, etw erledigen*
	to **demonstrate sth** [ˈdemənstreɪt]	to show sth	*etw nachweisen*
	(job) interview [ˈɪntəvjuː]	a question and answer session about a job	*Vorstellungsgespräch*
	to **apply for sth** [əˈplaɪ fə]	to try to get sth (esp. a job)	*sich für/um etw bewerben*
	to **monitor sth** [ˈmɒnɪtə]	to observe sth, to watch sth	*überwachen*
	range [reɪndʒ]	variety	*Vielfalt, Reihe*
	benefit [ˈbenɪfɪt]	an advantage, a helpful and useful effect that sth has	*Nutzen, Vorteil*
page 79	**applicant** [ˈæplɪkənt]	the person who applies for a job	*Bewerber/in*

TOPIC 3   Technology – risks and opportunities

BACKGROUND INFORMATION

page 80	**lifetime** [ˈlaɪftaɪm]	period when sb is alive	*Lebensdauer*
	to **discover sth** [dɪˈskʌvə]	be the first to find out about sth	*etw entdecken*
	defining force [dɪˌfaɪnɪŋ ˈfɔːs]	energy that sets sth apart	*bestimmende Kraft*
	to **drive progress** [ˌdraɪv ˈprəʊgres]	move things forward	*den Fortschritt antreiben*
	to **take sth for granted** [ˌteɪk fə ˈɡrɑːntɪd]	accept sth without question	*etw als selbstverständlich erachten*
	internal combustion engine [ɪnˌtɜːnl kəmˈbʌstʃən endʒɪn]	an engine which burns fuel within itself	*Verbrennungsmotor*
	flushing toilet [ˌflʌʃɪŋ ˈtɔɪlət]	a toilet which empties itself using water	*Wasserspültoilette*
	light bulb [ˈlaɪt bʌlb]	a glass ball which produces light using electricity	*Glühbirne*
	labour market [ˈleɪbə mɑːkɪt]	work force	*Arbeitsmarkt*
	working patterns pl [ˈwɜːkɪŋ pætnz]	the ways in which people work	*Arbeitsmuster, Arbeitsmodelle*
	life expectancy [ˈlaɪf ɪkspektənsi]	the length of time sb is expected to live	*Lebenserwartung*
	keyhole surgery [ˌkiːhəʊl ˈsɜːdʒəri]	surgery which is done through tiny cut in the body	*minimalinvasive Chirurgie*
	traumatic [trɔːˈmætɪk]	causing injury or pain	*traumatisch, traumatisierend*
	recovery time [rɪˈkʌvəri taɪm]	time it takes to get better	*Genesungszeit*
	X-ray [ˈeksreɪ]	photograph of the bones in the body	*Röntgengerät*
	genetic engineering [dʒəˌnetɪk ˌendʒɪˈnɪərɪŋ]	changing of genes in plants or animals for a desired effect	*Gentechnik, Gentechnologie*

controversial [ˌkɒntrə'vɜːʃl]	causing a lot of discussion and disagreement	*umstritten*	
to **screen sb** [skriːn]	test sb for potential problems	*jdn durchleuchten, jdn überprüfen*	
unborn [ʌn'bɔːn]	not yet born	*ungeboren*	
genetic flaw [dʒəˌnetɪk 'flɔː]	defect in a person's genes	*genetischer Defekt*	
to **raise ethical questions** [reɪz ˌeθɪkl 'kwestʃənz]	ask questions about morality	*ethische Fragen aufwerfen*	
to **overtake sb/sth** [ˌəʊvə'teɪk]	pass sb/sth	*jdn/etw überholen*	
preference ['prefrəns]	greater desire for sb/sth	*Vorliebe, Vorzug, Bevorzugung*	
mobile connectivity [ˌməʊbaɪl kɒnek'tɪvəti]	being connected without wires	*mobile Verbindung*	
social networking services pl [ˌsəʊʃl 'netwɜːkɪŋ sɜːvɪsɪz]	website that connects its users	*Anbieter sozialer Netzwerkdienste*	
to **generate sth** ['dʒenəreɪt]	create sth	*etw (Einkommen usw.) erwirtschaften*	
virtual world [ˌvɜːtʃuəl 'wɜːld]	computer/internet-based environment	*virtuelle Welt*	
privacy ['prɪvəsi]	keeping of information to yourself	*Privatsphäre*	**page 81**
security [sɪ'kjʊərəti]	safety	*Sicherheit*	
digital footprint [ˌdɪdʒɪtl 'fʊtprɪnt]	presence on the internet	*digitaler Fingerabdruck, digitale Spur*	
identity theft [aɪ'dentəti θeft]	stealing of sb's personal information	*Identitätsdiebstahl*	
cyber bullying ['saɪbə bʊliŋ]	intimidating of sb through the internet	*Cybermobbing*	
malware ['mælweə]	software that damages computers, software, etc	*Schadsoftware*	
to **arise** [ə'raɪz]	come about	*aufkommen, entstehen*	
on a vast scale [ɒn ə ˌvaːst 'skeɪl]	in large numbers	*in großem Maßstab*	
to **police sth** [pə'liːs]	regularly check sth	*etw überwachen*	
to **commit sth** [kə'mɪt]	do sth bad (esp. a crime)	*etw (Tat usw.) begehen*	
CCTV [ˌsiː siː tiː 'viː]	closed-circuit tv; tv used for surveillance	*Videoüberwachung*	
satellite observation ['sætəlaɪt ɒbzəveɪʃn]	watching sb/sth via satellite	*Satellitenüberwachung*	
drone [drəʊn]	flying robot	*Drohne*	
to **monitor sb/sth** ['mɒnɪtə]	watch sb/sth	*jdn/etw überwachen*	
public domain [ˌpʌblɪk də'meɪn]	open to the public	*öffentlicher Bereich*	
unprecedented [ʌn'presɪdentɪd]	that never happened before	*ohnegleichen*	
intrusion [ɪn'truːʒn]	act of going somewhere you are not wanted	*Eingriff, Eindringen*	
balance ['bæləns]	a situation in which different things exist in equal amounts	*Gleichgewicht*	
technophile ['teknəʊfaɪl]	sb very interested in technology	*Technikbegeisterte/r*	
technophobe ['teknəʊfəʊb]	sb who dislikes technology	*Technikfeind/in*	
geek [giːk]	nerd	*Computerfreak*	
early adopter [ˌɜːli ə'dɒptə]	sb who uses sth from the beginning	*frühzeitige(r) Anwender/in*	
technological innovation [teknəˌlɒdʒɪkl ɪnə'veɪʃn]	new development in technology	*technische Neuerung*	
online presence [ˌɒnlaɪn 'prezns]	existence on the internet	*Internetpräsenz*	
virtual reality gaming [ˌvɜːtʃuəl ri'æləti geɪmɪŋ]	games that exist in another world	*PC-Spiele in virtuellen Realitäten*	
digital immigrant [ˌdɪdʒɪtl 'ɪmɪgrənt]	sb who learned about internet communication when they were older	*jd, der den Umgang mit Computern erst im Erwachsenenalter erlernt hat*	

TEXT 1 Housing and technology

accommodation [əˌkɒmə'deɪʃn]	housing	*Unterkunft, Bleibe*	**page 83**
prefab housing [ˌpriːfæb 'haʊzɪŋ]	ready-made houses (that are quick and cheap to build)	*Fertighaus/-häuser*	
launch [lɔːntʃ]	introduction of sth (e.g. of a new product)	*Markteinführung*	
assumption [ə'sʌmpʃn]	belief	*Annahme, These, Unterstellung*	**page 84**
on sb's behalf [ɒn bɪ'haːf]	for or in the name of sb	*in jds Namen, für jdn*	
delay [dɪ'leɪ]	slow-down	*Verzögerung*	**page 85**

TEXT 2 Technology and materials

page 88	concrete ['kɒŋkriːt]	mix of cement, sand, gravel and water	*Beton*
	textile ['tekstaɪl]	cloth made by weaving	*Textilie, Stoff*
	to shiver ['ʃɪvə]	shake (e.g. because of cold or fear)	*zittern*
	to revert to sth [rɪ'vɜːt tə]	become sth again	*zu etw zurückkehren, in etw zurückfallen*
	apparent [ə'pærənt]	clear	*offensichtlich, augenscheinlich*
	disaster zone [dɪ'zɑːstə zəʊn]	area affected by a disaster (e.g. a fire or earthquake)	*Katastrophengebiet*
page 89	era ['ɪərə]	a period of history	*Epoche, Ära*
	breakthrough ['breɪkθruː]	an important new development	*Durchbruch*
	silicon chip [ˌsɪlɪkən 'tʃɪp]	small piece of silicon used in electronic devices	*Siliziumchip*
	to accelerate [ək'seləreɪt]	go much faster	*beschleunigen*
	collision [kə'lɪʒn]	meeting of two things that are very different	*Aufeinanderprallen*
	hip replacement ['hɪp rɪpleɪsmənt]	surgery to replace the hip joint	*Hüftprothese*
	feature ['fiːtʃə]	characteristic	*Merkmal*
	implant ['ɪmplɑːnt]	sth put inside sb's body	*Implantat*
	enlargement [ɪn'lɑːdʒmənt]	act of making sth bigger	*Vergrößerung*
	miniature ['mɪnətʃə]	very small	*sehr klein*
	at small scales [ət ˌsmɔːl 'skeɪlz]	having very small dimensions	*in kleinem Maßstab, in kleinen Dimensionen*
	to stumble upon sth ['stʌmbl əpɒn]	find sth by accident	*auf etw stoßen*
	manufacture [ˌmænju'fæktʃə]	the industrial process of making sth	*Fertigung, Herstellung*
page 90	to enhance sth [ɪn'hɑːns]	improve sth	*etw verbessern, etw stärken*
page 91	profound [prə'faʊnd]	very great	*tiefgreifend*

TEXT 3 GM foods

page 92	inherently [ɪn'hɪərəntli]	basically and essentially part of sth	*an (und für) sich, grundsätzlich*
	to be worth the risk [bi ˌwɜːθ ðə 'rɪsk]	believe the outcome is more important that the danger	*das Risiko wert sein*
page 93	spray [spreɪ]	fine mist	*Spritzmittel*
	to pretend [prɪ'tend]	act as though sth is true	*so tun, als ob*
	red herring [ˌred 'herɪŋ]	sth irrelevant and misleading	*Täuschungsmanöver*
	ecological footprint [iːkəˌlɒdʒɪkl 'fʊtprɪnt]	the impact your life and choices have on the environment	*Ökobilanz, ökologischer Fußabdruck*
	imperative [ɪm'perətɪv]	absolutely necessary	*absolutely necessary*
page 94	predictable [prɪ'dɪktəbl]	foreseeable	*vorhersagbar, voraussehbar*

TEXT 4 Space exploration

page 96	to jet off [ˌdʒet 'ɒf]	fly somewhere	*(ab)düsen*
	to found sth [faʊnd]	create sth	*etw gründen*
	to recoup sth [rɪ'kuːp]	get sth (esp. money) back	*(Geld) wieder hereinholen*
	fair share [ˌfeə 'ʃeə]	quite a lot	*gehörige Anzahl*
	hurdle ['hɜːdl]	obstacle, problem	*Hürde, Hindernis*
	to establish [ɪ'stæblɪʃ]	form sth, create sth	*gründen, etablieren*
	tough [tʌf]	difficult	*hart, schwer*
	to set in [ˌset 'ɪn]	start to become clear	*(Inhalt) begreifen, ankommen*
	to line up [ˌlaɪn 'ʌp]	queue	*anstehen, sich anstellen*
	in-laws pl ['ɪn lɔːz]	your wife's or husband's parents	*Schwiegereltern*
page 97	to come [tə 'kʌm]	in the future	*künftig*
	to leave sb/sth behind [ˌliːv bɪ'haɪnd]	go away without bringing sb/sth with you	*jdn/etw zurücklassen, jdn/etw hinterlassen*
	tedious ['tiːdiəs]	boring	*langweilig*
	profound [prə'faʊnd]	deep and important	*tiefsinnig, tiefschürfend*
	settlement ['setlmənt]	colony	*Ansiedlung, Siedlung*
	indefinitely [ɪn'defɪnətli]	for ever	*ewig*
	to skip sth [skɪp]	not do sth deliberately	*etw auslassen, etw unterlassen*

TEXT 5 Technology and our privacy

inversion [ɪnˈvɜːʃn]	act of changing sth to its opposite	*Umkehrung*	page 101
to **reassure sb** [ˌriːəˈʃʊə]	make sb feel less worried about sth	*jdn beruhigen*	
to **pledge** [pledʒ]	promise	*geloben*	page 102
surveillance [sɜːˈveɪləns]	act of watching others	*Überwachung*	

TEXT 6 Cyber crime

to **target sb/sth** [ˈtɑːgɪt]	focus on sb/sth	*jdn/etw ins Visier nehmen*	page 105
to **pose a danger** [ˌpəʊz ə ˈdeɪndʒə]	be dangerous	*eine Gefahr darstellen*	
attack [əˈtæk]	assault	*Angriff*	
to **address sth** [əˈdres]	deal with sth	*sich mit etw beschäftigen, etw thematisieren*	
opponent [əˈpəʊnənt]	person or thing you are fighting against	*Gegner*	
blackmail [ˈblækmeɪl]	crime of pressuring sb for money using the threat of revealing sth unpleasant	*Erpressung*	
ransom [ˈrænsəm]	money paid for the return of sb/sth	*Lösegeld*	
unfortunately [ʌnˈfɔːtʃənətli]	regrettably	*leider, unglücklicherweise*	page 106
authority [ɔːˈθɒrəti]	administration	*Behörde*	page 107
measure [ˈmeʒə]	procedure	*Maßnahme*	page 108
account [əˈkaʊnt]	record of incoming and outgoing money	*Konto*	
to **transfer sth** [trænsˈfɜː]	move sth (esp money) from one place to another	*etw (Geld) überweisen*	

TEXT 7 Messing with life

originally [əˈrɪdʒənəli]	at first	*ursprünglich*	page 109
to **consider sb/sth sth** [kənˈsɪdə]	believe sb/sth to be sth	*jdn/etw für etw halten*	
to **keep an eye on sb/sth** [kiːp ən ˈaɪ ɒn]	make sure you can see sb/sth	*jdn/etw im Auge behalten*	page 110
sweat [swet]	moisture that comes off the body when sb is hot	*Schweiß*	
to **crawl** [krɔːl]	walk on your hands and knees	*kriechen*	
to **disarm** [dɪsˈɑːm]	take a weapon from sb	*entwaffnen*	
duty [ˈdjuːti]	obligation	*Pflicht*	
educated [ˈedʒukeɪtɪd]	having learned a lot in school	*gebildet*	
memory [ˈmeməri]	recollections from the past	*Gedächtnis*	
to **whip sb** [wɪp]	hit sb with a strap or rod	*jdn auspeitschen*	
otherwise [ˈʌðəwaɪz]	if not	*sonst, andernfalls*	page 111
to **reason with sb** [ˈriːzn wɪð]	argue using logic	*mit jdm vernünftig reden*	
justified [ˈdʒʌstɪfaɪd]	done for a good reason	*gerechtfertigt*	
hideous [ˈhɪdiəs]	ugly	*grässlich*	
intellect [ˈɪntelekt]	ability to think logically	*Verstand*	page 112
inconsistent [ˌɪnkənˈsɪstənt]	often changing opinion	*widersprüchlich, unstimmig*	
to **infuriate sb** [ɪnˈfjʊərieɪt]	make sb very angry	*jdn wütend machen*	
revenge [rɪˈvendʒ]	act of hurting sb in return for them hurting you	*Rache*	

ENGLISH FOR WORK

honest [ˈɒnɪst]	telling the truth	*ehrlich, aufrichtig*	page 114
strength [streŋθ]	positive point	*Stärke*	
weakness [ˈwiːknəs]	negative point	*Schwäche*	

TOPIC 4 Striving for equality

BACKGROUND INFORMATION

page 116

minority [maɪˈnɒrəti]	a small group within a country that is different because of race, religion, etc.	Minderheit
class system [ˌklɑːs ˈsɪstəm]	a way of dividing people into different social and economic groups	Klassensystem
working class [ˌwɜːkɪŋ ˈklɑːs]	the people belonging to the social class that does physical work in industry	Arbeiterschicht
middle class [ˈmɪdl klɑːs]	the people belonging to the social class which is highly educated and includes professional and business people	Mittelschicht
upper class [ˌʌpə ˈklɑːs]	the people belonging to the social class that has the highest social status, wealth and power	Oberschicht
privileges pl [ˈprɪvəlɪdʒɪz]	special rights or advantages that a particular person or group of people has	Privilegien
inherited wealth [ɪnˌherɪtɪd ˈwelθ]	money and property received by a relative when a family member dies	geerbtes Vermögen
social mobility [ˌsəʊʃl məʊˈbɪləti]	the ability to move into a higher social class than the one you were born into	soziale Mobilität
outdated [ˌaʊtˈdeɪtɪd]	no longer useful because of being old-fashioned	überholt, veraltet
multiculturalism [ˌmʌltiˈkʌltʃərəlɪzm]	the practice of giving importance to all cultures in a society	Multikulturalismus
immigrant [ˈɪmɪgrənt]	a person who has come to live permanently in a country not their own	Einwanderer/in
colony [ˈkɒləni]	a country or area ruled by people from another, more powerful country	Kolonie
racism [ˈreɪsɪzəm]	unfair treatment of people who belong to a different race	Rassismus
to overrun sth [ˌəʊvəˈrʌn]	spread over sth (esp. an area) quickly and in large numbers	etw überfluten, etw überschwemmen
incident [ˈɪnsɪdənt]	something that happens, often unusual or unpleasant	Vorfall, Zwischenfall
to immigrate [ˈɪmɪgreɪt]	enter another country to live permanently after leaving your own.	einwandern
immigrant background [ˌɪmɪgrənt ˈbækgraʊnd]	a family history in which family members such as parents, grandparents moved to the present country	Migrationshintergrund
urban [ˈɜːbən]	connected with a town or city	städtisch
multicultural [ˌmʌltiˈkʌltʃərəl]	including people of several different races, religions and traditions	multikulturell
to expand [ɪkˈspænd]	become greater in size, number or importance	sich erweitern
to attract sb [əˈtrækt]	make sb come somewhere	jdn locken
to suffer racial discrimination [safə ˌreɪʃl dɪskrɪmɪˈneɪʃn]	experience unfair and negative treatment because of your race	unter Rassendiskriminierung leiden
abuse [əˈbjuːs]	unfair, cruel or violent treatment of sb	Beschimpfung(en)
to originate from [əˈrɪdʒɪneɪt frəm]	come from	stammen aus
religious extremist [rɪˌlɪdʒəs ɪkˈstriːmɪst]	a person whose religious opinions are extreme and who may act violently	religiöse/r Extremist/in
to treat sb with suspicion [ˌtriːt wɪð səˈspɪʃn]	behave in a negative way towards sb because you believe they have bad intentions	jdm mit Misstrauen begegnen
ethnically diverse [ˌeθnɪkli daɪˈvɜːs]	made up of members from many different races and cultures	ethnisch vielfältig
Native American [ˌneɪtɪv əˈmerɪkən]	a member of any of the races of people who were the original people living in North America.	amerikanische/r Ureinwohner/in

settler ['setlə]	a person who goes to live in a new place or region	*Siedler/in*
slave [sleɪv]	a person who is owned by another person and is forced to work for them	*Sklave/in*
plantation [plæn'teɪʃn]	a large area of land, esp. in a hot country where crops such as coffee, sugar, tobacco are grown	*Plantage*
slavery ['sleɪvəri]	the practice of buying and selling people as ,property'	*Sklaverei*
mistreatment [ˌmɪs'triːtmənt]	unfair, unkind or cruel behaviour towards a person or animal	*schlechte Behandlung*
shame [ʃeɪm]	a feeling of sadness, embarrassment and guilt about a past wrong action or situation	*Schande, Scham*
foundation [faʊn'deɪʃn]	the act of starting a new institution, organization or country	*Gründung*
Declaration of Independence [deklə,reɪʃn əv ɪndɪ'pendəns]	the document declaring the USA to be a free country	*Unabhängigkeitserklärung*
destination [ˌdestɪ'neɪʃn]	the place where sb/sth is going	*(Reise-)Ziel*
discriminate against sb [dɪ'skrɪmɪneɪt əgenst]	treat sb worse because they belong to a particular race, religion, etc	*jdn diskriminieren*
ethnic diversity [ˌeθnɪk daɪ'vɜːsəti]	a range of people from several different races and cultures	*ethnische Vielfalt*
melting pot ['meltɪŋ pɒt]	a situation in which people from different backgrounds are mixed together	*Schmelztiegel*
national identity [ˌnæʃnəl aɪ'dentəti]	the general character and qualities of a nation	*Nationalbewusstsein, nationales Selbstverständnis*
salad bowl ['sæləd bəʊl]	a large bowl for serving vegetables such as lettuce, tomato, cucumber etc.	*Salatschüssel*
pursuit of happiness [pə,sjuːt əv 'hæpinəs]	the act of looking for and trying to find happiness	*das Streben nach Glück*
arrival [ə'raɪvl]	coming or being brought to a place	*Ankunft, Eintreffen*
African-American [ˌæfrɪkən ə'merɪkən]	an American whose ancestors came from Africa	*Afro-Amerikaner/in*
equality [ɪ'kwɒləti]	the treatment of all people as having the same worth and value	*Gleichberechtigung*
to abolish sth [ə'bɒlɪʃ]	officially end sth	*etw abschaffen*
segregation [ˌsegrɪ'geɪʃn]	the act of separating people into different groups and treating them differently because of race	*Rassentrennung*
economic oppression [iːkə,nɒmɪk ə'preʃn]	the unfair or cruel treatment of people through the financial and employment system	*wirtschaftliche Unterdrückung*
"Jim Crow" laws pl [dʒɪm ˌkrəʊ 'lɔːz]	the former system of laws in the USA that were unfair to black people	*Gesetze zur Rassendiskriminierung*
to strike sth down [ˌstraɪk 'daʊn]	decide that sth (e.g. a law) is illegal and should not apply	*etw aufheben*
Civil Rights Movement [ˌsɪvl 'raɪts muːvmənt]	(esp. in the US) the campaign in the 1950s and 1960s to change the laws to give black people the same legal rights as others	*Bürgerrechtsbewegung*
Hispanic [hɪ'spænɪk]	connected with South and Central America	*Hispano-Amerikaner/in*
ethnic minority [ˌeθnɪk maɪ'nɒrəti]	a smaller group of people who share a particular race or culture within a larger society	*ethnische Minderheit*
prejudice ['predʒudɪs]	a fixed idea or image that people have of a particular type of person but which is often not true in reality	*Vorurteil*
immigration control [ɪmɪ'greɪʃn kəntrəʊl]	the system of checks and rules that limit and decide who can enter a country	*Grenzkontrolle*

page 117

blue-collar [ˌbluː ˈkɒlə]	connected with people who do physical work in industry	*in Arbeiterberufen*
illegal immigrant [ɪˌliːgl ˈɪmɪgrənt]	a person who comes to live in a new country without following the official rules and procedures	*illegale/r Einwanderer/in*
to move up in society [muːv ˌʌp ɪn səˈsaɪəti]	improve your social status	*gesellschaftlich aufsteigen*
notable [ˈnəʊtəbl]	important and interesting	*bedeutend, bemerkenswert*
poverty [ˈpɒvəti]	state of having no money or property	*Armut*
gender equality [ˈdʒendər ɪkwɒləti]	the treatment of men and women in the same way	*Gleichberechtigung der Geschlechter*
women's rights pl [ˌwɪmɪnz ˈraɪts]	equal opportunities for women	*Frauenrechte*
equal opportunities pl [ˌiːkwəl ɒpəˈtjuːnətiz]	giving the same chances in life, work and society to all people	*Chancengleichheit*
feminism [ˈfemənɪzəm]	the belief that women should have the same rights and opportunities as men	*Feminismus*
to close the gender gap [ˌkləʊz ðə ˈdʒendə gæp]	eliminate the unfair differences in incomes and opportunities of women compared to men	*geschlechtsspezifische Unterschiede beseitigen*
gender stereotype [ˌdʒendə ˈsteriətaɪp]	a fixed idea that people have of the roles of men and women, but which is often not true in reality	*geschlechtsspezifisches Klischee*
mentally/physically disabled [ˌmentli/ˌfɪzɪkli dɪsˈeɪbld]	people who have intellectual/physical difficulties often from birth	*geistig/körperlich behindert*
equal opportunity legislation [ˌiːkwəl ɒpəˌtjuːnəti ledʒɪsˈleɪʃn]	laws that give all people the right to be treated fairly and equally	*Gleichbehandlungsgesetz(e)*
gay [geɪ]	a person, normally a man, who is sexually attracted to other men	*schwuler Mann*
lesbian [ˈlezbiən]	a woman who is sexually attracted to other women	*lesbische Frau*
homosexual [ˌhəʊməˈsekʃuəl]	a person who is sexually attracted to people of the same gender	*homosexuell, gleichgeschlechtlich*
civil partnership [ˌsɪvl ˈpɑːtnəʃɪp]	the legal recognition given to a relationship between two people of the same sex	*eingetragene Lebenspartnerschaft*
same-sex marriage [ˌseɪm seks ˈmærɪdʒ]	the marriage of two people of the same sex	*gleichgeschlechtliche Ehe*
homosexuality [ˌhɒməˌsekʃuəˈæliti]	the sexual attraction between people of the same sex	*Homosexualität*
on moral/religious grounds [ɒn ˌmɒrəl/rɪˌlɪdʒəs ˈgraʊndz]	for reasons based on ethical and religious beliefs	*aus moralischen/religiösen Gründen*

TEXT 1 The class system in the UK

page 119	to range from … to … [ˈreɪndʒ frəm tə]	cover a variety of different things from sth to sth else	*von … zu/bis … reichen*
	elite [ɪˈliːt]	a small group of people in a society, etc. who are rich, powerful and influential	*Elite*
	occupation [ˌɒkjuˈpeɪʃn]	job	*Beschäftigung*
page 120	established [ɪˈstæblɪʃt]	respected or well-known because it has existed for many years	*etabliert*
	prosperous [ˈprɒspərəs]	rich and successful	*wohlhabend*
	affluent [ˈæfluənt]	rich, well-off	*reich, wohlhabend*
	deprived [dɪˈpraɪvd]	without enough food, money, education, etc. to live a happy and comfortable life	*unterprivilegiert, sozial benachteiligt*
	emergent [ɪˈmɜːdʒnt]	new and still developing	*aufstrebend*
	professional [prəˈfeʃənl]	an educated and qualified person	*Berufstätige/r (mit qualifizierter Ausbildung)*
	conventional [kənˈvenʃənl]	normal, traditional	*herkömmlich, konventionell*

de-industrialisation [ˌdiːɪndʌstriəlaɪˈzeɪʃn]	process of social and economic change caused by the reduction of industrial activity in a country, especially heavy industry	Deindustrialisierung	page 121
immigration [ˌɪmɪˈɡreɪʃn]	the movement of foreign people into a country to live permanently	Einwanderung	
to **socialize (with sb)** [ˈsəʊʃəlaɪz]	spend free time with sb	(mit jdm) Umgang pflegen, (mit jdm) gesellschaftlich verkehren	page 122
living standard [ˈlɪvɪŋ stændəd]	the quality and measure of how comfortable sb's life is	Lebensstandard	page 123

TEXT 2   Minorities in Britain

spiritual [ˈspɪrɪtʃuəl]	connected with religion	spirituell, geistlich	page 125
regardless of sth [rɪˈɡɑːdləs əv]	without taking sth into account	ungeachtet einer Sache, unabhängig von etw	
diverse [daɪˈvɜːs]	of very different kinds	vielfältig, unterschiedlich	page 126
rational [ˈræʃnəl]	able to think clearly	vernünftig, rational	
morality [məˈræləti]	principles concerning right and wrong or good and bad behaviour	Moral	
to **reject** [rɪˈdʒekt]	turn sth down	ablehnen, zurückweisen	
issue [ˈɪʃuː]	question, topic	Thema, Frage	
visible [ˈvɪzəbl]	able to be seen	sichtbar, erkennbar	
Islamophobic abuse [ɪzlæməˌfəʊbɪk əˈbjuːs]	cruel or violent treatment of Muslims	islamfeindliche Beschimpfungen	
community [kəˈmjuːnəti]	a group of people who feel they belong together because of some shared characteristics or situation	Gemeinde, Gemeinschaft	
to **persecute sb** [ˈpɜːsɪkjuːt]	treat sb in a cruel and unfair way, esp. because of their race, religion or political beliefs	jdn verfolgen, jdn schikanieren	page 127
to **mistrust sb** [ˌmɪsˈtrʌst]	not trust sb	jdm misstrauen	
prejudiced [ˈpredʒudɪst]	having an unreasonable dislike of sb/ sth, esp. based on race, religion, sex, etc.	voreingenommen, vorurteilsbehaftet	
upbringing [ˈʌpbrɪŋɪŋ]	the time during which children are raised and educated by parents, schools, etc.	Erziehung	
moral [ˈmɒrəl]	concerned with principles of right and wrong behaviour	moralisch	
to **be prepared to do sth** [bi prɪˈpeəd tə duː]	be ready/willing to do sth	bereit sein, etw zu tun	page 128

TEXT 3   Civil rights in the USA

unalienable [ʌnˈeɪliənəbl]	that cannot be taken away from you	unveräußerlich	page 130
intolerable [ɪnˈtɒlərəbl]	completely unacceptable	unerträglich	
environmentalist [ɪnˌvaɪrənˈmentəlɪst]	sb who tries to protect the environment	Umweltschützer/in	
peace activist [ˌpiːs ˈæktɪvɪst]	sb who works or protests for peace	Friedensaktivist/in	
disabled [dɪsˈeɪbld]	sb who has intellectual or physical difficulties through injury or birth	Behinderte/r	
overseas [ˌəʊvəˈsiːz]	connected with foreign countries, esp. when separated by the sea	Übersee-, im Ausland	
right of suffrage [ˌraɪt əf ˈsʌfrɪdʒ]	the right to vote	Wahlrecht	page 131
to **humiliate sb** [hjuːˈmɪlieɪt]	make sb feel ashamed or stupid and lose the respect of other people	jdn demütigen	

TEXT 4   Hispanics and the American Dream

epitome [ɪˈpɪtəmi]	perfect example of sth	Verkörperung	page 134
crock AE [krɒk]	sth that is not true	Schwachsinn	
faith [feɪθ]	strong religious belief	(religiöser) Glaube	

page 135	sacrifice ['sækrɪfaɪs]	the fact of giving up sth important in order to get or do something that seems more important	Opfer
	determined [dɪ'tɜːmɪnd]	ready to work hard to achieve a result and not allow sb/sth to stop you	entschlossen
	for the sake of sb [fə ðə 'seɪk əv]	for the benefit of sb	jdm zuliebe, um jds willen
	to drop out [ˌdrɒp 'aʊt]	leave high school or college without graduating	die Schule abbrechen
page 137	to emigrate ['emɪɡreɪt]	go to a different country to live permanently	auswandern

TEXT 5 Gender equality

page 138	to launch sth [lɔːntʃ]	begin sth new, e.g. a campaign, a project, selling a new product	etw (Aktion usw.) starten
	advocate ['ædvəkət]	sb who speaks in favour of sb/sth	Befürworter/in
page 139	to consider sb/sth sth [kən'sɪdə]	think about sb/sth in a particular way	jdn/etw für etw halten
	sheer privilege [ˌʃɪə 'prɪvəlɪdʒ]	the simple fact of having special advantages	absolutes Privileg
	women's rights pl [ˌwɪmɪnz 'raɪts]	providing equal opportunities and protections to women	Frauenrechte
	to participate in sth [pɑː'tɪsɪpeɪt ɪn]	take part in sth	an etw teilnehmen
	suicide ['suːɪsaɪd]	the act of killing yourself	Selbstmord
	submissive [səb'mɪsɪv]	willing to accept sb else's authority without question	unterwürfig
	sensitive ['sensətɪv]	able to understand other people's feelings	einfühlsam, empfindsam

TEXT 6 Gay rights

page 143	to come out (of the closet) [ˌkʌm 'aʊt]	no longer hide the fact that you are homosexual	sein Coming-out haben
	nightmare ['naɪtmeə]	a frightening, disturbing dream	Albtraum
	sexuality [ˌsekʃu'æləti]	feelings and activities connected with a person's sexual desires	Sexualität
	announcement [ə'naʊnsmənt]	a short public speech which gives people information	Durchsage
	coward ['kaʊəd]	sb who has no courage	Feigling
	anonymity [ˌænə'nɪməti]	state of remaining unknown to most other people	Anonymität
	bullying ['bʊliɪŋ]	use of strength or power to frighten or hurt weaker people	Mobbing
page 144	stuck in the closet [ˌstʌk ɪn ðə 'klɒzɪt]	unable to admit to being homosexual	unfähig, sich zu seiner Homosexualität zu bekennen
page 145	offensive [ə'fensɪv]	rude in a way that causes sb to feel upset or insulted	beleidigend
	insult ['ɪnsʌlt]	a statement that is said in order to offend, annoy and upset sb	Beleidigung
page 146	to elect sb [ɪ'lekt]	choose sb for a position by majority vote	jdn wählen

TOPIC 5 Britain – tradition and change

BACKGROUND INFORMATION

page 150	trade route ['treɪd ruːt]	a path over land or sea used to move products for sale	Handelsweg
	to leave sb/sth behind [ˌliːv bɪ'haɪnd]	make much better progress than sb/sth	jdn/etw überflügeln
	shipbuilding industry ['ʃɪpbɪldɪŋ ɪndəstri]	the large-scale manufacture of ships	Schiffbauindustrie

reign [reɪn]	the period of time a particular king or queen rules	*Herrschaft, Regentschaft*
to **claim sth** [kleɪm]	say that sth (e.g. land or possession) belong to you	*etw beanspruchen*
source of wealth [ˌsɔːs əv 'welθ]	the place where sb.'s riches and money come from	*Vermögensquelle, Wohlstandsquelle*
sugar plantation ['ʃʊgə plænteɪʃn]	a large area of land, where sugarcane is farmed	*Zuckerplantage*
slave trade [ˌsleɪv treɪd]	the selling and buying of people as property	*Sklavenhandel*
spice [spaɪs]	powder or seeds with a strong taste used in cooking	*Gewürz*
War of Independence [ˌwɔːr əv ɪndɪ'pendəns]	The war fought between 1775-1783 by American colonists to become independent from Britain	*Unabhängigkeitskrieg*
self-governing [ˌself'gʌvənɪŋ]	having a limited form of independence while remaining under official control of another country	*selbstverwaltet*
Indian mutiny [ˌɪndiən 'mjuːtəni]	a revolt by Indian soldiers against the the British in 1857	*indischer Aufstand*
steamship ['stiːmʃɪp]	a ship driven by a steam and coal-powered engine	*Dampfschiff*
bankrupt ['bæŋkrʌpt]	not having enough money to pay what is owed	*bankrott, pleite*
to **defend sb/sth** [dɪ'fend]	protect sb/sth against attack	*jdn/etw verteidigen*
to **request sth** [rɪ'kwest]	ask for sth	*um etw bitten*
partition [pɑː'tɪʃn]	official separation (e.g. of a country) into different independent parts	*Teilung*
population exchange [ˌpɒpju'leɪʃn ɪkstʃeɪndʒ]	the movement of people between two areas in order to unite ethnic groups	*Bevölkerungsaustausch*
intergovernmental [ˌɪntəgʌvən'mentl]	between two or more governments	*zwischenstaatlich*
member state [ˌmembə 'steɪt]	a country which is part of a larger grouping of countries e.g. the EU	*Mitgliedsstaat*
human rights pl [ˌhjuːmən 'raɪts]	the basic rights that everyone has to be treated fairly and not in a cruel way, especially by their government	*Menschenrechte*
free trade [ˌfriː 'treɪd]	international commerce without extra import taxes	*freier Handel*
parliamentary system [pɑːlə,mentri 'sɪstəm]	a system of government based upon a group of people who are elected to pass and change the laws of the country	*parlamentarisches System*
system of law [ˌsɪstəm əv 'lɔː]	the system of legal rules which a society follows to create order and stability	*Rechtssystem*
civil service [ˌsɪvl 'sɜːvɪs]	the departments of a country's government and the people who work for them	*öffentlicher Dienst, Staatsdienst*
wartime ['wɔːtaɪm]	the years when a country is at war with anther country	*Kriegszeiten*
defence [dɪ'fens]	the act of protecting sb/sth from attack	*Verteidigung*
intelligence sharing [ɪn'telɪdʒəns ʃeərɪŋ]	exchanging information gained from spying with a friendly country	*Informationsaustausch*
War on Terror [ˌwɔːr ɒn 'terə]	the name given by US President George W. Bush in 2001 to the US fight against terrorism	*Krieg gegen den Terror*
ambivalent [æm'bɪvələnt]	having or showing both good and bad feelings about sb/sth	*ambivalent, zweischneidig*
Europhile ['jʊərəfaɪl]	a person who admires supports participation in the European Union	*Befürworter/in Europas*
Eurosceptic ['jʊərəskeptɪk]	a person who is against closer links with the European Union	*Euroskeptiker/in*

page 151

	bloc [blɒk]	a group of countries that work closely together because they share common political interests	*Staatenblock*
	to **stand up to sb/sth** [ˌstænd ˈʌp tə]	not accept bad treatment from sb/sth	*jdm/etw die Stirn bieten*

TEXT 1 Immigration

page 153	**poll** [pəʊl]	a survey of people's opinions	*Meinungsumfrage*
	predictable [prɪˈdɪktəbl]	that could be known before	*vorhersagbar, voraussehbar*
page 154	to **be better off** [bi ˌbetər ˈɒf]	be in a better position	*es besser haben*
	lawless [ˈlɔːləs]	where there is no law	*rechtlos, gesetzlos*
	asylum seeker [əˈsaɪləm siːkə]	sb who wants to stay in a new country for safety reasons due to a threat in the home country	*Asylsuchende/r*
	continuously [kənˈtɪnjuəsli]	without stopping	*ständig, ununterbrochen*
	to **give sanctuary to sb** [ˌgɪv ˈsaŋtjʊəri tə]	offer a safe place to sb in danger	*jdm Zuflucht gewähren*
	to **botch sth** [bɒtʃ]	make a mess of sth	*etw vermasseln, etw verpfuschen*
	gamble [ˈgæmbl]	risk	*Wagnis, Risiko*
page 155	**language barrier** [ˈlæŋgwɪdʒ bæriə]	communication problems caused by differences in language	*Sprachbarriere*
	to **exploit sth** [ɪkˈsplɔɪt]	make use of sth	*etw ausschöpfen, etw nutzen*

TEXT 2 The Legacy of the British Empire

page 158	**ideal** [aɪˈdiːəl]	value, philosophy	*Wertvorstellung*
	scattered [ˈskætəd]	spread far apart over a wide area	*verstreut*
	to **crumble** [ˈkrʌmbl]	break up	*zerfallen*

TEXT 3 Britain's future influence

page 162	to **lose your grip on sth** [ˌluːz jɔː ˈgrɪp ɒn]	lose your power over sth	*etw nicht mehr im Griff haben*
	to **deliver sth** [dɪˈlɪvə]	provide sth	*etw (Macht) ausüben*
	diplomacy [dɪˈpləʊməsi]	the activity of managing relationships between countries	*Diplomatie*
	set [set]	group	*Kategorie, Gruppe*
	to **challenge sth** [ˈtʃælɪndʒ]	question sth	*etw infrage stellen*
	meaningful [ˈmiːnɪŋfl]	important	*sinnvoll, sinn*
page 163	to **make a strong case for sth** [meɪk ə ˌstrɒŋ ˈkeɪs fə]	make a positive argument for sth	*gute Argumente für etw anführen*
	proactively [ˌprəʊˈæktɪvli]	doing sth first on your initiative instead of waiting for sth to happen and then reacting	*vorausschauend, initiativ*
	mainstream [ˈmeɪnstriːm]	liked by the majority	*gängig*

TEXT 4 Britain and Europe

page 167	**consistently** [kənˈsɪstəntli]	always	*regelmäßig, beständig, durchweg*
	antagonistic [ænˌtagəˈnɪstɪk]	very negative	*feindselig*
	disinterested [ˌdɪsˈɪntrəstɪd]	with no particular interest in sth	*neutral, desinteressiert*
	pragmatic [prægˈmætɪk]	practical	*pragmatisch*
	to **rage against sth** [ˈreɪdʒ əgenst]	be angry with sth	*gegen etw wettern*
	to **struggle** [ˈstrʌgl]	find something difficult	*sich schwertun*
	twenty-something [ˈtwenti sʌmθɪŋ]	people aged 20-29	*jd im Alter zwischen 20 und 29*
	funnily enough [ˌfʌnəli ɪˈnʌf]	surprisingly	*komischerweise*
page 168	to **welcome sth** [ˈwelkəm]	feel positive about sth	*etw begrüßen*
	conversion rate [kənˈvɜːʃn reɪt]	exchange between currencies	*Wechselkurs*
	to **lose out** [ˌluːz ˈaʊt]	get a bad deal	*schlecht wegkommen*
	regardless [rɪˈgɑːdləs]	when something does not matter	*when something does*
	happen to be [ˈhæpən tə bi]	may be	*(zufällig) sein*
	cosmopolitan [ˌkɒzməˈpɒlɪtən]	with experience of different cultures	*Weltbürger/in*

TEXT 5 Britain's role in the world

outbreak ['aʊtbreɪk]	start (of a war)	*Ausbruch*	page 174
net [net]	that is the final number	*netto*	
to **fade** [feɪd]	become less important	*an Bedeutung verlieren*	
centrepiece ['sentəpiːs]	main part	*Herzstück, Kern*	
bulk [bʌlk]	majority	*Großteil, Masse*	
renowned [rɪ'naʊnd]	famous	*(für etw) berühmt, renommiert*	
contrary to popular belief [ˌkɒntrəri tə ˌpɒpjələ bɪ'liːf]	despite what people generally think	*entgegen der landläufigen Meinung*	
manufacturing sector [ˌmænjʊ'fæktʃərɪŋ sektə]	part of the economy that produces goods in large quantities	*Herstellungssektor, verarbeitende Industrie*	
island nation [ˌaɪlənd 'neɪʃn]	a country which is an island	*Inselstaat*	
trading bloc ['treɪdɪŋ blɒk]	group of partners in international business	*Handelsblock, Handelsmacht*	
undoubtedly [ʌn'daʊtɪdli]	without doubt	*zweifellos*	
labour costs pl ['leɪbə kɒsts]	costs of paying workers incl. salaries, social security, etc.	*Lohnkosten, Arbeitskosten*	
labour-intensive [ˌleɪbər ɪn'tensɪv]	work that needs a lot of people	*arbeitsaufwändig, lohnintensiv*	
aid [eɪd]	help and assistance	*(humanitäre) Hilfe*	page 176
target ['tɑːgɪt]	goal	*Ziel*	

TEXT 6 Accepting new arrivals

to **bleed** [bliːd]	lose blood	*bluten*	page 177
rust [rʌst]	reddish-brown substance caused by the effects of water and air on iron	*Rost*	
emergency accommodation [ɪˌmɜːdʒənsi əkɒmə'deɪʃn]	short-term shelter available at short notice	*Notunterkunft*	
stay [steɪ]	not move	*Aufenthalt*	
agent ['eɪdʒənt]	middle-man, negotiator	*Makler/in*	
sour ['saʊə]	not fresh	*sauer*	
to supervise sth ['suːpəvaɪz]	control sth	*etw beaufsichtigen*	
inhumanity [ˌɪnhjuː'mænəti]	cruel behaviour	*Grausamkeit, Unmenschlichkeit*	

ENGLISH FOR WORK

memorable ['memərəbl]	easily remembered because it is special	*einprägsam*	page 180
to **blame sb** [bleɪm]	to say that sb is responsible for sth bad	*jdm die Schuld geben*	

TOPIC 6 The USA – a fading superpower?

BACKGROUND INFORMATION

colonist ['kɒlənɪst]	a person who settles in a colony	*Siedler/in, Kolonist/in*	page 182
Puritan ['pjʊərɪtən]	a member of an English Protestant group who wanted to worship God in a simple way	*Puritaner/in*	
work ethic ['wɜːk eθɪk]	belief in the value of hard work	*Arbeitsmoral*	
religious faith [rɪˌlɪdʒəs 'feɪθ]	belief in God	*Glaube*	
constitution [ˌkɒnstɪ'tjuːʃn]	a system of laws and basic principles by which a country is governed	*Verfassung*	
Founding Fathers pl ['faʊndɪŋ fɑːðəz]	the group of men who signed the American Declaration of Independence	*Gründerväter*	
Revolutionary War [revəˌluːʃənəri 'wɔː]	The war fought between 1775-1783 by American colonists to become independent from Britain	*Revolutionskrieg*	
pioneer spirit [paɪəˌnɪə 'spɪrɪt]	adventurous nature that led to the opening up of unexplored areas of North America	*Pioniergeist*	

Wild West [ˌwaɪld 'west]	name given to western area of North America before the 20th century due to the lack of law	Wilder Westen
tribe [traɪb]	a group of people belonging to the same ethnic group sharing the same customs, traditions, etc.	Stamm
reservation [ˌrezə'veɪʃn]	an area of land set aside upon which certain people, such as Native Americans, live	Reservat
civil war [ˌsɪvl 'wɔː]	an internal war between the citizens of a country	Bürgerkrieg
secession [sɪ'seʃn]	the declaration of independence of an area from the country it belongs to	Abspaltung, Sezession
cotton ['kɒtn]	cloth made from soft white hairs of the cotton seed	Baumwolle
Confederacy [kən'fedərəsi]	the eleven southern states of the USA that left in 1860-1861 starting the American Civil War	Konföderation, die Konföderierten Staaten von Amerika
Union ['juːniən]	the twenty-three northern states of the USA who fought to preserve the country in the American Civil War	Union, die Nordstaaten
Civil Rights Movement [ˌsɪvl 'raɪts muːvmənt]	the campaign in the US in the 1950s and 1960s to gain the same rights for black people as white people	Bürgerrechtsbewegung
to escape poverty [ɪˌskeɪp 'pɒvəti]	improve your financial security to a more comfortable level	der Armut entfliehen
religious persecution [rɪˌlɪdʒəs pɜːsɪ'kjuːʃn]	unfair or bad treatment of sb because of their religious beliefs	Verfolgung aus religiösen Gründen
Great Depression [ˌgreɪt dɪ'preʃn]	a period of low economic activity that affected the world in the 1930s	Weltwirtschaftskrise (von 1929)
Wall Street Crash [wɔːl ˌstriːt 'kræʃ]	a financial crisis in October 1929 which saw stock markets lose significant value	Börsenkrach (von 1929)
war effort ['wɔːr efət]	the work of an entire country to help support its military forces	Kriegsanstrengungen
Hispanic [hɪ'spænɪk]	connected with South or Central America	Hispano-Amerikaner/in
salad bowl ['sæləd bəʊl]	a large bowl for serving vegetables such as lettuce, tomato, cucumber etc.	Salatschüssel
ethnic identity [ˌeθnɪk aɪ'dentəti]	character of a person or group based on their race and traditions	ethnische Identität
monolithic culture [mɒnəˌlɪθɪk 'kʌltʃə]	a cultural identity based upon one single ethnic, traditional source allowing no external influence	erstarrte, nicht wandlungsfähige Kultur
superpower ['suːpəpaʊə]	one of the most powerful countries in the world esp. during the Cold War, e.g. the USA and the Soviet Union	Supermacht
Cold War [ˌkəʊld 'wɔː]	period between 1945 and 1991 when tension existed between the Soviet Bloc and western countries such as the USA, the UK, etc.	Kalter Krieg
Soviet Union [ˌsəʊviət 'juːniən]	the union of 15 communist states led by the Russian Federation between 1922 and 1991	Sowjetunion
Vietnam War [ˌviːet'næm wɔː]	civil and international war between western forces incl. the USA, France, South Vietnam and pro-communist forces incl. North Korea, China and the USSR between 1955 and 1975	Vietnamkrieg
economic system [iːkəˌnɒmɪk 'sɪstəm]	a system of production and exchange of goods and services in a society	Wirtschaftssystem
diverse population [daɪˌvɜːs pɒpju'leɪʃn]	a population made up of many different racial, ethnic groups	vielfältige/multikulturelle Bevölkerung

page 183

Republican Party [rɪˈpʌblɪkən pɑːti]	the main right-wing political party in the USA	*Republikanische Partei*
Democratic Party [ˌdeməˈkrætɪk pɑːti]	the main centre-left political party in the US	*Demokratische Partei*
gun control [ˌgʌn kənˈtrəʊl]	limits and rules around the private ownership of guns	*Reglementierung von Waffenbesitz*
same-sex marriage [ˌseɪm seks ˈmærɪdʒ]	marriage between partners of the same sex	*gleichgeschlechtliche Ehe*
terrorist attack [ˌterərɪst əˈtæk]	a violent attack on a country (normally civilians) where the main goal is to inspire fear in its government and people	*Terroranschlag*
intervention [ˌɪntəˈvenʃn]	military action by a country in the affairs of another country when they have not been asked to do so	*Eingreifen, militärische Intervention*
unpatriotic [ˌʌnpætrɪˈɒtɪk]	being unsupportive of your own country	*unpatriotisch*
security agency [sɪˈkjʊərəti eɪdʒənsi]	state organization responsible for protecting the safety of the people and country	*Sicherheitsbehörde*
mass electronic surveillance [ˌmæs ɪlekˌtrɒnɪk sɜːˈveɪləns]	widespread monitoring of all electronic communications, e.g. internet, cell phones	*elektronische Massenüberwachung*
national debt [ˌnæʃnəl ˈdet]	the money owed by a country to international banks and creditors	*Staatsverschuldung*

TEXT 1 My homeland America

if it was up to me [ɪf ɪt wɒz ˌʌp tə ˈmiː]	used to express a hypothetical decision in a certain situation	*wenn's nach mir ginge*	**page 187**

TEXT 2 Economic dream or nightmare?

peer [pɪə]	person of the same age or social status	*sozial Gleichgestellte/r*	**page 189**
technological capabilities pl [teknəˌlɒdʒɪkl keɪpəˈbɪlətiz]	the ability to use technology to one's advantage	*technologische Möglichkeiten, technische Kompetenz*	**page 190**
to **fall behind sb** [ˌfɔːl bɪˈhaɪnd]	not do as well as sb	*hinter jdm zurückbleiben*	
social safety net [ˌsəʊʃl ˈseɪfti net]	a system of social security such as unemployment insurance that provides financial support for the poor	*soziales (Sicherheits-)Netz*	
health benefits pl [ˈhelθ benɪfɪts]	medical services available as part of health insurance or as extra work benefits	*Krankenversicherungsleistungen*	
retirement benefits pl [rɪˈtaɪəmənt benɪfɪts]	pensions schemes to support people when they stop working due to age	*Rentenversicherungsleistungen*	
shooting [ˈʃuːtɪŋ]	an attack carried out with a gun	*Schießerei*	**page 192**
dispute [dɪˈspjuːt]	argument, difference of opinion	*Streit, Auseinandersetzung*	

TEXT 3 Living on the 'rez'

beverage [ˈbevərɪdʒ]	any kind of drink (except water)	*Getränk*	**page 193**
nutritional value [njuˌtrɪʃənl ˈvæljuː]	a measure of how healthy a type of food is	*Nährwert*	
fresh produce [ˌfreʃ ˈprɒdjuːs]	fresh food particularly fruit and vegetables	*frische Lebensmittel*	**page 194**
diabetes [ˌdaɪəˈbiːtiːz]	medical condition which means the body cannot produce or control insulin	*Zucker(krankheit), Diabetes*	
obesity [əʊˈbiːsəti]	the state of being dangerously overweight	*Übergewicht(igkeit)*	
grocery store AE [ˈgrəʊsəri stɔː]	(small) supermarket	*Lebensmittelgeschäft*	
revenue [ˈrevənjuː]	income	*Einnahmen, Einkünfte*	
nutrition [njuˈtrɪʃn]	study of how food and diet helps people stay healthy	*Ernährung, Nahrung*	

to **make sb aware of sth** [ˌmeɪk əˈweər əv]	bring sth to sb.'s attention	*jdn auf etw aufmerksam machen, jdn auf etw hinweisen*
availability [əˌveɪləˈbɪləti]	the state of being able to be bought, got, found, etc.	*Verfügbarkeit*
demand [dɪˈmɑːnd]	how much customers want to buy a product or a service	*Nachfrage*
groceries pl [ˈɡrəʊsəriːz]	food and other household goods	*Lebensmittel*

TEXT 4 Hyphenated Americans

page 199	to **sever all ties to sth** [ˌsevər ɔːl ˈtaɪz tə]	have nothing to do with sth	*alle Bindungen zu etw abbrechen*
	roots pl [ruːts]	the place, country or culture sb or sb.'s family comes from originally	*Wurzeln*
	heritage [ˈherɪtɪdʒ]	history, traditions and culture of a country or society	*Erbe*
	hyphenated [ˈhaɪfəneɪtɪd]	linked with a hyphen	*mit Bindestrich*
page 200	**traitor** [ˈtreɪtə]	sb who betrays sb/sth, such as a friend or country	*Verräter/in*
	to **embrace a culture** [ɪmˌbreɪs ə ˈkʌltʃə]	adopt or make a new culture your own	*sich eine Kultur bereitwillig zu eigen machen*
	to **have a stake in sth** [həv ə ˈsteɪk ɪn]	have a part or a share in sth that is important to you	*an etw seinen Anteil haben*
page 201	to **pledge allegiance to sb/sth** [ˌpledʒ əˈliːdʒns tə]	promise to support sb/sth	*Treue schwören*

TEXT 5 "From my cold; dead hands"

page 205	**criminologist** [ˌkrɪmɪˈnɒlədʒɪst]	scientist who studies crimes and criminals	*Kriminologe/-in*
	death penalty [ˈdeθ penlti]	a legal punishment where the convicted person is killed	*Todesstrafe*
	background check [ˌbækɡraʊnd ˈtʃek]	when police or officials study sb's life history to see if they have broken the law in the past	*Nachforschungen, polizeiliche Überprüfung*
	to **be subject to sth** [bi ˈsʌbdʒɪkt tə]	be likely to be affected by sth	*einer Sache unterzogen werden*
	mental health [ˌmentl ˈhelθ]	psychological well-being of a person	*geistige Gesundheit*
	proliferation [prəˌlɪfəˈreɪʃn]	increase in numbers	*Ausbreitung, Verbreitung*
	combat-style weapon [ˌkɒmbæt staɪl ˈwepən]	gun etc. that can be used in wars	*Kriegswaffe*
	to **be obsessed with sth** [bi əbˈsest wɪð]	be always worrying about sth in a way that annoys other people	*auf etw fixiert sein*
	unconstitutional [ˌʌnˌkɒnstɪˈtjuːʃənl]	not allowed by the constitution of a country	*verfassungswidrig*
	to **misuse** [mɪsˈjuːz]	not use properly	*missbrauchen*
	mentally deranged [ˌmentli dɪˈreɪnʒd]	mentally ill	*geistesgestört*
page 206	**purchase** [ˈpɜːtʃəs]	sth that you have bought	*Kauf*
	to **obtain sth** [əbˈteɪn]	get sth	*bekommen, erlangen*
	partial [ˈpɑːʃl]	related to only a part of sth	*teilweise*
	concealed weapon [kənˌsiːld ˈwepən]	gun etc. that is hidden or not carried openly	*verborgen getragene Waffe*

TEXT 6 Surveillance or privacy?

page 209	**intelligence agency** [ɪnˈtelɪdʒəns eɪdʒənsi]	a department of a government that collects information about other countries, often secretly	*Geheimdienst*
	legitimacy [lɪˈdʒɪtɪməsi]	the quality of being allowed according to the law	*Rechtmäßigkeit, Gesetzmäßigkeit*
	hostile [ˈhɒstaɪl]	very unfriendly	*feindlich*
	capability [ˌkeɪpəˈbɪləti]	the ability to do sth	*Fähigkeit, Möglichkeit*
	law enforcement [ˌlɔː ɪnˈfɔːsmənt]	the police, FBI, etc.	*Exekutive*

to **prosecute sb** ['prɒsɪkjuːt]	officially charge sb with a crime in court	*jdn strafrechtlich verfolgen*	
excess ['ekses]	extreme behaviour that is unacceptable or illegal	*Exzess, Ausschweifung*	page 210
to **uphold our civil liberties** [ʌpˌhəʊld aʊə ˌsɪvl 'lɪbətiz]	keep individual freedoms safe	*die bürgerlichen Freiheitsrechte bewahren*	
to **pursue a lead** [pəˌsjuː ə 'liːd]	investigate a possible cause (of a crime)	*einem Hinweis nachgehen*	
abuse [ə'bjuːs]	use of sth in a way that is wrong or harmful	*Missbrauch*	
warrant ['wɒrənt]	legal document signed by a judge that gives the police authority to do sth	*Vollmacht*	
secrecy ['siːkrɪsi]	the fact of making sure that nothing is known about sth	*Geheimhaltung, Verschwiegenheit*	

A–Z WORD LIST

Dieses Worterverzeichnis enthält alle in *Crossover 2* Ausgabe Baden-Württemberg eingeführten in den Texten angegebenen Vokabeln in alphabetischer Reihenfolge. Wörter aus den Hörverständnisübungen sind mit einem T gekennzeichnet.

Abkürzungen:
AE = amerikanisches Englisch   jdm = jemandem   pl = plural
BE = britisches Englisch   jdn = jemanden   sb = somebody
etw = etwas   jds = jemandes   sth = something

A

to **abdicate your responsibilities** 190 *sich seiner Verantwortung entziehen*
to **abolish sth** 117 *etw abschaffen*
absence, in the ~ of sth 210 *in Ermangelung einer Sache*
to **absorb sth** 49 *etw aufnehmen, absorbieren*
abuse 116 *Beschimpfung(en)*; 210 *Missbrauch*; to **shout ~ at sb** 106 *jdm laut beschimpfen*
to **accelerate** 89 *beschleunigen*
access (to sth) 8 *Zugang (zu etw), Zugriff (auf etw)*
accessible 40 *erreichbar, zugänglich*
accommodation 83 *Unterkunft, Bleibe*; **emergency ~** 177 *Notunterkunft*
accomplishment, past ~s pl 35 *bisherige Leistungen/Erfolge*
according to 16 *(je) nach, gemäß, laut*
account 108T *Konto*
to **account for sth** 35 *etw ausmachen*
accountant 135 *Buchhalter/in, Steuerberater/in*
accurate 31 *genau*
to **achieve sth** 10 *etw erreichen, etw erzielen*
achievement 35 *Leistung, Erfolg*
acid rain 48 *saurer Regen*
acolyte 163 *Gefolgsmann, Anhänger/in*
acquaintance, chance ~ 130 *Zufallsbekanntschaft*
acquisition 102 *Erwerb, Kauf*
action 19T *Handlung, Tat*
acute 209 *akut*
ad hoc 32 *für den Einzelfall, von Fall zu Fall*
to **adapt** 52 *sich anpassen*
addicted, to be ~ to sth 16 *nach etw süchtig sein*
to **address sth** 105 *sich mit etw beschäftigen, etw thematisieren*
adequate 210 *angemessen, ausreichend*
to **admit sth** 65 *etw zugeben, etw eingestehen*
adopter, early ~ 81 *frühzeitige(r) Anwender/in*

advance 30 *Fortschritt, (Weiter-)Entwicklung*; **technological ~s pl** 210 *technologische Fortschritte*
advanced 23 *fortgeschritten, modern, weiterentwickelt*
advantage, competitive ~ 33 *Wettbewerbsvorteil*
advent 105 *Aufkommen, Auftreten*
adversity 32 *Widrigkeit(en)*
to **advise sb** 78 *jdn beraten*
advisor, strategic policy ~ 84 *Strategieberater/in*
advocate 138 *Befürworter/in*
to **advocate sth** 200 *etw befürworten, sich für etw aussprechen*
to **affect sth** 10 *etw beeinflussen, etw beeinträchtigen*
affiliation 200 *Zugehörigkeit, Mitgliedschaft*
affluent 120 *reich, wohlhabend*
to **afford sth** 10 *sich etw leisten*
affordability 84 *Erschwinglichkeit*
African-American 117 *Afro-Amerikaner/in*
aftermath, in the ~ of sth 209 *nach etw, in der Folge von etw*
agency, intelligence ~ 209 *Geheimdienst*; **security ~** 183 *Sicherheitsbehörde*
agent 177 *Makler/in*; **digital ~** 29 *digitale/r Händler/in*
aging 24 *alternd*
agreement 40 *Vereinbarung, Einigung, Abkommen, Vertrag*
agribusiness 48 *Agrarindustrie, industrielle Landwirtschaft*
agricultural chemicals pl 51 *landwirtschaftliche Chemikalien*
agriculture 23 *Landwirtschaft*
agrochemical 93 *agrochemisch*
aid 176T *(humanitäre) Hilfe*
aim 59 *Ziel, Zweck*
alarming 53 *beunruhigend, erschreckend*
algae blooms pl 57 *Algenblüten*
allegiance 168 *Zugehörigkeitsgefühl, Gefolgschaft*; to **pledge ~ to sb/sth** 201 *Treue schwören*
alternative sources of energy 49 *alternative Energiequellen*

aluminium alloy 89 *Aluminiumlegierung*
ambassador 139 *Botschafter/in*
ambiguous 158 *unklar, zweideutig*
ambition 46 *Ziel, Ehrgeiz, Ambition*
ambitious 23 *ehrgeizig*
ambivalent 151 *ambivalent, zweischneidig*
amount 14 *Menge, Betrag*
anachronism 56 *Anachronismus*
anaerobic digestion 74 *anaerobe Faulung/Vergärung*
to **analyse sth** 15 *analysieren*
ancient 73 *alt, historisch*
anguish 143 *Kummer, Qual(en)*
animal waste 48 *tierische Abfallstoffe, Exkremente*
to **animate** 88 *beleben*
announcement 143 *Durchsage*
annoying 12 *lästig, nervig, ärgerlich*
anonymity 143 *Anonymität*
antagonistic 167 *feindselig*
antique 57 *altertümlich*
apathy 120 *Gleichgültigkeit, Teilnahmslosigkeit*
apparent 88 *offensichtlich, augenscheinlich*
appliances pl, medical ~ 24 *medizinische Geräte*
applicant 79 *Bewerber/in*
to **apply: ~ for sth** 78 *sich für/um etw bewerben*; **~ sth to sth** 73 *etw auf etw anwenden*
approach 40 *Herangehensweise, Ansatz*
to **approach** 43 *näher kommen, sich nähern*
appropriate 12 *angemessen, passend*
archangel 110 *Erzengel*
to **arise** 81 *aufkommen, entstehen*
arrival 117 *Ankunft, Eintreffen*
artificial intelligence 28 *künstliche Intelligenz*
to **ascend** 109 *hochsteigen, besteigen*
aspiration 11 *Ziel, Bestreben*
to **aspire to sth** 9 *nach etw streben*
assembly line 130 *Fließband, Montageband*
assessment 105 *Einschätzung, Beurteilung*

to **assign sb to sth** 131 *jdm etw zuteilen*

to **associate with sb** 111 *mit jdm (gesellschaftlich) verkehren*

to **assume sth** 33 *etw annehmen, etw vermuten*

assumption 84 *Annahme, These, Unterstellung*

astonishing 126 *erstaunlich*

asylum seeker 154 *Asylsuchende/r*

atmosphere 48 *Atmosphäre*

attack 105 *Angriff;* **terrorist ~** 183 *Terroranschlag*

attitude 12 *Einstellung, Haltung*

to **attract sb** 116 *jdn locken*

to **attribute sth to sth** 54 *etw einer Sache zuschreiben*

austerity measures pl 25 *Sparmaßnahmen*

authority 32 *Autorität, Kompetenz, Macht;* 57 *Vollmacht;* 106 *Behörde*

availability 194 *Verfügbarkeit*

available 8 *verfügbar, erhältlich*

aware, to **be ~ of sth** 57 *sich einer Sache bewusst sein;* to **make sb ~ of sth** 194 *jdn auf etw aufmerksam machen, jdn auf etw hinweisen*

awareness 48 *Bewusstsein, Bekanntheit*

awash 70 *unter Wasser, überschwemmt*

B

backdrop 42 *Kulisse, Hintergrund*

background, immigrant ~ 116 *Migrationshintergrund;* **~ check** 205 *Nachforschungen, polizeiliche Überprüfung*

to **back-pedal** 101 *zurückrudern*

balance 81 *Gleichgewicht*

ban (on sth) 62 *Verbot (von etw)*

to **band around sth** 200 *sich um etw scharen*

bankrupt 151 *bankrott, pleite*

banter 143 *(humorvolles) Geplänkel*

baseline 51 *Ausgangswert*

basic 9 *grundsätzlich, einfach, Grund-;* **~ needs** pl 8 *Grundbedürfnisse*

to **batter sth** 70 *auf etw einschlagen, etw bombardieren*

battered 16 *mitgenommen, ramponiert*

battle-hardened 32 *kampferprobt*

to **bear sth** 177 *etw tragen*

beeline 200 *Luftlinie, kürzester Weg*

behalf, on sb's ~ 84 *in jds Namen, für jdn*

belief 52 *Glaube, Überzeugung;* **contrary to popular ~** 174 *entgegen der landläufigen Meinung*

to **belittle sb** 143 *jdn herabsetzen, jdn schlechtmachen*

beloved 135 *geliebt*

to **benefit: ~ (from sth)** 9 *(von etw) profitieren;* **~ sb** 43 *jdm nützen*

benefit 78 *Nutzen, Vorteil*

benefits pl, **health ~** 190 *Krankenversicherungsleistungen;* **retirement ~** 190 *Rentenversicherungsleistungen*

benign 101 *harmlos*

to **berate sb** 143 *jdn beschimpfen, jdn ausschimpfen*

beverage 193 *Getränk*

bias 210 *Voreingenommenheit, Befangenheit*

bile 110 *Galle*

to **billow** 109 *sich aufblähen*

biodegradable 49 *biologisch abbaubar*

biofuel 49 *Biotreibstoff*

biologist, plant molecular ~ 92 *Pflanzenmolekularbiologe/-in*

biomethane 74 *Biomethan, Bioerdgas*

blackmail 105 *Erpressung*

to **blame: ~ sb** 180T *jdm die Schuld geben;* **~ sth on sb/sth** 58 *jdm/einer Sache für etw die Schuld geben*

bland 201 *fade, farblos*

blanket 130 *Decke*

to **bleed** 177 *bluten*

blight-resistant 93 *resistent gegen Fäule*

bloc 151 *Staatenblock;* **trading ~** 174 *Handelsblock, Handelsmacht*

blot 163 *Makel*

blue-collar 117 *in Arbeiterberufen*

boarding house 130 *Pension, Gästehaus*

to **bolster sth** 163 *etw stärken*

to **boost sth** 65 *etw ankurbeln, etw antreiben*

bossy 138 *rechthaberisch, herrisch*

to **botch sth** 154 *etw vermasseln, etw verpfuschen*

boundary 127 *Grenze*

bounds pl, **within the ~ of** 29 *innerhalb*

bounty 190 *Fülle, Belohnung*

bout 144 *Anfall, kurze Phase (einer Krankheit)*

brand 9 *Marke, Markenlogo*

brashness 57 *Unverfrorenheit, Dreistigkeit*

braying 143 *(wie ein Esel) schreiend*

breach, security ~ 106 *Sicherheitslücke, Sicherheitsverletzung*

breakthrough 89 *Durchbruch*

breath 109 *Atem;* to **draw ~** 110 *Atem holen, hier: den ersten Atemzug machen*

breeding, selective ~ 92 *Auslesezüchtung, Selektionszüchtung*

breezy 32 *locker, unbeschwert*

bridge fuel 64 *Überbrückungs-Energieträger*

broadcast media, public ~ 17 *öffentliche Rundfunkmedien*

to **broaden your horizons** 12 *den eigenen Horizont erweitern*

brunt, to **bear the ~ of sth** 126 *Hauptleidtragende/r sein*

bubble 11 *Blase*

to **buck the trend** 17 *sich dem Trend widersetzen, gegen den Strom schwimmen*

bulb, light ~ 80 *Glühbirne*

bulk 174 *Großteil, Masse*

bullying 143 *Mobbing;* **cyber ~** 81 *Cybermobbing*

to **burden** 131 *belasten*

business leader 9 *Betriebsleiter/in, Führungskraft*

buying habits pl 8 *Konsumgewohnheiten*

C

calamitous 70 *katastrophal*

to **call** 69 *zu Besuch kommen, besuchen*

camera shutter 16 *Kameraverschluss*

campaign 59 *Kampagne*

to **campaign for sth** 39T *sich für etw engagieren, für etw auf die Straße gehen*

capability 209 *Fähigkeit, Möglichkeit;* **technological ~ies** pl 190 *technologische Möglichkeiten, technische Kompetenz*

cape 109 *Umhang*

capita, per ~ income 24 *Pro-Kopf-Einkommen*

carbon 49 *Kohlenstoff;* **~ dioxide (CO_2)** 48 *Kohlendioxid;* **~ fibre composite** 89 *Kohlefaserverbundwerkstoff*

carcass, rodent ~es pl 57 *Nagetierkadaver*

career 14 *berufliche Laufbahn, Karriere*

cartel 17 *Kartell*

case, to **make a strong ~ for sth** 163 *gute Argumente für etw anführen*

to **cast sb out** 110 *jdn verstoßen*

category 23 *Rubrik, Kategorie*

cause 48 *Ursache*

CCTV 81 *Videoüberwachung*

to **cease** 89 *aufhören*

celestial 110 *himmlisch, Himmels-*

cemetery 57 *Friedhof*

centrally planned economy 23 *Planwirtschaft*

centre of gravity 174 *Schwerpunkt*

centrepiece 174 *Herzstück, Kern*

century 9 *Jahrhundert*

CEO (Chief Executive Officer) 32 *Geschäftsführer/in*

ceramics, dental ~ 89 *Zahnkeramik*

to **certify sb (as sth) 200** *jdn offiziell zu etw erklären*

to **challenge:** ~ **sb 29** *jdn herausfordern, es mit jdm aufnehmen;* ~ **sth 162** *etw infrage stellen*

chain, food ~ **60** *Nahrungskette*

chance acquaintance 130 *Zufallsbekanntschaft*

chant, homophobic ~**s** *pl* **143** *schwulenfeindliche Gesänge*

chemicals *pl,* **agricultural** ~ **51** *landwirtschaftliche Chemikalien*

child labour 8 *Kinderarbeit*

chord, to strike a ~ **144** *einen Nerv treffen, Anklang finden*

to **circulate 60** *zirkulieren*

cityscape 73 *Stadtbild*

civil: ~ **liberties** *pl* **131** *bürgerliche Freiheitsrechte;* to **uphold our** ~ **liberties 210** *die bürgerlichen Freiheitsrechte bewahren;* ~ **partnership 117** *eingetragene Lebenspartnerschaft;* **C**~ **Rights Movement 117** *Bürgerrechtsbewegung;* ~ **service 151** *öffentlicher Dienst, Staatsdienst;* ~ **war 182** *Bürgerkrieg*

to **claim sth 48** *etw fordern;* **65** *etw behaupten;* **150** *etw beanspruchen*

class, middle ~ **9** *Mittelschicht;* **upper** ~ **116** *Oberschicht;* **working** ~ **116** *Arbeiterschicht;* ~ **system 116** *Klassensystem*

classifiable 177 *klassifizierbar*

to **cleave sth from sth 57** *etw von etw abschneiden*

climate: ~ **change 48** *Klimawandel;* ~**-change refugee 48** *Klimaflüchtling;* ~ **crisis 49** *Klimakrise*

to **climb the ladder 135** *(gesellschaftlich) aufsteigen*

clime 110 *Gefilde*

closet, to **come out of the** ~ **143** *sein Coming-out haben;* **stuck in the** ~ **144** *unfähig, sich zu seiner Homosexualität zu bekennen*

coastal 177 *Küsten-, an der Küste*

to **cocoon yourself 200** *sich einkapseln*

code enforcement 57 *Durchsetzung von Vorschriften*

cohesion, social ~ **127** *sozialer Zusammenhalt*

coincidence 32 *Zufall*

Cold War 183 *Kalter Krieg*

collar, blue-~ **117** *in Arbeiterberufen*

to **collect sth 58** *etw sammeln, etw zusammentragen*

collision 89 *Aufeinanderprallen*

colonist 182 *Siedler/in, Kolonist/in*

colony 116 *Kolonie*

to **combat sth 105** *etw bekämpfen*

combat-style weapon 205 *Kriegswaffe*

combination 24 *Verbindung, Verknüpfung, Kombination*

combustion, internal ~ **engine 80** *Verbrennungsmotor*

to **come:** ~ **out (of the closet) 143** *sein Coming-out haben;* **to** ~ **97** *künftig*

comforts *pl,* **creature** ~ **190** *(durch Wohlstand ermöglichte) Annehmlichkeiten*

to **commit sth 81** *etw (Tat usw.) begehen*

commitment 102 *Zusage, Verpflichtung*

committee, select ~ **162** *Sonderausschuss*

commodity 40 *(Handels-)Ware*

common, to **have sth in** ~ **73** *etw gemeinsam haben;* ~ **law 158** *(geltendes) Recht*

commonality 127 *Gemeinsamkeit*

community 126 *Gemeinde, Gemeinschaft*

comparative 174 *relativ, verhältnismäßig*

compelled, to **feel** ~ **to do sth 139** *sich genötigt sehen, etw zu tun*

to **compete 45T** *konkurrieren*

competitive advantage 33 *Wettbewerbsvorteil*

component, core ~ **51** *Kernbestandteil*

composite, carbon fibre ~ **89** *Kohlefaserverbundwerkstoff*

to **compost 49** *kompostieren*

computer-related skills *pl* **8** *Computerkenntnisse*

concealed weapon 206 *verborgen getragene Waffe*

conceivable 200 *denkbar*

to **concentrate on sth 19** *sich auf etw konzentrieren*

concern 57 *Sorge, Besorgnis;* ~ **for sth 45T** *Rücksicht auf etw*

concise 33 *prägnant, kurz (und bündig)*

conclusion 22 *Schluss*

concrete 88 *Beton*

condescending 126 *herablassend*

conditions *pl,* **working** ~ **8** *Arbeitsbedingungen*

condominium *AE* **70** *Wohnblock mit Eigentumswohnungen*

to **conduct sth 32** *etw durchführen, etw ausführen*

conduit 177 *Kanal*

Confederacy 182 *Konföderation, die Konföderierten Staaten von Amerika*

confidence 32 *Selbstbewusstsein, Zuversicht*

confident 59 *zuversichtlich*

confined, to **be** ~ **to sth 52** *auf etw beschränkt sein*

congressional oversight 210 *Kontrolle durch den Kongress*

to **connect dots 33** *Zusammenhänge herstellen*

connection 15 *Verbindung*

connectivity, mobile ~ **80** *mobile Verbindung*

to **consent 111** *zustimmen, einwilligen*

consequence 13 *Folge, Konsequenz*

to **conserve sth 49** *etw sparen*

to **consider sb/sth sth 109** *jdn/etw für etw halten*

considerable 19T *beträchtlich, erheblich*

consideration 125 *Rücksicht*

to **consist of sth 73** *aus etw bestehen*

consistently 34 *durchweg, beständig, konsequent*

consistently 167 *regelmäßig, beständig, durchweg*

conspicuous consumption 8 *beträchtlicher Konsum*

constant 12 *ständig*

to **constitute sth 9** *etw zahlenmäßig ausmachen*

constitution 182 *Verfassung*

to **constrain sb/sth 210** *jdn/etw einschränken*

constraint 210 *Einschränkung*

construction 70 *Bau*

consultation 24 *Beratung*

consulting firm 29 *Beratungsunternehmen*

consumer society 8 *Konsumgesellschaft*

consumption, conspicuous ~ **8** *beträchtlicher Konsum;* **pattern of** ~ **8** *Konsumverhalten;* **unfit for human** ~ **74** *nicht für menschlichen Verzehr geeignet*

to **contaminate the soil 48** *den Erdboden verseuchen*

to **contend with sth 126** *mit etw kämpfen, mit etw zu kämpfen haben*

continuously 154 *ständig, ununterbrochen*

contract 24 *Vertrag*

to **contradict 210** *widersprechen*

contrary to popular belief 174 *entgegen der landläufigen Meinung*

contrast 38 *Gegensatz*

to **contribute to sth 53** *zu etw beitragen*

contribution 24 *Beitrag*

control, strict ~**s** *pl* **9** *strenge Kontrollen;* **immigration** ~ **117** *Grenzkontrolle;* **gun** ~ **183** *Reglementierung von Waffenbesitz;* to **spiral out of** ~ **143** *außer Kontrolle geraten*

controversial 80 *umstritten*

convenient **11** *praktisch, bequem*

convention **35** *Übereinkommen*

conventional **120** *herkömmlich, konventionell*

conversion rate **168** *Wechselkurs*

to convert sth into sth **74** *etw in etw umwandeln*

to convince sb of sth **17** *jdn von etw überzeugen*

to cooperate **41** *zusammenarbeiten, kooperieren*

cooperation **41** *Zusammenarbeit*

coordination, muscular ~ **110** *Muskelkoordination*

core: ~ body temperature **52** *Körpertemperatur;* ~ component **51** *Kernbestandteil*

corn **49** *Mais*

coronary heart disease **139** *koronare Herzerkrankungen*

corporation, major ~ **29** *Großunternehmen*

correlation **126** *Zusammenhang, Wechselbeziehung*

corresponding **29** *entsprechend*

corrosive **70** *aggressiv, korrosiv, zersetzend*

cosmopolitan **168** *Weltbürger/in*

cost-effective **74** *wirtschaftlich, rentabel, kostengünstig*

cotton **182** *Baumwolle*

counterintuitive **190** *widersinnig*

counterpart **105** *Amtskollege;* male ~ **139** *männliches Pendant*

to cover sth up **187** *etw vertuschen, (Fehler usw.) überspielen*

coward **143** *Feigling*

to cram sth into sth **73** *etw in etw hineinstopfen*

crane **70** *Kran*

crash, Wall Street C~ **183** *Börsenkrach (von 1929)*

to crawl **110** *kriechen*

to creak **42** *ächzen, es kaum schaffen*

creation, wealth ~ **24** *Vermögensbildung, Schaffung von Wohlstand*

creature comforts pl **190** *(durch Wohlstand ermöglichte) Annehmlichkeiten*

credibility **163** *Glaubwürdigkeit*

crime **31** *Kriminalität, Verbrechen*

criminologist **205** *Kriminologe/-in*

critic **14** *Kritiker/in*

critical **52** *entscheidend (für etw)*

to criticize **58** *kritisieren*

crock AE **134** *Schwachsinn*

crop **19T** *(Nutz-, Anbau-)Pflanze, Ernte*

crowdsourced **29** *durch Crowdfunding finanziert*

crucially **36** *vor allem, von entscheidender Bedeutung ist*

to crumble **158** *zerfallen*

crux **200** *Kern*

cue **153** *Stichwort*

culinary **126** *kulinarisch*

to curb **210** *zügeln, eindämmen*

curious **32** *neugierig*

current **60** *Strömung;* **14** *gegenwärtig, derzeitig, aktuell*

to curse **110** *verfluchen*

to curtail sth **110** *etw abbrechen*

curve, behind the ~ **163** *hinterherhinken*

cyber bullying **81** *Cybermobbing*

D

damage **17** *Schaden, Schäden*

damaging **19T** *schädlich*

day of rest **8** *Ruhetag*

de-industrialisation **121** *Deindustrialisierung*

death penalty **205** *Todesstrafe*

debatable **125** *fraglich, strittig*

debate, to host a disruptive ~ **84** *eine kontraproduktive Debatte veranstalten*

debt, national ~ **183** *Staatsverschuldung;* personal ~ **8** *Privatverschuldung*

decade **29** *Jahrzehnt*

deception **144** *(vorsätzliche) Täuschung*

decisively **40** *entscheidend*

Declaration of Independence **116** *Unabhängigkeitserklärung*

decline **27** *Rückgang, Abnahme;* **42** *Verfall, Niedergang*

decorator, painter and ~ **134** *Maler/in und Tapezierer/in*

to decrease **40** *sinken, zurückgehen*

to decry sth **42** *verdammen*

to dedicate yourself to sth **111** *sich einer Sache verschreiben*

defence **151** *Verteidigung*

to defend sb/sth **151** *jdn/etw verteidigen*

defining force **80** *bestimmende Kraft*

deforestation **49** *Entwaldung*

deformed **111** *missgebildet*

to degrade **51** *abbauen, zersetzen*

degrading **36** *entwürdigend*

delay **85** *Verzögerung*

deliberate(ly) **17** *absichtlich, vorsätzlich*

to deliver **33** *liefern, bieten;* **162** *(Macht) ausüben*

demand **194** *Nachfrage;* growing ~ **8** *wachsende Nachfrage*

democracy **57** *Demokratie*

Democratic Party **183** *Demokratische Partei*

demography **41** *Demografie, Bevölkerungsstatistik*

to demonstrate sth **78** *etw nachweisen*

denial **131** *Verweigerung, Vorenthaltung;* to be in ~ **70** *etw nicht wahrhaben wollen, die Augen vor der Wahrheit verschließen*

dental ceramics **89** *Zahnkeramik*

to deny sth **66** *etw leugnen, etw betreiten*

to depend on sb/sth **24** *von jdm/etw abhängen*

dependence **49** *Abhängigkeit*

dependent on sth **23** *abhängig von*

to depict sth **15** *abbilden, darstellen*

to deplete sth **16** *aufbrauchen, erschöpfen*

depression, Great D~ **183** *Weltwirtschaftskrise (von 1929)*

deprived **120** *unterprivilegiert, sozial benachteiligt*

deranged, mentally ~ **205** *geistesgestört*

desertification **48** *Wüstenbildung*

designed, to be ~ to do sth **16** *dazu gedacht sein, etw zu tun*

desolate **56** *öde*

to desolate sth **111** *etw verwüsten*

destination **116** *(Reise-)Ziel*

to destroy sth **29** *etw zerstören*

determined **135** *entschlossen*

detestation **112** *Abscheu, Verachtung*

devastating **70** *verheerend*

development **9** *Entwicklung*

device **17** *Gerät*

diabetes **194** *Zucker(krankheit), Diabetes*

digestion, anaerobic ~ **74** *anaerobe Faulung/Vergärung*

digital: ~ agent **29** *digitale/r Händler/in;* ~ footprint **81** *digitaler Fingerabdruck, digitale Spur;* ~ immigrant **81** *jd, der den Umgang mit Computern erst im Erwachsenalter erlernt hat*

diligent **33** *fleißig, sorgfältig*

diplomacy **162** *Diplomatie*

direction **56** *Richtung*

disabled **130** *Behinderte/r;* mentally/physically ~ **117** *geistig/körperlich behindert*

disadvantage **10** *Nachteil*

to disappear **29** *verschwinden*

to disarm **110** *entwaffnen*

to disassemble sth **17** *etw auseinanderbauen, etw demontieren*

disaster, natural ~ **48** *Naturkatastrophe;* ~ zone **88** *Katastrophengebiet*

disclaimer **153** *Einschränkung, Richtigstellung*

to discredit, to sb's ~ **36** *zu jds Schande*

to discover sth **80** *etw entdecken*

discriminate against sb 116 *jdn diskriminieren*

discrimination 35 *Diskriminierung, Benachteiligung;* to **suffer racial ~** 116 *unter Rassendiskriminierung leiden*

disease, coronary heart ~ 139 *koronare Herzerkrankungen*

to **disengage** 42 *sich abkoppeln, sich lösen*

to **disintegrate** 60 *zerfallen, sich auflösen*

disinterested 167 *neutral, desinteressiert*

to **disown sb/sth** 200 *jdn/etw verleugnen*

to **displace sth** 29 *etw verdrängen, etw ersetzen*

disposal, waste ~ 49 *Abfallentsorgung*

to **dispose of sth** 19T *etw entsorgen*

dispute 192T *Streit, Auseinandersetzung*

to **disqualify sb** 200 *prevent sb (from*

to **disregard sth** 127 *etw ausklammern, etw außer Acht lassen*

to **disrupt sth** 29 *etw stören, etw zerstören*

disruptive, to **host a ~ debate** 84 *eine kontraproduktive Debatte veranstalten*

dissatisfaction 12 *Unzufriedenheit*

distinct from sth 120 *von etw abgegrenzt*

distinctive 120 *eigen, markant, charakteristisch*

distinguished by sth 120 *durch etw gekennzeichnet sein*

to **distort sth** 126 *etw verzerren*

distorted 139 *verzerrt*

distribution network 65 *Leitungsnetz*

disturbing 126 *beunruhigend, alarmierend*

to **ditch sth** 89 *etw wegschmeißen*

diverse 126 *vielfältig, unterschiedlich;* **ethnically ~** 116 *ethnisch vielfältig;* **~ population** 183 *vielfältige/ multikulturelle Bevölkerung*

diversity 36 *Vielfalt;* **ethnic ~** 116 *ethnische Vielfalt*

divisive 125 *polarisierend, kontrovers*

domain, public ~ 81 *öffentlicher Bereich*

domestic 74 *relating to the home;* **~ service** 131 *Arbeit als Hausangestellte/r*

to **dominate sb/sth** 12 *jdn/etw beherrschen, jdn/etw dominieren*

dominating factor 153 *beherrschender Faktor*

dot, to **connect ~s** 33 *Zusammenhänge herstellen*

to **double** 9 *(sich) verdoppeln*

doubt 16 *Zweifel*

to **drain** 57 *entleeren*

drain, storm ~ 70 *(Regenwasser-) Kanal, Kanalisation*

dramatic(ally) 19 *dramatisch*

to **draw breath** 110 *Atem holen, hier: den ersten Atemzug machen*

drinking water 48 *Trinkwasser*

to **drive progress** 80 *den Fortschritt antreiben*

drone 81 *Drohne*

to **drop out** 135 *die Schule abbrechen*

drought 48 *Dürre*

drought-hit 56 *von Trockenheit/Dürre heimgesucht*

durable 17 *langlebig, robust*

dust 16 *Staub*

duty 110 *Pflicht*

E

early adopter 81 *frühzeitige(r) Anwender/in*

to **earmark sth for sth** 194 *etw für etw vorsehen*

to **earn** 8 *verdienen*

to **eclipse sth** 139 *etw in den Schatten stellen*

ecological footprint 93 *Ökobilanz, ökologischer Fußabdruck*

economic: ~ oppression 117 *wirtschaftliche Unterdrückung;* **~ system** 183 *Wirtschaftssystem*

economy 23 *Wirtschaft;* **centrally planned ~** 23 *Planwirtschaft*

ecosystem 49 *Ökosystem*

edge, on ~ 12 *gereizt*

educated 110 *gebildet*

effect 11 *Auswirkung, Effekt*

effeminate 189 *unmännlich, weibisch*

efficiency, energy ~ 64 *Energieeffizienz*

to **elect sb** 146 *jdn wählen*

election 71 *Wahl*

electric grid 209 *Stromnetz*

electricity 19T *Strom*

elimination 35 *Beseitigung*

elite 119 *Elite;* **wealthy ~** 8 *wohlhabende Elite*

to **embrace a culture** 200 *sich eine Kultur bereitwillig zu eigen machen*

to **embrace sth** 32 *etw annehmen*

to **emerge** 126 *bekannt werden, zum Vorschein kommen*

emergence 29 *Entstehung, Aufkommen*

emergency accommodation 177 *Notunterkunft*

emergent 120 *aufstrebend*

emerging powers pl 174 *Schwellenländer*

to **emigrate** 137 *auswandern*

eminently 29 *ausgesprochen, in hohem Maße*

emission 48 *Ausstoß*

to **emit sth** 51 *etw ausstoßen*

to **emphasize sth** 76 *etw betonen*

empirical 93 *empirisch*

employee 32 *Angestellte/r, Arbeitnehmer/in*

to **empower sb** 35 *jdn stärken*

to **enable** 73 *ermöglichen, möglich machen*

to **enclose sth** 70 *umhüllen, einschließen*

to **encourage** 10 *ermuntern, auffordern, ermutigen*

endeavour 110 *Bemühung*

endowed, to **be ~ with sth** 130 *mit etw ausgestattet sein, etw besitzen*

energising 127 *belebend*

energy: alternative sources of ~ 49 *alternative Energiequellen;* **nuclear ~** 49 *Atomenergie;* **renewable ~** 49 *erneuerbare Energie(quellen);* **~ efficiency** 64 *Energieeffizienz;* **~ source** 49 *Energiequelle*

enforcement, code ~ 57 *Durchsetzung von Vorschriften;* **law ~** 209 *Exekutive*

engagement 121 *Engagement, Teilhabe;* **~ with sb** 168 *Auseinandersetzung mit jdm*

engine, internal combustion ~ 80 *Verbrennungsmotor*

engineering, genetic ~ 80 *Gentechnik, Gentechnologie*

to **engulf sth** 37 *einhüllen, umschließen*

to **enhance sth** 90 *etw verbessern, etw stärken*

enlargement 89 *Vergrößerung*

enormous 8 *gewaltig, enorm*

to **ensure sth** 51 *etw gewährleisten, für etw sorgen*

enterprise, local ~ 9 *lokales Unternehmen*

to **entertain sth** 101 *etw erwägen*

entirely 74 *vollständig, völlig*

entry-level 35 *für Berufseinsteiger*

to **enunciate** 168 *äußern*

environment 49 *Umwelt*

environmentalist 130 *Umweltschützer/in*

to **envision sth** 29 *sich etw vorstellen, sich etw ausmalen*

epitome 134 *Verkörperung*

to **epitomise sth** 125 *etw verkörpern*

equal: ~ opportunities pl 117 *Chancengleichheit;* **~ opportunity legislation** 117 *Gleichbehandlungsgesetz(e)*

equality 117 *Gleichberechtigung;* **gender ~** 117 *Gleichberechtigung der Geschlechter*

equitable society 36 *gerechte/ gleichberechtigte Gesellschaft*
era 89 *Epoche, Ära*
to **erase sth** 209 *etw auslöschen*
to **escape poverty** 182 *der Armut entfliehen*
to **eschew sth** 89 *einer Sache aus dem Weg gehen, etw meiden*
essence, in ~ 125 *im Wesentlichen*
essentials pl 8 *notwendige Güter*
to **establish** 96 *gründen, etablieren*
established 120 *etabliert*
ethic, work ~ 182 *Arbeitsmoral*
ethical, to raise ~ questions 80 *ethische Fragen aufwerfen*
ethnic: ~ diversity 116 *ethnische Vielfalt;* **~ identity** 183 *ethnische Identität;* **~ minority** 117 *ethnische Minderheit*
ethnically diverse 116 *ethnisch vielfältig*
Europhile 151 *Befürworter/in Europas*
Eurosceptic 151 *Euroskeptiker/in*
to **evade sth** 205 *etw umgehen, sich einer Sache entziehen*
to **evaporate** 56 *verdunsten*
evasive 64 *ausweichend*
event 9 *Veranstaltung, Ereignis*
eventually 60 *schließlich, am Ende, irgendwann*
everyday 16 *alltäglich, Alltags-*
eviction 135 *Zwangsräumung*
evidence 52 *Beweis(e)*
to **evolve** 29 *entstehen, sich entwickeln*
to **exceed sth** 51 *etw übersteigen, etw übertreffen*
excess 210 *Exzess, Ausschweifung*
excessive 54 *übermäßig, überhöht*
exchange, population ~ 151 *Bevölkerungsaustausch*
executive 64 *Manager/in*
exhaust 48 *Abgas(e)*
to **exist** 17 *(es) geben, vorhanden sein, bestehen, existieren*
existing 17 *vorhanden*
to **expand** 116 *sich erweitern*
expectancy, life ~ 80 *Lebenserwartung*
to **expire** 194 *ablaufen, auslaufen*
to **exploit sth** 24 *etw ausnutzen;* **155T** *etw ausschöpfen, etw nutzen*
exposure 11 *Ausgesetztsein; Kontakt*
to **extend: ~ to sth** 81 *sich auf etw erstrecken;* **~ an invitation to sb** 139 *jdn einladen*
extent 9 *Umfang, Maßstab*
extinct, to become ~ 51 *aussterben*
extinction of species 49 *Artensterben*
extortion 105 *Erpressung*
extract 40 *Auszug, Ausschnitt*
to **extract sth** 74 *etw (aus etw) gewinnen, etw entziehen*

extraction 23 *Abbau (von Rohstoffen)*
extreme, at the opposite ~ 120 *am anderen Ende der Skala*
eye, in the public ~ 9 *im Bewusstsein der Öffentlichkeit;* to **keep an ~ on sb/sth** 110 *jdn/etw im Auge behalten*

F

fabled 200 *legendär, sagenumwoben*
to **face sth** 10 *mit etw konfrontiert werden, einer Sache gegenüberstehen*
to **facilitate sth** 112 *etw ermöglichen, etw unterstützen*
factor, by a ~ of five 51 *um den Faktor fünf*
to **factor sth in** 153 *etw berücksichtigen, etw miteinbeziehen*
factory 8 *Fabrik, Werk*
to **fade** 174 *an Bedeutung verlieren*
to **fail** 17 *versagen, ausfallen*
failure 32 *Versagen, Misserfolg*
fair share 96 *gehörige Anzahl*
(religious) faith 134 *(religiöser) Glaube*
to **fall behind sb** 190 *hinter jdm zurückbleiben*
fallout, radioactive ~ 49 *radioaktiver Niederschlag*
to **fare** 41 *ergehen (es ergeht jdm)*
feature 89 *Merkmal*
feeling 72 *Ansicht, Meinung*
feminism 117 *Feminismus*
fertiliser 51 *Dünger*
fictitious 11 *fiktiv*
figure 26 *Zahl*
fine 21 *Geldstrafe, Bußgeld*
to **fine sb** 57 *jdn zu einer Geldstrafe verurteilen*
finite 12 *endlich, begrenzt;* **~ natural resource** 48 *begrenzte Naturressource;* **~-resource use** 17 *Verbrauch endlicher Ressourcen*
fiscal issue 154 *finanzpolitisches Problem*
fit for purpose 29 *zweckdienlich, tauglich*
fixture 143 *Spiel*
flaw, genetic ~ 80 *genetischer Defekt*
flawed 52 *fehlerhaft, mit Mängeln behaftet*
to **flood** 70 *(über)strömen, (über)fluten*
flooding 48 *Hochwasser*
to **flourish** 17 *florieren*
to **flush sth away** 71 *etw wegspülen*
flushing toilet 80 *Wasserspültoilette*
food chain 60 *Nahrungskette*
footprint, digital ~ 81 *digitaler Fingerabdruck, digitale Spur;* **ecological ~** 93 *Ökobilanz, ökologischer Fußabdruck*
force, defining ~ 80 *bestimmende Kraft;* **labour ~** 23 *Arbeitskräfte*

fore, to bring an issue to the ~ 209 *ein Problem in den Vordergrund rücken*
to **forecast** 24 *vorhersagen*
forefront, to be at the ~ 210 *an vorderster Front stehen, an der Spitze stehen*
foreign direct investment 173 *Direktinvestitionen im Ausland*
Foreign Office 163 *Außenministerium*
forensic techniques pl 105 *gerichtsmedizinische Verfahren*
forestry 23 *Forstwirtschaft*
to **forge sth** 163 *etw schmieden, etw (Freundschaft usw.) schließen*
former 70 *ehemalig, früher*
fossil fuel 49 *fossile Brennstoffe*
to **foster** 93 *begünstigen*
to **found sth** 96 *etw gründen*
foundation 116 *Gründung*
Founding Fathers pl 182 *Gründerväter*
fragile 139 *schwach, zerbrechlich*
to **fragment** 121 *zersplittern, in Bruchstücke zerlegen*
free trade 151 *freier Handel*
freelancer 29 *Selbstständige/r*
fresh produce 194 *frische Lebensmittel*
frontage 177 *Fassade*
frustrated 135 *frustriert*
fuel, bridge ~ 64 *Überbrückungs-Energieträger;* **fossil ~** 49 *fossile Brennstoffe*
to **fund sth** 71 *finanzieren*
fundamental 8 *grundlegend*
fundamentally 36 *grundsätzlich*
funnily enough 167 *komischerweise*
furnace 56 *Ofen*
fuzzy 121 *unscharf*

G

gadget 16 *Gerät, technische Spielerei*
to **galvanize sb to do sth** 138 *jdm den Anstoß geben, etw zu tun*
gamble 154 *Wagnis, Risiko*
game face 32 *(professionelle) Maske, Pokerface*
gaming, virtual reality ~ 81 *PC-Spiele in virtuellen Realitäten*
gay 117 *schwuler Mann*
GDP (Gross Domestic Product) 29 *BIP (Bruttoinlandsprodukt)*
geek 81 *Computerfreak*
gender: ~ equality 117 *Gleichberechtigung der Geschlechter;* **~ gap** 35 *Kluft (zwischen den Geschlechtern), Ungleichbehandlung;* to **close the ~ gap** 117 *geschlechtsspezifische Unterschiede beseitigen;* **~ stereotype** 117 *geschlechtsspezifisches Klischee;* **~-based** 138 *geschlechtsspezifisch*
to **generate sth** 12 *etw erzeugen;* **80** *etw (Einkommen usw.) erwirtschaften*

generous 70 *großzügig, hier: rasant*
genetic: ~ engineering 80 *Gen-technik, Gentechnologie;* **~ flaw** 80 *genetischer Defekt*
given sth 13 *angesichts von etw*
glacier, melting of ~s 48 *Gletscherschmelze*
global warming 48 *Erderwärmung*
gloom 110 *Finsternis*
glory, to wallow in ~ 101 *sich in Ruhm sonnen*
glued-in 17 *eingeklebt*
to gnaw at sth 177 *an etw nagen*
to go: ~ the way of sth 190 *es einer Sache gleichtun, das Schicksal von etw teilen;* **~ to waste** 74 *ungenutzt bleiben, im Müll landen*
goal 10 *Ziel*
goodwill 163 *Wohlwollen*
governor 199 *Gouverneur/in (eines US-Bundesstaates)*
grace 110 *Eleganz*
graduate 24 *Hochschulabsolvent/in*
grain 48 *Getreide*
to grant sb sth 42 *jdm etw gewähren*
granted 190 *zugegeben;* **to take sth for ~** 80 *etw als selbstverständlich erachten*
to grapple with sth 143 *mit etw kämpfen, mit etw zu kämpfen haben*
gravity, centre of ~ 174 *Schwerpunkt*
Great Depression 183 *Weltwirtschaftskrise (von 1929)*
greenhouse gas 48 *Treibhausgas*
gregarious 120 *gesellig*
grid, electric ~ 209 *Stromnetz*
grim 206 *düster, trostlos*
grip, to lose your ~ on sth 162 *etw nicht mehr im Griff haben*
groceries *pl* 194 *Lebensmittel*
grocery store *AE* 194 *Lebens-mittelgeschäft*
grounds *pl,* **on moral/religious ~** 117 *aus moralischen/religiösen Gründen*
groundwater 48 *Grundwasser*
growing demand 8 *wachsende Nachfrage*
growth 24 *Wachstum*
guarantee 17 *Garantie*
gun: ~ control 183 *Reglementierung von Waffenbesitz;* **~ show** 206 *Waffenmesse*
gutter 70 *Regenrinne, Rinnstein*
gyre 60 *Wirbel*

H

habit, buying ~s *pl* 8 *Konsum-gewohnheiten;* **spending ~s** *pl* 8 *Konsumgewohnheiten*
habitat 49 *Lebensraum*
to hail sth as sth 89 *etw als etw feiern*

to handle sth 78 *etw bearbeiten, etw erledigen*
handset 17 *Handy, Mobilgeräte*
to hang out with sb 136 *sich mit jdm herumtreiben*
happen to be 168 *(zufällig) sein*
happiness, pursuit of ~ 117 *das Streben nach Glück*
harbinger 42 *Vorbote*
harmful 19T *schädlich*
harvest 73 *Ernte*
havoc, to wreak ~ 190 *verheerenden Schaden anrichten*
head of state 35 *Staatsoberhaupt*
heading, to be ~ towards sth 53 *zu etw unterwegs sein, auf dem Weg zu etw sein*
health benefits *pl* 190 *Kranken-versicherungsleistungen*
healthcare 8 *Gesundheitsfürsorge*
heatwave 48 *Hitzewelle*
herbicide 48 *Unkrautbekämpfungs-mittel, Herbizid*
heritage 199 *Erbe*
herring, red ~ 93 *Täuschungsmanöver*
hideous 111 *grässlich*
hip replacement 89 *Hüftprothese*
Hispanic 117 *Hispano-Amerikaner/in*
homophobe 143 *Schwulenhasser*
homophobic chants *pl* 143 *schwulen-feindliche Gesänge*
homosexual 117 *homosexuell, gleich-geschlechtlich*
homosexuality 117 *Homosexualität*
honest 114T *ehrlich, aufrichtig*
hose 71 *Schlauch*
hospitable to sth 52 *günstig für etw, wirtlich für etw*
to host a disruptive debate 84 *eine kontraproduktive Debatte veranstalten*
host country 200 *Gastland*
hostile 209 *feindlich*
House of Lords 162 *Oberhaus*
to howl 109 *heulen*
hue 130 *Farbton*
human rights *pl* 151 *Menschenrechte*
human-driven 51 *von Menschen verursacht*
the humanities 35 *Geisteswissen-schaften*
humanity 70 *Menschheit*
humble 135 *bescheiden*
to humiliate sb 131 *jdn demütigen*
humorous 15 *witzig, humorvoll*
hurdle 96 *Hürde, Hindernis*
hurricane 70 *Orkan*
hyphenated 199 *mit Bindestrich*

I

ice cap 52 *Polkappe*
iconography 56 *Bilderwelt, Ikonographie*
ideal 158 *Wertvorstellung*

identical 41 *identisch*
to identify sth 26 *etw genau bestimmen;* 51 *etw herausfinden, etw feststellen*
identity: ethnic ~ 183 *ethnische Identität;* **national ~** 117 *National-bewusstsein, nationales Selbstver-ständnis;* **~ statement** 8 *Produkt-identität (seinen Sozialstatus durch teuren Konsum definieren);* **~ theft** 81 *Identitätsdiebstahl*
ignorance of materiality 89 *Miss-achtung/Unkenntnis der Materialität*
to ignore: to be hard to ~ 9 *schwer zu übersehen sein*
illegal immigrant 117 *illegale/r Einwanderer/in*
illiteracy 126 *Analphabetismus*
to illustrate sth 15 *veranschaulichen, illustrieren*
illustrative 167 *anschaulich*
imagination, to spark sb's ~ 84 *jds Phantasie anregen*
immense 45T *gewaltig, immens*
to immerse sth 70 *(Wasser:) in etw eindringen, in etw laufen*
immigrant 116 *Einwanderer/in;* **digital ~** 81 *jd, der den Umgang mit Computern erst im Erwachsenalter erlernt hat;* **illegal ~** 117 *illegale/r Einwanderer/in;* **~ background** 116 *Migrationshintergrund*
to immigrate 116 *einwandern*
immigration 121 *Einwanderung;* **~ control** 117 *Grenzkontrolle*
immoderate 111 *maßlos*
impact 19T *Auswirkung(en), Einfluss*
to impact on sth 126 *sich auf etw auswirken*
impending 210 *bevorstehend*
imperative 93 *absolutely necessary*
implant 89 *Implantat*
import-reliant 12 *importabhängig*
imposition 12 *Zumutung*
impression 15 *Eindruck*
to imprint sth 36 *prägen*
to improve 10 *verbessern*
improvement 8 *Verbesserung*
in circulation 17 *in/im Umlauf*
in-laws *pl* 96 *Schwiegereltern*
inadvertent 101 *unbeabsichtigt, versehentlich*
incident 116 *Vorfall, Zwischenfall*
incineration 49 *Abfallverbrennung;* **~ plant** 74 *Müllverbrennungsanlage*
to include sth 15 *beinhalten, umfassen, einschließen*
income 24 *Einkommen;* **per capita ~** 24 *Pro-Kopf-Einkommen*
inconsistent 112 *widersprüchlich, unstimmig*
to increase 8 *zunehmen, steigen, steigern*

increasingly 16 *zunehmend, immer +
Komparativ*
indefinitely 97 *ewig*
Indian mutiny 150 *indischer
Aufstand*
indicator 52 *Anzeichen, Indikator*
indifference (to sth) 190 *Gleichgültigkeit (einer Sache gegenüber)*
independence, Declaration of I~ 116
Unabhängigkeitserklärung
indispensable 16 *unverzichtbar,
unerlässlich*
indulgent 57 *maßlos*
Industrial Revolution 8 *industrielle
Revolution*
industrialisation, de- ~ 121
Deindustrialisierung
inefficient 30 *ineffizient,
unwirtschaftlich*
inevitable 210 *unvermeidlich*
influence, pole of ~ 163
Einflussfaktor; **significant ~ 12**
erheblicher Einfluss
influx 154 *Zustrom*
infrastructure 24 *Infrastruktur*
infringe (on) sth 204 *etw
beeinträchtigen*
to **infuriate sb 112** *jdn wütend
machen*
ingenious 16 *einfallsreich, genial*
ingrained 17 *tief verwurzelt*
inherently 92 *an (und für) sich,
grundsätzlich*
inheritance 130 *Erbe*
inherited wealth 116 *geerbtes
Vermögen*
inhospitable 55 *unwirtlich*
inhumanity 177 *Grausamkeit,
Unmenschlichkeit*
innards pl 70 *das Innere*
innovation, technological ~ 81
technische Neuerung
innovative 127 *innovativ*
to **insist 66** *darauf bestehen*
to **institute sth 210** *etw einrichten*
institutional requirement 210
gesetzliche Vorschrift
insular 201 *borniert*
insult 145 *Beleidigung*
insurance underwriter 29
Versicherer/in
insurmountable 126 *unüberwindbar*
to **integrate 41** *integrieren, eingliedern*
intellect 112 *Verstand*
intelligence: artificial ~ 28 *künstliche
Intelligenz;* ~ **agency 209** *Geheimdienst;* ~ **sharing 151** *Informationsaustausch*
interconnectedness 105 *Vernetzung*
interdependent 9 *voneinander
abhängig, verflochten*
intergovernmental 151
zwischenstaatlich

internal combustion engine 80
Verbrennungsmotor
internet-driven 162 *durch das
Internet getrieben/ermöglicht*
interrogation technique 209
Verhörmethode
intervention 183 *Eingreifen,
militärische Intervention*
interview 78 *Vorstellungsgespräch*
intestines pl 60 *Eingeweide*
intolerable 130 *unerträglich*
intrinsic 96 *innewohnend, zugehörig*
introduction 22 *Einleitung*
intrusion 81 *Eingriff, Eindringen*
to **inundate sth 70** *etw überfluten,
etw überschwemmen*
inventory 194 *Warenbestand*
inversion 101 *Umkehrung*
to **invest 23** *investieren*
investment 14 *Investition;* **foreign
direct ~ 173** *Direktinvestitionen im
Ausland*
invitation, to extend an ~ to sb 139
jdn einladen
involved, to be ~ in sth 19T *zu etw
dazugehören, an etw beteiligt sein*
irresolute 189 *unentschlossen, zaghaft*
to **irrigate sth 19T** *etw bewässern*
Islamophobic abuse 126 *islam-
feindliche Beschimpfungen*
island nation 174 *Inselstaat*
isolated 143 *einzelne/r/s*
isolating 139 *ausgrenzend, abweisend*
issue 16 *Problem;* **126** *Thema, Frage;*
to **bring an ~ to the fore 209** *ein
Problem in den Vordergrund rücken;*
to **rule on an ~ 205** *(Justiz:) in einer
Frage entscheiden*
to **issue sth 17** *etw ausstellen, etw
ausgeben*
item 14 *Artikel, Ware;* **luxury ~ 8**
Luxusgut

J

jam, to be in a ~ 187 *in der Klemme
sitzen*
to **jet off 96** *(ab)düsen*
"Jim Crow" laws 117 *Gesetze zur
Rassendiskriminierung*
job: ~ for life 8 *lebenslange
Beschäftigung;* ~ **interview 78**
Vorstellungsgespräch
journal 110 *Tagebuch*
justified 111 *gerechtfertigt*

K

to **keep an eye on sb/sth 110** *jdn/
etw im Auge behalten*
keeping, in ~ with 73 *in Übereinstimmung mit*
kelp 74 *Kelp, Seetang*
keyhole surgery 80 *minimalinvasive
Chirurgie*

knowledge 15 *Wissen;* ~**-based 24**
wissensbasiert

L

laborious 131 *anstrengend, mühsam*
labour: child ~ 8 *Kinderarbeit;* ~
costs pl 174 *Lohnkosten,
Arbeitskosten;* ~ **force 23**
Arbeitskräfte; ~ **market 80**
Arbeitsmarkt; ~**-intensive 174**
arbeitsaufwändig, lohnintensiv
lack 30 *Mangel*
ladder, to climb the ~ 135
(gesellschaftlich) aufsteigen
lag 33 *Verzögerung, Hinterherhinken*
to **lag behind sb 189** *hinter jdm
zurückbleiben*
landfill site 49 *Mülldeponie*
landowner 84 *Grundbesitzer/in*
language barrier 155T *Sprachbarriere*
to **last 17** *halten, andauern*
launch 83 *Markteinführung*
to **launch sth 138** *etw (Aktion usw.)
starten*
law, common ~ 158 *(geltendes)
Recht;* **"Jim Crow" ~s 117** *Gesetze
zur Rassendiskriminierung;* **system of
~ 151** *Rechtssystem;* ~ **enforcement
209** *Exekutive*
law-abiding 205 *unbescholten*
lawless 154 *rechtlos, gesetzlos*
to **lay sth out 177** *etw ausbreiten*
lead, to pursue a ~ 210 *einem Hinweis
nachgehen*
leader 32 *Führungskraft*
leak 57 *Leck, Undichtigkeit*
to **leak away 41** *schwinden, weniger
werden*
leakage 65 *Verlust durch Auslaufen*
to **leave sb/sth behind 97** *jdn/etw
zurücklassen, jdn/etw hinterlassen;*
150 *jdn/etw überflügeln*
ledge 177 *Felsvorsprung, Kante*
legal 35 *gesetzlich, rechtlich*
legislation, equal opportunity ~ 117
Gleichbehandlungsgesetz(e)
legitimacy 209 *Rechtmäßigkeit,
Gesetzmäßigkeit*
leisure activity 8 *Freizeitaktivitäten*
leper 130 *Aussätzige/r*
lesbian 117 *lesbische Frau*
level 8 *Niveau, Stand, Höhe;* **entry-~
35** *für Berufeinsteiger;* **rising sea ~s
pl 48** *steigende Meeresspiegel;* to **do
your ~ best 130** *sein Möglichstes tun*
to **leverage sth 29** *sich etw (voll) zu
Nutze machen, etw zur Gänze
ausschöpfen*
liability 57 *Haftung, Haftpflicht*
liberty, civil ~ies pl 131 *bürgerliche
Freiheitsrechte;* to **uphold our civil
~ies 210** *die bürgerlichen
Freiheitsrechte bewahren*

life expectancy 80 *Lebenserwartung*
lifestyle 9 *Lebensstil, -führung, -art*
lifetime 80 *Lebensdauer*
light bulb 80 *Glühbirne*
likely 18 *wahrscheinlich*
linchpin 189 *wesentliche Stütze*
to **line up 96** *anstehen, sich anstellen*
linear 17 *geradlinig, linear*
literally 74 *buchstäblich*
litter 60 *Abfall, Müll*
livelihood 29 *Lebensgrundlage, Lebensunterhalt*
living standard 123T *Lebensstandard*
local enterprise 9 *lokales Unternehmen*
to **look up to sb 9** *zu jdm aufsehen*
to **loom 41** *sich abzeichnen, drohen*
loop, tape ~ 143 *Tonbandschleife*
to **loose sb/sth 111** *jdn/etw loslassen*
lord, House of L~s 162 *Oberhaus*
to **lose out 168** *schlecht wegkommen*
loss 31 *Verlust*
lucky stars *pl*, to **thank your ~ 186** *sich glücklich schätzen, dem Schicksal danken*
luxury item 8 *Luxusgut*

M

mainstream 163 *gängig*
to **maintain sth 12** *etw aufrechterhalten, etw (finanziell) unterhalten*
major 9 *groß, bedeutend;* ~ **corporation 29** *Großunternehmen*
malaise 190 *Missstand*
male counterpart 139 *männliches Pendant*
malware 81 *Schadsoftware*
to **manifest 89** *sich zeigen, sichtbar werden*
manifestation 143 *Ausdruck, Erscheinung*
to **manipulate sb/sth 12** *jdn/etw manipulieren*
man-made 48 *von Menschen verursacht*
manual, service ~ 17 *Serviceanleitung, Wartungshandbuch*
manufacture 89 *Fertigung, Herstellung*
manufacturing 23 *Herstellung, Produktion;* ~ **sector 174** *Herstellungssektor, verarbeitende Industrie*
to **marginalise sb 127** *jdn ausgrenzen*
marine 60 *Meeres-, See-*
marine life 48 *Meereslebewesen*
marked out, to be ~ by sth 168 *sich durch etw auszeichnen*
market based 23 *marktwirtschaftlich*
to **maroon 57** *stranden, auf Grund setzen*
marvel, technological ~ 89 *technisches Wunderwerk*

mass: ~ electronic surveillance 183 *elektronische Massenüberwachung;* ~ **production 8** *Massenproduktion*
massive 39T *groß, gewaltig*
mate 112 *Partner/in, Gefährte/-in*
mayhem 71 *(fürchterliches) Chaos*
meaning 18 *Bedeutung, Sinn*
meaningful 162 *sinnvoll, sinn*
means 15 *Mittel*
measure 107 *Maßnahme;* **austerity ~s** *pl* **25** *Sparmaßnahmen*
medical appliances *pl* **24** *medizinische Geräte*
to **meld sth together with sth 154** *etw mit etw in einen Topf werfen, etw mit etw kombinieren*
melting: ~ of glaciers 48 *Gletscherschmelze;* ~ **pot 116** *Schmelztiegel*
member: ~ of parliament 35 *(Parlaments-)Abgeordnete/r;* ~ **state 151** *Mitgliedsstaat*
memorable 180 *einprägsam*
memory 110 *Gedächtnis;* ~ **card 16** *Speicherkarte*
mental health 205 *geistige Gesundheit*
mental input 11 *geistige Anreize*
mentally: ~ deranged 205 *geistesgestört;* ~ **disabled 117** *geistig behindert*
to **mention sth 16** *etw erwähnen, etw nennen*
mercy, to be at the ~ of sb/sth 57 *jdm/einer Sache ausgeliefert sein*
metaphysical 126 *metaphysisch*
methane 65 *Methangas*
method 19 *Verfahren, Methode*
microplastics *pl* **60** *Mikroplastikteile*
middle: ~ class 9 *Mittelschicht;* ~ **management 29** *mittleres Management*
mind-boggling 70 *unglaublich, unfassbar*
miniature 89 *sehr klein*
minority 116 *Minderheit;* **ethnic ~ 117** *ethnische Minderheit*
misplaced 57 *deplatziert, unangebracht*
mistreatment 116 *schlechte Behandlung*
to **mistrust sb 127** *jdm misstrauen*
to **misuse 205** *missbrauchen*
mixed bag 153 *uneinheitlich, sehr gemischt*
mobile connectivity 80 *mobile Verbindung*
mobility, social ~ 116 *soziale Mobilität*
modification 206 *Änderung, Abwandlung*
molecular biologist, plant ~ 92 *Pflanzenmolekularbiologe/-in*
money-spinning 74 *gewinnbringend, hoch profitabel*

moniker 93 *Spitzname*
to **monitor sb/sth 81** *jdn/etw überwachen*
to **monitor sth 78** *überwachen*
monolithic 93 *groß, mächtig;* ~ **culture 183** *erstarrte, nicht wandlungsfähige Kultur*
moral 127 *moralisch*
morality 126 *Moral*
motivational 144 *motivierend*
to **mould sb/sth 11** *jdn/etw formen*
mound 177 *Hügel, Haufen*
mournful 110 *traurig*
to **move up in society 117** *gesellschaftlich aufsteigen*
multicultural 116 *multikulturell*
multiculturalism 116 *Multikulturalismus*
multinational company 9 *multinationales Unternehmen, Konzern*
muscular coordination 110 *Muskelkoordination*
mushy 199 *schmalzig, kitschig*
mutiny, Indian ~ 150 *indischer Aufstand*

N

national: ~ debt 183 *Staatsverschuldung;* ~ **identity 117** *Nationalbewusstsein, nationales Selbstverständnis*
Native American 116 *amerikanische/r Ureinwohner/in*
natural disaster 48 *Naturkatastrophe*
needs *pl* **12** *Bedürfnisse, Bedarf;* **basic ~ 8** *Grundbedürfnisse*
negligible 153 *vernachlässigbar, unerheblich*
net 174 *netto*
networking services *pl,* **social ~ 80** *Anbieter sozialer Netzwerkdienste*
nickel superalloy 89 *Nickel-Superlegierung*
nightmare 143 *Albtraum*
nitrogen 51 *Stickstoff*
nominee 189 *Kandidat/in*
non-essentials *pl* **8** *Unwesentliches*
Nordic 35 *nordeuropäisch*
norm 51 *Regel, Norm*
nostalgic portrayal 190 *verklärte Darstellung*
notable 117 *bedeutend, bemerkenswert*
noticeable 35 *erkennbar, merklich, spürbar*
notion 32 *Gedanke, Auffassung*
notwithstanding 57 *trotz*
novel 209 *neu, neuartig*
nowadays 10 *heutzutage, heute*
nuclear: ~ energy 49 *Atomenergie;* ~ **waste 49** *Atommüll*
numerous 23 *zahlreich*
nutrition 194 *Ernährung, Nahrung*
nutritional value 193 *Nährwert*

O

obesity **194** *Übergewicht(igkeit)*
obligation **76** *Verpflichtung*
obliged, to be ~ to do sth **130** *gezwungen sein, etw zu tun; etw tun müssen*
oblivious, to be ~ of sth **70** *etw nicht wahrnehmen*
obsessed, to be ~ with sth **205** *auf etw fixiert sein*
obsolescence, planned ~ **17** *geplanter Verschleiß, eingebaute Alterung*
obstacle **35** *Hindernis*
to obtain sth **206** *bekommen, erlangen*
occupation **119** *Beschäftigung*
to occur **29** *vorkommen, auftreten*
off, to be better ~ **154** *es besser haben*
offensive **145** *beleidigend*
offer, on ~ **8** *im Angebot*
oil **49** *Erdöl*
old folks *pl* **131** *die Alten*
online presence **81** *Internetpräsenz*
open source **83** *(Software:) quelloffen*
opponent **105** *Gegner*
opportunity **32** *Chance, Gelegenheit*
opposite, at the ~ extreme **120** *am anderen Ende der Skala*
to oppress sb **36** *jdn unterdrücken*
oppression, economic ~ **117** *wirtschaftliche Unterdrückung*
organic waste **49** *Biomüll*
organization **10** *Unternehmen, Organisation*
originally **109** *ursprünglich*
to originate from **116** *stammen aus*
ostentatious **190** *prahlerisch, pompös*
otherwise **111** *sonst, andernfalls*
outbreak **174** *Ausbruch*
outdated **116** *überholt, veraltet*
outlet **41** *Laden, Geschäft*
to outpace sb **35** *jdn überholen, jdn abhängen*
outward looking **168** *außenorientiert*
outward-facing **174** *nach außen orientiert*
to overcome sth **32** *etw überwinden*
overdrive, to go into ~ **52** *auf Hochtouren laufen*
overdue notice **135** *Zahlungserinnerung, Mahnung*
to overpump **48** *abpumpen, trockenpumpen*
overreach **209** *Überreaktion, Übergriff(e)*
to override sth **36** *Vorrang vor etw haben*
to overrun sth **116** *etw überfluten, etw überschwemmen*
overseas **130** *Übersee-, im Ausland*
to overshare **101** *zu viele persönliche Informationen preisgeben*
oversight, congressional ~ **210** *Kontrolle durch den Kongress*
to overtake sb/sth **80** *jdn/etw überholen*
to own sth **35** *etw besitzen*
ownership, to take ~ of sth **32** *sich etw zu eigen machen*

P

painter and decorator **134** *Maler/in und Tapezierer/in*
palm oil **49** *Palmöl*
to pander to sb/sth **200** *sich bei jdm/ etw anbiedern*
paradigm shift **93** *Paradigmenwechsel*
paragraph **22** *(Text:) Absatz*
parliament, member of ~ **35** *(Parlaments-)Abgeordnete/r*
parliamentary system **151** *parlamentarisches System*
parochial **201** *beschränkt, engstirnig*
partial **206** *teilweise*
to participate in sth **139** *an etw teilnehmen*
particular **11** *speziell, bestimmt*
partition **151** *Teilung*
partnership, civil ~ **117** *eingetragene Lebenspartnerschaft*
party, Democratic P~ **183** *demokratische Partei;* **Republican P~** **183** *Republikanische Partei*
to pass sth **22** *etw (Gesetz) verabschieden, etw beschließen*
passenger liner **89** *Passagierdampfer*
Passover **201** *Passah*
past accomplishments *pl* **35** *bisherige Leistungen/Erfolge*
patch **60** *Stück (Land), Fläche*
patch **130** *Flicken (Stück Stoff)*
pattern: ~ of consumption **8** *Konsumverhalten;* **working ~s** *pl* **80** *Arbeitsmuster, Arbeitsmodelle*
peace activist **130** *Friedensaktivist/in*
peak standard of living **41** *höchstmöglicher Lebensstandard*
peer **189** *sozial Gleichgestellte/r*
penalty, death ~ **205** *Todesstrafe*
penitentiary *AE* **187** *Gefängnis*
per capita income **24** *Pro-Kopf-Einkommen*
to perceive **139** *wahrnehmen, verstehen*
percentage **9** *Prozentsatz, Anteil*
to perform sth **28** *etw ausführen*
performance **32** *Leistung(en), Abschneiden*
permanent **18** *dauerhaft*
perpetrator **106** *Täter/in*
perpetuation **36** *Aufrechterhaltung, Fortschreibung*
to persecute sb **127** *jdn verfolgen, jdn schikanieren*
persecution, religious ~ **182** *Verfolgung aus religiösen Gründen*
personal debt **8** *Privatverschuldung*

to persuade sb **17** *jdn überzeugen, jdn überreden*
pesticide **48** *Schädlingsbekämpfungsmittel, Pestizid*
petrol *BE* **45T** *Benzin*
physically disabled **117** *körperlich behindert*
picture, the big ~ **32** *das große Ganze*
to pinpoint sth **51** *etw genau bestimmen;* **210** *etw genau lokalisieren*
pioneer spirit **182** *Pioniergeist*
pivotal **36** *zentral, ausschlaggebend*
plain **19T** *einfach*
plant molecular biologist **92** *Pflanzenmolekularbiologe/-in*
plantation **116** *Plantage;* **sugar ~** **150** *Zuckerplantage*
to pledge **102** *geloben;* **~ allegiance to sb/sth** **201** *Treue schwören*
to plummet **71** *abstürzen, stark fallen*
to plunge in **56** *hineinspringen*
point, to get to the ~ **33** *(direkt) zur Sache kommen*
poisonous **48** *giftig*
pole of influence **163** *Einflussfaktor*
to police sth **81** *etw überwachen*
policy advisor, strategic ~ **84** *Strategieberater/in*
poll **153** *Meinungsumfrage*
pollutant **48** *Schadstoff*
to pollute sth **49** *etw verschmutzen*
pollution **48** *(Umwelt-)Verschmutzung*
poo **74** *A-a, Kacke*
pool of human resources **36** *Gesamtvorrat an Humanvermögen*
population, diverse ~ **183** *vielfältige/ multikulturelle Bevölkerung;* **urban ~** **48** *städtische Bevölkerung;* **~ exchange** **151** *Bevölkerungsaustausch*
porous **101** *durchlässig*
portrayal, nostalgic ~ **190** *verklärte Darstellung*
to pose a danger **105** *eine Gefahr darstellen*
possession **8** *Besitztum*
post-apocalyptic **71** *Weltuntergangs-*
potentially **12** *möglicherweise*
pottery **37** *Töpferwaren, Keramik*
to pour **70** *fließen, strömen*
poverty **117** *Armut;* **to escape ~** **182** *der Armut entfliehen;* **urban ~** **8** *Stadtarmut*
power, solar ~ **49** *Solarenergie;* **emerging ~s** *pl* **174** *Schwellenländer*
powerless **58** *machtlos*
pragmatic **167** *pragmatisch*
precedent **195** *vergleichbarer Fall, Beispiel*
precious **130** *kostbar, wertvoll*
predecessor **174** *Vorgänger/in*

rein, to give full ~ to sb **89** *jdm alle Freiheiten bieten*

to **reject 126** *ablehnen, zurückweisen*

related to sth 41 *mit etw verbunden, im Zusammenhang mit etw*

to **release sth 17** *veröffentlichen, auf den Markt bringen;* **48** *etw abgeben;* **51** *etw freisetzen*

relentless 32 *unermüdlich, unablässig*

relevant 30 *nötig (für etw), wichtig (für etw), relevant*

reliable 31 *zuverlässig*

religious: ~ extremist 116 *religiöse/r Extremist/in;* **faith 182** *Glaube;* **~ persecution 182** *Verfolgung aus religiösen Gründen*

to **relish sth 32** *etw genießen*

to **relocate 37** *verlagern, verlegen, umsiedeln*

to **rely on sth 10** *auf etw angewiesen sein*

remorse 111 *Reue*

to **render 106** *machen*

renewable energy 49 *erneuerbare Energie(quellen)*

renewables *pl* **64** *erneuerbare Energiequellen*

renowned 174 *(für etw) berühmt, renommiert*

to **repair sth 16** *etw reparieren*

to **replace sth 17** *etw ersetzen*

to **represent sth 26** *etw darstellen, etw repräsentieren*

representative 167 *repräsentativ*

Republican Party 183 *Republikanische Partei*

to **request sth 151** *um etw bitten*

to **require sth 19T** *etw erfordern, etw benötigen*

requirement, institutional ~ 210 *gesetzliche Vorschrift;* **regulatory ~s** *pl* **92** *behördliche/gesetzliche Anforderungen*

reservation 182 *Reservat*

reservoir 57 *Stausee*

resolution, solemn ~ 131 *feierlicher Beschluss*

resource-scarce 42 *arm an Ressourcen*

resources *pl* **9** *Rohstoffe, Mittel, Ressourcen*

to **respond to sth 70** *auf etw reagieren*

responsibility, to abdicate your ~ies 190 *sich seiner Verantwortung entziehen*

rest, day of ~ 8 *Ruhetag*

to **restrict sth 12** *etw einschränken*

restructuring 121 *Umstrukturierung*

result 19 *Ergebnis, Resultat*

to **resume sth 144** *etw wiederaufnehmen*

retail 23 *Einzelhandel*

to **reticulate 177** *netzförmig anlegen*

retired 25 *im Ruhestand*

retiree 73 *Rentner/in*

retirement benefits *pl* **190** *Rentenversicherungsleistungen*

reuse sth 49 *etw wiederverwenden*

revenge 112 *Rache*

revenue 194 *Einnahmen, Einkünfte*

reverence 33 *Ehrfurcht*

to **reverse sth 70** *etw umkehren*

to **revert to sth 88** *zu etw zurückkehren, in etw zurückfallen*

Revolutionary War 182 *Revolutionskrieg*

rewarding 29 *lohnend, bereichernd*

rhetoric 125 *Sprache, Rhetorik, Phrasendrescherei*

rifle 204 *Gewehr*

right of suffrage 131 *Wahlrecht*

righteousness 201 *Rechtschaffenheit*

rip 16 *Riss*

rising sea levels *pl* **48** *steigende Meeresspiegel*

risk, to be worth the ~ 92 *das Risiko wert sein*

road, on the ~ 134 *unterwegs*

robust 52 *widerstandsfähig, robust*

rodent carcasses *pl* **57** *Nagetierkadaver*

rooted 168 *verwurzelt*

roots *pl* **199** *Wurzeln*

to **rot sth 70** *etw verrotten lassen*

rotate 73 *sich drehen, rotieren*

routine 210 *alltäglich*

row 29 *Reihe*

rubbish 15 *Müll*

rugged 189 *rau, robust*

to **rule on an issue 205** *(Justiz:) in einer Frage entscheiden*

to **run: ~ out 16** *zu Ende gehen, knapp werden;* **~ rampant 36** *um sich greifen, an der Tagesordnung sein*

rural 64 *ländlich*

rust 177 *Rost*

S

sacrifice 135 *Opfer*

safeguard 210 *Schutzmaßnahme*

safety net, social ~ 190 *soziales (Sicherheits-)Netz*

sake, for the ~ of sb 135 *jdm zuliebe, um jds willen*

salad bowl 117 *Salatschüssel*

salary 10 *Gehalt*

same-sex marriage 117 *gleichgeschlechtliche Ehe*

sanctuary, to give ~ to sb 154 *jdm Zuflucht gewähren*

sanitation 48 *sanitäre Anlagen*

satellite observation 81 *Satellitenüberwachung*

to **saturate sth 9** *etw durchdringen*

saturation, to reach ~ 17 *Sättigung erreichen*

to **save: ~ sb/sth 63** *jdn/etw retten;* **~ sth 58** *etw sparen, etw einsparen*

savings *pl* **119** *Ersparnisse*

scaffolding 70 *Gerüst*

scale 29 *Umfang, Maßstab;* **at small ~s 89** *in kleinem Maßstab, in kleinen Dimensionen;* **on a vast ~ 81** *in großem Maßstab*

scales *pl*, to **tilt the ~ toward sb 190** *die Waage zu jds Gunsten neigen*

scarce 41 *knapp;* **resource-~ 42** *arm an Ressourcen*

scare tactics *pl* **93** *Panikmache*

scattered 158 *verstreut*

scenario 70 *Szenarium, Szenario*

to **screen sb 80** *jdn durchleuchten, jdn überprüfen*

scrub 56 *Gestrüpp*

scrutiny, to come under ~ 96 *auf dem Prüfstand stehen;* **social ~ 102** *Überwachung des sozialen Lebens*

sea turtle 60 *Meeresschildkröte, Seeschildkröte*

seal 60 *Seehund, Robbe*

seaweed 73 *Seetang*

secession 182 *Abspaltung, Sezession*

secrecy 210 *Geheimhaltung, Verschwiegenheit*

sectarianism 126 *Sektierertum, Sektenwesen*

secure 39T *sicher*

to **secure sth 174** *etw sichern*

security 81 *Sicherheit;* **~ agency 183** *Sicherheitsbehörde;* **~ breach 106** *Sicherheitslücke, Sicherheitsverletzung*

to **seek to do sth 42** *versuchen, etw zu tun*

segregation 117 *Rassentrennung*

select committee 162 *Sonderausschuss*

selective breeding 92 *Auslesezüchtung, Selektionszüchtung*

self-evident 130 *selbstverständlich, offensichtlich*

self-governing 150 *selbstverwaltet*

self-interest 42 *Egoismus, Eigennutz*

self-interested 41 *eigennützig*

self-pity 144 *Selbstmitleid*

sense, to make ~ 76 *sinnvoll sein, vernünftig sein;* **~ of moral purpose 190** *moralisches Empfinden*

sensibilities *pl* **200** *Empfinden, Wertvorstellungen*

sensitive 139 *einfühlsam, empfindsam*

service, civil ~ 151 *öffentlicher Dienst, Staatsdienst;* **domestic ~ 131** *Arbeit als Hausangestellte/r;* **~ manual 17** *Serviceanleitung, Wartungshandbuch*

service-based 174 *dienstleistungsorientiert*

set 162 *Kategorie, Gruppe*

to **set: ~ in 96** *(Inhalt) begreifen,*

ankommen; ~ **sth aside** 32 *etw vergessen, auf etw verzichten*
setback 42 *Rückschlag*
settlement 97 *Ansiedlung, Siedlung*
settler 116 *Siedler/in*
seven-fold 51 *siebenfach*
to **sever all ties to sth** 199 *alle Bindungen zu etw abbrechen*
severe 57 *schwer, heftig, ernst*
sewage 48 *Ab-/Schmutzwasser;* ~ **system** 71 *Abwassersystem*
sexuality 143 *Sexualität*
to **sexualize** 138 *sexualisieren*
shaken, to be ~ by sth 209 *von etw erschüttert werden*
shale gas 64 *Schiefergas*
shame 116 *Schande, Scham;* S~ **on you!** 199 *Pfui (Teufel)!*
shape, to be in bad ~ 135 *in schlechter Verfassung sein*
to **shape sth** 40 *etw formen, etw gestalten*
share 17 *Anteil;* **fair ~** 96 *gehörige Anzahl*
sharing, intelligence ~ 151 *Informationsaustausch*
sheer 36 *schier, rein;* ~ **privilege** 139 *absolutes Privileg*
shift 23 *Verlagerung;* **paradigm ~** 93 *Paradigmenwechsel*
to **shift** 52 *(sich) verlagern, (sich) verschieben*
shipbuilding industry 150 *Schiffbauindustrie*
shipping 173 *Schifffahrt*
to **shiver** 88 *zittern*
to **shoot up** 52 *hochschnellen*
shooting 192T *Schießerei*
shopaholic 8 *Kaufsüchtige/r*
short, to be well ~ of sth 35 *weit unter etw liegen*
shortage 29 *Mangel;* **water ~** 48 *Wasserknappheit*
short-term 18 *kurzfristig*
shutter, camera ~ 16 *Kameraverschluss*
siege, to be under ~ 102 *belagert werden*
to **sift through sth** 210 *etw durchsuchen*
significant influence 12 *erheblicher Einfluss*
silicon chip 89 *Siliziumchip*
similarly 40 *ebenso, auf gleiche Weise*
simplistic 119 *(zu) simpel, (zu) einfach*
to **skip sth** 97 *etw auslassen, etw unterlassen*
slave 116 *Sklave/in;* ~ **trade** 150 *Sklavenhandel*
slavery 116 *Sklaverei*
to **slip into sth** 11 *in etw hineinrutschen*

slowly and steadily 35 *langsam und stetig*
to **slump** 177 *abrutschen, absacken*
slur 135 *Beleidigung, Verunglimpfung*
to **snap sb** 102 *jdn ablichten, jdn knipsen*
to **soak sth up** 60 *etw aufnehmen, etw absorbieren*
to **soar** 51 *in die Höhe schnellen, sprunghaft ansteigen*
sobering 189 *ernüchternd*
social: ~ cohesion 127 *sozialer Zusammenhalt;* ~ **mobility** 116 *soziale Mobilität;* ~ **networking services** pl 80 *Anbieter sozialer Netzwerkdienste;* ~ **safety net** 190 *soziales (Sicherheits-)Netz;* ~ **scrutiny** 102 *Überwachung des sozialen Lebens*
to **socialize (with sb)** 122 *(mit jdm) Umgang pflegen, (mit jdm) gesellschaftlich verkehren*
societal 153 *gesellschaftlich*
society, consumer ~ 8 *Konsumgesellschaft;* **equitable ~** 36 *gerechte/gleichberechtigte Gesellschaft*
soda AE 193 *alkoholfreies Getränk*
soil 110 *Erde, Erdboden;* to **contaminate the ~** 48 *den Erdboden verseuchen*
solar: ~ power 49 *Solarenergie;* ~ **technology** 24 *Solartechnik*
solemn resolution 131 *feierlicher Beschluss*
to **solve sth** 49 *etw lösen*
sophisticated 17 *raffiniert, ausgeklügelt*
sordid 131 *schmutzig*
sour 177 *sauer*
source 26 *Quelle;* ~ **of wealth** 150 *Vermögensquelle, Wohlstandsquelle;* **alternative ~s of energy** 49 *alternative Energiequellen;* **energy ~** 49 *Energiequelle;* **open ~** 83 *(Software:) quelloffen*
Soviet Union 183 *Sowjetunion*
to **spark sb's imagination** 84 *jds Phantasie anregen*
species 42 *Art, Gattung;* **extinction of ~** 49 *Artensterben*
specs pl, **tech ~** 102 *technische Daten*
speed 28 *Geschwindigkeit*
spending habits pl 8 *Konsumgewohnheiten*
spice 150 *Gewürz*
to **spiral out of control** 143 *außer Kontrolle geraten*
spirit, pioneer ~ 182 *Pioniergeist*
spiritual 125 *spirituell, geistlich*
to **spoil sth** 12 *etw verderben, etw ruinieren*
sponsorship 9 *Unterstützung, Förderung, Sponsoring*

to **spot sth** 32 *etw erkennen, etw entdecken*
sprawl, urban ~ 89 *Zersiedlung*
spray 93 *Spritzmittel*
to **squabble over sth** 42 *sich wegen etw zanken/streiten*
stability, price ~ 84 *Preisstabilität*
stable 53 *stabil*
stage 19T *Phase, Stadium, Etappe;* 22 *Bühne*
stake, to have a ~ in sth 200 *an etw seinen Anteil haben*
to **stall sb** 177 *jdn aufhalten*
stance, stooping ~ 69 *gebeugte Haltung*
to **stand up to sb/sth** 151 *jdm/etw die Stirn bieten*
standard of living 8 *Lebensstandard;* **peak ~** 41 *höchstmöglicher Lebensstandard*
stark 51 *unangenehm, krass*
to **state sth** 22 *etw angeben, etw nennen*
state, head of ~ 35 *Staatsoberhaupt;* **member ~** 151 *Mitgliedsstaat*
statecraft 163 *staatliche (internationale) Politik*
statement 23 *Aussage;* **identity ~** 8 *Produktidentität (seinen Sozialstatus durch teuren Konsum definieren)*
status 9 *Status, Stand, Stellung;* ~ **quo** 33 *gegenwärtiger Zustand, Ist-Zustand*
stay 177 *Aufenthalt*
steadily, slowly and ~ 35 *langsam und stetig*
steady 27 *stetig, beständig*
steamship 150 *Dampfschiff*
steeply banked terraces pl 143 *steile Zuschauertribüne*
stereotype, gender ~ 117 *geschlechtsspezifisches Klischee*
stinging 189 *scharf, verletzend*
stooping stance 69 *gebeugte Haltung*
storm drain 70 *(Regenwasser-)Kanal, Kanalisation*
strain 93 *Züchtung, Sorte*
strategic policy advisor 84 *Strategieberater/in*
strength 114T *Stärke*
strict controls pl 9 *strenge Kontrollen*
to **strike: ~ sth down** 117 *etw aufheben;* ~ **a chord** 144 *einen Nerv treffen, Anklang finden*
to **stroll** 41 *schlendern, spazieren*
to **structure sth** 21 *etw strukturieren*
struggle 39T *Kampf*
to **struggle** 25 *kämpfen, sich abmühen;* 167 *sich schwertun*
stuck, to be ~ 153 *festsitzen;* ~ **in the closet** 144 *unfähig, sich zu seiner Homosexualität zu bekennen*
stuff 15 *Zeug, Sachen*

to **stumble upon sth** 89 *auf etw stoßen*
subdued 111 *bedrückt*
subject, to **be ~ to sth** 205 *einer Sache unterzogen werden*
submissive 139 *unterwürfig*
to **subscribe to sth** 199 *etw abonnieren*
subsidiary 40 *Niederlassung*
substandard 24 *minderwertig*
substantial 23 *bedeutend, erheblich*
suburbanite 190 *Vorstadtbewohner/in*
success 14 *Erfolg*
successive 158 *nachfolgend*
to **suck sth up** 101 *etw aufsaugen*
to **suffer racial discrimination** 116 *unter Rassendiskriminierung leiden*
sufficient 19T *genügend, hinreichend*
suffrage, right of ~ 131 *Wahlrecht*
sugar plantation 150 *Zuckerplantage*
to **suggest** 39T *vorschlagen;* **~ sth** 23 *darauf hindeuten*
suggestion 27 *Vorschlag*
suicide 139 *Selbstmord*
suitable 47 *geeignet*
superalloy, nickel ~ 89 *Nickel-Superlegierung*
superpower 183 *Supermacht*
to **supervise sth** 177 *etw beaufsichtigen*
supply, water ~ 48 *Wasserversorgung*
to **supply** 53 *liefern, beliefern, (mit etw) versorgen*
to **surge** 70 *rasch anschwellen*
surge 158 *Welle, starker Anstieg*
surgery, keyhole ~ 80 *minimalinvasive Chirurgie*
surveillance 102 *Überwachung;* **mass electronic ~** 183 *elektronische Massenüberwachung*
survey 14 *Umfrage*
survival 50 *Überleben*
suspension bridge 89 *Hängebrücke*
suspicion, to **treat sb with ~** 116 *jdm mit Misstrauen begegnen*
to **sustain** 53 *erhalten, aufrechterhalten*
sustainable 36 *nachhaltig*
sustained 24 *kontinuierlich, anhaltend*
suture 110 *Naht*
to **swagger** 190 *stolzieren*
swathe 29 *große Zahl, breite Schicht*
sweat 110 *Schweiß*
to **sweep** 70 *(Wasser:) schießen, rauschen*
to **switch to sth** 65 *auf etw umstellen*
to **swivel** 110 *schwenken, sich drehen*
to **symbolize sth** 59 *etw symbolisieren*
synonymous with 138 *gleichbedeutend mit*
to **synthesise sth** 33 *etw zusammen-fassen*
system of law 151 *Rechtssystem*

T

to **tackle sth** 71 *etw bekämpfen*
take, a modern ~ on sth 83 *eine moderne Herangehensweise an etw*
to **tamper with sth** 105 *etw manipulieren*
tangible 138 *greifbar, konkret, handfest*
to **tap sth** 36 *anzapfen, nutzen*
tape loop 143 *Tonbandschleife*
target 176T *Ziel*
to **target sb/sth** 105 *jdn/etw ins Visier nehmen*
tasklist 163 *Liste von/mit Aufgaben*
tattered 110 *zerschlissen*
taunt 143 *Spott, Hohn*
tax 21 *Steuer*
tech specs pl 102 *technische Daten*
technological: ~ advances pl 210 *technologische Fortschritte;* **~ capabilities** pl 190 *technologische Möglichkeiten, technische Kompetenz;* **~ innovation** 81 *technische Neuerung;* **~ marvel** 89 *technisches Wunderwerk*
technology, solar ~ 24 *Solartechnik*
technophile 81 *Technikbegeisterte/r*
technophobe 81 *Technikfeind/in*
tedious 97 *langweilig*
telemarketer 29 *Telefonverkäufer/in*
tenacious 190 *hartnäckig*
tenacity 177 *Hartnäckigkeit*
tendency 42 *Neigung, Tendenz;* to **have a ~ to do sth** 126 *dazu neiten, etw zu tun*
terrace, steeply banked ~s pl 143 *steile Zuschauertribüne*
terrorist attack 183 *Terroranschlag*
textile 88 *Textilie, Stoff*
to **thank your lucky stars** 186 *sich glücklich schätzen, dem Schicksal danken*
theft, identity ~ 81 *Identitätsdiebstahl*
thoroughfare 70 *Haupstraße, Durchgangsstraße*
thread 130 *Faden, Garn*
threat 22 *Bedrohung*
to **thrive** 17 *gedeihen, florieren*
to **thrust sb out** 130 *jdn hinauswerfen, jdn ausstoßen*
to **thwart sth** 210 *etw durchkreuzen, einer Sache entgegenwirken*
tide 70 *Gezeiten, Ebbe und Flut*
tie, to **sever all ~s to sth** 199 *alle Bindungen zu etw abbrechen*
tier 189 *(soziale) Schicht, Stufe*
tight 47 *eng*
to **tilt the scales toward sb** 190 *die Waage zu jds Gunsten neigen*
tipping point 52 *kritischer Punkt, Wendepunkt*

tissue 110 *Gewebe*
tool 29 *Werkzeug*
tough 96 *hart, schwer*
toxic 48 *giftig*
trade: slave ~ 150 *Sklavenhandel;* **free ~** 151 *freier Handel;* **~ route** 150 *Handelsweg;* **~ union** 8 *Gewerkschaft*
trading: ~ bloc 174 *Handelsblock, Handelsmacht;* **~ nation** 174 *Handelsnation*
training 25 *Schulung, Ausbildung*
trait 32 *Charakterzug*
traitor 200 *Verräter/in*
to **transfer sth** 108T *etw (Geld) überweisen*
to **transform sth** 23 *verwandeln*
to **transplant** 153 *verpflanzen, versetzen*
transportation 8 *Transportwesen*
to **trap sb** 11 *jdn fangen*
trash 49 *Müll*
traumatic 80 *traumatisch, traumatisierend*
to **treat sb with suspicion** 116 *jdm mit Misstrauen begegnen*
tribe 182 *Stamm*
to **trigger** 56 *auslösen*
tropical rainforest 49 *tropischer Regenwald*
troubling 42 *beunruhigend*
truism 32 *Binsenweisheit*
turmoil 33 *Aufruhr*
to **turn out** 154 *(gut/schlecht) ausgehen;* **~ (for a team)** 143 *(für eine Mannschaft) auflaufen*
turtle 60 *Schildkröte*
twenty-something 167 *jd im Alter zwischen 20 und 29*
twisted reading 205 *einseitige Auslegung*
typically 27 *üblicherweise, normalerweise*

U

ubiquitous 23 *allgegenwärtig*
unalienable 130 *unveräußerlich*
unborn 80 *ungeboren*
unconstitutional 205 *verfassungswidrig*
to **uncouple sth** 17 *etw entkoppeln*
to **underpin sth** 51 *die Grundlage von etw bilden*
to **undertake sth** 29 *etw übernehmen, etw durchführen*
underwriter, insurance ~ 29 *Versicherer/in*
undoubtedly 174 *zweifellos*
to **unearth sth** 37 *ausgraben, finden*
unemployed 29 *arbeitslos, ohne Arbeit*
unfamiliar 135 *ungewohnt, unbekannt, fremd*

IRREGULAR VERBS

be – was/were – been	*sein*
beat – beat – beaten	*schlagen, besiegen*
become – became – become	*werden*
begin – began – begun	*anfangen, beginnen*
behold – beheld – beheld	*erblicken, beobachten*
bend – bent – bent	*(sich) beugen*
bind – bound – bound	*binden*
break – broke – broken	*brechen*
build – built – built	*bauen*
burn – burned/burnt – burned/burnt	*(ver)brennen*
buy – bought – bought	*kaufen*
catch – caught – caught	*fangen, verstehen*
choose – chose – chosen	*(aus)wählen*
come – came – come	*kommen*
cost – cost – cost	*kosten*
creep – crept – crept	*(ein)schleichen*
cut – cut – cut	*schneiden*
do – did – done	*tun, machen*
deal – dealt – dealt	*sich befassen; handeln; austeilen*
draw – drew – drawn	*zeichnen*
dream – dreamt – dreamt	*träumen*
drink – drank – drunk	*trinken*
drive – drove – driven	*fahren*
eat – ate – eaten	*essen*
fall – fell – fallen	*fallen*
feed – fed – fed	*füttern, ernähren*
feel – felt – felt	*(sich) fühlen, empfinden*
fight – fought – fought	*kämpfen*
find – found – found	*finden*
fit – fit/fitted – fit/fitted	*passen*
fly – flew – flown	*fliegen*
forget – forgot – forgotten	*vergessen*
freeze – froze – frozen	*(ge)frieren*
frolic – frolicked – frolicked	*(herum)tollen, toben*
get – got – got (AE gotten)	*bekommen*
give – gave – given	*geben*
go – went – gone	*gehen, fahren*
grow – grew – grown	*wachsen*
hang – hung – hung	*hängen*
have – had – had	*haben*
hear – heard – heard	*hören*
hide – hid – hidden	*(sich) verstecken*
hit – hit – hit	*schlagen; treffen auf*
hold – held – held	*halten, festhalten*
hurt – hurt – hurt	*verletzen, weh tun*
keep – kept – kept	*behalten*
know – knew – known	*kennen, wissen*
lay – laid – laid	*legen*
lead – led – led	*führen*
learn – learnt/learned – learnt/learned	*lernen*
leave – left – left	*abfahren, verlassen, weggehen*
let – let – let	*lassen*
lie – lay – lain	*liegen*
light – lit – lit	*anzünden, beleuchten*
lose – lost – lost	*verlieren*
make – made – made	*machen*
mean – meant – meant	*meinen, bedeuten*
meet – met – met	*treffen*
offset – offset – offset	*ausgleichen*
pay – paid – paid	*bezahlen*
put – put – put	*setzen, stellen, legen*
quit – quit/quitted – quit/quitted	*verlassen, aufhören*
read – read – read	*lesen*
ride – rode – ridden	*reiten, fahren*
rise – rose – risen	*(an)steigen*
ring – rang – rung	*läuten, klingeln*
run – ran – run	*laufen, rennen*
say – said – said	*sagen*
see – saw – seen	*sehen*
seek – sought – sought	*suchen*
sell – sold – sold	*verkaufen*
send – sent – sent	*senden, schicken*
set – set – set	*setzen, stellen*
shake – shook – shaken	*schütteln*
show – showed – shown	*zeigen*
shut – shut – shut	*schließen*
sing – sang – sung	*singen*
sink – sank/sunk – sunk/sunken	*sinken*
sit – sat – sat	*sitzen*
sleep – slept – slept	*schlafen*
smell – smelt/smelled – smelt/smelled	*riechen*
speak – spoke – spoken	*sprechen*
spell – spelt/spelled – spelt/spelled	*buchstabieren*
spend – spent – spent	*ausgeben, verbringen*
stand – stood – stood	*stehen*
steal – stole – stolen	*stehlen*
stride – strode – stridden	*schreiten*
strive – strove/strived – striven/strived	*streben (nach)*
swim – swam – swum	*schwimmen*
take – took – taken	*nehmen*
teach – taught – taught	*unterrichten, beibringen*
tell – told – told	*sagen, erzählen*
think – thought – thought	*denken*
thrive – thrived – thrived	*florieren*
throw – threw – thrown	*werfen*
thrust – thrust – thrust	*stoßen*
understand – understood – understood	*verstehen*
wake – woke/waked – woken/waked	*aufwachen, wecken*
wear – wore – worn	*tragen*
win – won – won	*gewinnen*
withhold – withheld – withheld	*verweigern, vorenthalten*
write – wrote – written	*schreiben*

QUELLENVERZEICHNIS

Bildquellen:

S. 8/shutterstock/Dimitry Kalinovsky; S. 9/1/shutterstock/Syda Productions, S. 9/2/shutterstock/Sean Pavone; S. 10/shutterstock/bymandesigns; S. 11/1/shutterstock/AllenG, S. 11/2/shutterstock/wavebreak-media, S. 11/3/shutterstock/pruciatti, S. 11/4/shutterstock/Andrey Popov, S. 12/shutterstock/Oleksiy Mark, S. 13/1/shutterstock/Rido, S. 13/2/shutterstock/bikeriderlondon; S. 15/Cartoonstock/Fran; S. 16/1/shutterstock/Ansis Klucis, S. 16/2/shutterstock/Gilmar, S. 16/3/shutterstock/Zentilia, S. 16/4/shutterstock/chris-dorney, S. 16/5/shutterstock/Chiyacat, S. 16/6/shutterstock/Lovegraphic; S. 17/shutterstock/Fotos593; S. 18/1/shutterstock/rzstudio, S. 18/2/shutterstock/Fotofermer; S. 20/shutterstock/P.Chinnapong, S. 22/shutterstock/Lightboxx; S. 23/1/shutterstock/xtock, S. 23/2/shutterstock/Tomazino; S. 24/1/Image Source/Hemant Mehta, S. 24/2/Glow Images/Cultura; S. 25/shutterstock/Carmen Karin; S. 28/1/shutterstock/VectorLifestylepic, S. 28/2/shutterstock/Monkey Business Images, S. 28/3/shutterstock/with God, S. 28/4/shutterstock/Pavel LPhoto, S. 28/5/shutterstock/maggee, S. 28/5/shutterstock/Angelo Giampiccolo, S. 30/1/3/4/shutterstock/Tatiana Shepeleva, S. 30/2/shutterstock/RTimages; S. 32/shutterstock/Monkey Business Images; S. 33/shutterstock/Hasloo Group; S. 34/cartoonstock/Roy Delgado; S. 35/shutterstock/ra2studio; S. 38/2/Fotolia/C.Georghiou; S. 39/Interfoto/Sammlung Rauch; S. 40/1/Fotolia/E.Kalvinbacak, S. 40/2/shutterstock/Chris Parypa, S. 40/3/Fotolia/Adrian_ilie825, S. 40/4/Fotolia/adam21, S. 40/5/Laif/Johann Rousselot; S. 42/Fotolia/FengYu; S. 43/S. 44/cartoonstock/Len Hawkins; S. 46/Fotolia/Casper1774; S. 48/1/shutterstock/Lane Erickson, S. 48/2/shutterstock/Gigira; S. 49/1/shutterstock/Grynold, S. 49/2/shutterstock/WDGPhoto; S. 50/shutterstock/Designsstock; S. 51/shutterstock/Mopic; S. 53/ shutterstock/erwinf.; S. 54/1/shutterstock/TTstudio, S. 54/2/shutterstock/rorem, S. 54/3/shutterstock/Peter Gudella, S. 54/4/shutterstock/Tony Campell; S. 57/1/shutterstock/Lane Erickson, S. 57/2/Imaga Source/Claire Keeley; S. 59/1/Corbis, S. 59/2/Lookfoto/age fotostock; S. 61/shutterstock/Richard Whitcombe; S. 62/Wildlife/Minden/juniors; S. 63/ S. 65/shutterstock/A.Nika; S. 67/shutterstock/Thaiview; S. 68/1/Cagle/Monte Woverton, S. 68/2/Cagle/Joe Heller; S. 69/Paul Cumes; S. 71/1/2/Reuters; S. 73/1/Reuters/Edgar Su, S. 73/2/Corbis/Michael Ready; S. 74/Laif/Paul Box; S. 75/Lookfoto/agefotostock; S. 77/1/shutterstock/Ekkachai, S. 77/2/Fotolia/adam121; S. 80/shutterstock/Stokkete; S. 81/1/shutterstock/canpipat, S. 81/2/shutterstock/Sergey Nivens, S. 81/3/shutterstock/Sergey Nivens; S. 82/shutterstock/Sergey Nivens; S. 83/1/shutterstock/kostasgr, S. 83/2/shutterstock/Pres Panayotov, S. 83/3/shutterstock/olan, S. 83/4/shutterstock/mubus7; S. 84/picture-alliance/dpa; S. 85/shutterstock/Nattle; S. 87/Fotolia/Furnada S. 88/1/action-press/Nasa/Planetpiactionpress, S. 88/2/shutterstock/gabriel12; S. 88/3/shutterstock/zeljkadan, S. 88/4/shutterstock/Pete Saloutos, S. 88/5/shutterstock/Mike Flipp, S. 88/6/shutterstock/michaeljung; S. 91/1/Fotolia/david rawcliffe, S. 91/2/Mauritius/Alamy, S. 91/3/ddp images, S. 91/4/shutterstock/AgnesKantaruk; S. 91/5/NikoNomad, S. 91/6/shutterstock/Sean Pavone, S. 92/Fotolia/G.Dawes; S. 93/Lookfoto/age Fotostock; S. 94/cartoonstock; S. 95/1/shutterstock/Vuk Varuna, S. 95/2/Fotolia/Ivanov Alexandr; S. 96/1/shutterstock/Niko Nomand, S. 96/2/shutterstock/Rachel Sanderoff; S. 97/shutterstock/Holbox; S. 99/1/cartoonstock/Kresten Forsman, S. 99/2/Chris Madden; S. 100/shutterstock/Olyy; S. 101/1/shutterstock/Edyta Pawlowska, S. 101/2/shutterstock/Bill McKelvie, S. 101/3/shutterstock/aodoodoud; S. 106/Fotolia/tiero; S. 103/1/Fotolia/sarayuth, S. 103/2/shutterstock7Andrey Popov; S. 104/1/cartoonstock/grin, S. 104/2/shutterstock/bluebay; S. 106/1/shutterstock/zimmytws, S. 106/2/Fotolia/Family Business; S. 107/shutterstock/illustratorkris; S. 108/cartoonstock/Loren Fishman; S. 109/1/Mauritus Images/Alamy/ S. 109/2/Corbis/Robbie Jack, S. 109/3/A.P.L.-Allstar/Picture Library; S. 110/shutterstock/Bob Orsilo; S. 111/shutterstock/Bob Orsilo, S. 114/1/Fotolia/eenevski, S. 114/2/Fotolia/ty; S. 115/Fotolia/Edward Samuel; S. 116/mauritius images/Alamy; S. 117/1/shutterstock/Curioso, S. 117/2/Image Source/Jonathan Gibson; S. 118/action press; S. 119/shutterstock/Andrey Popov; S. 120 © The Independent; S. 122/1/Fotolia/TTLmedia, S. 122/2/shutterstock/SGM, S. 122/3/shutterstock/Monkey Business Business, S. 122/4/Fotolia/Billion Photos, S. 122/5/Fotolia/JJAVA, S. 122/6/Fotolia/Goir, S. 122/7/Fotolia/Das Fotowerk; S. 125/ INTERTOPICS/Photoshot; S. 127/Corbis/Toby Melville/Reuters S. 128/Mauritius/Alamy; S. 130/Picture-alliance/AP Photo; S. 131/1/Photoshot/Bruce Coleman, S. 131/2/culture-images/United Archiv, S. 131/3/picture-alliance/Everett Collection, S. 131/4/culture-images/Photo12, S. 131/5/Photoshot/photoshot, S. 131/6/culture-images/Helga Esteb, S. 131/7/Photoshot/Xinhua; S. 132/1/AKG-images/Florelegius, S. 132/2/culture-images/Photos12, S. 132/3/culture-images Photos12, S. 132/4/Visum/The Image Works; S. 133/1/Action press/Courtesy Everett Collection, S. 133/2/ddp images, S. 133/3/ddp images; S. 134/1/shutterstock/Vacclav, S. 134/2/shutterstock/Bart Everett, S. 134/3/Corbis/Bradbury/Ocean, S. 134/4/Laif/Robert Gallagher/Aurora Photos, S. 134/5/action press/ZUMA Press; S. 135/Corbis/ERproduction; S. 138/1/shutterstock, S. 138/2/picture-alliance/Photoshot; S. 139/shutterstock/Skovoroda; S. 140/cartoonstock/Wilfred Hildonen; S. 141/shutterstock; S. 142/cartoonstock/Rona Chadwick; S. 143/Imago/Andrew Winning/Reuters; S. 144/Corbis/Catharinne Jill; S. 145/Fotolia/J.Ibrakovic; S. 146/Corbis/Andrew Winning; S. 147/1/Fotolia/iculig, S. 147/2/Fotolia/yellomello; S. 148/1/Fotolia/dacasdo, S. 148/2/Fotolia/Africa Studio; S. 149/Fotolia/bbbastian; S. 150/1/Interfoto/Imagebroker, S. 150/2/shutterstock/pruciatti; S. 151/1/Fotolia/Speedfighter, S. 151/2/shutterstock/S. Borisov; S. 152/shutterstock/pjhpix; S. 153/shutterstock/DeVisu; S. 154/shutterstock/FatManPhoto; S. 155/shutterstock/Family Business; S. 158/Mauritius images/

Alamy; S. 159/Bridgeman-imageS.com; S. 160/1/Mauritius-images/Alamy, S. 160/2/Mauritius-images/Alamy; S. 161/1/Interfoto/Mary Evans, S. 161/2/Interfoto/Mary Evans, S. 161/3/Mauritius-images/United Archives; S. 162/1/shutterstock/Mukhina Viktoria, S. 162/2/shutterstock/Pressmaster, S. 162/3/shutterstock/Olyy, S. 162/4/shutterstock/Oleg Zabielin, S. 162/5/shutterstock/EDHAR, S. 162/6/shutterstock/Leungchopan; S. 166/1/Fotolia/WavebreakMedia, S. 166/2/Mauritius-images/Alamy; S. 167/shutterstock/simobs; S. 168/shutterstock/somchaij; S. 169/Fotolia/oliy; S. 171/Nicolas Vadot; S. 173/shutterstock/Leonard Zhukovsky; S. 174/shutterstock/Tashatuvango; S. 175/shutterstock/xtock; S. 177/shutterstock/Kamira; S. 178/shutterstock/SGM; S. 180/shutterstock/iQoncept; S. 181/Fotolia/kues1; S. 182/shutterstock/steve estvanik S. 183/1/AKG-images, S. 183/2/Bridgeman-imgeS.com, S. 183/3/Reuters; S. 184/Fotolia/Steve Allen; S. 185/1/Fotolia/somchaij, S. 185/2/Fotolia/Alexandro Lanuzio, S. 185/3/Mirko Vitau; S. 186/1/ddp-images, S. 186/2/Glow Images/imagebroker, S 186/3/shutterstock/Gemenacom S. 187/1/ddp-images, S. 187/2/shutterstock/Philipimage; S. 188/Glow Images; S. 189/1/shutterstock/Joseph Sohm; S. 189/2/shutterstock/mandritoiu, S. 189/3/shutterstock/Alexey Stiop, S. 189/4/shutterstock/Action Sports photography, S. 189/5/shutterstock/N. Murmakova, S. 189/6/shutterstock/Stuart Monk, S. 189/7/shutterstock/Stone Photos, S. 189/8/shutterstock/logoboom; S. 191/Fotolia/inna_astakhora; S. 192/shutterstock kamira; S. 193/1/picture-alliance/United Archiv, S. 193/2/Interfoto/Granger, S. 193/3/shutterstock/aceshot1, S. 193/4/picture-alliance/DesignPics; S. 195/shutterstock/imageFlow; S. 196/1/Fotolia/Stillfx, S. 196/2/Laif/Mark Peterson; S. 197/1/Imago/Zuma Press, S. 197/2/shutterstock/PK Photography, S. 197/3/action press/copyright2000, S. 197/4/Intertopics, S. 197/5/Interfoto/Granger; S. 198/cartoonstock/Steve Kelley; S. 199/1/shutterstock/Stuart Monk, S. 199/2/shutterstock/a katz, S. 199/3/shutterstock/Chuck Wagner, S. 199/4/Fotolia/Monkey Business, S. 199/5/Fotolia/Hill Street Studios, S. 199/6/shutterstock/Kobby Doyan, S. 200/ddp-images, S. 202/picture-alliance/AP Photo S. 204/1/Image Source/Adam Sternin, S. 204/2 ddp images/ColoradoSpringsGazette/MCT/Sip, S. 204/3/shutterstock/Burlington, S. 204/4/action-press, S. 204/5/ddp images/dapd, S. 207/mauritius images/moedboard S. 209/shutterstock/Christopher Halloran, S. 212/shutterstock/Stephen Clarke, S. 213/Paul Fell; S. 214/Fotolia/VadimGuzha Anhang: S. 216/1/Carlson, S. 216/2/Cagle/Mil Prigee; S. 218/cartoonstock/Marty Bucella; S. 219/cartoonstock/John Morris; S. 220/cartoonstock, S. 221/cartoonstock/Harley; S. 238/cartoonstock/Martha Campbell, S. 239/1/Jim Sizemore, S. 239/2/Dave Carpenter; S. 240/action press/SWNS; S. 241/cartoonstock/Mark Lynch; S. 242/cartoonstock/Guy&Rodd; S. 243/1/cartoonstock/Robert Thompson, S. 243/2/cartoonstock/Jesse Springer, S. 244/cartoonstock/Aaron Bacal, S. 245/1/Cagle/Andy Singer, S. 245/2/cartoonstock/Steve Greenberg; S. 247/1//cartoonstock/Bill Proud, S. 247/2/cartoonstock/Lindsay Foyle; S. 248/1/picture-alliance/dpa, S. 248/2/Fotolia/menfis, S. 249/1/Cagle, S. 249/2/Greenberg; S. 262/cartoonstock/Mike Baldwin; Landkarten: Carlos Borrell

Textquellen:
1/1 Richard Docwra, The effects of consumerism, life squared, 2009, used by permission; 1/2 Gaia Vince, The high cost of our throwaway society, BBC future, 2012, used by permission; 1/4 Jenny Awford, Will your job still exist in 2025?, The Daily Mail, 2014, used by permission; 1/5 Adam Bryant © Guardian News & Media Ltd 2011; 1/6 Valbona Zeneli, Why is it right and smart to empower women?, The Globalist, 2014, used by permission; 1/7 Mark Pagel, Does globalization mean we will become one culture?, BBC future, 2012, used by permission; 2/1 Oliver Milman, Rate of environmental degradation puts life on Earth at risk, say scientists, The Guardian, 2015, used by permission; 2/2 Rory Carroll, They were the last word in glamour, but has the sun set on LA's swimming pools?, The Guardian 2014, used by permission; 2/5 Pat Moon, Earth's Clock, Earth Lines, Pimlico Books, 1991, used by permission; 2/5 Robin McKie, Miami Beach – a city affected by climate change, The Guardian, 2014, used by permission; 3/1 Jonathan Owen, 3D-printed WikiHouse 4.0: £50,000 house you can download from the internet, The Independent, 2014, used by permission; 3/2 Mark Miodownik, Why the story of materials is really the story of civilisation, The Guardian, used by permission; 3/3 Karl Mathiesen, Is a ban on GM crops more harmful than growing them?, The Guardian, 2014, used by permission; 3/4 Carmen Fishwick, Mission to colonise Mars, The Guardian, 2013, used by permission; 3/5 Jemima Kiss, Worried about your privacy? Wait until the drones start stalking you, The Guardian, 2014, used by permission; 3/6 Paul Peachey, Cyber Crime: First online murder will happen by the end of the year, warns US firm, The Guardian, 2014, used by permission; 3/7 Nick Dear, Frankenstein, 2011, used by permission; 4/1 Huge Survey Reveals Seven Social Classes in the UK, BBC News, 2014, used by permission; 4/2 Emma Howard, What is it like to be a Muslim in Britain today?, The Guardian, 2014, used by permission; 4/3e Mary McLeod Bethune (1875-1955), speech: 'What Does American Democracy Mean to Me?' at America's Town Meeting of the Air, New York City, 23 Nov 1939; 4/3b Mary Church Terrell, 'What It Means to be Colored in Capital of the U.S.', delivered 10 October 1906, United Women's Club, Washington, D.C.; 4/5 Emma Watson speech by UN Women Goodwill Ambassador, a special event for the HeForShe campaign, United Nations Headquarters, New York, 20 September 2014; 4/6 Darren Devine, Gareth Thomas' new autobiography Proud: Alfie reveals pain of cruel gay jibes he endured after coming out, Wales Online, 2014, used by permission; 5/1 Douglas Murray,Who do we let in? It's time to choose, The Spectator, 2014, used by permission; 5/3 Indra Adnan, Soft power: Britain is losing its grip on this key asset, The Guardian 2014, used by permission; 5/3 task 9 © The British Council 2015; 5/4 Michael Skey, British attitudes towards Europe are being shaped by new ways of thinking about

The World

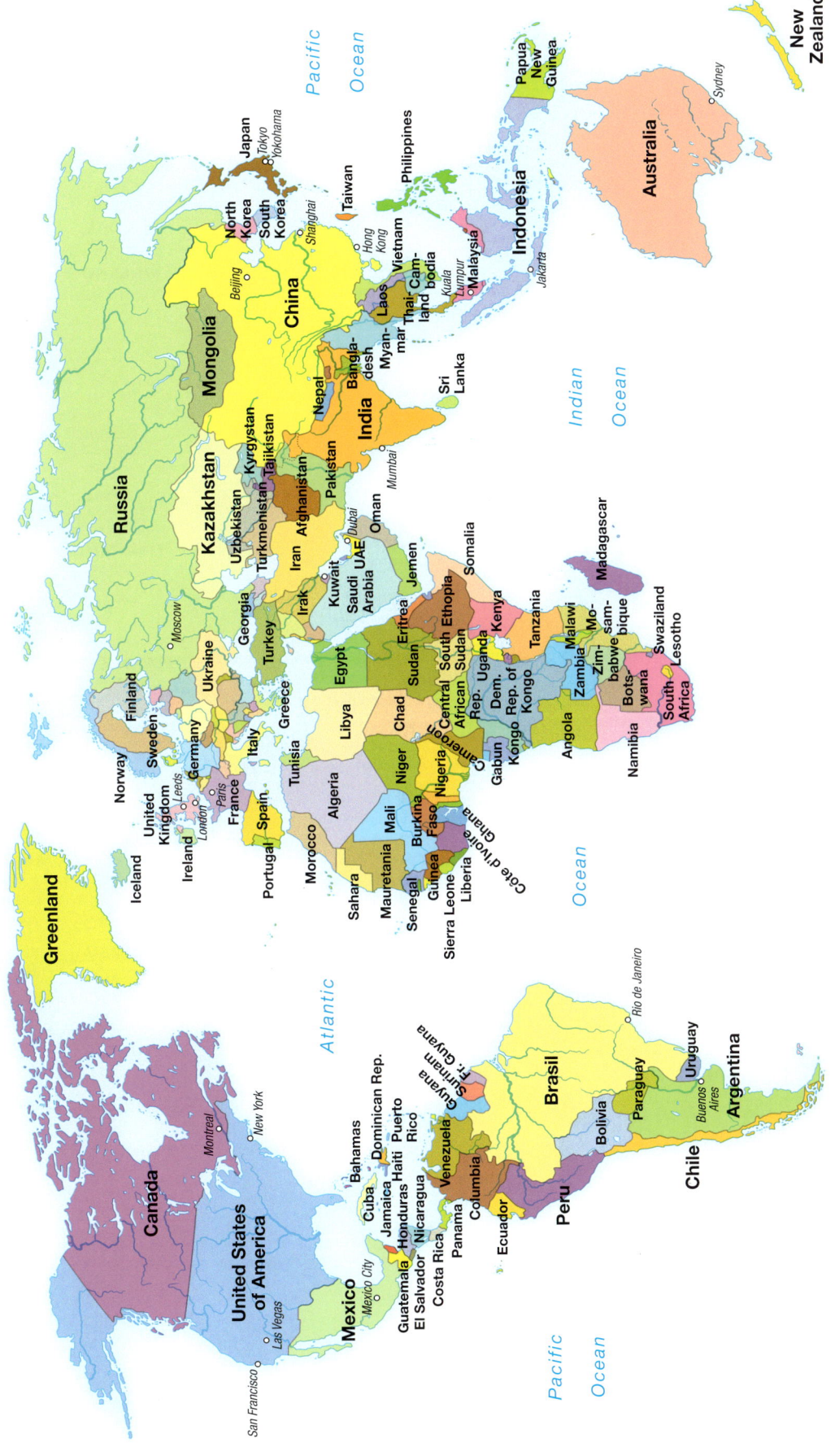

New Zealand

Australia

Sydney

Papua New Guinea

Indonesia

Jakarta

Philippines

Taiwan

Japan
Tokyo
Yokohama

North Korea
South Korea

Beijing

Shanghai

China

Mongolia

Hong Kong

Vietnam
Laos
Thai-Cam-
Myan- land bodia
mar
Kuala Lumpur
Malaysia

Bangla-
desh

Nepal

India

Sri Lanka

Mumbai

Russia

Kazakhstan

Uzbekistan
Kyrgystan
Turkmenistan Tadjikistan

Afghanistan

Pakistan

Iran

Dubai
UAE
Oman

Somalia

Madagascar

Kenya
Tanzania

Mo-
sam-
Zim- bique
babwe
Swaziland
Lesotho

Kuwait
Saudi Arabia Yemen

Eritrea
Ethiopia
South Sudan

Angola

Bots-
wana

South Africa

Namibia

Zambia
Malawi

Dem.
Rep. of
Kongo

Gabun

Central
African
Rep. Uganda

Georgia

Turkey

Greece

Irak

Ukraine

Moscow

Finland

Sweden

Norway

United Kingdom
Ireland
London
Leeds

Germany
Paris
France

Italy

Spain

Portugal

Sudan

Egypt

Libya

Chad

Niger

Nigeria

Cameroon

Côte d'Ivoire
Ghana

Tunisia

Algeria

Morocco

Mali

Burkina
Faso

Guinea

Sierra Leone
Liberia

Senegal

Mauretania

Sahara

Indian Ocean

Ocean

The World

Greenland

Iceland

Atlantic

Canada

Montreal

New York

United States of America

Las Vegas

San Francisco

Mexico City

Mexico

Bahamas
Cuba
Jamaica
Dominican Rep.
Haiti Puerto
Rico

Guatemala Honduras Nicaragua
El Salvador
Costa Rica
Panama

Columbia

Venezuela

Ecuador

Peru

Guyana
Surinam
Fr. Guyana

Rio de Janeiro

Brasil

Bolivia

Paraguay

Chile

Buenos Aires

Uruguay

Argentina

Pacific Ocean

Pacific Ocean

EUROPEAN UNION

0 100 200 300 400 500
km

ICELAND

NORWAY

SWEDEN

FINLAND

Helsinki

Stockholm

RUSSIA

Tallinn
ESTONIA

LATVIA
Riga

LITHUANIA
Vilnius

RUSSIA

BELARUS

DENMARK
Copenhagen

NETHER-
LANDS
Amsterdam
Utrecht
Antwerp
Brussels
BELGIUM

UNITED
KINGDOM

Dublin
IRELAND

London

Rostock

Hamburg

Berlin

GERMANY

Cologne

Frankfurt

Dresden

Warsaw

POLAND

UKRAINE

Prague
CZECH
REPUBLIC

SLOVAKIA
Bratislava

MOLDOVA

Luxembourg
LUXEM-
BOURG

Rouen
Paris

Stuttgart
Strasbourg

LIECHTEN-
STEIN

Munich

Vienna

Budapest

ROMANIA

FRANCE

SWITZER-
LAND

The Alps

Innsbruck
AUSTRIA

HUNGARY

Bucharest

Genoa

SAN
MARINO

SLOVENIA
Ljubljana

Zagreb
CROATIA

BOSNIA-
HERZE-
GOVINA

SERBIA

BULGARIA
Sofia

MONACO

MONTE-
NEGRO

KOSOVO

MACE-
DONIA

PORTUGAL

Madrid

ANDORRA

ITALY
Rome

ALBANIA

TURKEY

Lisbon

SPAIN

GREECE
Athens

ALGERIA

MOROCCO

Valletta
MALTA

TUNISIA

Canary Islands (Spain)

Tenerife

MOROCCO

LIBYA

TURKEY

Nicosia
CYPRUS

SYRIA

LEBANON